THE NORTON BOOK OF
PERSONAL ESSAYS

THE NORTON BOOK OF PERSONAL ESSAYS

Edited by JOSEPH EPSTEIN

W · W · NORTON & COMPANY · NEW YORK · LONDON

Copyright © 1997 by Joseph Epstein
All rights reserved

Printed in the United States of America

First Edition

Since this page cannot legibly accommodate all the copyright
notices, pages 474–77 constitute an extension of the
copyright page.

The text of this book is composed in Electra
with the display set in Bernhard Modern.
Composition and manufacturing by The Maple-Vail Book Manufacturing Group.
Book design by Antonina Krass adapted by Jack Meserole.

Library of Congress Cataloging-in-Publication Data
The Norton book of personal essays / edited by Joseph Epstein.
        p.   cm.
        ISBN 0-393-03654-5
    1. American essays—20th century.   2. English essays—20th century.
        I. Epstein, Joseph, 1937–   .
                PS688.N67   1997
814'.508—dc20   96-26975
                                                                            CIP

W. W. Norton & Company, Inc., 500 Fifth Avenue, New York, N.Y. 10110
http://www.wwnorton.com

W. W. Norton & Company Ltd., 10 Coptic Street, London WC1A 1PU

1 2 3 4 5 6 7 8 9 0

CONTENTS

Contents

THE NORTON BOOK OF
PERSONAL ESSAYS

THE PERSONAL ESSAY:
A FORM OF DISCOVERY
BY JOSEPH EPSTEIN

The personal essay is a happy accident of literature. I call it an accident because it seems to have come into the world without anything like a clear line of descent. Michel de Montaigne (1530–1590) was its first great practitioner, the first man to make plain that he did not intend to be either exhaustive or definitive in his writing and to use the first-person singular in a fairly regular way. Montaigne once referred to himself, in fact, as "an accidental philosopher."

Writing that comes very close to the personal essay appears in the letters of the Roman philosopher Seneca; and of course the first person was used in great autobiographies such as Saint Augustine's. But neither Seneca's letters nor Augustine's autobiography is quite the same as the personal essay. Both were written under the constraints of very different forms. I have called the personal essay "a happy accident," and invoked the word *happy* because it is free, the freest form in all of literature. A form that is itself intrinsically formless, the personal essay is able to take off on any tack it wishes, building its own structure as it moves along, rebuilding and remaking itself—and its author—each time out.

Adding to its accidental quality, no one, I think, sets out in life to become an essayist. One might, at an early age, wish to be a poet or a dramatist or a novelist, or even possibly a critic. One somehow wanders or stumbles into becoming an essayist. But,

11

given the modest reputation of the essay and the way it has tended to be taught in schools, it is quite amazing that anyone should ever again wish to read essays, let alone write them.

My own introduction to the personal essay—one, I suspect, shared by many in my generation—was by way of the bloated, vatic, never less than pompous Ralph Waldo Emerson and the rather precious Charles Lamb. Few things are more efficient at killing the taste for a certain kind of literature than being force-fed it in school at an early age. (Willa Cather, one of the contributors to this volume, would not allow her books to be reproduced in inexpensive student editions because she felt that, forced to read her when young, students would never again read her of their own volition when they had grown up.) Although I have come to have a higher opinion of Lamb and an even lower one of Emerson, having to read them at an early age all but effectively killed the essay for me.

When I think about my own reintroduction to the personal essay, it is connected with my having begun to read, in my junior year at the University of Chicago, the so-called little magazines. This was in the late 1950s, when these magazines—among them *Partisan Review, Kenyon Review, Encounter* (in England), and *Commentary*—were going through a rich period. These magazines contributed more to my education than anything that went on in the classroom, and classrooms at the University of Chicago weren't all that bad. (Like Mark Twain, another of the contributors to this book, I was one of those students who tried never to allow school to get in the way of his education and generally seemed to find more interesting things to read outside the classroom than those offered within it.) The little magazines ran political articles, short stories, much literary criticism, but also occasional memoirs and personal essays. The last, with their strong personal note, especially excited me.

I came too late to read George Orwell when he was still alive and regularly wrote a personal essay of a sort under the rubric of "London Letter" for *Partisan Review.* But through that magazine's pages I learned about Orwell the essayist, who was much greater, if less famous, as a writer of essays than as a novelist— or, more precisely, as the political novelist who wrote *Animal*

Farm and 1984. But even as a critic, Orwell invariably struck the personal note: every word he wrote outside his fiction bore his beliefs, his point of view, his strong personal trademark.

Orwell is not alone in being a writer who—though famous for work in other forms—was really superior as an essayist. To consider only contributors to this volume: With the single, towering exception of *The Adventures of Huckleberry Finn*, a strong case can be made for Mark Twain's having been a greater essayist than novelist. About Edmund Wilson, who also wrote fiction, no such argument need even be made. James Baldwin is stronger in the essay than as either a novelist or a playwright. I tend to think the same is true of Joan Didion. It may well be true, too, of Cynthia Ozick.

I'm not at all sure how any of these writers would take the judgment that they are better essayists than novelists. Literary forms, like stocks, rise and fall, not in value of course but in prestige. Until very recently, the prestige of the essay was much lower than that of the novel. The novel was the art of the imagination; it was, in the loaded term taken up by university writing programs, "creative" writing. The essay, in contradistinction, was thought mundane, earth-bound, pedestrian—cut it any way you like, nowhere near so elevated. This, one begins to sense, is changing.

Of course, poetry once held first place in the form, or genre, sweepstakes, rivaled only by drama. The prestige of any single kind of writing is in good part dependent upon who its practitioners are at any given moment in history. The appearance of another Shakespeare would doubtless catapult drama back to the top position it held in Elizabethan England. Yet a Shakespeare of our day might not choose to write drama at all. He might just possibly discover a new form not yet known but perfectly suited to our times. Why certain forms rise and fall as they do is itself a question of immense complication.

V. S. Naipaul, also represented by an essay in this volume, has said that lucky is the writer who has found his or her true form. What makes this remark especially interesting is that V. S. Naipaul, who in such books as *A House for Mr. Biswas* and *A Bend in the River* has written some of the best novels of the last half of the twentieth century, has recently announced that he no longer considers the novel a useful form for conveying the complex truths of our day. I myself tend to doubt that this is so. What I think may be the case is that people do not seem to have the patience for so lengthy a form as the novel, which is a shame. Naipaul, meanwhile, has said that he plans to write no more fiction. Now in his sixties, what new form of nonfiction, or perhaps amalgam of fiction and nonfiction, Naipaul will turn to is itself a question of genuine interest.

Near the beginning of this century now ending, Georg Lukacs, the Hungarian critic, prophesied that the essay was likely to be the reigning form of the modern age. He had in mind less the personal than the cultural-philosophical essay, but behind his prophecy was the notion that the essay, with its tentativeness and its skeptical spirit, was really the ideal form for those times when people were less certain about matters that were once thought fundamental and fixed: family, love, religion, loyalty, happiness among them. Theodor Adorno, another central European thinker, felt that the essay was well suited to the modern spirit because it shied away from what he called "the violence of dogma." The essay, in short, was—and perhaps remains—the ideal form for ages of transition and uncertain values. Such an age, for better *and* for worse, is the one in which we now live.

The personal essay has this single quality of difference from fiction: it is bounded—some might say grounded—by reality. There are no unreliable narrators in personal essays; in a personal essay an unreliable narrator is just another name for a bad writer. We believe—we have to believe—what the writer tells us, though we are of course at liberty not to be persuaded by the way he tells it. We believe, too, in the facts in his essay as facts that have an existence in reality, unlike the "details" ("caress the details" Vladimir Nabokov instructs all writers of fiction) in stories and novels, whose ultimate existence resides in their authors' minds, whatever their origin in reality. The subject matter of the personal essay, then, is actual, palpable, real, and this, from a reader's standpoint, can be an immense advantage.

The first personal essay I ever wrote was written when I was thirty-one and was, in fact, closer to a memoir than to a personal essay. But I found myself greatly elated in writing about that sweetest of subjects—my own experience. Thirty-one, it occurs to me now, may be young to write personal essays. The personal essay is perhaps intrinsically a middle-aged or older writer's form in that it calls for a certain experience of life and the disposition to reflect upon that experience. Since that time, I have written perhaps a hundred personal essays, and I wonder if I mightn't convey something of what, from the writer's point of view, has gone into the making of these essays.

I agree with Phyllis Rose, another contributor to this book, who, writing about Montaigne, called him "the father of jazz." By this she meant that he was "the inventor of the verbal riff, the man who elevated organic form over inherited structures and first made art by letting one thing lead to another." That is, in my own experience, precisely how writing the personal essay works. I sometimes make notes recalling anecdotes, facts, oddities of one kind or another that I wish to include in an essay, but where precisely in the essay they will be used I cannot say in advance. As for a previous design or ultimate goal for my essays, before I write them I have neither. I would no more use an outline in writing a personal essay than I would take a thesaurus to a pro basketball game.

The personal essay is, in my experience, a form of discovery. What one discovers in writing such essays is where one stands on complex issues, problems, questions, subjects. In writing the essay, one tests one's feelings, instincts, thoughts in the crucible of composition.

For example, I plan before long to write an essay on the subject of talent. Just now I know very little about the subject apart from the fact that it fascinates me. "We need a word between talent and genius," Valéry once said. He may well be correct, but just now I am myself not even clear on the precise definition of the word "talent." I know only that talent tends to be something magical, or at least confers magic on its possessors, no matter in what realm: art, athletics, crime. In this essay, I intend to speak of my own admiration for the talented, question the extent to which I may myself have any spark of talent, try to figure out the meaning of talent in the larger scheme of existence. Through this essay I hope to learn what I really think about this complex subject and, while doing so, to learn perhaps something new about myself and the world. Talent, in any case, seems to me a fine subject for a personal essay—a fine subject, that is to say, for personal exploration.

In recent years, I have taken to writing short stories, which has caused me to wonder why certain kinds of material seem better suited to essays than to stories. As with my writing of essays, when I begin a story I generally do not have anything like a clear notion of its direction. I suspect the same may be true of poetry. I have always been impressed by a remark of Robert Frost's to the effect that whenever he knew the ending of a poem in advance of writing it, the poem turned out to be a damn poor one.

When I set out to write a story, I am usually motivated by a strong yet somewhat vague curiosity; often behind this curiosity lies complex emotion of a kind that I have felt but not yet sorted out, at least not in any way I find satisfactory. Sometimes in a story a character will be at the center of my attention, sometimes a question still in the flux of controversy.

Consider a live and rivening issue of our day—that of abortion. It is not a subject upon which I brood, and my "political" position on it, if I were pressed to give it, is that I am "pro-choice"; I believe a woman ought to be allowed to decide if she wishes to go through with a pregnancy; I also believe that there are too many instances in which to deny the possibility of abortion is to bring about unhappiness of a kind that is avoidable—unhappiness for the unborn child as well as for its parents. I do not believe that the decision to have an abortion ought to be entered into frivolously, though I rather doubt that many women who choose to have abortions do so without giving it serious thought. I guess my true position on abortion is that I am not against it, yet I also think it a private matter that people do well to keep to themselves.

Having said this, I have to go on to say that, if I had a young daughter, I would hate to learn that she had had an abortion. It would more than bother me; it would tear me up. Why? I have no religious objections to abortion. I do not believe that an early fetus is quite truly human. I do not even believe that all people must accept the responsibility for their actions, especially when this acceptance entails possible hardship for an entirely innocent third party, the poor child. Medically meticulous abortion, thoughtfully entered into, therefore seems to be intelligent, sensible, even enlightened. All very well, except, as I say, I would be torn apart if I learned a still young daughter of mine had put herself through an abortion.

I suppose I could write an essay—even a personal essay—about abortion, but I am certain it would be a flop. My opinions and point of view on the subject are not all that interesting; my personal experience of the subject is nil. Still, how to resolve my inchoate feelings on the subject? The way I chose to do it was through a short story. What I did was draw a character, a serious businessman, to whom I gave a daughter whom he much loved and also supplied him with my own general views on abortion and sat back and watched how he would react when he learned that his nineteen-year-old child, so dear to him, had had an abortion. Whether I succeeded in this story is not for me to say, but I do think I was correct in deciding that this was material appropriate for fiction.

On the other hand, when, five or so years ago, my mother died, it did not for an instant occur to me to put her into a short story. Instead I wrote an essay about the remarkable woman who was my mother. Nothing would be gained—a good deal might have been lost—had I chosen to disguise my mother through the transformative powers of fiction. Behind my decision was my belief that writing about my mother, about whom I felt uncomplicated love, was best done directly—that is, in the form of the personal essay; while writing about things about which I had somewhat confused, unresolved, less than fully formed thoughts was best done indirectly—that is, in the form of fiction. All this may be a roundabout way of saying that stories are about what happens to characters, while essays are about what happens to one character: the essayist him- or herself.

None of this is meant to circumscribe the territory of the personal essay. "My idea of a writer," Susan Sontag has written, is "someone who is interested in everything," and it is true that the field of subjects available to the essayist is as wide as life itself.

The Norton Book of Personal Essays, I hope, bears this out. Some of its essays are about large subjects; some are about small; and in some what seems a small subject—see, for example, E. B. White's "Once More to the Lake"—turns out to be very large indeed. Some subjects are exotic (Truman Capote's "Tangier," Cyril Connolly's "Revisiting Greece"), others absolutely home-bound (Eudora Welty's "The Little Store," Scott Russell Sanders's "The Inheritance of Tools"). Family relations is a great subject for the personal essayist: in this volume, Virginia Woolf and Doris Lessing write about their fathers, Graham Greene about his childhood, and John Gregory Dunne and Nancy Mairs about their children.

Whatever the ostensible subject of a personal essay, at bottom the true subject is the author of the essay. In all serious writing, no matter how strenuous the attempt to attain objectivity, the author leaves his or her fingerprints. But in the personal essay, all claims to objectivity are dropped at the outset, all masks removed, and the essayist proceeds with shameless subjectivity. This direct presentation of the self, when it comes off, gives the personal essay both its charm and its intimacy.

Perhaps it is this intimacy that makes the personal essay an almost irresistible form. The novelist Rosellen Brown, who edited a collection of personal essays for the magazine *Plough-shares,* makes this same point when, in the preface to the issue of the magazine, she wrote: "Mediocre essays, I can swear after months of reading, are never as boring as mediocre fiction because, even in the hands of the inept, the lives we actually live or witness are more interesting than the ones most of us can (or dare to) invent from scratch." Brown adds that "essays can be badly written and banal, too, but (to mix metaphors wantonly) the wildly unpredictable movements of real event and outcome tend to poke through and make a lively choreography."

The essays in this volume share some of "the wildly unpredict-able movements" about which Rosellen Brown speaks, but, pleasing to report, none is badly written. Which brings us to the matter of how a personal essay ought to be written. The obvious answer, to mimic those old jokes about how do you feed a seven-hundred-pound gorilla, is as carefully and as well as possible. But to take things a step further, there is a general style for personal essays, and it is that which William Hazlitt, one of the great practitioners of the personal essay, termed, nearly two centuries ago, "familiar style." In his essay "On Familiar Style," Hazlitt notes that, to write in a truly familiar style "is to write as any one would speak in common conversation, who had a thorough command and choice of words, or who could discourse with ease, force, and perspicuity, setting aside all pedantic and oratorical flourishes." A familiar style, in other words, is a natural style — natural to conversation, very superior conversation to be sure, and without artifice, pomposity, any bull whatsoever. To be natural in prose, it turns out, much practice is required. The first thing one must learn — and here the exercise of the personal essay is a help — before one can be oneself is who oneself really is.

Not, let me hasten to add, that there is only one familiar style. Although all the essays in this volume were written within the past century, the styles employed by their authors range widely, from the plain to the ornate, to the sensitive, to the anti-nonsensical, to the aggressive, to the penetrating, to the bemused. There are as many styles as there are different temperaments. (Maurice Ravel, when accused of composing music that sounded artificial, replied that what his accuser didn't seem to understand was that he, Ravel, was "naturally artificial.") What unites all the styles of the best personal essayists, though, is that they have found the best way, for them, to recount their experience with the greatest honesty.

What the personal essayist must do straightaway is establish his honesty. Honesty for a writer is rather different from honesty for others. Honesty, outside literature, means not lying, establishing trust through honorable conduct, absolute reliability in personal and professional dealings. In writing, honesty implies something rather different: it implies the accurate, altogether truthful, reporting of feelings, for in literature only the truth is finally persuasive and persuasiveness is at the same time the measure of truth. One might think this would be easy enough to do, but it isn't, especially when one is under the added pressure of making both the feelings and the reporting of them keenly interesting.

Two of the chief ways an essayist can prove interesting are, first, by telling readers things they already know in their hearts but have never been able to formulate for themselves; and, second, by telling them things they do not know and perhaps have never even imagined. Sometimes the personal essayist is announcing, in effect: "Please to notice that I am not so different from you in my feelings toward my father [music, food, sleep, aging, etc.]." When this happens, an amiable community is built up between essayist and audience. Sometimes the personal essayist is announcing, also in effect: "Something truly extraordinary has happened to me that I think you will find no less extraordinary than did I." When this happens, the reader, through the mediation of the essayist, finds his or her own experience enlarged. Sometimes, too, the essayist will admit to ignorance, which is a way of asserting sincerity, and this also makes for an atmosphere of congeniality between essayist and reader. On the matter of a writer's audience, Gertrude Stein once said that she wrote for herself and strangers. The personal essayist writes, I think, for himself and people—even though he has never met them—he assumes are potentially his friends.

Often the personal essayist will begin with a small subject, which grows into something much larger. A perfect example of this phenomenon in this volume is Max Beerbohm's essay "Something Indefeasible," which begins with the essayist observing a child building castles in the sand and leads gently but firmly into a profound observation about the need for destruction in human nature. This magical trick of the personal essay of turning the small into the large has been well described by the essayist Philip Lopate in a nice reversal of an old metaphor: "The personal essay is the reverse of that set of Chinese boxes that you keep opening, only to find a smaller one within. Here you start with the small . . . and suddenly find a slightly larger container, insinuated by the essay's successful articulation and the writer's self-knowledge." Yet from where, the question is, does this self-knowledge derive?

Many years ago I read, in a biography of the philosopher Hannah Arendt, that every afternoon, in her apartment in Manhattan, Arendt would lie down on a couch for an hour and do nothing but think. What a sensible arrangement this seemed! I thought to test it myself. But when I set myself down on my own couch, I discovered that I could come nowhere near an hour's concentrated thought on a specific subject. Five or six minutes seemed my outer limit. Soon my mind would drift off to stray subjects, irrelevant preoccupations, food, fantasies, sheer dreaminess. I suspect that I am not entirely alone in this deficiency.

I have often felt, in fact, that the only coherent, consecutive thought I am capable of comes about through my own writing and through reading other writers. Here I return to my earlier point about the personal essay as a mode or method of discovery—of discovering such truth as is available to the essayist and to his readers. Some writers do not begin a composition—be it a magazine article or a full-blown book—until all the fact-finding that goes by the pretentious name of research is completed. The personal essayist—if my own experience is in any way exemplary—stumbles into facts as he goes along. He writes out of his experience, seen through the lens of his character, projected onto the page through the filter of his style. Experience, character, style—these things, if the personal essayist is lucky, will come together to supply a point of view.

A point of view, which is very different from a collection of opinions, is a distinct way of viewing the world. It is the *sine qua non* of the personal essayist. It can be the making or the breaking of him. All the strong personal essayists—from Montaigne through Hazlitt through Beerbohm through George Orwell— have had a clear and strong and often subtle point of view.

If one has a defect in one's personality, the personal essay is likely to show it up. (Self-congratulation, or the imputation of virtue to oneself, is one of the great traps of the personal essay.) Just possibly all personal essayists suffer from the defect of wishing to talk—or, what is much the same thing, write—about themselves. Apart from those whose egotism is entirely out of control, every personal essayist has had to have thought about this. "I think some people find the essay the last resort of the egoist," wrote E. B. White, "a much too self-conscious and self-serving form for their taste; they feel that it is presumptuous of a writer to assume that his little excursions or his small observations will interest the reader. There is some justice in their complaint."

When the complaint is most just, of course, is when the experience described by the personal essayist has no generalizing quality. By this I mean when the essay isn't really about anything more than the essayist's experience, merely, solely, wholly, and only. The trick of the personal essay—I call it a trick, but I really think true magic is entailed—is to make the particular experience of the essayist part of universal experience. The subject of the personal essay—one's self—may be one in which the personal essayist is the world's leading expert, but if that is his only subject of expertise, the essayist won't remain in business long.

For more than twenty years, I have written a personal essay every three months for *The American Scholar* magazine. Each time I do so, I wonder if the readers of the magazine don't pick it up and, with a half-exasperated sigh, mutter to themselves, "Him again," to be followed, if they decide to read the essay anyway, by such unhappy (for me) exclamations as "Give him the hook!" "Enough already!" and (most terrifying of all) "Who cares!" Where, the question is, does the personal essayist acquire the effrontery to believe—and, more astonishing still, to act on the belief—that his or her interests, concerns, quirks, passions matter to anyone else in the world? If you happen to write personal essays, it's rather an embarrassing question.

The answer, at least for me, comes in part out of two utterly contradictory beliefs. The first is my complete confidence that I am, in the larger scheme of things, an altogether insignificant and fairly ordinary being; the second is my belief that, even in my insignificance and ordinariness—possibly even because of it—what I think is worthy of interest. Another contradiction: I am a man committed to understanding the world and how it operates, all the while knowing that I haven't much chance in succeeding in this endeavor. What I do know is that the world is too rich, too various, too multifaceted and many-layered for a fellow incapable of an hour's sustained thought to hope to comprehend it. Still, through the personal essay, I can take up one or another of its oddities, unresolved questions, or occasional larger subjects, hoping against hope to chip away at true knowledge by obtaining some modicum of self-knowledge.

"The world exists," said Mallarmé, "in order to become a book." For the personal essayist, the first use for experience is for it to be translated into essays. In struggling to make sense of personal experience, the essayist must also fight off adopting the notion of being in any way a star, at center stage. By its very nature, the essay is modest in its assaults upon the world. It is modest, to begin with, in being an attempt (*essayer*, in French, of course, means just that: to attempt) and, to end with, in being content not to answer anywhere near all the questions the essayist's own work, let alone the world, raises. Like the painter Vermeer, the personal essayist is most profound, at least for me, when his intentions are most modest.

An element of confession resides in the personal essay, but, in my view, it ought not to dominate. Confession leads to excessive self-dramatization, and behind most literary work in which self-dramatization plays a key role is the plea, not always entirely out in the open but always hovering in the background, for the sensitivity, soulfulness, and sweet virtue of the essayist. The etiquette for confession in the essay, again in my view, ought to be the same as that for confession in religion: be brief, be blunt, be gone.

What the essayist confronting a subject usually has to confess is that he or she is not quite like other men or women—but then, it turns out, neither are most men and women like other men and women. That seems to me perhaps the chief value of personal essayists: by displaying their individuality, they remind readers of their own individuality.

My hope, of course, is that this is precisely what *The Norton Book of Personal Essays* will do for its readers—remind them that their own lives exist in a world never dreamed of by social science, journalism, or any sort of academic thought. Not that the essays in this book were chosen primarily to illustrate this crucial point. They were chosen because I liked them, found them interesting, touching, pleasing, amusing, delightful—above all, entertaining.

A few words on the plan and rationale of this book. My assignment simply was to select good essays, all originally written in English and published in this century. Insofar as possible, I tried not to allow too much duplication in the subject matter of the essays; I also tried to avoid republishing essays that have already appeared too often in other collections of essays, which meant leaving out Virginia Woolf's essay on the moth, and George Orwell on a hanging or on the political nature of language, and H. L. Mencken on the South. Working my way round this, in some instances I have chosen lesser-known essays by famous writers; in other instances, I have chosen works by good writers who are not as well known as they ought to be. Some of my selections are fairly lengthy; others are brief. Variety, which is the essence of a successful prose style, ought also to be the essence of an entertaining collection of essays. My hope is that I have got everything—content, length, writers—in roughly the right mixture and that the essays in this book give their readers the same pleasure they gave their editor.

I have two acknowledgments to make: The first is to Frederick T. Courtright, who is in charge of rights and permissions for the firm of W. W. Norton, and whose negotiations for the reprint rights for this book proved immensely helpful. The second is to Carol Houck Smith—my excellent editor, my dear friend—who contributed her skill and good judgment to this book from first to last and without whom it would never have come into existence.

MARK TWAIN

ITALIAN WITHOUT A MASTER

It is almost a fortnight now that I am domiciled in a mediæval villa in the country, a mile or two from Florence. I cannot speak the language; I am too old now to learn how, also too busy when I am busy, and too indolent when I am not; wherefore some will imagine that I am having a dull time of it. But it is not so. The "help" are all natives; they talk Italian to me, I answer in English; I do not understand them, they do not understand me, consequently no harm is done, and everybody is satisfied. In order to be just and fair, I throw in an Italian word when I have one, and this has a good influence. I get the word out of the morning paper. I have to use it while it is fresh, for I find that Italian words do not keep in this climate. They fade toward night, and next morning they are gone. But it is no matter; I get a new one out of the paper before breakfast, and thrill the domestics with it while it lasts. I have no dictionary, and I do not want one; I can select my words by the sound, or by orthographic aspect. Many of them have a French or German or English look, and these are the ones I enslave for the day's service. That is, as a rule. Not always. If I find a learnable phrase that has an imposing look and warbles musically along I do not care to know the meaning of it; I pay it out to the first applicant, knowing that if I pronounce it carefully *he* will understand it, and that's enough.

Yesterday's word was *avanti*. It sounds Shakespearian, and probably means Avaunt and quit my sight. To-day I have a whole phrase: *sono dispiacentissimo*. I do not know what it means, but it seems to fit in everywhere and give satisfaction. Although as a rule my words and phrases are good for one day and train only, I have several that stay by me all the time, for some unknown reason, and these come very handy when I get into a long conversation and need things to fire up with in monotonous stretches. One of the best ones is *Dov' è il gatto*. It nearly always produces a pleasant surprise, therefore I save it up for places where I want to express applause or admiration. The fourth word has a French sound, and I think the phrase means "that takes the cake."

During my first week in the deep and dreamy stillness of this woodsy and flowery place I was without news of the outside world, and was well content without it. It had been four weeks since I had seen a newspaper, and this lack seemed to give life a new charm and grace, and to saturate it with a feeling verging upon actual delight. Then came a change that was to be expected: the appetite for news began to rise again, after this invigorating rest. I had to feed it, but I was not willing to let it make me its helpless slave again; I determined to put it on a diet, and a strict and limited one. So I examined an Italian paper, with the idea of feeding it on that, and on that exclusively. On that exclusively, and without help of a dictionary. In this way I should surely be well protected against overloading and indigestion.

A glance at the telegraphic page filled me with encouragement. There were no scare-heads. That was good—supremely good. But there were headings—one-liners and two-liners—and that was good too; for without these, one must do as one does with a German paper—pay out precious time in finding out what an article is about, only to discover, in many cases, that there is nothing in it of interest to you. The headline is a valuable thing.

Necessarily we are all fond of murders, scandals, swindles, robberies, explosions, collisions, and all such things, when we know the people, and when they are neighbors and friends, but when they are strangers we do not get any great pleasure out of them, as a rule. Now the trouble with an American paper is that it has no discrimination; it rakes the whole earth for blood and garbage, and the result is that you are daily overfed and suffer a surfeit. By habit you stow this muck every day, but you come by and by to take no vital interest in it—indeed, you almost get tired of it. As a rule, forty-nine-fiftieths of it concerns strangers only—people away off yonder, a thousand miles, two thousand miles, ten thousand miles from where you are. Why, when you come to think of it, who cares what becomes of those people? I would not give the assassination of one personal friend for a whole massacre of those others. And, to my mind, one relative or neighbor mixed up in a scandal is more interesting than a whole Sodom and Gomorrah of outlanders gone rotten. Give me the home product every time.

Very well. I saw at a glance that the Florentine paper would suit me: five out of six of its scandals and tragedies were local; they were adventures of one's very neighbors, one might almost say one's friends. In the matter of world news there was not too much, but just about enough. I subscribed. I have had no occasion to regret it. Every morning I get all the news I need for the day; sometimes from the headlines, sometimes from the text. I have never had to call for a dictionary yet. I read the paper with ease. Often I do not quite understand, often some of the details escape me, but no matter, I get the idea. I will cut out a passage or two, then you will see how limpid the language is:

Il ritorno dei Reali d'Italia
Elargizione del Re all' Ospedale italiano

The first line means that the Italian sovereigns are coming back—they have been to England. The second line seems to mean that they enlarged the King at the Italian hospital. With a banquet, I suppose. An English banquet has that effect. Further:

Il ritorno dei Sovrani
a Roma

ROMA, 24, ore 22,50. - I Sovrani e le Principessine Reali si attendono a Roma domani alle ore 15,51.

Return of the sovereigns to Rome, you see. Date of the telegram, Rome, November 24, ten minutes before twenty-three o'clock. The telegram seems to say, "The Sovereigns and the Royal Children expect themselves at Rome tomorrow at fifty-one minutes after fifteen o'clock."

I do not know about Italian time, but I judge it begins at midnight and runs through the twenty-four hours without breaking bulk. In the following ad. the theatres open at half past twenty. If these are not matinées, 20.30 must mean 8.30 P.M., by my reckoning.

Spettacoli del dì 25

TEATRO DELLA PERGOLA — (Ore 20,30)
— Opera: *Bohème.*
TEATRO ALFIERI. — Compagnia drammatica Drago — (Ore 20,30) — *La Legge.*
ALHAMBRA — (Ore 20,30) — Spettacolo variato.
SALA EDISON — Grandioso spettacolo Cinematografico: *Quo-Vadis?* — Inaugurazione della Chiesa Russa — In coda al Direttissimo — Vedute di Firenze con gran movimento — America: Trasporto tronchi giganteschi — I ladri in casa del Diavolo — Scene comiche.
CINEMATOGRAFO — Via Brunelleschi n. 4. — Programma straordinario, *Don Chisciotte* — Prezzi popolari.

The whole of that is intelligible to me—and sane and rational, too—except the remark about the Inauguration of a Russian Cheese. That one oversizes my hand. Gimme five cards.

This is a four-page paper; and as it is set in long primer leaded and has a page of advertisements, there is no room for the crimes, disasters, and general sweepings of the outside world—thanks be! To-day I find only a single importation of the off-color sort:

Una principessa
che fugge con un cocchiere

PARIGI, 24. - Il *Matin* ha da Berlino che la principessa Schovenbare-Waldenbure scomparve il 9 novembre. Sarebbe partita col suo cocchiere.
La principessa ha 27 anni.

Twenty-seven years old, and scomparve—scampered—on the 9th November. You see by the added detail that she departed with her coachman. I hope Sarebbe has not made a mistake, but I am afraid the chances are that she has. *Sono dispiacentissimo.*

There are several fires; also a couple of accidents. This is one of them:

Grave disgrazia sul Ponte Vecchio

Stamattina, circa le 7,30, mentre Giuseppe Sciatti, di anni 55, di Casellina e Torri, passava dal Ponte Vecchio, stando seduto sopra un barroccio carico di verdura, perse l'equilibrio e cadde al suolo, rimanendo con la gamba destra sotto una ruota del veicolo.

Lo Sciatti fu subito raccolto da alcuni cittadini, che, per mezzo della pubblica vettura n. 365, lo trasportarono a San Giovanni di Dio.

Ivi il medico di guardia gli riscontrò la frattura della gamba destra e alcune lievi escoriazioni giudicandolo guaribile in 50 giorni salvo complicazioni.

What it seems to say is this: "Serious Disgrace on the Old Old Bridge. This morning about 7.30, Mr. Joseph Sciatti, aged 55, of Casellina and Torri, while standing up in a sitting posture on top of a carico barrow of verdure (foliage? hay? vegetables?), lost his equilibrium and fell on himself, arriving with his left leg under one of the wheels of the vehicle.

"Said Sciatti was suddenly harvested (gathered in?) by several citizens, who by means of public cab No. 365 transported him to St. John of God."

Paragraph No. 3 is a little obscure, but I think it says that the medico set the broken left leg—right enough, since there was nothing the matter with the other one—and that several are encouraged to hope that fifty days will fetch him around in quite giudicandolo-guaribile way, if no complications intervene.

I am sure I hope so myself.

There is a great and peculiar charm about reading news-scraps in a language which you are not acquainted with—the charm that always goes with the mysterious and the uncertain. You can never be absolutely sure of the meaning of anything you read in such circumstances; you are chasing an alert and gamy riddle all the time, and the baffling turns and dodges of the prey make the life of the hunt. A dictionary would spoil it. Sometimes a single word of doubtful purport will cast a veil of dreamy and golden uncertainty over a whole paragraph of cold and practical certainties, and leave steeped in a haunting and adorable mystery an

incident which had been vulgar and commonplace but for that
benefaction. Would you be wise to draw a dictionary on that
gracious word? Would you be properly grateful?

After a couple of days' rest I now come back to my subject and
seek a case in point. I find it without trouble, in the morning
paper; a cablegram from Chicago and Indiana by way of Paris.
All the words save one are guessable by a person ignorant of
Italian:

Revolverate in teatro

PARIGI, 27. - La *Patrie* ha da Chicago:
Il guardiano del teatro dell'opera di Wallace (Indiana), avendo voluto espellere uno
spettatore che continuava a fumare malgrado
il divieto, questo spalleggiato dai suoi amici
tirò diversi colpi di rivoltella. Il guardiano
rispose. Nacque una scarica generale. Grande
panico fra gli spettatori. Nessun ferito.

Translation. — "REVOLVERATION IN THEATRE. *Paris. 27th. La
Patrie* has from Chicago: The cop of the theatre of the opera of
Wallace, Indiana, had willed to expel a spectator which continued to smoke in spite of the prohibition, who, spalleggiato by his
friends, tirò (Fr. *tiré,* Anglice *pulled*) manifold revolver-shots.
The cop responded. Result, a general scare; great panic among
the spectators. Nobody hurt."

It is bettable that that harmless cataclysm in the theatre of the
opera of Wallace, Indiana, excited not a person in Europe but
me, and so came near to not being worth cabling to Florence by
way of France. But it does excite me. It excites me because I
cannot make out, for sure, what it was that moved that spectator
to resist the officer. I was gliding along smoothly and without
obstruction or accident, until I came to that word spalleggiato,
then the bottom fell out. You notice what a rich gloom, what a
sombre and pervading mystery, that word sheds all over the
whole Wallachian tragedy. That is the charm of the thing, that
is the delight of it. This is where you begin, this is where you
revel. You can guess and guess, and have all the fun you like;
you need not be afraid there will be an end to it; none is possible,
for no amount of guessing will ever furnish you a meaning for

that word that you can be sure is the right one. All the other words give you hints, by their form, their sound, or their spelling—this one doesn't, this one throws out no hints, this one keeps its secret. If there is even the slightest slight shadow of a hint anywhere, it lies in the very meagrely suggestive fact that spalleggiato carries our word "egg" in its stomach. Well, make the most out of it, and then where are you at? You conjecture that the spectator which was smoking in spite of the prohibition and become reprohibited by the guardians, was "egged on" by his friends, and that it was owing to that evil influence that he initiated the revolveration in theatre that has galloped under the sea and come crashing through the European press without exciting anybody but me. But are you sure, are you dead sure, that that was the way of it? No. Then the uncertainty remains, the mystery abides, and with it the charm. Guess again.

If I had a phrase-book of a really satisfactory sort I would study it, and not give all my free time to undictionarial readings, but there is no such work on the market. The existing phrase-books are inadequate. They are well enough as far as they go, but when you fall down and skin your leg they don't tell you what to say.

MAX BEERBOHM

Something Defeasible

The cottage had a good trim garden in front of it, and another behind it. I might not have noticed it at all but for them and their emerald greenness. Yet itself (I saw when I studied it) was worthy of them. Sussex is rich in fine Jacobean cottages; and their example, clearly, had not been lost on the builder of this one. Its proportions had a homely grandeur. It was long and wide and low. It was quite a yard long. It had three admirable gables. It had a substantial and shapely chimney-stack. I liked the look that it had of honest solidity all over, nothing anywhere scamped in the workmanship of it. It looked as though it had been built for all time. But this was not so. For it was built on sand, and of sand; and the tide was coming in.

Here and there in its vicinity stood other buildings. None of these possessed any points of interest. They were just old-fashioned "castles," of the bald and hasty kind which I myself used to make in childhood and could make even now—conic affairs, with or without untidily-dug moats, the nullities of convention and of unskilled labour. When I was a child the charm of a castle was not in the building of it, but in jumping over it when it was built. Nor was this an enduring charm. After a few jumps one abandoned one's castle and asked one's nurse for a bun, or picked a quarrel with some child even smaller than oneself, or went paddling. As it was, so it is. My survey of the sands this morning showed me that forty years had made no difference. Here was plenty of animation, plenty of scurrying and gambolling, of laughter and tears. But the actual spadework was a mere empty form. For all but the builder of that cottage. For him, manifestly, a passion, a rite.

He stood, spade in hand, contemplating, from one angle and another, what he had done. He was perhaps nine years old; if so, small for his age. He had very thin legs in very short grey knickerbockers, a pale freckled face, and hair that matched the sand. He was not remarkable. But with a little good-will one can always find something impressive in anybody. When Mr. Mallaby-Deeley won a wide and very sudden fame in connexion with Covent Garden, an awe-stricken reporter wrote of him for *The Daily Mail,* "he has the eyes of a dreamer." I believe that Mr. Cecil Rhodes really had. So, it seemed to me, had this little boy. They were pale grey eyes, rather prominent, with an unwavering light in them. I guessed that they were regarding the cottage rather as what it should be than as what it had become. To me it appeared quite perfect. But I surmised that to him, artist that he was, it seemed a poor thing beside his first flushed conception.

He knelt down and, partly with the flat of his spade, partly with the palm of one hand, redressed some (to me obscure) fault in one of the gables. He rose, stood back, his eyes slowly endorsed the amendment. A few moments later, very suddenly, he scudded away to the adjacent breakwater and gave himself to the task of scraping off it some of the short green sea-weed wherewith he had made the cottage's two gardens so pleasantly realistic, oases so refreshing in the sandy desert. Were the lawns somehow imperfect? Anon, when he darted back, I saw what it was that his taste had required: lichen, moss, for the roof. Sundry morsels and patches of green he deftly disposed in the angles of roof and gables. His stock exhausted, off to the breakwater he darted, and back again, to and fro with the lightning directness of a hermit-bee making its nest of pollen. The low walls that enclosed the two gardens were in need of creepers. Little by little, this grace was added to them. I stood silently watching.

I kept silent for fear of discommoding him. All artists—by which I mean, of course, all good artists—are shy. They are trustees of something not entrusted to us others; they bear fragile treasure, not safe in a jostling crowd; they must ever be wary. And especially shy are those artists whose work is apart from words. A man of letters can mitigate his embarrassment among us by a certain glibness. Not so can the man who works through the medium of visual form and colour. Not so, I was sure, could the young architect and landscape-gardener here creating. I would have moved away had I thought my mere presence was a bother to him; but I decided that it was not: being a grown-up person, I did not matter; he had no fear that I should offer violence to his work. It was his coevals that made him uneasy. Groups of these would pause in their wild career to stand over him and watch him in a fidgety manner that hinted mischief. Suppose one of them suddenly jumped—onto the cottage!

Fragile treasure, this, in a quite literal sense; and how awfully exposed! It was spared, however. There was even legible on the faces of the stolid little boys who viewed it a sort of reluctant approval. Some of the little girls seemed to be forming with their lips the word "pretty," but then they exchanged glances with one another, signifying "silly." No one of either sex uttered any word of praise. And so, because artists, be they never so agoraphobious, do want praise, I did at length break my silence to this one. "I think it splendid," I said to him.

He looked up at me, and down at the cottage. "Do you?" he asked, looking up again. I assured him that I did; and to test my opinion of him I asked whether he didn't think so too. He stood the test well. "I wanted it rather diff'rent," he answered.

"In what way different?"

He searched his vocabulary. "More comf'table," he found.

I knew now that he was not merely the architect and builder of the cottage, but also, by courtesy of imagination, its tenant; but I was tactful enough not to let him see that I had guessed this deep and delicate secret. I did but ask him, in a quite general way, how the cottage could be better. He said that it ought to have a porch—"but porches tumble in." He was too young an artist to accept quite meekly the limits imposed by his material. He pointed along the lower edge of the roof: "It ought to stick out," he said, meaning that it wanted eaves. I told him not to worry about that: it was the sand's fault, not his. "What really *is* a pity," I said, "is that your house can't last for ever." He was tracing now on the roof, with the edge of his spade, a criss-cross pattern, to represent tiles, and he seemed to have forgotten my presence and my kindness. "Aren't you sorry," I asked, raising my voice rather sharply, "that the sea is coming in?"

He glanced at the sea. "Yes." He said this with a lack of emphasis that seemed to me noble though insincere.

The strain of talking in words of not more than three syllables had begun to tell on me. I bade the artist good-bye, wandered away up the half-dozen steps to the Parade, sat down on a bench, and opened the morning paper that I had brought out unread. During the War one felt it a duty to know the worst before breakfast; now that the English polity is threatened merely from within, one is apt to dally. . . . Merely from within? Is that a right phrase when the nerves of unrestful Labour in any one land are interplicated with its nerves in any other, so vibrantly? News of the dismissal of an erring workman in Timbuctoo is enough nowadays to make us apprehensive of vast and dreadful effects on our own immediate future. How pleasant if we had lived our lives in the nineteenth century and no other, with the ground all firm under our feet! True, the people who flourished then had recurring alarms. But their alarms were quite needless; whereas ours—! Ours, as I glanced at this morning's news from Timbuctoo and elsewhere, seemed odiously needful. Withal, our Old Nobility in its pleasaunces was treading once more the old graceful measure which the War arrested; Bohemia had resumed its motley; even the middle class was capering, very noticeably. . . . To gad about smiling as though he were quite well, thank you, or to sit down, pull a long face, and make his soul—which, I wondered, is the better procedure for a man knowing that very soon he will have to undergo a vital operation at the hands of a wholly unqualified surgeon who dislikes him personally? I inclined to think the gloomier way the less ghastly. But then, I asked myself, was my analogy a sound one? We are at the mercy of Labour, certainly; and Labour does not love us; and Labour is not deeply versed in statecraft. But would an unskilled surgeon, however ill-wishing, care to perform a drastic operation on a patient by whose death he himself would forthwith perish? Labour is wise enough—surely?—not to will us destruction. Rus-

sia has been an awful example. Surely! And yet, Labour does not
seem to think the example so awful as I do. Queer, this; queer
and disquieting. I rose from my bench, strolled to the railing,
and gazed forth.

The unrestful, the well-organised and minatory sea had been
advancing quickly. It was not very far now from the cottage. I
thought of all the civilisations that had been, that were not, that
were as though they had never been. Must it always be thus?—
always the same old tale of growth and greatness and overthrow,
nothingness? I gazed at the cottage, all so solid and seemly, so
full of endearing character, so like to the "comf'table" polity of
England as we have known it. I gazed away from it to a large-ish
castle that the sea was just reaching. A little, then quickly much,
the waters swirled into the moat. Many children stood by, all a-
dance with excitement. The castle was shedding its sides, lapsing,
dwindling, landslipping—gone. O Ninevah! And now another—
O Memphis? Rome?—yielded to the cataclysm. I listened to the
jubilant screams of the children. What rapture, what wantoning!
Motionless beside his work stood the builder of the cottage, gazing seaward, a pathetic little figure. I hoped the other children
would have the decency not to exult over the unmaking of what
he had made so well. This hope was not fulfilled. I had not
supposed it would be. What did surprise me, when anon the sea
rolled close up to the cottage, was the comportment of the young
artist himself. His sobriety gave place to an intense animation.
He leapt, he waved his spade, he invited the waves with wild
gestures and gleeful cries. His face had flushed bright, and now,
as the garden walls crumbled, and the paths and lawns were mingled by the waters' influence and confluence, and the walls of
the cottage itself began to totter, and the gables sank, and all, all
was swallowed, his leaps were so high in air that they recalled to
my memory those of a strange religious sect which once visited
London; and the glare of his eyes was less indicative of a dreamer
than of a triumphant fiend.

I myself was conscious of a certain wild enthusiasm within
me. But this was less surprising for that *I* had not built the cottage, and *my* fancy had not enabled me to dwell in it. It was the
boy's own enthusiasm that made me feel, as never before, how

deep-rooted in the human breast the love of destruction, of mere destruction, is. And I began to ask myself: "Even if England as we know it, the English polity of which that cottage was a symbol to me, were the work of (say) Mr. Robert Smillie's own unaided hands"—but I waived the question coming from that hypothesis, and other questions that would have followed; for I wished to be happy while I might.

BERTRAND RUSSELL

Joseph Conrad

I made the acquaintance of Joseph Conrad in September 1913, through our common friend Lady Ottoline Morrell. I had been for many years an admirer of his books, but should not have ventured to seek acquaintance without an introduction. I traveled down to his house near Ashford in Kent in a state of somewhat anxious expectation. My first impression was one of surprise. He spoke English with a very strong foreign accent, and nothing in his demeanor in any way suggested the sea. He was an aristocratic Polish gentleman to his finger tips. His feeling for the sea, and for England, was one of romantic love—love from a certain distance, sufficient to leave the romance untarnished. His love for the sea began at a very early age. When he told his parents that he wished for a career as a sailor, they urged him to go into the Austrian navy, but he wanted adventure and tropical seas and strange rivers surrounded by dark forests; and the Austrian navy offered him no scope for these desires. His family were horrified at his seeking a career in the English merchant marine, but his determination was inflexible.

He was, as anyone may see from his books, a very rigid moralist and politically far from sympathetic with revolutionaries. He and I were in most of our opinions by no means in agreement, but in something very fundamental we were extraordinarily at one.

My relation to Joseph Conrad was unlike any other that I have ever had. I saw him seldom, and not over a long period of years. In the outworks of our lives, we were almost strangers, but we shared a certain outlook on human life and human destiny, which, from the very first, made a bond of extreme strength. I may perhaps be pardoned for quoting a sentence from a letter that he wrote to me very soon after we had become acquainted. I should feel that modesty forbids the quotation except for the fact that it expresses so exactly what I felt about him. What he expressed and I equally felt was, in his words, "A deep admiring affection which, if you were never to see me again and forgot my existence tomorrow, would be unalterably yours *usque ad finem*."

Of all that he had written I admired most the terrible story called *The Heart of Darkness,* in which a rather weak idealist is driven mad by horror of the tropical forest and loneliness among savages. This story expresses, I think, most completely his philosophy of life. I felt, though I do not know whether he would have accepted such an image, that he thought of civilized and morally tolerable human life as a dangerous walk on a thin crust of barely cooled lava which at any moment might break and let the unwary sink into fiery depths. He was very conscious of the various forms of passionate madness to which men are prone, and it was this that gave him such a profound belief in the importance of discipline. His point of view, one might perhaps say, was the antithesis of Rousseau's: "Man is born in chains, but he can become free." He becomes free, so I believe Conrad would have said, not by letting loose his impulses, not by being casual and uncontrolled, but by subduing wayward impulse to a dominant purpose.

He was not much interested in political systems, though he had some strong political *feelings.* The strongest of these were love of England and hatred of Russia, of which both are expressed in *The Secret Agent:* and the hatred of Russia, both Czarist and revolutionary, is set forth with great power in *Under Western Eyes.* His dislike of Russia was that which was traditional in Poland. It went so far that he would not allow merit to either Tolstoy or Dostoievsky. Turgeniev, he told me once, was the only Russian novelist he admired.

Except for love of England and hatred of Russia, politics did not much concern him. What interested him was the individual human soul faced with the indifference of nature, and often with the hostility of man, and subject to inner struggles with passions

both good and bad that led toward destruction. Tragedies of loneliness occupied a great part of his thought and feeling. One of
his most typical stories is *Typhoon*. In this story the captain, who
is a simple soul, pulls his ship through by unshakable courage
and grim determination. When the storm is over, he writes a
long letter to his wife telling about it. In his account his own part
is, to him, perfectly simple. He has merely performed his captain's duty as, of course, anyone would expect. But the reader,
through his narrative, becomes aware of all that he has done and
dared and endured. The letter, before he sends it off, is read
surreptitiously by his steward, but is never read by anyone else at
all because his wife finds it boring and throws it away unread.

The two things that seem most to occupy Conrad's imagination are loneliness and fear of what is strange. *An Outcast of the
Islands* like *The Heart of Darkness* is concerned with fear of what
is strange. Both come together in the extraordinarily moving story
called *Amy Foster*. In this story a South-Slav peasant, on his way
to America, is the sole survivor of the wreck of his ship, and is
cast away in a Kentish village. All the village fears and ill treats
him, except Amy Foster, a dull, plain girl who brings him bread
when he is starving and finally marries him. But she, too, when,
in fever, her husband reverts to his native language, is seized with
a fear of his strangeness, snatches up their child and abandons
him. He dies alone and hopeless. I have wondered at times how
much of this man's loneliness Conrad had felt among the
English and had suppressed by a stern effort of will.

Conrad's point of view was far from modern. In the modern
world there are two philosophies: the one, which stems from
Rousseau, and sweeps aside discipline as unnecessary; the other,
which finds its fullest expression in totalitarianism, which thinks
of discipline as essentially imposed from without. Conrad
adhered to the older tradition, that discipline should come from
within. He despised indiscipline, and hated discipline that was
merely external.

In all this I found myself closely in agreement with him. At
our very first meeting, we talked with continually increasing intimacy. We seemed to sink through layer after layer of what was
superficial, till gradually both reached the central fire. It was an

experience unlike any other that I have known. We looked into each other's eyes, half appalled and half intoxicated to find ourselves together in such a region. The emotion was as intense as passionate love, and at the same time all-embracing. I came away bewildered, and hardly able to find my way among ordinary affairs.

I saw nothing of Conrad during the war or after it until my return from China in 1921. When my first son was born in that year I wished Conrad to be as nearly his godfather as was possible without a formal ceremony. I wrote to Conrad saying: "I wish, with your permission, to call my son John Conrad. My father was called John, my grandfather was called John, and my great-grandfather was called John; and Conrad is a name in which I see merits." He accepted the position and duly presented my son with the cup which is usual on such occasions.

I did not see much of him, as I lived most of the year in Cornwall, and his health was failing. But I had some charming letters from him, especially one about my book on China. He wrote: "I have always liked the Chinese, even those that tried to kill me (and some other people) in the yard of a private house in Chantabun, even (but not so much) the fellow who stole all my money one night in Bangkok, but brushed and folded my clothes neatly for me to dress in the morning, before vanishing into the depths of Siam. I also received many kindnesses at the hands of various Chinese. This with the addition of an evening's conversation with the secretary of His Excellency Tseng on the verandah of a hotel and a perfunctory study of a poem, "The Heathen Chinee" is all I know about Chinese. But after reading your extremely interesting view of the Chinese Problem I take a gloomy view of the future of their country." He went on to say that my views of the future of China "strike a chill into one's soul," the more so, he said, as I pinned my hopes on international socialism—"The sort of thing," he commented, "to which I cannot attach any sort of definite meaning. I have never been able to find in any man's book or any man's talk anything convincing enough to stand up for a moment against my deep-seated sense of fatality governing this man-inhabited world." He went on to say that although man has taken to flying, "He doesn't fly like an eagle, he flies like a beetle. And you must have noticed how ugly, ridiculous and fatuous is the flight of a beetle." In these pessimistic remarks, I felt that he was showing a deeper wisdom than I had shown in my somewhat artificial hopes for a happy issue in China. It must be said that so far events have proved him right.

This letter was my last contact with him. I never again saw him to speak to. Once I saw him across the street, in earnest conversation with a man I did not know, standing outside the door of what had been my grandmother's house, but after her death had become the Arts Club. I did not like to interrupt what seemed a serious conversation, and I went away. When he died, shortly afterward, I was sorry I had not been bolder. The house is gone, demolished by Hitler. Conrad, I suppose, is in process of being forgotten. But his intense and passionate nobility shines in my memory like a star seen from the bottom of a well. I wish I could make his light shine for others as it shone for me.

WILLA CATHER

A Chance Meeting

I

It happened at Aix-les-Bains, one of the pleasantest places in the world. I was staying at the Grand-Hôtel d'Aix, which opens on the sloping little square with the bronze head of Queen Victoria, commemorating her visits to that old watering-place in Savoie. The Casino and the Opera are next door, just across the gardens. The hotel was built for the travellers of forty years ago, who liked large rooms and large baths, and quiet. It is not at all smart, but very comfortable. Long ago I used to hear old Pittsburghers and Philadelphians talk of it. The newer hotels, set on the steep hills above the town, have the fashionable trade; the noise and jazz and dancing.

In the dining-room I often noticed, at a table not far from mine, an old lady, a Frenchwoman, who usually lunched and dined alone. She seemed very old indeed, well over eighty, and somewhat infirm, though not at all withered or shrunken. She was not stout, but her body had that rather shapeless heaviness which for some detestable reason often settles upon people in old age. The thing one especially noticed was her fine head, so well set upon her shoulders and beautiful in shape, recalling some of the portrait busts of Roman ladies. Her forehead was low and straight, her nose made just the right angle with it, and there was something quite lovely about her temples, something one very rarely sees.

As I watched her entering and leaving the dining-room I observed that she was slightly lame, and that she utterly disregarded it—walked with a quick, short step and great impatience, holding her shoulders well back. One saw that she was contemptuously intolerant of the limitations of old age. As she passed my table she often gave me a keen look and a half-smile (her eyes were extremely bright and clear), as if she were about to speak. But I remained blank. I am a poor linguist, and there would be no point in uttering commonplaces to this old lady; one knew that much about her, at a glance. If one spoke to her at all, one must be at ease.

Several times in the early morning I happened to see her leave the hotel in her motor, and each time her chauffeur brought down and placed in the car a camp chair, an easel, and canvases and colour boxes strapped together. Then they drove off toward the mountains. A plucky old lady, certainly, to go sketching in that very hot weather—for this was in the latter part of August 1930, one of the hottest seasons Aix-les-Bains had ever known. Every evening after dinner the old lady disappeared into the lift and went to her own rooms. But often she reappeared later, dressed for the opera, and went out, attended by her maid.

One evening, when there was no opera, I found her smoking a cigarette in the lounge, where I had gone to write letters. It was a very hot night, and all the windows were open; seeing her pull her lace shawl closer about her shoulders, I went to shut one of them. Then she spoke to me in excellent English:—

"I think that draught blows out from the dining-room. If you will ask the boy to close the doors, we shall not feel the air."

I found the boy and had the doors closed. When I returned, the old lady thanked me, motioned to a chair at her side, and asked if I had time for a cigarette.

"You are stopping at Aix for some time, I judge?" she asked as I sat down.

I replied that I was.

"You like it, then? You are taking a cure? You have been here before?"

No, I was not taking a cure. I had been here before, and had come back merely because I liked the place.

"It has changed less than most places, I think," she remarked. "I have been coming here for thirty-five years; I have old associations with Aix-les-Bains. Besides, I enjoy the music here. I live in the South, at Antibes. You attend the Grand-Cercle? You heard the performance of *Tristan and Iseult* last night?"

I had not heard it. I told her I had thought the evening too frightfully hot to sit in a theatre.

"But it was no hotter there than anywhere else. I was not uncomfortable."

There was a reprimand in her tone, and I added the further excuse that I had thought the principals would probably not be very good, and that I liked to hear that opera well sung.

"They were well enough," she declared. "With Wagner I do not so much care about the voices. It is the orchestra I go to hear. The conductor last night was Albert Wolff, one of our best *Kapellmeister.*"

I said I was sorry I had missed the opera.

"Are you going to his classical concert tomorrow afternoon? He will give a superb rendering of Ravel's *La Valse*—if you care for modern music."

I hastily said that I meant to go.

"But have you reserved your places? No? Then I would advise you to do so at once. The best way here is to have places for the entire chain of performances. One need not go to all, of course; but it is the best way. There is little else to do here in the evening, unless one plays at the gaming tables. Besides, it is almost September; the days are lowering now, and one needs the theatre." The old lady stopped, frowned, and made an impatient gesture with her very interesting hand. "What should I have said then? Lowering is not the word, but I seldom have opportunity to speak English."

"You might say the days are growing shorter, but I think lowering a very good word."

"*Mais un peu poétique, n'est-ce pas?*"

"Perhaps; but it is the right kind of poetic."

"And by that you mean?"

"That it's not altogether bookish or literary. The country people use it in some parts of England, I think. I have heard old-fashioned farmers use it in America, in the South."

The old lady gave a dry little laugh. "So if the farmers use a word it is quite safe, eh?"

Yes, I told her, that was exactly what I meant; safe.

We talked a little longer on that first occasion. She asked if I had been to Chamonix, and strongly advised me to go to a place near Sallanches, where she had lately been visiting friends, on her way to Aix-les-Bains. In replying to her questions I fell into the stupid way one sometimes adopts when speaking to people of another language; tried to explain something in very simple words. She frowned and checked me with: "Speak idiomatically, please. I knew English quite well at one time. If I speak it badly, it is because now I have no practice."

I said good-night and sat down at a desk to write letters. But on the way to my room I stopped to tell the friend with whom I was travelling that the old French lady we had so often admired spoke very good English, and spoke it easily; that she seemed, indeed, to have a rather special feeling for language.

II

The next day was intensely hot. In the morning the beautiful mountain ridges which surround Aix stood out sharp and clear, but the vineyards looked wilted. Toward noon the hills grew misty, and the sun poured down through a slightly milky atmosphere. I rather dreaded the heat of a concert hall, but at two o'clock I went to Albert Wolff's concert, and heard such a rendition of Ravel's *La Valse* as I do not expect to hear again; a small orchestra, wonderfully trained, and a masterly conductor.

The program was long, with two intermissions. The last group did not seem to be especially interesting, and the concert was quite long enough, and fine enough, without those numbers. I decided that I could miss them. I would go up to the Square and have tea beside the Roman arch. As I left the hall by the garden entrance, I saw the old French lady seated on the veranda with her maid, wearing a white dress and a white lace garden hat, fanning herself vigorously, the beads of moisture on her face making dark streaks in the powder. She beckoned to me and asked whether I had enjoyed the music. I told her that I had, very much indeed; but now my capacity for enjoying, or even listening, was quite spent, and I was going up to the Square for tea.

"Oh, no," said she, "that is not necessary. You can have your tea here at the Maison des Fleurs quite well, and still have time to go back for the last group."

I thanked her and went across the garden, but I did not mean to see the concert through. Seeing things through was evidently a habit with this old lady: witness the way she was seeing life through, going to concerts and operas in this wilting heat; being concerned that other people should go, moreover, and caring about the way in which Ravel was played, when in the course of nature her interest in new music should have stopped with César Franck, surely.

I left the Casino gardens through a grotto that gave into the street, went up to the Square, and had tea with some nice English people I had met on Mont Revard, a young business man and his wife come over for their holiday. I felt a little as if I had escaped from an exacting preceptress. The old lady took it for granted that one wished to accomplish as much as possible in a given space of time. I soon found that, to her, life meant just that—accomplishing things; "doing them always a little better and better," as she once remarked after I came to know her.

While I was dressing for dinner I decided to go away for a few days, up into the high mountains of Haute-Savoie, under Mont Blanc. That evening, when the old lady stopped me to discuss the concert, I asked her for some suggestions about the hotels there, since at our first meeting she had said I must certainly go to some of the mountain places easily reached from Sallanches.

She at once recommended a hotel that was very high and cool, and then told me of all the excursions I must make from that place, outlining a full program which I knew I should not follow. I was going away merely to escape the heat and to regard Mont Blanc from an advantageous point—not to become acquainted with the country.

III

My trip into the mountains was wholly successful. All the suggestions the old lady had given me proved excellent, and I felt very grateful to her. I stayed away longer than I had intended. I returned to Aix-les-Bains late one night, got up early the next morning, and went to the bank, feeling that Aix is always a good place to come back to. When I returned to the hotel for lunch, there was the old lady, sitting in a chair just outside the door, looking worn and faded. Why, since she had her car and her driver there, she had not run away from the heat, I do not know. But she had stayed through it, and gone out sketching every morning. She greeted me very cordially, asked whether I had an engagement for the evening, and suggested that we should meet in the salon after dinner.

I was dining with my friend, and after dinner we both went into the writing-room where the old lady was awaiting us. Our acquaintance seemed to have progressed measurably in my absence, though neither of us as yet knew the other's name. Her name, I thought, would mean very little; she was what she was. No one could fail to recognize her distinction and authority; it was in the carriage of her head, in her fine hands, in her voice, in every word she uttered in any language, in her brilliant, very piercing eyes. I had no curiosity about her name; that would be an accident and could scarcely matter.

We talked very comfortably for a time. The old lady made some comment on the Soviet experiment in Russia. My friend remarked that it was fortunate for the great group of Russian writers that none of them had lived to see the Revolution; Gogol, Tolstoi, Turgeniev.

"Ah, yes," said the old lady with a sigh, "for Turgeniev, especially, all this would have been very terrible. I knew him well at one time."

I looked at her in astonishment. Yes, of course, it was possible. She was very old. I told her I had never met anyone who had known Turgeniev.

She smiled. "No? I saw him very often when I was a young girl. I was much interested in German, in the great works. I was making a translation of *Faust*, for my own pleasure, merely, and Turgeniev used to go over my translation and correct it from time to time. He was a great friend of my uncle. I was brought up in my uncle's house." She was becoming excited as she spoke, her face grew more animated, her voice warmer, something flashed in her eyes, some strong feeling awoke in her. As she went on, her voice shook a little. "My mother died at my birth, and I was brought up in my uncle's house. He was more than father to me. My uncle also was a man of letters, Gustave Flaubert, you may perhaps know . . ." She murmured the last phrase in a curious tone, as if she had said something indiscreet and were evasively dismissing it.

The meaning of her words came through to me slowly; so this must be the "Caro" of the *Lettres à sa Nièce Caroline*. There was nothing to say, certainly. The room was absolutely quiet, but there was nothing to say to this disclosure. It was like being suddenly brought up against a mountain of memories. One could not see round it; one could only stupidly realize that in this mountain which the old lady had conjured up by a phrase and a name or two lay most of one's mental past. Some moments went by. There was no word with which one could greet such a revelation. I took one of her lovely hands and kissed it, in homage to a great period, to the names that made her voice tremble.

She laughed an embarrassed laugh, and spoke hurriedly. "Oh, that is not necessary! That is not at all necessary." But the tone of distrust, the faint challenge in that "you may perhaps know . . ." had disappeared. "*Vous connaissez bien les œuvres de mon oncle?*"

Who did not know them? I asked her.

Again the dry tone, with a shrug. "Oh, I almost never meet anyone who really knows them. The name, of course, its place in our literature, but not the works themselves. I never meet anyone now who cares much about them."

Great names are awkward things in conversation, when one is a chance acquaintance. One cannot be too free with them; they have too much value. The right course, I thought, was to volunteer nothing, above all to ask no questions; to let the old lady say what she would, ask what she would. She wished, it seemed, to talk about *les œuvres de mon oncle*. Her attack was uncertain; she touched here and there. It was a large subject. She told me she had edited the incomplete *Bouvard et Pécuchet* after his death, that *La Tentation de Saint Antoine* had been his own favourite among his works; she supposed I would scarcely agree with his choice?

No, I was sorry, but I could not.

"I suppose you care most for *Madame Bovary?*"

One can hardly discuss that book; it is a fact in history. One knows it too well to know it well.

"And yet," she murmured, "my uncle got only five hundred francs for it from the publisher. Of course, he did not write for money. Still, he would have been pleased . . . Which one, then, do you prefer?"

I told her that a few years ago I had reread *L'Éducation sentimentale,* and felt that I had never risen to its greatness before.

She shook her head. "Ah, too long, prolix, *trop de conversation.* And Frédéric is very weak."

But there was an eagerness in her face, and I knew by something in her voice that this was like Garibaldi's proclamation to his soldiers on the retreat from Rome, when he told them he could offer them cold and hunger and sickness and misery. He offered something else, too, but the listeners must know that for themselves.

It had seemed to me when I last read *L'Éducation sentimentale* that its very faults were of a noble kind. It is too cold, certainly, to justify the subtitle, *Roman d'un jeune homme;* for youth, even when it has not generous enthusiasm, has at least fierce egotism. But I had wondered whether this cool, dispassionate, almost contemptuous presentation of Frédéric were not a protest against the overly sympathetic manner of Balzac in his stories of young men: Eugène de Rastignac, Lucien de Rubempré, Horace Bianchon, and all the others. Certainly Balzac's habit of playing up his characters, of getting into the ring and struggling and sweating with them, backing them with all his animal heat, must have been very distasteful to Flaubert. It was perhaps this quality of salesmanship in Balzac which made Flaubert say of him in a letter to this same niece Caroline: "He is as ignorant as a pot, and bourgeois to the marrow."

Of course, a story of youth, which altogether lacks that gustatory zest, that exaggerated concern for trivialities, is scarcely successful. In *L'Éducation* the trivialities are there (for life is made up of them), but not the voracious appetite which drives young people through silly and vulgar experiences. The story of Frédéric is a story of youth with the heart of youth left out; and of course it is often dull. But the latter chapters of the book justify one's journey through it. Then all the hero's young life becomes more real than it was as one followed it from year to year, and the story ends on a high plateau. From that great and quiet last scene, seated by the fire with the two middle-aged friends (who were never really friends, but who had been young together), one looks back over Frédéric's life and finds that one has it all, even the dull stretches. It is something one has lived through, not a story one has read; less diverting than a story, perhaps, but more inevitable. One is "left with it," in the same way that one is left with a weak heart after certain illnesses. A shadow has come into one's consciousness that will not go out again.

The old French lady and I talked for some time about *L'Édu-cation sentimentale*. She spoke with warm affection, with tenderness, of Madame Arnoux.

"Ah yes, Madame Arnoux, she is beautiful!" The moisture in her bright eyes, the flush on her cheeks, and the general softening of her face said much more. That charming and good woman of the middle classes, the wife who holds the story together (as she held Frédéric himself together), passed through the old lady's mind so vividly that it was as if she had entered the room. Madame Arnoux was there with us, in that hotel at Aix, on the evening of September 5, 1930, a physical presence, in the charming costume of her time, as on the night when Frédéric first dined at 24 rue de Choiseul. The niece had a very special feeling for this one of her uncle's characters. She lingered over the memory, recalling her as she first appears, sitting on the bench of a passenger boat on the Seine, in her muslin gown sprigged with green and her wide straw hat with red ribbons. Whenever the old lady mentioned Madame Arnoux it was with some mark of affection; she smiled, or sighed, or shook her head as we do when we speak of something that is quite unaccountably fine: "Ah yes, she is lovely, Madame Arnoux! She is very complete."

The old lady told me that she had at home the corrected manuscript of *L'Éducation sentimentale*. "Of course I have many others. But this he gave me long before his death. You shall see it when you come to my place at Antibes. I call my place the Villa Tanit, *pour la déesse*," she added with a smile.

The name of the goddess took us back to *Salammbô*, which is the book of Flaubert I like best. I like him in those great reconstructions of the remote and cruel past. When I happened to speak of the splendid final sentence of *Hérodias*, where the fall of the syllables is so suggestive of the hurrying footsteps of John's disciples, carrying away with them their prophet's severed head, she repeated that sentence softly: *"Comme elle était très lourde, ils la portaient al-ter-na-tiv-e-ment."*

The hour grew late. The maid had been standing in the corridor a long while, waiting for her mistress. At last the old lady rose and drew her wrap about her.

"Good-night, madame. May you have pleasant dreams. As for me, I shall not sleep; you have recalled too much." She went toward the lift with the energetic, unconquered step with which she always crossed the dining-room, carrying with hardihood a body no longer perfectly under her control.

When I reached my room and opened my windows I, too, felt that sleep was far from me. The full moon (like the moon in *Salammbô*) stood over the little square and flooded the gardens and quiet streets and the misty mountains with light. The old lady had brought that great period of French letters very near; a period which has meant so much in the personal life of everyone to whom French literature has meant anything at all.

IV

Probably all those of us who had the good fortune to come upon the French masters accidentally, and not under the chilling guidance of an instructor, went through very much the same experience. We all began, of course, with Balzac. And to young people, for very good reasons, he seems the final word. They read and reread him, and live in his world; to inexperience, that world is neither overpeopled nor overfurnished. When they begin to read Flaubert—usually *Madame Bovary* is the introduction—they resent the change of tone; they miss the glow, the ardour, the temperament. (It is scarcely exaggeration to say that if one is not a little mad about Balzac at twenty, one will never live; and if at forty one can still take Rastignac and Lucien de Rubempré at

Balzac's own estimate, one has lived in vain.) We first read *Bovary* with a certain hostility; the wine is too dry for us. We try, perhaps, another work of Flaubert, and with a shrug go back to Balzac. But young people who are at all sensitive to certain qualities in writing will not find the Balzac they left. Something has happened to them which dampens their enjoyment. For a time it looks as if they had lost both Balzac and Flaubert. They recover both, eventually, and read each for what he is, having learned that an artist's limitations are quite as important as his powers; that they are a definite asset, not a deficiency, and that both go to form his flavour, his personality, the thing by which the ear can immediately recognize Flaubert, Stendhal, Mérimée, Thomas Hardy, Conrad, Brahms, César Franck.

The fact remains that Balzac, like Dickens and Scott, has a strong appeal for the great multitudes of humanity who have no feeling for any form of art, and who read him only in poor translations. This is overwhelming evidence of the vital force in him, which no rough handling can diminish. Also it implies the lack in him of certain qualities which matter to only a few people, but matter very much. The time in one's life when one first began to sense the things which Flaubert stood for, to admire (almost against one's will) that peculiar integrity of language and vision, that coldness which, in him, is somehow noble—that is a pleasant chapter of one's life to remember, and Madame Franklin Grout had brought it back within arm's length of me that night.

V

For that was her name. Next morning the *valet de chambre* brought me a visiting card on which was engraved:

MADAME FRANKLIN GROUT
ANTIBES

In one corner *Villa Tanit* was written in purple ink.

In the evening we sat in the writing-room again, and Madame Grout's talk touched upon many things. On the Franco-Prussian War, for instance, and its effect upon her uncle. He had seen to it that she herself was comfortably settled in England through most of that troubled time. And during the late war of 1914 she had been in Italy a great deal. She loved Italian best of all the languages she spoke so well. (She spoke Swedish, even; she had lived for a time in Sweden during the life of her first husband, who had business interests there.)

She talked of Turgeniev, of her uncle's affection for him and great admiration for him as an artist.[1] She liked to recall his pleasant visits to Croisset, which were the reward of long anticipation on the part of the hosts. Turgeniev usually fixed the date by letter, changed it by another letter, then again by telegram—and sometimes he did not come at all. Flaubert's mother prepared for these visits by inspecting all the beds in the house, but she never found one long enough to hold "le Moscove" comfortably.

Madame Grout seemed to remember with especial pleasure the evenings when he used to sit at the table with her, going over her translation of *Faust*: "That noble man, to give his time to my childish efforts!" She well remembered the period during which he was writing *Les Eaux printanières*, and her own excitement when she first read that work. Like Henry James, she seemed to resent Turgeniev's position in the Viardot household; recalling it, even after such a long stretch of time, with vexation. "And when they gave a hunt, he looked after the dogs!" she murmured under her breath. She talked one evening of his sad latter years: of his disappointment in his daughter, of his long and painful illness, of the way in which the death of his friends, going one after another, contracted his life and made it bleak. But these were very personal memories, and if Madame Grout had wished to make them public, she would have written them herself.

Madame Viardot she had known very well, and for many years after Turgeniev's death. "Pauline Viardot was a superb artist, very

[1] Madame Grout's regard for Turgeniev seems to have been warmly returned. In a letter written to her in 1873, immediately after one of Turgeniev's visits to Croisset, Flaubert says: "Mon Moscove m'a quitté ce matin. . . . Tu l'as tout à fait séduit, mon loulou! car à plusieurs reprises il m'a parlé de 'mon adorable nièce,' de 'ma charmante nièce,' 'ravissante femme,' etc., etc. Enfin le Moscove t'adore! ce qui me fait bien plaisir, car c'est un homme exquis. Tu ne t'imagines pas ce qu'il sait! Il m'a répété, par cœur, des morceaux des tragédies de Voltaire, et de Luce de Lancival! Il connaît, je crois, *toutes* les littératures jusque dans leurs bas-fonds! Et si modeste avec tout cela! si bonhomme! si *vache*!"

intelligent and engaging as a woman, with a great charm—and, *au fond*, very Spanish!" she said. Of Monsieur Louis Viardot she did not think highly. I gathered that he was agreeable, but not much more than that. When I asked her whether Monsieur Viardot had not translated some of Turgeniev's books into French, the old lady lifted her brows and there was a mocking glint in her eyes.

"Turgeniev himself translated them; Viardot may have looked over his shoulder!"

George Sand she did not like. Yes, she readily admitted, her men friends were very loyal to her, had a great regard for her; *mon oncle* valued her comradeship; but Madame Grout found the lady's personality distasteful.

I gathered that, for Madame Grout, George Sand did not really fill any of the great rôles she assigned herself: the devoted mistress, the staunch comrade and "good fellow," the self-sacrificing mother. George Sand's men friends believed her to be all these things; and certainly she herself believed that she was. But Madame Grout seemed to feel that in these various relations Madame Dudevant was self-satisfied rather than self-forgetful; always self-admiring and a trifle unctuous. Madame Grout's distaste for this baffling kind of falseness was immediate and instinctive—it put her teeth on edge. Turgeniev, that penetrating reader of women, seems never to have felt this shallowness in his friend. But in Chopin's later letters one finds that he, to his bitter cost, had become aware of it—curiously enough, through Madame Dudevant's behaviour toward her own children! It is clear that he had come upon something so subtly false, so excruciatingly aslant, that when he briefly refers to it his sentences seem to shudder.

Though I tried to let Madame Grout direct our conversations without suggestion from me, and never to question her, I did ask her whether she read Marcel Proust with pleasure.

"*Trop dur et trop fatigant,*" she murmured, and dismissed the greatest French writer of his time with a wave of her hand.

When I made some reference to Anatole France she said quickly: "Oh, I like him very much! But I like him most where he is most indebted to my uncle!"

When she was tired, or deeply moved, Madame Grout usually spoke French; but when she spoke English it was as flexible as it was correct. She spoke like an Englishwoman, with no French accent at all.

What astonished me in her was her keen and sympathetic interest in modern music; in Ravel, Scriabin, Albéniz, Stravinsky, De Falla. Only a few days before I quitted Aix I found her at the box office in person, getting exactly the seats she wanted for a performance of *Boris Godounov.* She must change her habitual seat, as she had asked some friends to come over from Sallanches to hear the opera with her. "You will certainly hear it? Albert Wolff is conducting for the last time this season, and he does it very well," she explained.

It was interesting to observe Madame Grout at the opera that night, to watch the changes that went over her face as she listened with an attention that never wandered, looking younger and stronger than she ever did by day, as if the music were some very potent stimulant. Any form of pleasure, I had noticed, made her keener, more direct and positive, more authoritative, revived in her the stamp of a period which had achieved a great style in art. In a letter which Flaubert wrote her when she was a young woman, he said:—

> "C'est une joie profonde pour moi, mon pauvre loulou, que de t'avoir donné le goût des occupations intellectuelles. Que d'ennuis et de sottises il vous épargne!"

Certainly those interests had stood her in good stead, and for many more years than the uncle himself lived through. She had still, at eighty-four, a capacity for pleasure such as very few people in this world ever know at all.

VI

The next morning I told Madame Grout that, because of the illness of a friend, I must start at once for Paris.

And when, she asked, could I return and go south to Antibes and the Villa Tanit, to see her Flaubert collection, and the interior of his study, which she had brought down there thirty-five years ago?

I told her I was afraid that visit must be put off until next summer.

She gave a very charming laugh. "At my age, of course, the future is somewhat uncertain!" Then she asked whether, on her return to Antibes, she could send me some souvenir of our meeting; would I like to have something that had belonged to her uncle, or some letter written by him?

I told her that I was not a collector; that manuscripts and autographed letters meant very little to me. The things of her uncle that were valuable to me I already had, and had had for years. It rather hurt me that she should think I wanted any material reminder of her or of Flaubert. It was the Flaubert in her mind and heart that was to give me a beautiful memory.

On the following day, at *déjeuner*, I said good-bye to Madame Grout; I was leaving on the two o'clock train. It was a hurried and mournful parting, but there was real feeling on both sides. She had counted upon my staying longer, she said. But she did not for a moment take on a slightly aggrieved tone, as many privileged old ladies would have done. There was nothing "wayward" or self-indulgent about Madame Grout; the whole discipline of her life had been to the contrary. One had one's objective, and one went toward it; one had one's duty, and one did it as best one could.

The last glimpse I had of her was as she stood in the dining-room, the powder on her face quite destroyed by tears, her features agitated, but her head erect and her eyes flashing. And the last words I heard from her expressed a hope that I would always remember the pleasure we had had together in talking unreservedly about *les œuvres de mon oncle*. Standing there, she seemed holding to that name as to a staff. A great memory and a great devotion were the things she lived upon, certainly; they were her armour against a world concerned with insignificant matters.

VII

When I got back to Paris and began to reread the *Lettres de Flaubert à sa Nièce Caroline*, I found that the personality of Madame Grout sent a wonderful glow over the pages. I was now almost startled (in those letters written her when she was still a child) by his solicitude about her progress in her English lessons—those lessons by which I was to profit seventy-three years afterward!

The five hundred pages of that book were now peopled for me with familiar figures, like the chronicles of a family I myself had known. It will always be for me one of the most delightful of books; and in none of his letters to other correspondents does Gustave Flaubert himself seem so attractive.

In reading over those letters, covering a stretch of twenty-four years, with the figure of Madame Grout in one's mind, one feels a kind of happiness and contentment about the whole situation—yes, and gratitude to Fate! The great man might have written very charming and tender and warmly confidential letters to a niece who was selfish, vain, intelligent merely in a conventional way—because she was the best he had! One can never be sure about such things; a heartless and stupid woman may be so well educated, after all!

But having known Madame Grout, I know that she had the root of the matter in her; that no one could be more sensitive than she to all that was finest in Flaubert's work, or more quick to admit the qualities he did not have—which is quite as important.

During all his best working years he had in his house beside him, or within convenient distance for correspondence, one of his own blood, younger and more ardent than he, who absolutely understood what he was doing; who could feel the great qualities of his failures, even. Could any situation be happier for a man of letters? How many writers have found one understanding ear among their sons or daughters?

Moreover, Caroline was the daughter of a sister whom Flaubert had devotedly loved. He took her when she was an infant into his house at Croisset, where he lived alone with his old mother. What delight for a solitary man of letters and an old lady to have a baby to take care of, the little daughter of a beloved daughter! They had all the pleasure of her little girlhood—and she must have been an irresistible little girl! Flaubert spent a great deal of time attending to her early education, and when he was seated at his big writing-table, or working in bed, he liked to have her in the room, lying on a rug in the corner with her book. For hours she would not speak, she told me; she was so passionately proud of the fact that he wanted her to be there. When she was just beginning to read, she liked to think, as she lay in her corner, that she was shut in a cage with some powerful wild animal, a tiger or a lion or a bear, who had devoured his keeper and would spring upon anyone else who opened his door, but with whom she was "quite safe and conceited," as she said with a chuckle.

During his short stays in Paris, Flaubert writes to Caroline about her favourite rabbit, and the imaginary characters with whom she had peopled the garden at Croisset. He sends his greetings to Caroline's doll, Madame Robert:—

> "Remercie de ma part Mme. Robert qui a bien voulu se rappeler de moi. Présente-lui mes respects et conseille-lui un régime fortifiant, car elle me paraît un peu pale, et je ne suis pas sans inquiétude sur sa santé."

In a letter from Paris, dated just a year later, when Caroline was eleven, he tells her that he is sending her Thierry's *Récits des temps mérovingiens*, and adds:—

> "Je suis bien aise que les *Récits mérovingiens* t'amusent; relis-les quand tu auras fini; *apprends des dates*, tu as tes programmes, et passe tous les jours quelque temps à regarder une carte de géographie."

One sees from the letters with what satisfaction Flaubert followed every step of Caroline's development. Her facility in languages was a matter of the greatest pride to him, though even after she is married and living abroad he occasionally finds fault with her orthography:—

> "Un peu d'orthographe ne te nuirait pas, mon bibi! car tu écris *aplomb* par deux *p:* 'Moral et physique sont d'applomb,' trois *p* marqueraient encore plus d'énergie! Ça m'a amusé, parce que ça te ressemble."

Yes, it was like her, certainly; like her as she walked across the floor of that hotel dining-room in Aix-les-Bains, so many years afterward.

Though she had been married twice, Madame Grout, in our

conversations, did not talk of either of her husbands. Her uncle had always been the great figure in her life, and even a short acquaintance with her made me feel that she possessed every quality for comradeship with him. Besides her devotion to him, her many gifts, her very unusual intelligence and intuition in art, she had moral qualities which he must have loved: poise, great good sense, and a love of fairness and justice. She had the habit of searching out facts and weighing evidence, for her own satisfaction. Her speech, when she was explaining something, had the qualities of good Latin prose: economy, elegance, and exactness. She was not an idealist; she had lived through two wars. She was one of the least visionary and sentimental persons I have ever met. She knew that conditions and circumstances, not their own wishes, dictate the actions of men. In her mind there was a kind of large enlightenment, like that of the many-windowed workroom at Croisset, with the cool, tempered northern light pouring into it. In her, Flaubert had not only a companion, but a "daughter of the house" to cherish and protect. And he had her all his life, until the short seizure which took him off in an hour. And she, all her life, kept the handkerchief with which they had wiped the moisture from his brow a few moments before he died.

VIII

I sailed for Quebec in October. In November, while I was at Jaffrey, New Hampshire, a letter came from Madame Grout; the envelope had been opened and almost destroyed. I have received letters from Borneo and Java that looked much less travel-worn. She had addressed it to me in care of an obscure bookseller, on a small street in Paris, from whom she had got one of my books. (I suppose, in her day, all booksellers were publishers.) The letter had been forwarded through three publishing houses, and a part of its contents had got lost. In her letter Madame Grout writes that she is sending me "ci-joint une lettre de mon oncle Gustave Flaubert adressée à George Sand—elle doit être, je crois, de 1866. Il me semble qu'elle vous fera plaisir et j'ai plaisir à vous l'envoyer."

This enclosure had been removed. I regretted its loss chiefly because I feared it would distress Madame Grout. But I wrote her, quite truthfully, that her wish that I should have one of her uncle's letters meant a great deal more to me than the actual possession of it could mean. Nevertheless, it was an awkward explanation to make, and I delayed writing it until late in December. I did not hear from her again.

In February my friends in Paris sent me a clipping from the *Journal des Débats* which read:—

Mort de Mme. Franklin-Grout

Nous apprenons avec tristesse la mort de Mme. Franklin-Grout, qui s'est éteinte à Antibes, à la suite d'une courte maladie.

Nièce de Gustave Flaubert, Mme. Franklin-Grout a joué un rôle important dans la diffusion et le succès des œuvres de son oncle. Exécutrice testamentaire du grand romancier, qui l'avait élevée et instruite, Mme. Franklin-Grout a publié la correspondance de son oncle, si précieuse pour sa psychologie littéraire, et qui nous a révélé les doctrines de Flaubert et sa vie de travail acharné. Mme. Franklin-Grout publia aussi *Bouvard et Pécuchet*. . . . Mme. Franklin-Grout était une personne charmante et distinguée, très attachée à ses amis et qui, jusqu'à la plus extrême vieillesse, avait conservé l'intelligence et la bonté souriante d'une spirituelle femme du monde.

WINSTON CHURCHILL

THE DREAM

One foggy afternoon in November 1947 I was painting in my studio at the cottage down the hill at Chartwell. Someone had sent me a portrait of my father which had been painted for one of the Belfast Conservative Clubs about the time of his visit to Ulster in the Home Rule crisis of 1886. The canvas had been badly torn, and though I am very shy of painting human faces I thought I would try to make a copy of it.

My easel was under a strong daylight lamp, which is necessary for indoor painting in the British winter. On the right of it stood the portrait I was copying, and behind me was a large looking glass, so that one could frequently study the painting in reverse. I must have painted for an hour and a half, and was deeply concentrated on my subject. I was drawing my father's face, gazing at the portrait, and frequently turning round right-handed to check progress in the mirror. Thus I was intensely absorbed, and my mind was freed from all other thoughts except the impressions of that loved and honoured face now on the canvas, now on the picture, now in the mirror.

I was just trying to give the twirl to his moustache when I suddenly felt an odd sensation. I turned round with my palette in my hand, and there, sitting in my red leather upright armchair, was my father. He looked just as I had seen him in his prime, and as I had read about him in his brief year of triumph. He was small and slim, with the big moustache I was just painting, and all his bright, captivating, jaunty air. His eyes twinkled and shone. He was evidently in the best of tempers. He was engaged in filling his amber cigarette-holder with a little pad of cotton-wool before putting in the cigarette. This was in order to stop the nicotine, which used to be thought deleterious. He was so exactly like my memories of him in his most charming moods that I could hardly believe my eyes. I felt no alarm, but I thought I would stand where I was and go no nearer.

"Papa!" I said.

"What are you doing, Winston?"

"I am trying to copy your portrait, the one you had done when you went over to Ulster in 1886."

"I should never have thought it," he said.

"I only do it for amusement," I replied.

"Yes, I am sure you could never earn your living that way." There was a pause.

"Tell me," he asked, "what year is it?"

"Nineteen forty-seven."

"Of the Christian era, I presume?"

"Yes, that all goes on. At least, they still count that way."

"I don't remember anything after ninety-four. I was very confused that year. . . . So more than fifty years have passed. A lot must have happened."

"It has indeed, Papa."

"Tell me about it."

"I really don't know where to begin," I said.

"Does the Monarchy go on?" he asked.

"Yes, stronger than in the days of Queen Victoria."

"Who is King?"

"King George the Sixth."

"What! Two more Georges?"

"But, Papa, you remember the death of the Duke of Clarence."

"Quite true; that settled the name. They must have been clever to keep the Throne."

"They took the advice of the Ministers who had majorities in the House of Commons."

"That all goes on still? I suppose they still use the Closure and the Guillotine?"

"Yes, indeed."

"Does the Carlton Club go on?"

"Yes, they are going to rebuild it."

"I thought it would have lasted longer; the structure seemed quite solid. What about the Turf Club?"

"It's OK."

"How do you mean, OK?"

"It's an American expression, Papa. Nowadays they use initials for all sorts of things, like they used to say RSPCA and HMG."

"What does it mean?"

"It means all right."

"What about racing? Does that go on?"

"You mean horse-racing?"

"Of course," he said. "What other should there be?"

"It all goes on."

"What, the Oaks, the Derby, the Leger?"

"They have never missed a year."

"And the Primrose League?"

"They have never had more members."

He seemed to be pleased at this.

"I always believed in Dizzy, that old Jew. He saw into the future. He had to bring the British working man into the centre of the picture." And here he glanced at my canvas.

"Perhaps I am trespassing on your art?" he said, with that curious, quizzical smile of his, which at once disarmed and disconcerted.

Palette in hand, I made a slight bow.

"And the Church of England?"

"You made a very fine speech about it in eighty-four." I quoted, " 'And, standing out like a lighthouse over a stormy ocean, it marks the entrance to a port wherein the millions and masses of those who at times are wearied with the woes of the world and tired of the trials of existence may seek for, and may find, that peace which passeth all understanding".'

"What a memory you have got! But you always had one. I remember Dr Welldon telling me how you recited the twelve hundred lines of Macaulay without a single mistake."

After a pause. "You are still a Protestant?" he said.

"Episcopalian."

"Do the bishops still sit in the House of Lords?"

"They do indeed, and make a lot of speeches."

"Are they better than they used to be?"

"I never heard the ones they made in the old days."

"What party is in power now? Liberals or Tories?"

"Neither, Papa. We have a Socialist Government, with a very large majority. They have been in office for two years, and will probably stay for two more. You know we have changed the Septennial Act to five years."

"Socialist!" he exclaimed. "But I thought you said we still have a Monarchy."

"The Socialists are quite in favour of the Monarchy, and make generous provisions for it."

"You mean in regard to Royal grants, the Civil List, and so forth? How can they get those through the Commons?"

"Of course they have a few rebels, but the old Republicanism of Dilke and Labby is dead as mutton. The Labour men and the trade unions look upon the Monarchy not only as a national but a nationalised institution. They even go to the parties at Buckingham Palace. Those who have very extreme principles wear sweaters."

"How very sensible. I am glad all that dressing up has been done away with."

"I am sorry, Papa," I said, "I like the glitter of the past."

"What does the form matter if the facts remain? After all, Lord Salisbury was once so absent-minded as to go to a levée in uniform with carpet slippers. What happened to old Lord Salisbury?"

"Lord Salisbury leads the Conservative party in the House of Lords."

"What!" he said. "He must be a Methuselah!"

"No. It is his grandson."

"Ah, and Arthur Balfour? Did he ever become Prime Minister?"

"Oh, yes. He was Prime Minister, and came an awful electoral cropper. Afterwards he was Foreign Secretary and held other high posts. He was well in the eighties when he died."

"Did he make a great mark?"

"Well, Ramsay MacDonald, the Prime Minister of the first Socialist Government, which was in office at his death, said he 'saw a great deal of life from afar".'

"How true! But who was Ramsay MacDonald?"

"He was the leader of the first and second Labour-Socialist Governments, in a minority."

"The first Socialist Government? There has been more than one?"

"Yes, several. But this is the first that had a majority."

"What have they done?"

"Not much. They have nationalised the mines and railways and a few other services, paying full compensation. You know, Papa, though stupid, they are quite respectable, and increasingly bourgeois. They are not nearly so fierce as the old Radicals, though of course they are wedded to economic fallacies."

"What is the franchise?"

"Universal," I replied. "Even the women have votes."

"Good gracious!" he exclaimed.

"They are a strong prop to the Tories."

"Arthur was always in favour of Female Suffrage."

"It did not turn out as badly as I thought," I said.

"You don't allow them in the House of Commons?" he inquired.

"Oh, yes. Some of them have even been Ministers. There are not many of them. They have found their level."

"So Female Suffrage has not made much difference?"

"Well, it has made politicians more mealy-mouthed than in your day. And public meetings are much less fun. You can't say the things you used to."

"What happened to Ireland? Did they get Home Rule?"

"The South got it, but Ulster stayed with us."

"Are the South a republic?"

"No one knows what they are. They are neither in nor out of the Empire. But they are much more friendly to us than they used to be. They have built up a cultured Roman Catholic system in the South. There has been no anarchy or confusion. They are getting more happy and prosperous. The bitter past is fading."

"Ah," he said, "how vexed the Tories were with me when I observed that there was no English statesman who had not had his hour of Home Rule." Then, after a pause, "What about the Home Rule meaning 'Rome Rule'?"

"It certainly does, but they like it. And the Catholic Church has now become a great champion of individual liberty."

"You must be living in a very happy age. A Golden Age, it seems."

His eye wandered round the studio, which is entirely panelled with scores of my pictures. I followed his travelling eye as it rested now on this one and on that. After a while: "Do you live in this cottage?"

"No," I said, "I have a house up on the hill, but you cannot see it for the fog."

"How do you get a living?" he asked. "Not, surely, by these?" indicating the pictures.

"No, indeed, Papa. I write books and articles for the Press."

"Ah, a reporter. There is nothing discreditable in that. I myself wrote articles for the *Daily Graphic* when I went to South Africa. And well I was paid for them. A hundred pounds an article!"

Before I could reply: "What has happened to Blenheim? Blandford [his brother] always said it could only become a museum for Oxford."

"The Duke and Duchess of Marlborough are still living there."

He paused again for a while, and then: "I always said 'Trust the people'. Tory democracy alone could link the past with the future."

"They are only living in a wing of the Palace," I said. "The rest is occupied by MI5."

"What does that mean?"

"A Government department formed in the war."

"War?" he said, sitting up with a startled air. "War, do you say? Has there been a war?"

"We have had nothing else but wars since democracy took charge."

"You mean real wars, not just frontier expeditions? Wars where tens of thousands of men lose their lives?"

"Yes, indeed, Papa," I said. "That's what has happened all the time. Wars and rumours of war ever since you died."

"Tell me about them."

"Well, first there was the Boer War."

"Ah, I would have stopped that. I never agreed with 'Avenge Majuba'. Never avenge anything, especially if you have the power to do so. I always mistrusted Joe."

"You mean Mr Chamberlain?"

"Yes. There is only one Joe, or only one I ever heard of. A Radical turned Jingo is an ugly and dangerous thing. But what happened in the Boer War?"

"We conquered the Transvaal and the Orange Free State."

"England should never have done that. To strike down two independent republics must have lowered our whole position in the world. It must have stirred up all sorts of things. I am sure the Boers made a good fight. When I was there I saw lots of them. Men of the wild, with rifles, on horseback. It must have taken a lot of soldiers. How many? Forty thousand?"

"No, over a quarter of a million."

"Good God! What a shocking drain on the Exchequer!"

"It was," I said. "The Income Tax went up to one and three-pence." He was visibly disturbed. So I said that they got it down to eightpence afterwards.

"Who was the General who beat the Boers?" he asked.

"Lord Roberts," I answered.

"I always believed in him. I appointed him Commander-in-Chief in India when I was Secretary of State. That was the year I annexed Burma. The place was in utter anarchy. They were just butchering one another. We had to step in, and very soon there was an ordered, civilised Government under the vigilant control of the House of Commons." There was a sort of glare in his eyes as he said "House of Commons".

"I have always been a strong supporter of the House of Commons, Papa. I am still very much in favour of it."

"You had better be, Winston, because the will of the people must prevail. Give me a fair arrangement of the constituencies, a wide franchise, and free elections—say what you like, and one part of Britain will correct and balance the other."

"Yes, you brought me up to that."

"I never brought you up to anything. I was not going to talk politics with a boy like you ever. Bottom of the school! Never passed any examinations, except into the Cavalry! Wrote me stilted letters. I could not see how you would make your living on the little I could leave you and Jack, and that only after your mother. I once thought of the Bar for you but you were not clever enough. Then I thought you might go to South Africa. But of course you were very young, and I loved you dearly. Old people are always very impatient with young ones. Fathers always expect their sons to have their virtues without their faults. You were very fond of playing soldiers, so I settled for the Army. I hope you had a successful military career."

"I was a Major in the Yeomanry."

He did not seem impressed.

"However, here you are. You must be over seventy. You have a roof over your head. You seem to have plenty of time on your hands to mess about with paints. You have evidently been able to keep yourself going. Married?"

"Forty years."

"Children?"

"Four."

"Grandchildren?"

"Four."

"I am so glad. But tell me more about these other wars."

"They were the wars of nations, caused by demagogues and tyrants."

"Did we win?"

"Yes, we won all our wars. All our enemies were beaten down. We even made them surrender unconditionally."

"No one should be made to do that. Great people forget sufferings, but not humiliations."

"Well, that was the way it happened, Papa."

"How did we stand after it all? Are we still at the summit of the world, as we were under Queen Victoria?"

"No, the world grew much bigger all around us."

"Which is the leading world-power?"

"The United States."

"I don't mind that. You are half American yourself. Your mother was the most beautiful woman ever born. The Jeromes were a deep-rooted American family."

"I have always," I said, "worked for friendship with the United States, and indeed throughout the English-speaking world."

"English-speaking world," he repeated, weighing the phrase. "You mean, with Canada, Australia and New Zealand, and all that?"

"Yes, all that."

"Are they still loyal?"

"They are our brothers."

"And India, is that all right? And Burma?"

"Alas! They have gone down the drain."

He gave a groan. So far he had not attempted to light the cigarette he had fixed in the amber holder. He now took his matchbox from his watch-chain, which was the same as I was wearing. For the first time I felt a sense of awe. I rubbed my brush in the paint on the palette to make sure that everything was real. All the same I shivered. To relieve his consternation I said:

"But perhaps they will come back and join the English-speaking world. Also, we are trying to make a world organisation in which we and America will be quite important."

But he remained sunk in gloom, and huddled back in the chair. Presently: "About these wars, the ones after the Boer War, I mean. What happened to the great States of Europe? Is Russia still the danger?"

"We are all very worried about her."

"We always were in my day, and in Dizzy's before me. Is there still a Tsar?"

"Yes, but he is not a Romanoff. It's another family. He is much more powerful, and much more despotic."

"What of Germany? What of France?"

"They are both shattered. Their only hope is to rise together."

"I remember," he said, "taking you through the Place de la Concorde when you were only nine years old, and you asked me about the Strasbourg monument. You wanted to know why this one was covered in flowers and crape. I told you about the lost provinces of France. What flag flies in Strasbourg now?"

"The Tricolor flies there."

"Ah, so they won. They had their revanche. That must have been a great triumph for them."

"It cost them their life blood," I said.

"But wars like these must have cost a million lives. They must have been as bloody as the American Civil War."

"Papa," I said, "in each of them about thirty million men were killed in battle. In the last one seven million were murdered in cold blood, mainly by the Germans. They made human slaughter-pens like the Chicago stockyards. Europe is a ruin. Many of her cities have been blown to pieces by bombs. Ten capitals in Eastern Europe are in Russian hands. They are Communists now, you know—Karl Marx and all that. It may well be that an even worse war is drawing near. A war of the East against the West. A war of liberal civilisation against the Mongol hordes. Far gone are the days of Queen Victoria and a settled world order. But, having gone through so much, we do not despair."

He seemed stupefied, and fumbled with his matchbox for what seemed a minute or more. Then he said:

"Winston, you have told me a terrible tale. I would never have believed that such things could happen. I am glad I did not live to see them. As I listened to you unfolding these fearful facts you seemed to know a great deal about them. I never expected that you would develop so far and so fully. Of course you are too old now to think about such things, but when I hear you talk I really wonder you didn't go into politics. You might have done a lot to help. You might even have made a name for yourself."

He gave me a benignant smile. He then took the match to light his cigarette and struck it. There was a tiny flash. He vanished. The chair was empty. The illusion had passed. I rubbed my brush again in my paint, and turned to finish the moustache. But so vivid had my fancy been that I felt too tired to go on. Also my cigar had gone out, and the ash had fallen among all the paints.

H. L. MENCKEN

REFLECTIONS ON JOURNALISM

1

Looking back over a dull life, mainly devoted to futilities, I can discern three gaudy and gorgeous years. They were my first three years as a newspaper reporter in Baltimore, and when they closed I was still short of twenty-two. I recall them more and more brightly as I grow older, and take greater delight in the recalling. Perhaps the imagination of a decaying man has begun to gild them. But gilded or not, they remain superb, and it is inconceivable that I'll ever see their like again. It is the fate of man, I believe, to be wholly happy only once in his life. Well, I had my turn while I was still fully alive, and could enjoy every moment.

It seems to me that the newspaper reporters of today know very little of the high adventure that bathed the reporters of my time, now nearly thirty years ago. The journalism of that era was still somewhat wild-cattish: all sorts of mushroom papers sprang up; any man with a second-hand press and a few thousand dollars could start one. Thus there was a steady shifting of men from paper to paper, and even the most sober journals got infected with the general antinomianism of the craft. Salaries were low, but nobody seemed to care. A reporter who showed any sign of opulence was a sort of marvel, and got under suspicion. The theory was that journalism was an art, and that to artists money was somehow offensive.

Now all that is past. A good reporter used to make as much as a bartender or a police sergeant; he now makes as much as the average doctor or lawyer, and probably a great deal more. His view of the world he lives in has thus changed. He is no longer a free-lance in human society, thumbing his nose at its dignitaries; he has got a secure lodgment in a definite stratum, and his wife, if he has one, maybe has social ambitions. The highest sordid aspiration that any reporter had, in my time, was to own two complete suits of clothes. Today they have dinner coats, and some of them even own plug hats.

II

This general poverty, I suspect, bore down harshly upon some of my contemporaries, especially older ones, but as for me, I never felt it as oppressive, for no one was dependent on me, and I could always make extra money by writing bad fiction and worse verse. I had enough in Summer to take a holiday. In Winter, concerts and the theaters were free to me. Did I dine in a restaurant? Then I know very well that opinion in the craft frowned upon any bill beyond 50 cents. I remember clearly, and with a shudder still, how Frank Kent once proposed to me that we debauch ourselves at a place where the dinner was $1. I succumbed, but with an evil conscience. And Frank, too, looked over his shoulder when we sneaked in.

The charm of the life, in those remote days, lay in the reporter's freedom. Today he is at the end of a telephone wire, and his city editor can reach him and annoy him in ten minutes. There were very few telephones in 1899, and it was seldom that even the few were used. When a reporter was sent out on a story, the whole operation was in his hands. He was expected to get it without waiting for further orders. If he did so, he was rewarded with what, in newspaper offices, passed for applause. If he failed, he stood convicted of incompetence or worse. There was no passing of the buck. Every man faced a clear and undivided responsibility.

That responsibility was not oppressive to an active young man: it was flattering to him. He felt himself a part of important events, with no string tied to him. Through his eyes thousands of people would see what was happening in this most surprising and fascinating of worlds. If he made a good job of it, the fact would be noticed by the elders he respected. If he fell down, then those same elders would not hesitate to mark the fact profanely. In either case, he was almost completely his own man. There was no rewrite-man at the other end of a telephone wire to corrupt his facts and spoil his fine ideas. Until he got back with his story there was no city editor's roar in his ear, and even after he had got back that roar tended to be discreetly faint until he had got his noble observations on paper. There was, of course, such a thing then as rattling a reporter, but it was viewed as evil. Today the problem is to derattle him.

III

I believe that a young journalist, turned loose in a large city, had more fun a quarter of a century ago than any other man. The Mauve Decade was just ending, and the new era of standardization and efficiency had not come in. Here in Baltimore life was unutterably charming. The town was still a series of detached neighborhoods, many of them ancient and with lives all their own. Marsh Market was as distinct an entity as Cairo or Samarkand. The water-front was immensely romantic. The whole downtown region was full of sinister alleys, and in every alley there were mysterious saloons. One went out with the cops to fires, murders, and burglaries, riding in their clumsy wagon. Any reporter under twenty-five, if not too far gone in liquor, could overtake the fire-horses.

I do not recall that crime was common in Baltimore in those days, but certainly the town was not as mercilessly policed as it is today. Now the cops are instantly alert to every departure, however slight, from the Y.M.C.A.'s principles of decorum, but in that era they were very tolerant to eccentricity. The dance-halls that then flourished in the regions along the harbor would shock them to death today, and they'd be horrified by some of the old-time saloons. In such places rough-houses were common, and where a rough-house began the cops flocked, and where the cops flocked young reporters followed. It was, to any youngster with humor in him, a constant picnic. Odd fish were washed up by the hundred. Strange marvels unrolled continuously. And out of marvels copy was made, for the newspapers were not yet crowded with comic strips and sporting pages. What was on the police blotter was only the half of it. The energetic young reporter was supposed to go out and see for himself. In particular, he was supposed to see what the older and duller men failed to see. If it was news, well and good. But if it was not news, then it was better than news.

IV

The charm of journalism, to many of its practitioners, lies in the contacts it gives them with the powerful and eminent. They enjoy communion with men of wealth, high officers of state, and other such magnificoes. The delights of that privilege are surely not to be cried down, but it seems to me that I got a great deal more fun, in my days on the street, out of the lesser personages who made up the gaudy life of the city. A mayor was thrilling once or twice, but after that he tended to become a stuffed shirt, speaking platitudes out of a tin throat. But a bartender was different every day, and so was a police sergeant, and so were the young doctors at the hospital, and so were the catchpolls in the courts, and so were the poor wretches who passed before the brass rail in the police station.

There was no affectation about these lesser players in the endless melodrama. They were not out to make impressions even upon newspaper reporters; their aim, in the phrase of Greenwich Village, was to lead their own lives. I recall some astounding manifestations of that yearning. There was the lady who celebrated her one-hundredth arrest for drunkenness by stripping off all her clothes and throwing them at the police lieutenant booking her. There was the policeman who, on a bet, ate fifty fried hard crabs. There was the morgue-keeper who locked himself in his morgue, drunk and howling, and had to be clawed out by firemen. There was the detective who spent his Sundays exhorting in Methodist churches. There was the Irish lad who lived by smuggling bottles of beer to prisoners in the old Central

Police Station. There was the saloon-keeper who so greatly vener-
ated journalists that he set them a favored rate of three drinks for
the price of two. Above all, there was the pervasive rowdiness
and bawdiness of the town—the general air of devil-may-care
freedom—the infinite oddity and extravagance of its daily, and
especially nightly, life.

It passed with the fire of 1904. I was a city editor by that time
and the show had begun to lose its savor. But I was still sufficiently interested in it to mourn the change. The old Baltimore
had a saucy and picturesque personality; it was unlike any other
American city. The new Baltimore that emerged from the ashes
was simply a virtuoso piece of Babbitts. It put in all the modern
improvements, especially the bad ones. Its cops climbed out of
the alleys behind the old gin-mills and began harassing decent
people on the main streets. I began to lose interest in active journalism in 1905. Since 1906, save as an occasional sentimental
luxury, I have never written a news story or a headline.

VIRGINIA WOOLF

LESLIE STEPHEN

By the time that his children were growing up the great days of my father's life were over. His feats on the river and on the mountains had been won before they were born. Relics of them were to be found lying about the house—the silver cup on the study mantelpiece; the rusty alpenstocks that leant against the bookcase in the corner; and to the end of his days he would speak of great climbers and explorers with a peculiar mixture of admiration and envy. But his own years of activity were over, and my father had to content himself with pottering about the Swiss valleys or taking a stroll across the Cornish moors.

That to potter and to stroll meant more on his lips than on other people's is becoming obvious now that some of his friends have given their own version of those expeditions. He would start off after breakfast alone, or with one companion. Shortly before dinner he would return. If the walk had been successful, he would have out his great map and commemorate a new short cut in red ink. And he was quite capable, it appears, of striding all day across the moors without speaking more than a word or two to his companion. By that time, too, he had written the *History of English Thought in the Eighteenth Century*, which is said by some to be his masterpiece; and the *Science of Ethics*—the book which interested him most; and *The Playground of Europe*, in which is to be found "The Sunset on Mont Blanc"—in his opinion the best thing he ever wrote.

He still wrote daily and methodically, though never for long at a time. In London he wrote in the large room with three long windows at the top of the house. He wrote lying almost recumbent in a low rocking chair which he tipped to and fro as he wrote, like a cradle, and as he wrote he smoked a short clay pipe, and he scattered books round him in a circle. The thud of a book dropped on the floor could be heard in the room beneath. And often as he mounted the stairs to his study with his firm, regular tread he would burst, not into song, for he was entirely unmusical, but into a strange rhythmical chant, for verse of all kinds, both "utter trash," as he called it, and the most sublime words of Milton and Wordsworth stuck in his memory, and the act of walking or climbing seemed to inspire him to recite whichever it was that came uppermost or suited his mood.

But it was his dexterity with his fingers that delighted his children before they could potter along the lanes at his heels or read his books. He would twist a sheet of paper beneath a pair of scissors and out would drop an elephant, a stag, or a monkey with trunks, horns, and tails delicately and exactly formed. Or, taking a pencil, he would draw beast after beast—an art that he practised almost unconsciously as he read, so that the fly-leaves of his books swarm with owls and donkeys as if to illustrate the "Oh, you ass!" or "Conceited dunce," that he was wont to scribble impatiently in the margin. Such brief comments, in which one may find the germ of the more temperate statements of his essays, recall some of the characteristics of his talk. He could be very silent, as his friends have testified. But his remarks, made suddenly in a low voice between the puffs of his pipe, were extremely effective. Sometimes with one word—but his one word was accompanied by a gesture of the hand—he would dispose of the tissue of exaggerations which his own sobriety seemed to provoke. "There are 40,000,000 unmarried women in London alone!" Lady Ritchie once informed him. "Oh, Annie, Annie!" my father exclaimed in tones of horrified but affectionate rebuke. But Lady Ritchie, as if she enjoyed being rebuked, would pile it up even higher next time she came.

The stories he told to amuse his children of adventures in the Alps—but accidents only happened, he would explain, if you were so foolish as to disobey your guides—or of those long walks, after one of which, from Cambridge to London on a hot day, "I drank, I am sorry to say, rather more than was good for me," were told very briefly, but with a curious power to impress the scene. The things that he did not say were always there in the background. So, too, though he seldom told anecdotes, and his memory for facts was bad, when he described a person—and he had known many people, both famous and obscure—he would convey exactly what he thought of him in two or three words. And what he thought might be the opposite of what other people thought. He had a way of upsetting established reputations and disregarding conventional values that could be disconcerting, and sometimes perhaps wounding, though no one was more respectful of any feeling that seemed to him genuine. But when, suddenly opening his bright blue eyes, and rousing himself from what had seemed complete abstraction, he gave his opinion, it was difficult to disregard it. It was a habit, especially when deafness made him unaware that this opinion could be heard, that had its inconveniences.

"I am the most easily bored of men," he wrote, truthfully as usual: and when, as was inevitable in a large family, some visitor threatened to stay not merely for tea but also for dinner, my father would express his anguish at first by twisting and untwisting a certain lock of hair. Then he would burst out, half to himself, half to the powers above, but quite audibly, "Why can't he go? Why can't he go?" Yet such is the charm of simplicity—and did he not say, also truthfully, that "bores are the salt of the earth"?—that the bores seldom went, or, if they did, forgave him and came again.

Too much, perhaps, has been said of his silence; too much stress has been laid upon his reserve. He loved clear thinking; he hated sentimentality and gush; but this by no means meant that he was cold and unemotional, perpetually critical and condemnatory in daily life. On the contrary, it was his power of feeling strongly and of expressing his feeling with vigour that made him sometimes so alarming as a companion. A lady, for instance, complained of the wet summer that was spoiling her tour in Cornwall. But to my father, though he never called himself a democrat, the rain meant that the corn was being laid; some poor man was being ruined; and the energy with which he expressed his sympathy—not with the lady—left her discomfited. He had something of the same respect for farmers and fishermen that he had for climbers and explorers. So, too, he talked little of patriotism, but during the South African War—and all wars were hateful to him—he lay awake thinking that he heard the guns on the battlefield. Again, neither his reason nor his cold common sense helped to convince him that a child could be late for dinner without having been maimed or killed in an accident. And not all his mathematics, together with a bank balance which he insisted must be ample in the extreme, could persuade him, when it came to signing a cheque, that the whole family was not "shooting Niagara to ruin," as he put it. The pictures that he would draw of old age and the bankruptcy court, of ruined men of letters who have to support large families in small houses at Wimbledon (he owned a very small house at Wimbledon) might have convinced those who complain of his understatements that hyperbole was well within his reach had he chosen.

Yet the unreasonable mood was superficial, as the rapidity with which it vanished would prove. The chequebook was shut; Wimbledon and the workhouse were forgotten. Some thought of a humorous kind made him chuckle. Taking his hat and his stick, calling for his dog and his daughter, he would stride off into Kensington Gardens, where he had walked as a little boy, where his brother Fitzjames and he had made beautiful bows to young Queen Victoria and she had swept them a curtsey, and so, round the Serpentine, to Hyde Park Corner, where he had once saluted the great Duke himself; and so home. He was not then in the least "alarming"; he was very simple, very confiding; and his silence, though one might last unbroken from the Round Pond to the Marble Arch, was curiously full of meaning, as if he were thinking half aloud, about poetry and philosophy and people he had known.

He himself was the most abstemious of men. He smoked a pipe perpetually, but never a cigar. He wore his clothes until they were too shabby to be tolerable; and he held old-fashioned and rather puritanical views as to the vice of luxury and the sin of idleness. The relations between parents and children today have a freedom that would have been impossible with my father. He expected a certain standard of behaviour, even of ceremony, in family life. Yet if freedom means the right to think one's own thoughts and to follow one's own pursuits, then no one respected and indeed insisted upon freedom more completely than he did. His sons, with the exception of the Army and Navy, should follow whatever professions they chose; his daughters, though he cared little enough for the higher education of women, should have the same liberty. If at one moment he rebuked a daughter sharply for smoking a cigarette—smoking was not in his opinion a nice habit in the other sex—she had only to ask him if she might become a painter, and he assured her that so long as she took her work seriously he would give her all the help he could. He had no special love for painting; but he kept his word. Freedom of that sort was worth thousands of cigarettes.

It was the same with the perhaps more difficult problem of literature. Even today there may be parents who would doubt the wisdom of allowing a girl of fifteen the free run of a large and quite unexpurgated library. But my father allowed it. There were certain facts—very briefly, very shyly he referred to them. Yet "Read what you like," he said, and all his books, "mangy and worthless," as he called them, but certainly they were many and various, were to be had without asking. To read what one liked because one liked it, never to pretend to admire what one did not—that was his only lesson in the art of reading. To write in the fewest possible words, as clearly as possible, exactly what one meant—that was his only lesson in the art of writing. All the rest must be learnt for oneself. Yet a child must have been childish in the extreme not to feel that such was the teaching of a man of great learning and wide experience, though he would never impose his own views or parade his own knowledge. For, as his tailor remarked when he saw my father walk past his shop up Bond Street, "There goes a gentleman that wears good clothes without knowing it."

In those last years, grown solitary and very deaf, he would sometimes call himself a failure as a writer; he had been "jack of all trades, and master of none." But whether he failed or succeeded as a writer, it is permissible to believe that he left a distinct impression of himself on the minds of his friends. Meredith saw him as "Phoebus Apollo turned fasting friar" in his earlier days; Thomas Hardy, years later, looked at the "spare and desolate figure" of the Schreckhorn and thought of

> him,
> Who scaled its horn with ventured life and limb,
> Drawn on by vague imaginings, maybe,
> Of semblance to his personality
> In its quaint glooms, keen lights, and rugged trim.

But the praise he would have valued most, for though he was an agnostic nobody believed more profoundly in the worth of human relationships, was Meredith's tribute after his death: "He was the one man to my knowledge worthy to have married your mother." And Lowell, when he called him "L.S., the most lovable of men," has best described the quality that makes him, after all these years, unforgettable.

REBECCA WEST

A Visit to a Godmother

What I chiefly want to do when I write is to contemplate character: either by inventing my own characters in novels and short stories based on my own experience, or by studying characters in history, ancient or, by preference, modern. This is an inborn tendency in me, I am sure, but various events have stimulated it, and one among them was a visit to my godmother which I paid more than half a century ago. When I was thirteen my godmother invited me and my elder sister Winifred to stay with her. The prospect filled me with excitement. I had never met her since I was a very small child, but I had reason to have more grateful and romantic feelings for her than most god-children feel for their sponsors. She had a picturesque connection with my mother's early life. When my mother was in her late twenties she had had a nervous breakdown caused by her grief at the loss of a brother, and she had given up her career as a musician and had become for two or three years what was then known as "a musical governess." It was a pleasant post such as this age, so mistakenly called affluent, could never afford. She was engaged by a rich city banker, whom we may call Mr Kastner, to live with his family and give piano lessons to his two daughters, Amanda and Charlotte, who were in their late teens and had finished their general education; she had also to take them to concerts and the opera and talk French, German, and Italian with them. It was perhaps the most tranquil time in my mother's life.

The family had a house in Belgravia and a country place in the South Downs with a great park full of splendid trees and far views, which my mother always remembered with delight.

It happened that the mother of her pupils was a very unhappy woman. She came from the southern states of America. She was thus three thousand miles from her own relatives, and her husband suffered from an internal malady which made him irritable and morose; and he had alienated most of his family by his temper. The arrival of my mother, gifted, witty, full of vitality, and kind, was a godsend to her. Mrs Kastner was very sad indeed when after three years or so my mother's own family reclaimed her, and the two women never lost touch with each other. When my mother was left a penniless widow with three children, Mrs Kastner immediately made her an allowance, not a large one, for she had little money of her own, but it was all she could do and it meant a great deal to us.

But only a short time afterwards she died. My mother had wept for the loss of a friend, and later had been chilled by the thought that in the future she was going to be poorer. But then the elder Kastner daughter, Amanda, who had been my godmother, wrote and announced her intention of continuing the allowance. This was remarkably kind. She had married late, a man not at all rich, whom I shall call Bolton, who was working as a not very successful cattle-breeder in South America. She had inherited no great fortune from her father, whose fortunes had declined in his last years. My mother exclaimed at Amanda's generosity and refused it, but resolutely Amanda had sent the allowance as before through a London solicitor.

Now, when I was thirteen, my godmother and her family had returned from South America and had settled in the Midlands, and I was eager to see her.

I had so often between sleeping and waking seen these four women, dressed in the be-bustled fashions of the eighties, pacing a lawn under great cedars or resting on the seat under the beech tree at the turn of the high path where a break in the downs showed a blue triangle of distant sea. Mrs Kastner I saw as a melancholy and graceful woman, an ageing Mariana in the Moated Grange. Charlotte was faceless for me because I knew nothing about her, she was an invalid who lived in Switzerland, but Amanda was very visible. I saw her bland as her name, like a Jane Austen character, but with a Brontëan nobility, which I imputed to her because it had been impressed on me that to continue our allowance after her mother's death she must be making sacrifices. I knew that when my sister and I visited her in the Midlands we would see her in a very different setting. But I expected some of the glory of that setting to have clung to her.

My sister and I were nervous as we travelled down from Edinburgh towards the Midlands. We knew the Boltons would be poor, but they certainly would not be as poor as we were. We never came across anybody who was as poor as we were. We therefore had to take it for granted that they would think our clothes were awful. But we also took it for granted that my godmother's family would be too nice to mind about them. But if there were visitors they might not be so nice. This, I must explain, was a real point. In those days there were no attractive cheap ready-made clothes. If you were poor you had to wear clothes run up by sewing-women, and you looked terrible. But on the other hand I was aware we had a trump card to play. My sister Winifred was very beautiful, in the style of an early Victorian beauty, with smooth chestnut hair and an oval face and regular features. It seemed to me that if people asked two girls they had never seen to stay with them they would be bound to be pleased if one of them turned up looking like Winifred.

For the rest, we wondered what the talk would be about; we had grown up in air thick with conversation about literature, politics, music, painting. I took it for granted that we would step into a house where people were discussing their pet ideas, and imagined that, as we would arrive in the evening, they would be engaged in an argument, probably with the reference books got out.

It was not at all like that. To begin with, we were disconcerted by the landscape. We knew London, we knew Edinburgh, we knew the superb hill ranges of Lowland Scotland and the lochs and mountains of the Highlands. But we had never before been in country in which, no matter in what direction one looked, one saw nothing but flat fields and hedges. We could not think why my godmother and her husband should have chosen to live in such a god-forsaken corner of the country, as the dog-cart carried us along five flat miles to the house.

This was pleasant. It was one of those comfortable rectories that were built in the second half of the eighteenth century. But once we entered the house we received a shock. We were met by a big, bouncing woman in dull clothes who uttered words of mechanical welcome without taking the smallest trouble to pretend that she meant them.

We wondered why the godmother we imagined should have such a dreary person in her house, and then the authority in her voice as she spoke to the groom warned us that this was Amanda. Her eyes ran over us and did not seem to notice anything special about my sister's appearance. She asked us how our mother was and before we could answer turned away and told a housemaid to take us to our rooms. My sister insisted on delaying for a moment to give her the presents my mother had sent her, the classic Edinburgh presents, shortbread and Edinburgh rock. Mrs Bolton made the proper acknowledgements but her manner expressed a conviction that whatever it was that we had brought her it could not interest her.

Our visit lasted a fortnight and at no time was my godmother much more gracious to us, nor was her husband, nor were her children. Two guests arrived, two young women in their late twenties, daughters of relatives. I realize now, from my recollection of remarks which my godmother and her husband exchanged over our heads, that these girls were in the miserable plight which befell Edwardian young women who failed to marry in their first youth and were not very well off. They would never have married at all if they had gone out to work, so they either sat at home doing nothing or bumping round the country staying with friends who were doing nothing, quite simply waiting and hoping. I then felt no pity for their humiliating lot. We had hoped they would give us some companionship, but when they arrived they whispered together in corners and glowered at us, particularly at my poor pretty sister. They quite rudely stared at our clothes, they were indeed sometimes rude in words, so rude that my sister and I did not like to speak to each other about it. But once my sister said to me, when we had taken refuge in our bedrooms, "Well, it's probably true, that bit about Lady Blanche being so rude to Jane Eyre."

Nobody in the whole house was agreeable to us except the nursery governess, a gay little creature. Everybody seemed in favour of our alliance with her, and we understood why when we took some flowers down to the church and the vicar's wife said, "Ah, yes, you're the *old* governess' children, aren't you." This put us in a psychologically difficult position. From a snobbish point of view, my sister and I were at least as well-born as my godmother. But we couldn't resent this classification of us because our whole disposition was to consider such a distinction absurd, and we hadn't the slightest wish to dissociate ourselves from the dear little nursery governess.

It was not only such incivilities which irked us. One day a newcomer to the district, the wife of an engineer employed on some large construction nearby, a reservoir, came to return my godmother's call. She was amazingly beautiful. I am not wrong about that, for I was to come across her a few years later in circumstances which proved it. She went on the stage and George Bernard Shaw and Granville-Barker put her into the first production of *Androcles and the Lion* as a flower-seller who was to go to and fro at the back of the stage offering her wares to a crowd while the actors talked to each other in the front of the stage. Shaw and Barker had to take her out of the part because as long as she was on the stage the audience paid no attention to the actors.

My sister and I were fascinated, and sat with our eyes and our ears open, for she was a delightful talker. When she left my sister and I were deputed to go and help her get her little donkey-cart out into the road, and once out of the house my sister dared to say to her, "You're not English, are you?"

"No, I'm Russian." This was something tremendous. Then, not less than now, Russia was the country of mysterious enchantment. But she did better than that. She added, "Before I married I was Vera Tchaikovsky." "Not . . . ?" "His niece." We chattered until the donkey brayed with impatience and she had to go. Was St Petersburg as marvellously beautiful as people said? Did she know the wonderful people at the Conservatory of Music in St Petersburg? Did she know Rubinstein? Had she read Gorky? He was just then bursting on the world of the young in England.

When she had finally left we hurried back to the drawing-room to make known our marvellous discovery. Dead faces looked at us and not a word was spoken. I have recalled that moment every time I have come across the lines, "Like a party in a parlour, all silent and all damned." Then my godmother said, "Well, who-ever she may be, she was returning a first call; she should have stayed only twenty minutes, and she stayed forty."

Sometimes the household mollified me by amusing me. Once, when my godmother's husband seemed less surly than usual, I tried, delicately, to find out why they lived in that partic-ular flat and unexciting part of England. He explained that he and his wife had chosen to live there because it was hunting country. "Oh, do you hunt?" I asked. "But where are the horses?" No, he didn't hunt. He had long ago suffered an injury to his leg which prevented him from doing more than sit a horse. "I see. You like to be with people who hunt." No, the hunting set round there had not much use for people who didn't hunt. He didn't see much of them. "But you like to be where hunting is going on?" Yes, that was it. This tickled me; so might a devout old lady who was bedridden choose to live near a cathedral so that she could hear the chimes. To keep the conversation going I went on, "But I suppose you hunted a great deal at one time." No. He had injured his leg at his preparatory school. He had never hunted at all. I still think that such abstract piety, such reverence for the mere idea of hunting, was very funny.

They were sometimes funny and they were good. I realized that, for it became clear that the allowance they made my mother did inconvenience them to some extent. They were able to live in a comfortable house with a cook, a butler, a housemaid, a knife-boy, a groom, and a gardener. But on the other hand they were not even able to go and stay in London as often as they would have liked, much less go abroad. And I was so deeply familiar with the technique of poverty in my own home that I recognized it elsewhere. The carpets here and the curtains and the loose covers all needed replacing. I felt guilty and grateful.

But they would not let me feel just that. They were, as it proved, too rude. One morning they were going to a neighbour-ing town to conclude some business with a solicitor, and had to take an early train. They had left the breakfast room when I came down. When they were all ready to leave in the dog-cart they sent in a message to ask me if I would care to drive with them to the station. I put on my coat and hat and hurried out and took my place on the high seat beside the groom, and immediately passed into an unexpected ecstasy. It was quite early in the morning. The rabbits were still out in the fields. There had been rain in the night and now there was sun, and the grass was shining like wet paint and the flooded dykes were like blue crystal. Above us there was a tremendous sky-battle of what we at home called clouds-of-war, and the wind was fresh as if it had come straight off the sea. The horse was a lovely little cob a rich relative had given my godmother, and it brought down its hooves on the roadway as if it thought it was playing a percussion instrument in a band. I had never enjoyed anything much more in my life, and I remember regretting that my sister was not there.

When we got to the station the groom slipped off the seat and ran to open the dog-car door, and I hastened to clamber down so that I could thank my godmother for the treat. But before I got to the ground they had walked past me towards the platform, as if I were not there. I had opened my mouth to thank them, and it remained open. I stared at them to see if I had offended them, but it was not that. Their faces were not tense. They simply could not be bothered to say good-bye to me, they could not be bothered to recognize the presence of someone who meant nothing to them, who was both a child and the child of an unimportant person. I told myself that I must have made a mistake. Perhaps people didn't say good-bye to each other in such circumstances. But the groom sucked in his breath through his teeth, and I had the final shame of knowing that he thought they were being very rude to me and had probably seen that I was having hard work not to cry.

Through tears of rage I stared at the two square, unyielding, ungenial figures standing on the platform beside a cluster of milk churns, with hatred in my heart. But it was soon displaced. I found there was something more interesting to do than hate my godmother. I remember my mind sliding out towards her, palpating her character with my mind as a surgeon's hand palpates his patient's body. What was the pattern of this curious woman's attributes? She was a boor and she had behaved boorishly to me; she behaved boorishly to everybody not in her family, so far as I could see; she was so unresponsive to human beings that she remained unmoved when a beautiful niece of Tchaikovsky strayed in sparkling from the Leicestershire lanes. How on earth did it happen that she was giving my mother an allowance she could ill afford? She was even, I perceived, trying to do more than that. She certainly had planned no pleasure for herself when she invited my sister and myself to stay with her.

She must have been moved by benevolence. But what could be the nature of the benevolent impulse which took the curious form of inviting children to her house to insult their power-lessness? I felt, I remember, excited at the spectacle of such inconsistencies. I felt greedy for some revelation which would make me able to account for them. Of course I never did. I was to learn later that though she seemed incapable of emotion, she had deeply cared for her children; she broke her heart when one of them died. There was also a moving explanation for her generosity to my mother. It seemed that she had passionately loved her mother, and had resented her father's treatment of her, with such warmth that years afterwards, she was willing to impose sacrifices on herself in order to give my mother some reward for having given *her* mother two or three years of happiness. She was in fact far more loving than the bland Amanda I had visualized walking on the lawn. But how could she love a woman as gra-cious as Mrs Kastner must have been, from all accounts, without absorbing any of her graciousness? How could such love exist without creating some loveliness? But even in her ungracious-ness, she had charm, for she had her own mystery, as each human being does. My writing is about that.

KATHERINE ANNE PORTER

St. Augustine and the Bullfight

Adventure. The word has become a little stale to me, because it
has been applied too often to the dull physical exploits of professional "adventurers" who write books about it, if they know how
to write; if not, they hire ghosts who quite often can't write either.

I don't read them, but rumors of them echo, and re-echo. The
book business at least is full of heroes who spend their time,
money and energy worrying other animals, manifestly their bet-
ters such as lions and tigers, to death in trackless jungles and
deserts only to be crossed by the stoutest motorcar; or another
feeds hooks to an inedible fish like the tarpon; another crosses
the ocean on a raft, living on plankton and seaweed. Why ever,
I wonder? And always always, somebody is out climbing mountains, and writing books about it, which are read by quite millions of persons who feel, apparently, that the next best thing to
going there yourself is to hear from somebody who went. And I
have heard more than one young woman remark that, though
she did not want to get married, still, she would like to have a
baby, for the adventure: not lately though. That was a pose of the
1920s and very early '30s. Several of them did it, too, but I do not
know of any who wrote a book about it—good for them.

W. B. Yeats remarked—I cannot find the passage now, so must
say it in other words—that the unhappy man (unfortunate?) was
one whose adventures outran his capacity for experience—
capacity for experience being, I should say, roughly equal to the
faculty for understanding what has happened to one. The difference then between mere adventures and a real experience might

be this? That adventure is something you seek for pleasure, or even for profit, like a gold rush or invading a country; for the illusion of being more alive than ordinarily, the thing you *will* to occur; but experience is what really happens to you in the long run; the truth that finally overtakes you.

Adventure is sometimes fun, but not too often. Not if you can remember what really happened; all of it. It passes, seems to lead nowhere much, is something to tell to friends to amuse them, maybe. "Once upon a time," I can hear myself saying, for I once said it, "I scaled a cliff in Boulder, Colorado, with my bare hands, and in Indian moccasins, bare-legged. And at nearly the top, after six hours of feeling for toe- and fingerholds, and the gayest feeling in the world that when I got to the top I should see something wonderful, something that sounded awfully like a bear growled out of a cave, and I scuttled down out of there in a hurry." This is a fact. I had never climbed a mountain in my life, never had the least wish to climb one. But there I was, for perfectly good reasons, in a hut on a mountainside in heavenly sunny though sometimes stormy weather, so I went out one morning and scaled a very minor cliff; alone, unsuitably clad, in the season when rattlesnakes are casting their skins; and if it was not a bear in that cave, it was some kind of unfriendly animal who growls at people; and this ridiculous escapade, which was nearly six hours of the hardest work I ever did in my life, toeholds and fingerholds on a cliff, put me to bed for just nine days with a complaint the local people called "muscle poisoning." I don't know exactly what they meant, but I do remember clearly that I could not turn over in bed without help and in great agony. And did it teach me anything? I think not, for three years later I was climbing a volcano in Mexico, that celebrated unpronounceably named volcano which everybody who comes near it climbs sooner or later; but was that any reason for me to climb it? No. And I was knocked out for weeks, and that finally did teach me: I am not supposed to go climbing things. Why did I not know in the first place? For me, this sort of thing must come under the head of Adventure.

I think it is pastime of rather an inferior sort; yet I have heard men tell yarns like this only a very little better: their mountains were higher, or their sea was wider, or their bear was bigger and noisier, or their cliff was steeper and taller, yet there was no point whatever to any of it except that it had happened. This is not enough. May it not be, perhaps, that experience, that is, the thing that happens to a person living from day to day, is anything at all that sinks in? is, without making any claims, a part of your growing and changing life? whatever it is that happens in your mind, your heart?

Adventure hardly ever seems to be that at the time it is happening: not under that name, at least. Adventure may be an afterthought, something that happens in the memory with imaginative trimmings if not downright lying, so that one should suppress it entirely, or go the whole way and make honest fiction of it. My own habit of writing fiction has provided a wholesome exercise to my natural, incurable tendency to try to wangle the sprawling mess of our existence in this bloody world into some kind of shape: almost any shape will do, just so it is recognizably made with human hands, one small proof the more of the validity and reality of the human imagination. But even within the most limited frame what utter confusion shall prevail if you cannot take hold firmly, and draw the exact line between what really happened, and what you have since imagined about it. Perhaps my soul will be saved after all in spite of myself because now and then I take some unmanageable, indigestible fact and turn it into fiction; cause things to happen with some kind of logic—my own logic, of course—and everything ends as I think it should end, and no back talk, or very little, from anybody about it. Otherwise, and except for this safety device, I should be the greatest liar unhung. (When was the last time anybody was hanged for lying?) What is Truth? I often ask myself, and Echo answers, Who knows?

A publisher asked me a great while ago to write a kind of autobiography, and I was delighted to begin; it sounded very easy when he said, "Just start, and tell everything you remember until now!" I wrote about a hundred pages before I realized, or admitted, the hideous booby trap into which I had fallen. First place, I remember quite a lot of stupid and boring things: there were other times when my life seemed merely an endurance test, or a quite mysterious but not very interesting and often monotonous effort at survival on the most primitive terms. There are dozens of things that might be entertaining but I have no intention of telling them because they are nobody's business; and endless little gossipy incidents that might entertain indulgent friends for a minute, but in print they look as silly as they really are. Then, there are the tremendous, unmistakable, life-and-death crises, the scalding, the bone-breaking events, the lightnings that shatter the landscape of the soul—who would write *that* by request? No, that is for a secretly written manuscript to be left with your papers, and if your executor is a good friend, who has probably been brought up on St. Augustine's *Confessions*, he will read it with love and attention and gently burn it to ashes for your sake.

Yet I intend to write something about my life, here and now, and so far as I am able without one touch of fiction, and I hope to keep it as shapeless and unforeseen as the events of life itself from day to day. Yet, look! I have already betrayed my occupation, and dropped a clue in what would be the right place if this *were* fiction, by mentioning St. Augustine when I hadn't meant to until it came in in its right place in life, not in art. Literary art, at least, is the business of setting human events to rights and giving them meanings that, in fact, they do not possess, or not obviously, or not the meanings the artist feels they should have— we do understand so little of what is really happening to us in any given moment. Only by remembering, comparing, waiting to know the consequences can we sometimes, in a flash of light, see what a certain event really meant, what it was trying to tell us. So this will be notes on a fateful thing that happened to me when I was young and did not know much about the world or about myself. I had been reading St. Augustine's *Confessions* since I was able to read at all, and I thought I had read every word, perhaps because I did know certain favorite passages by heart. But then, it was something like having read the Adventures by Rabelais when I was twelve and enjoying it; when I read it again at thirty-odd, I was astounded at how much I had overlooked in the earlier reading, and wondered what I thought I had seen there.

So it was with St. Augustine and my first bullfight. Looking back nearly thirty-five years on my earliest days in Mexico, it strikes me that, for a fairly serious young woman who was in the country for the express purpose of attending a Revolution, and studying Mayan temple art, I fell in with a most lordly gang of fashionable international hoodlums. Of course I had Revolution-ist friends and artist friends, and they were gay and easy and poor as I was. This other mob was different: they were French, Span-ish, Italian, Polish, and they all had titles and good names: a duke, a count, a *marqués*, a baron, and they all were in some flashy money-getting enterprise like importing cognac wholesale, or selling sports cars to newly rich politicians; and they all drank like fish and played fast games like polo or tennis or jaialai; they haunted the wings of theatres, drove slick cars like maniacs, but expert maniacs, never missed a bullfight or a boxing match; all were reasonably young and good-looking; and they had ladies to match, mostly imported and all speaking French. These persons stalked pleasure as if it were big game—they took their fun exactly where they found it, and the way they liked it, and they worked themselves to exhaustion at it. A fast, tough, expensive, elegant, high low-life they led, for the ladies and gentlemen each in turn had other friends you would have had to see to believe; and from time to time, without being in any way involved or engaged, I ran with this crowd of shady characters and liked their company and ways very much. I don't like gloomy sinners, but the merry ones charm me. And one of them introduced me to Shelley. And Shelley, whom I knew in the most superficial way, who remained essentially a stranger to me to the very end, led me, without in the least ever knowing what he had done, into one of the most important and lasting experiences of my life.

He was British, a member of the poet's family; said to be authentic great-great-nephew; he was rich and willful, and had come to Mexico young and wild, and mad about horses, of course. Coldly mad—he bred them and raced them and sold them with the stony detachment and merciless appraisal of the true horse lover—they call it love, and it could be that: but he did not like them. "What is there to like about a horse but his good points? If he has a vice, shoot him or send him to the bull ring; that is the only way to work a vice out of the breed!"

Once, during a riding trip while visiting a ranch, my host gave me a stallion to ride, who instantly took the bit in his teeth and bolted down a steep mountain trail. I managed to stick on, held an easy rein, and he finally ran himself to a standstill in an open field. My disgrace with Shelley was nearly complete. Why? Because the stallion *was not a good horse.* I should have refused to mount him. I said it was a question how to refuse the horse your host offered you—Shelley thought it no question at all. "A lady," he reminded me, "can always excuse herself gracefully from anything she doesn't wish to do." I said, "I wish that were really true," for the argument about the bullfight was already well started. But the peak of his disapproval of me, my motives, my temperament, my ideas, my ways, was reached when, to provide a diversion and end a dull discussion, I told him the truth: that I had liked being run away with, it had been fun and the kind of thing that had to happen unexpectedly, you couldn't arrange for it. I tried to convey to him my exhilaration, my pure joy when this half-broken, crazy beast took off down that trail with just a hoofhold between a cliff on one side and a thousand-foot drop on the other. He said merely that such utter frivolity surprised him in someone whom he had mistaken for a well-balanced, intelligent girl; and I remember thinking how revoltingly fatherly he sounded, exactly like my own father in his stuffier moments.

He was a stocky, red-faced, muscular man with broad shoulders, hard-jowled, with bright blue eyes glinting from puffy lids; his hair was a grizzled tan, and I guessed him about fifty years old, which seemed a great age to me then. But he mentioned that his Mexican wife had "died young" about three years before, and that his eldest son was only eleven years old. His whole appearance was so remarkably like the typical horsy, landed-gentry sort of Englishman one meets in books by Frenchmen or Americans, if this were fiction I should feel obliged to change his looks altogether, thus falling into one stereotype to avoid falling into another. However, so Shelley did look, and his clothes were magnificent and right beyond words, and never new-looking and never noticeable at all except one could not help observing sooner or later that he was beyond argument the best-dressed man in America, North or South; it was that kind of typical British inconspicuous good taste: he had it, superlatively. He was evidently leading a fairly rakish life, or trying to, but he was of a cast-iron conventionality even in that. We did not fall in love — far from it. We struck up a hands-off, quaint, far-fetched, tetchy kind of friendship which consisted largely of good advice about worldly things from him, mingled with critical marginal notes on my character — a character of which I could not recognize a single trait; and if I said, helplessly, "But I am not in the least like that," he would answer, "Well, you should be!" or "Yes, you are, but you don't know it."

This man took me to my first bullfight. I'll tell you later how St. Augustine comes into it. It was the first bullfight of that season; Covadonga Day; April; clear, hot blue sky; and a long procession of women in flower-covered carriages; wearing their finest lace veils and highest combs and gauziest fans; but I shan't describe a bullfight. By now surely there is no excuse for anyone who can read or even hear not to know pretty well what goes on in a bull ring. I shall say only that Sanchez Mejías and Rudolfo Gaona each killed a bull that day; but before the Grand March of the toreros, Hattie Weston rode her thoroughbred High School gelding into the ring to thunders of shouts and brassy music.

She was Shelley's idol. "*Look* at that girl, for God's sake," and his voice thickened with feeling, "the finest rider in the world," he said in his dogmatic way, and it is true I have not seen better since.

She was a fine buxom figure of a woman, a highly colored blonde with a sweet, childish face; probably forty years old, and perfectly rounded in all directions; a big round bust, and that is the word, there was nothing plural about it, just a fine, warm-looking bolster straight across her front from armpit to armpit; fine firm round hips — again, why the plural? It was an ample seat born to a sidesaddle, as solid and undivided as the bust, only more of it. She was tightly corseted and her waist was small. She wore a hard-brimmed dark gray Spanish sailor hat, sitting straight and shallow over her large golden knot of hair; a light gray bolero and a darker gray riding skirt — not a Spanish woman's riding dress, nor yet a man's, but something tight and fit and formal and appropriate. And there she went, the most elegant woman in the saddle I have ever seen, graceful and composed in her perfect style, with her wonderful, lightly dancing, learned horse, black and glossy as shoe polish, perfectly under control—no, not under control at all, you might have thought, but just dancing and showing off his paces by himself for his own pleasure.

"She makes the bullfight seem like an anticlimax," said Shelley, tenderly.

I had not wanted to come to this bullfight. I had never intended to see a bullfight at all. I do not like the slaughtering of animals as sport. I am carnivorous, I love all the red juicy meats and all the fishes. Seeing animals killed for food on the farm in summers shocked and grieved me sincerely, but it did not cure my taste for flesh. My family for as far back as I know anything about them, only about 450 years, were the huntin', shootin', fishin' sort: their houses were arsenals and their dominion over the animal kingdom was complete and unchallenged. When I was older, my father remarked on my tiresome timidity, or was I just pretending to finer feelings than those of the society around me? He hardly knew which was the more tiresome. But that was perhaps only a personal matter. Morally, if I wished to eat meat I should be able to kill the animal—otherwise it appeared that I was willing to nourish myself on other people's sins? For he supposed I considered it a sin. Otherwise why bother about it? Or was it just something unpleasant I wished to avoid? Maintaining my own purity—and a very doubtful kind of purity he found it, too—at the expense of the guilt of others? Altogether, my father managed to make a very sticky question of it, and for some years at intervals I made it a matter of conscience to kill an animal or bird, something I intended to eat. I gave myself and the beasts some horrible times, through fright and awkwardness, and to my shame, nothing cured me of my taste for flesh. All forms of cruelty offend me bitterly, and this repugnance is inborn, absolutely impervious to any arguments, or even insults, at which the red-blooded lovers of blood sports are very expert; they don't admire me at all, any more than I admire them. . . . Ah, me, the contradictions, the paradoxes! I was once perfectly capable of keeping a calf for a pet until he outgrew the yard in the country and had to be sent to the pastures. His subsequent fate I leave you to guess. Yes, it is all revoltingly sentimental, and worse than that, confused. My defense is that no matter whatever else this world seemed to promise me, never once did it promise to be simple.

So, for a great tangle of emotional reasons I had no intention of going to a bullfight. But Shelley was so persistently unpleasant about my cowardice, as he called it flatly, I just wasn't able to take the thrashing any longer. Partly, too, it was his natural snobbery: smart people of the world did not have such feelings; it was to him a peculiarly provincial if not downright Quakerish attitude. "I have some Quaker ancestors," I told him. "How absurd of you!" he said, and really meant it.

The bullfight question kept popping up and had a way of spoiling other occasions that should have been delightful. Shelley was one of those men, of whose company I feel sometimes that I have had more than my fair share, who simply do not know how to drop a subject, or abandon a position once they have declared it. Constitutionally incapable of admitting defeat, or even its possibility, even when he had not the faintest shadow of right to expect a victory—for why should he make a contest of my refusal to go to a bullfight?—he would start an argument during the theatre intermissions, at the frontón, at a street fair, on a stroll in the alameda, at a gay restaurant over coffee and brandy; there was no moment so felicitous he could not shatter it with his favorite gambit: "If you would only see *one*, you'd get over this nonsense."

So there I was, at the bullfight, with cold hands, trembling innerly, with painful tinglings in the wrists and collarbone: yet my excitement was not altogether painful; and in my happiness at Hattie Weston's performance I was calmed and off guard when the heavy barred gate to the corral burst open and the first bull charged through. The bulls were from the Duke of Veragua's ranch, as enormous and brave and handsome as any I ever saw afterward. (This is not a short story, so I don't have to maintain any suspense.) This first bull was a beautiful monster of brute courage: his hide was a fine pattern of black and white, much enhanced by the goad with fluttering green ribbons stabbed into his shoulder as he entered the ring; this in turn furnished an interesting design in thin rivulets of blood, the enlivening touch of scarlet in his sober color scheme, with highly aesthetic effect.

He rushed at the waiting horse, blindfolded in one eye and standing at the proper angle for the convenience of his horns, the picador making only the smallest pretense of staving him off, and disemboweled the horse with one sweep of his head. The horse trod in his own guts. It happens at least once every bull-fight. I could not pretend not to have expected it; but I had not been able to imagine it. I sat back and covered my eyes. Shelley, very deliberately and as inconspicuously as he could, took both my wrists and held my hands down on my knees. I shut my eyes and turned my face away, away from the arena, away from him, but not before I had seen in his eyes a look of real, acute concern and almost loving anxiety for me—he really believed that my feelings were the sign of a grave flaw of character, or at least an unbecoming, unworthy weakness that he was determined to overcome in me. He couldn't shoot me, alas, or turn me over to the bull ring; he had to deal with me in human terms, and he did it according to his lights. His voice was hoarse and fierce: "Don't you dare come here and then do this! You *must* face it!"

Part of his fury was shame, no doubt, at being seen with a girl who would behave in such a pawky way. But at this point he was, of course, right. Only he had been wrong before to nag me into this, and I was altogether wrong to have let him persuade me. Or so I felt then. "You have *got* to face this!" By then he was right; and I did look and I did face it, though not for years and years.

During those years I saw perhaps a hundred bullfights, all in Mexico City, with the finest bulls from Spain and the greatest bullfighters—but not with Shelley—never again with Shelley, for we were not comfortable together after that day. Our odd, mismatched sort of friendship declined and neither made any effort to revive it. There was bloodguilt between us, we shared an evil secret, a hateful revelation. He hated what he had revealed in me to himself, and I hated what he had revealed to me about myself, and each of us for entirely opposite reasons; but there was nothing more to say or do, and we stopped seeing each other.

I took to the bullfights with my Mexican and Indian friends. I sat with them in the cafés where the bullfighters appeared; more

than once went at two o'clock in the morning with a crowd to
see the bulls brought into the city; I visited the corral back of the
ring where they could be seen before the corrida. Always, of
course, I was in the company of impassioned adorers of the sport,
with their special vocabulary and mannerisms and contempt for
all others who did not belong to their charmed and chosen cult.
Quite literally there were those among them I never heard speak
of anything else; and I heard then all that can be said—the topic
is limited, after all, like any other—in love and praise of bull-
fighting. But it can be tiresome, too. And I did not really live in
that world, so narrow and so trivial, so cruel and so unconscious;
I was a mere visitor. There was something deeply, irreparably
wrong with my being there at all, something against the grain of
my life; except for this (and here was the falseness I had finally
to uncover): I loved the spectacle of the bullfights, I was drunk
on it, I was in a strange, wild dream from which I did not want
to be awakened. I was now drawn irresistibly to the bull ring as
before I had been drawn to the race tracks and the polo fields at
home. But this had death in it, and it was the death in it that I
loved. . . . And I was bitterly ashamed of this evil in me, and
believed it to be in me only—no one had fallen so far into cruelty
as this! These bullfight buffs I truly believed did not know what
they were doing—but I did, and I knew better because I had *once*
known better; so that spiritual pride got in and did its deadly
work, too. How could I face the cold fact that at heart I was just
a killer, like any other, that some deep corner of my soul consented not just willingly but with rapture? I still clung obstinately
to my flattering view of myself as a unique case, as a humane,
blood-avoiding civilized being, somehow a fallen angel, perhaps?
Just the same, what was I doing there? And why was I beginning
secretly to abhor Shelley as if he had done me a great injury,
when in fact he had done me the terrible and dangerous favor of
helping me to find myself out?

  In the meantime I was reading St. Augustine; and if Shelley
had helped me find myself out, St. Augustine helped me find
myself again. I read for the first time then his story of a friend of
his, a young man from the provinces who came to Rome and
was taken up by the gang of clever, wellborn young hoodlums
Augustine then ran with; and this young man, also wellborn but

severely brought up, refused to go with the crowd to the gladiatorial combats; he was opposed to them on the simple grounds that they were cruel and criminal. His friends naturally ridiculed such dowdy sentiments; they nagged him slyly, bedeviled him openly, and, of course, finally some part of him consented—but only to a degree. He would go with them, he said, but he would not watch the games. And he did not, until the time for the first slaughter, when the howling of the crowd brought him to his feet, staring: and afterward he was more bloodthirsty than any.

Why, of course: oh, it might be a commonplace of human nature, it might be it could happen to anyone! I longed to be free of my uniqueness, to be a fellow-sinner at least with someone: I could not bear my guilt alone—and here was this student, this boy at Rome in the fourth century, somebody I felt I knew well on sight, who had been weak enough to be led into adventure but strong enough to turn it into experience. For no matter how we both attempted to deceive ourselves, our acts had all the ear-marks of adventure: violence of motive, events taking place at top speed, at sustained intensity, under powerful stimulus and a willful seeking for pure sensation; willful, I say, because I was not kidnapped and forced, after all, nor was that young friend of St. Augustine's. We both proceeded under the power of our own weakness. When the time came to kill the splendid black and white bull, I who had pitied him when he first came into the ring stood straining on tiptoe to see everything, yet almost blinded with excitement, and crying out when the crowd roared, and kissing Shelley on the cheekbone when he shook my elbow and shouted in the voice of one justified: "Didn't I tell you? Didn't I?"

DOROTHY PARKER

The Middle or Blue Period

And what was it I had to remember, the minute I woke up? I know there was something, something pretty terrible, too. Not just plain terrible. This was fancy terrible; this was terrible with raisins in it. Ah, yes, I have it. This is my birthday. Here's the anniversary of my nativity, come around again on that cosmic belt. The Lord knows I didn't ask for it. Like a hole in the head I need another birthday. I'm birthday poor as it is.

Well. The best you can do about it is the best you can do about it. Many happy returns, my dear; there, that made you laugh out loud, didn't it? Well, that's better. What place have those salt tears on your cheek, on this, your day of fete? This is fiesta. See, the fountains run wine, and already there is dancing in the square. Come, then, a song, a song! Happy birthday to you, happy birthday to you, happy birthday, poor bastard, happy birthday to-o-o you!

This is it, you know, baby. This is the one that does it. You have said farewell to the thirties for the tenth and last time. Now you face it, baby. Now you take it smack in the teeth, baby. Quote baby unquote.

A fine lot of good that ever did, trying to lie about your age. The most you could plausibly knock off was a couple of years, and what's a couple of sandspits to an archipelago? Perhaps, if you had moved to a strange city and given it out that you had had a terribly tragic life, spent mostly in the tropics, you might have been able to subtract something worthwhile.

No; you couldn't have done it. Though the city were Trebi-

zond, you would have met there someone who used to be in your
class in school. They go all over the earth, those schoolmates of
yours; there can't be a soul left in Upper Montclair. Close your
eyes and put your finger anywhere on the spinning globe, and
whatever spot it touches, land or sea, someone who used to be
in your class in school is there. It passes credibility that fourteen
dirty little girls could have grown up to be so far-flung.

Even at home, there is no safety from them. Put on your best
and walk out your door into the tender light, all set to sign "Faithfully, Katharine Hepburn" in any proffered autograph books; and
there, waiting to pounce, will be something that used to sit next
to you at the Jackson Whites' Academy for the Digitally Over-
Privileged, Native Clay Lunches a Feature, which you seem to
have attended in your youth. You can tell your fellow alumnae a
block off by their gait, which is that of those assisted by prison
guards along the last mile. Other show points are the hair like
blown ashes, the mouth like a horseshoe with the luck running
out, and the general air, no matter how glorious the weather, of
being dressed in the expectation of heavy rains. Oh, Oh, God.
Maybe you look like that to them. No; no, of course you don't.
Stop it. You don't, you don't, you don't.

You know perfectly well they look like that because that's the
way they are and the way they always have been; years have nothing to do with it. Years are only garments, and you either wear
them with style all your life, or else you go dowdy to the grave.
And these are the prettiest years, the most becoming, these that
are about to be given you. Can't you get that through your head,
you poor cluck? Oh, the gratitude with which you are going to
look back on this day! You're going to think of it as the delicate
arch through which you passed into the enchanted garden. Sure
you are. You know what's happening today? The birthday of your
life is come, as Miss Rossetti has it. If you had any sense, your
heart would be like a singing bird whose nest is in the watered
shoot. (Dear Christina Rossetti: we are taking up English poets,
in school, and I have chosen you for the subject of a composition. Please write me any interesting facts you can remember
about yourself, also how you came to make up poetry, and what
the hell a watered shoot is.) Very well, then, *don't* go around all

day with your heart like a soaking wet bird, if that's the way you feel about it. But you might at least have the decency to show a little enthusiasm. Why, you've got the world by the tail. Everything is going to be fine for you from now on. You will have all that you never had before—tranquillity and grace and usefulness and tribute. You're going to have the true time of your life. Oh, you'll love it. Honestly, you will. Honestly.

Well, all right, Middle Age. You've been hanging around here for ten years. Take your foot out of the door and come on in . . . No—please wait a minute . . . Please, just another minute . . . I can't quite . . .

It's that word "middle." Any phrase it touches becomes the label of the frump; middle of the road, middle class, middle age. If only you could leap these dreary decades and land up in the important numbers. There is chic to seventy, elegance to eighty.

People ought to be one of two things, young or old. No; what's the good of fooling? People ought to be one of two things, young or dead.

Well. Taking it like a little soldier, aren't you? And what is there to take, for heaven's sake? If you hadn't ripped the back pages off the calendar last night, you'd never have known the difference.

You probably don't even look any more than twenty-four hours older than you did yesterday. It's only your personal piece of hard luck that you are what you are today, when, inside, you never felt cuter.

You're just the same, within, as you were fifteen years ago, twenty; does any gentleman want to make it thirty? The only noticeable differences are a tendency to believe that your friends are several years older than they say they are, and a disposition to regard sixty as the age of consent. There are certain outer changes you could make, if you feel up to it. You might, for instance, give away that apple-blossom hat; some poor tot would be glad to have it for Sunday school. And now is the time to throw in the towel and stop ordering your dresses a little too big, so you can grow into them.

Take it easy, that's all you have to do. Don't fight it. You're the only one who is passionately interested in your age; other people have their own troubles. The matter will probably never come up, unless you fetch it up. After all, how often does the McKinley Inaugural normally creep into the conversation?

Pretty behavior. The best years of your life opening before you like a painted fan, and here you are, sulking. Look at the women who were famous long after they became, shall we say, full-blown. Look at Ninon de Lenclos. No; don't go off thinking about all the other poor souls who sought to cheer themselves by looking at Ninon de Lenclos. Just keep your eye on Ninon de Lenclos, and you can't go wrong; what woman has done, woman can do. And keep thinking about what's ahead of you. There will be friends and work and communication and laughter. There might very well be a series of rather stately adventures. It is not even impossible that you will be invited to take part in the dance. For God's sake, there must be somebody, somewhere, who has read Benjamin Franklin's letter to the young man!

Your path stretches so smooth, so gracious. There are no more ways for you to make a fool of yourself; you have assembled the complete set. There are no more mistakes; you have made them all. There are, for you, only ease and fulfillment and tenderness. And you did not work to gain them. They are given to you as gifts for this, your happiest birthday.

Oh, come in, Middle Age, come in, come in! Come close to me, give me your hand, let me look in your face . . . Oh . . . Is that what you are really like? . . . Oh, God help me . . . help me . . .

EDMUND WILSON

A Preface to Persius

Maudlin Meditations in a Speakeasy

The other evening I had to dine out alone, and, stopping in on my way at a bookstore, bought a little eighteenth-century edition of Persius, with notes and a translation. The editor and translator was a man named William Drummond, who had also been a member of Parliament. The attractive duodecimo was bound in green morocco and stamped in gold, and, inside the cover, had gray marbled paper with green and yellow runnings. There was a medallion of Aulus Persius Flaccus, with crisp metallic curls on the title-page, and the whole volume, with the edges of its pages gilded on all three sides and its well-spaced and small clear type, had the aspect of a little casket in which something precious was kept. I went to an Italian restaurant and, while I was waiting for the antipasto, I began to read the preface. "In offering to the public," it ran, "a new English version of Persius, my object has rather been to express his meaning clearly, than either to translate his words literally, or to copy his manner servilely. The sentiments of this satirist are indeed admirable, and deserve to be better known than they are; but his poetry cannot be praised for its elegance, nor his language for its urbanity."

The plate arrived, with a glistening sardine, little purple olives, two pearly leeks, bronze anchovies and bright red pimiento slices that looked like little tongues, all against a lining of pale lettuce. There were also a bottle of yellow wine and a goblet of pale green glass. I wondered what had become of the sort of thing that this

editor of Persius represented. In the middle of the room where I
sat was a party of men and women, all pink and of huge size,
who were uncorking loud sour laughter; across the room was a
quite pretty young girl, of an obviously simple nature, who had
some sort of keen professional interest in pleasing a rather defec-
tive-looking half-aquiline man, whose eyes one couldn't see
through his eyeglasses. Craning around behind me, however, I
caught sight of E. E. Cummings. Cummings, I reflected, was a
cultivated fellow and a good writer and came from Boston, but
was not a bit like William Drummond. For a point of view like
that of Drummond, who would have reproached the inelegance
of Persius's poetry yet applauded his admirable sentiments, one
would have to go to our own eighteenth-century literature—to
Joel Barlow or Philip Freneau. But Drummond was a fancier of
letters and a political figure at the same time—Jefferson might
have thought and written so. Some of the logic, some of the
elegance, some of the moderate and equable opinion which
seemed to be the qualities—here found, as it were, in their pure
state—of this preface to an ancient classic had gone to the
announcement of our national policies and the construction of
our constitution. But new interests had taken over the government; and I had been reading in the paper that day of a typical
example of their methods—an assault by the state constabulary
on a meeting of Italian miners; men clubbed insensible, children
gassed, old people badly beaten, a nursing woman knocked
down. With the exception, I reflected, of Cummings, and possibly the Italian waiters, there was probably not a person in that
room who would not either approve this action or refuse to
believe that it had happened; and Cummings was as powerless
to prevent its recurrence as the illiterate waiters would be. Perhaps the only element in sight which had anything in common
with Drummond on Persius was the Italian dinner itself, of
which a bowl of minestrone, with its cabbage, big brown beans
and round noodles, had just reached me as the second course,
and in the richness and balance of whose composition I could
still see the standards of a civilization based on something more
comfortably human than commercial and industrial interests.
Yet how few generations of Italians speaking English and com-

peting with the natives would it take for them to forget their cooking and their ideal of a good dinner and to go in, as one already saw them beginning to do, for expensive à la carte restaurants with heterogeneous and uninteresting menus?

"The defects of Persius, considered with respect to composition, cannot perhaps be easily defended. Even Casaubon, his fondest admirer, and most successful interpreter, admits that his style is obscure. If, however, any apology can be made for this first sin against good writing, it is in the case of a satirist, and above all, of a satirist who dared to reprobate the crimes, and to ridicule the follies of a tyrant. If Persius be obscure, let it be remembered, he lived in the time of Nero. But it has been remarked, that this author is not obscure, only when he lashes and exposes the Roman emperor. It was very well, it has been said, to employ hints, and to speak in half sentences, while he censured the vices of a cruel and luxurious despot; but there could be no occasion for enveloping himself in obscurity, while he expounded the doctrines of the Stoics to his friend Cornutus, or expatiated to the poet Bassus on the true use of riches."—I looked up, as the chicken and greens were being set down before me, and saw Cummings, who had finished and was leaving. If they had felt that way about Persius, what would they have thought of Cummings? And what was the use, in the eighteenth century, of the critics' having cultivated those standards, if Cummings was what the future had in store? He stopped at my table, and I asked him where he had spent the summer. "I thought of going to Boston," he ejaculated, "to see the machine-guns!*— but we've all seen plenty of machine-guns!—commonest thing in the world!—so I walked around New York, expecting to be blown up any moment—be a fine thing to blow the subways up!—of course, my attitude toward this whole thing—I mean, it's just unfortunate—it's a bore; like somebody losing his pants— it's embarrassing, but it oughtn't to be a surprise to anybody— what surprises me is that they managed to stay alive for seven

---

* Sacco and Vanzetti had been executed in Boston on August 23, 1927, and the demonstrations in protest against this had alarmed the city authorities to the point of having the State House guarded with tommy-guns.

years!—why, I've seen them shoot people first and search them
afterwards—and if they've got any bullets in them, they arrest
them for carrying concealed weapons!" He slipped away with his
spirited crest of hair and his narrow self-regarding eyes. I
addressed myself to the salad. So Persius, in another age that
combined moral anarchy with harsh repression, had, it seemed,
expressed himself confusedly, inelegantly and obscenely. And it
is Persius who is the writer and not the complacent Drummond,
as it is Cummings and not the persons who publish books on
American poetry. Where life is disorderly, the poets will express
themselves in nonsense. I had looked at the beginning of Persius—"*O curas hominum! O quantum est in rebus inane!*"—it
seemed to me entirely in the modern spirit.

I went on reading the preface: "While, therefore, I fully admit
the charge against Persius, I cannot allow to it that weight, which
it would have in most other cases. Indeed, we may as well complain of the rust on an ancient coin, as of the obscurity of an
ancient satire. Nature, it is true, always holds up the same mirror,
but prejudice, habit, and education, are continually changing
the appearance of the objects seen in it. The objections which
have been made to my author in some other respects, are more
difficult to answer. His unpolished verses, his coarse compari-
sons, and his ungraceful transitions from one subject to another,
manifest, it is said, either his contempt or his ignorance of elegant composition. It cannot, indeed, be contended, that Persius
displays the politeness of Horace, or that he shows himself an
adept in the *callida junctura*. His poetry is a strong and rapid
torrent, which pours in its infracted course over the rocks and
precipices, and which occasionally, like the waters of the Rhone,
disappears from view, and loses itself underground." Yes: like
Cummings's poetry and conversation. Yet Drummond had his
poetry, too: "the rust on an ancient coin," "a strong and rapid
torrent, which pours in its infracted course"—and it appeared
that he was, after all, sympathetic with the unpolished Persius
and had earnestly undertaken to defend him against the taste of
the time. That was the paradox of literature: provoked only by
the anomalies of reality, by its discord, its chaos, its pain, it
attempted, from poetry to metaphysics, to impose on that chaos

some order, to find some resolution for that discord, to render that pain acceptable—to strike some permanent mark of the mind on the mysterious flux of experience which escapes beneath our hand. So with Persius, poised, as it were, on the edge of the collapse of the Empire, for whom the criticism of the satirist, the philosophy of the Stoic—at the least, the hexameter itself—were all ways, for even so "inelegant" a poet, of introducing some logic and some meaning into the ceaseless struggles of men to make themselves at home in the universe. Then, as it were, relieving the poet, the critic who studies him, in turn, must stand firm against these miseries and horrors, these disquieting shocks of reality—he must pick up the poet's verses, all twisted where disaster has struck them, and he must carry them further, like Drummond, to where there is tranquillity and leisure enough for him to point out what form and what sense the poet had tried to give them, to supply by his own judicial comments the straightness and the soundness they lack. Yet, even beneath the shelter of that firmament of eighteenth-century order, he, too, has felt the shock of reality—the dullness of a rusted coin, the turbulence of a river. For without the impulse from reality, neither criticism nor poetry nor any other human work can be valid.

I had finished the apple, the Brie cheese and the little black demi-tasse, and I turned to the book again: "I cannot conclude this Preface, without lamenting that an early and untimely death should have prevented the Poet, whom I have translated, from giving a more finished appearance to his works." How extraordinary that William Drummond, almost two thousand years after Christ, should have felt this solidarity with Persius, that, bridging the ruin of Rome, bridging the confusion of the Middle Ages, we should find him lamenting this early death as if it were that of some able young man whom he had known in his time in London, some young man who had been educated at the same institutions and shared with him the same values. The discord and chaos of reality! From the point of view of civilization, the whole of the West had caved in. The geographical void of Europe had been too big for Rome to fill; and then later—to change the metaphor, as my wine made it easy to do—when plantations that had been ploughed under had scattered their seed abroad, and at last there had been bred all through Europe such a race as had formerly flourished only on the Mediterranean, a new race to whom Persius could speak as men of his own education—when this had been achieved, there opened, as it were in another dimension, a new void, the social void, below the class of educated people to which Persius and Drummond belonged, and into that yawning gulf of illiteracy and mean ambitions, even while Drummond wrote—the book was dated 1797—Europe heavily and dully sank, not without some loud crackings of her structure. America, in a sense, was that gulf.

I had finished the bottle of wine, which was certainly better than they had had last year—they were really making an effort, I thought, to improve the quality of their wine. How much, I wondered, was it due to the wine that I now myself felt so warmed by this sense of continuity with the past, with Persius and William Drummond, by this spirit of stubborn endurance? Suppose that the federal agents should succeed in suppressing these restaurants where pretty good wine was still served. These restaurants were run by Italians, and it had lately been against Italians that the machine-guns of the State had been trained and the police incited to butchery. In the meantime, there was nothing to do save to work with the dead for allies, and at odds with the ignorance of most of the living, that that edifice, so many times begun, so discouragingly reduced to ruins, might yet stand as the headquarters of humanity!

I left the restaurant in meditation, and, on my way out, had a collision that jarred me with a couple of those bulky pink people who had stopped laughing and were dancing to the radio.

F. SCOTT FITZGERALD

SLEEPING AND WAKING

When some years ago I read a piece by Ernest Hemingway called *Now I Lay Me*, I thought there was nothing further to be said about insomnia. I see now that that was because I had never had much; it appears that every man's insomnia is as different from his neighbor's as are their daytime hopes and aspirations.

Now if insomnia is going to be one of your naturals, it begins to appear in the late thirties. Those seven precious hours of sleep suddenly break in two. There is, if one is lucky, the "first sweet sleep of night" and the last deep sleep of morning, but between the two appears a sinister, ever widening interval. This is the time of which it is written in the Psalms: *Scuto circumdabit te veritas eius: non timebis a timore nocturno, a sagitta volante in die, a negotio perambulante in tenebris.*

With a man I knew the trouble commenced with a mouse; in my case I like to trace it to a single mosquito.

My friend was in course of opening up his country house unassisted, and after a fatiguing day discovered that the only practical bed was a child's affair—long enough but scarcely wider than a crib. Into this he flopped and was presently deeply engrossed in rest *but* with one arm irrepressibly extending over the side of the crib. Hours later he was awakened by what seemed to be a pinprick in his finger. He shifted his arm sleepily and dozed off again—to be again awakened by the same feeling.

This time he flipped on the bed-light—and there attached to the bleeding end of his finger was a small and avid mouse. My friend, to use his own words, "uttered an exclamation," but probably he gave a wild scream.

The mouse let go. It had been about the business of devouring the man as thoroughly as if his sleep were permanent. From then on it threatened to be not even temporary. The victim sat shivering, and very, very tired. He considered how he would have a cage made to fit over the bed and sleep under it the rest of his life. But it was too late to have the cage made that night and finally he dozed, to wake in intermittent horrors from dreams of being a Pied Piper whose rats turned about and pursued him.

He has never since been able to sleep without a dog or cat in the room.

My own experience with night pests was at a time of utter exhaustion—too much work undertaken, interlocking circumstances that made the work twice as arduous, illness within and around—the old story of troubles never coming singly. And ah, how I had planned that sleep that was to crown the end of the struggle—how I had looked forward to the relaxation into a bed soft as a cloud and permanent as a grave. An invitation to dine *à deux* with Greta Garbo would have left me indifferent.

But had there been such an invitation I would have done well to accept it, for instead I dined alone, or rather was dined upon by one solitary mosquito.

It is astonishing how much worse one mosquito can be than a swarm. A swarm can be prepared against, but *one* mosquito takes on a personality—a hatefulness, a sinister quality of the struggle to the death. This personality appeared all by himself in September on the twentieth floor of a New York hotel, as out of place as an armadillo. He was the result of New Jersey's decreased appropriation for swamp drainage, which had sent him and other younger sons into neighboring states for food.

The night was warm—but after the first encounter, the vague slappings of the air, the futile searches, the punishment of my own ears a split second too late, I followed the ancient formula and drew the sheet over my head.

And so there continued the old story, the bitings through the sheet, the sniping of exposed sections of hand holding the sheet in place, the pulling up of the blanket with ensuing suffocation—followed by the psychological change of attitude, increasing wakefulness, wild impotent anger—finally a second hunt.

This inaugurated the maniacal phase—the crawl under the bed with the standing lamp for torch, the tour of the room with final detection of the insect's retreat on the ceiling and attack with knotted towels, the wounding of oneself—my God!

—After that there was a short convalescence that my opponent seemed aware of, for he perched insolently beside my head—but I missed again.

At last, after another half hour that whipped the nerves into a frantic state of alertness came the Pyrrhic victory, and the small mangled spot of blood, *my* blood, on the headboard of the bed.

As I said, I think of that night, two years ago, as the beginning of my sleeplessness—because it gave me the sense of how sleep can be spoiled by one infinitesimal incalculable element. It made me, in the now archaic phraseology, "sleep-conscious." I worried whether or not it was going to be allowed me. I was drinking, intermittently but generously, and on the nights when I took no liquor the problem of whether or not sleep was specified began to haunt me long before bedtime.

A typical night (and I wish I could say such nights were all in the past) comes after a particularly sedentary work-and-cigarette day. It ends, say without any relaxing interval, at the time for going to bed. All is prepared, the books, the glass of water, the extra pajamas lest I awake in rivulets of sweat, the luminol pills in the little round tube, the note book and pencil in case of a night thought worth recording. (Few have been—they generally seem thin in the morning, which does not diminish their force and urgency at night.)

I turn in, perhaps with a night-cap—I am doing some comparatively scholarly reading for a coincident work so I choose a lighter volume on the subject and read till drowsy on a last cigarette. At the yawning point I snap the book on a marker, the cigarette at the hearth, the button on the lamp. I turn first on the left side, for that, so I've heard, slows the heart, and then—coma.

So far so good. From midnight until two-thirty peace in the room. Then suddenly I am awake, harassed by one of the ills or functions of the body, a too vivid dream, a change in the weather for warm or cold.

The adjustment is made quickly, with the vain hope that the continuity of sleep can be preserved, but no—so with a sigh I

flip on the light, take a minute pill of luminol and reopen my
book. The *real* night, the darkest hour, has begun. I am too tired
to read unless I get myself a drink and hence feel bad next day—
so I get up and walk. I walk from my bedroom through the hall
to my study, and then back again, and if it's summer out to my
back porch. There is a mist over Baltimore; I cannot count a
single steeple. Once more to the study, where my eye is caught
by a pile of unfinished business: letters, proofs, notes, etc. I start
toward it, but No! this would be fatal. Now the luminol is having
some slight effect, so I try bed again, this time half circling the
pillow on edge about my neck.

"Once upon a time" (I tell myself) "they needed a quarterback
at Princeton, and they had nobody and were in despair. The
head coach noticed me kicking and passing on the side of the
field, and he cried: 'Who is *that* man—why haven't we noticed
him before?' The under coach answered, 'He hasn't been out,'
and the response was: 'Bring him to me.'

". . . we go to the day of the Yale game. I weigh only one
hundred and thirty-five, so they save me until the third quarter,
with the score—"

—But it's no use—I have used that dream of a defeated dream
to induce sleep for almost twenty years, but it has worn thin at
last. I can no longer count on it—though even now on easier
nights it has a certain lull . . .

The war dream then: the Japanese are everywhere victori-
ous—my division is cut to rags and stands on the defensive in a
part of Minnesota where I know every bit of the ground. The
headquarters staff and the regimental battalion commanders
who were in conference with them at the time have been killed
by one shell. The command devolved upon Captain Fitzgerald.
With superb presence . . .

—but enough; this also is worn thin with years of usage. The
character who bears my name has become blurred. In the dead
of the night I am only one of the dark millions riding forward in
black buses toward the unknown.

Back again now to the rear porch, and conditioned by intense
fatigue of mind and perverse alertness of the nervous system—
like a broken-stringed bow upon a throbbing fiddle—I see the
real horror develop over the roof-tops, and in the strident horns

of night-owl taxis and the shrill monody of revelers' arrival over the way. Horror and waste —

—Waste and horror — what I might have been and done that is lost, spent, gone, dissipated, unrecapturable. I could have acted thus, refrained from this, been bold where I was timid, cautious where I was rash.

I need not have hurt her like that.

Nor said this to him.

Nor broken myself trying to break what was unbreakable.

The horror has come now like a storm — what if this night prefigured the night after death — what if all thereafter was an eternal quivering on the edge of an abyss, with everything base and vicious in oneself urging one forward and the baseness and viciousness of the world just ahead. No choice, no road, no hope — only the endless repetition of the sordid and the semi-tragic. Or to stand forever, perhaps, on the threshold of life unable to pass it and return to it. I am a ghost now as the clock strikes four.

On the side of the bed I put my head in my hands. Then silence, silence — and suddenly — or so it seems in retrospect — suddenly I am asleep.

Sleep — real sleep, the dear, the cherished one, the lullaby. So deep and warm the bed and the pillow enfolding me, letting me sink into peace, nothingness — my dreams now, after the catharsis of the dark hours, are of young and lovely people doing young, lovely things, the girls I knew once, with big brown eyes, real yellow hair.

> *In the fall of '16 in the cool of the afternoon*
> *I met Caroline under a white moon*
> *There was an orchestra — Bingo-Bango*
> *Playing for us to dance the tango*
> *And the people all clapped as we arose*
> *For her sweet face and my new clothes —*

Life *was* like that, after all; my spirit soars in the moment of its oblivion; then down, down deep into the pillow . . .

". . . Yes, Essie, yes. — Oh, My God, all right, I'll take the call myself."

Irresistible, iridescent — here is Aurora — here is another day.

DAWN POWELL

WHAT ARE YOU DOING IN MY DREAMS?

The best time to run away is September. When you run away in July the good people are off someplace else. Their daughters or wives are on guard, and one of them will be blocking the front door, arms folded, yelling at you, "Where do you think you're going, missy, with that suitcase? If you think you're going to throw your clothes around my house you got another think coming." What you have to do is to walk right on down the street, keeping your eyes straight ahead, pretending you're on your way someplace a lot better.

And that's the way it turns out, too; wherever you land is sure to be better than the place you left.

I found that out the first time I ran away. I was four and the running away wasn't my own idea at all. My sister and her girlfriend, who were nearly six, found a stack of old colored circus handbills in the woodshed and they dressed me up in them over my pantywaist. Then they led me to the middle of the road and said, "Here's a comb for you to play 'Yankee Doodle' on. Go ahead, now, and be a parade."

I was scared stiff but at the same time proud at being given this assignment. I started marching, playing "Yankee Doodle" on the comb big as you please. They followed me until I turned down a forbidden corner and then it was their turn to get scared. I could hear them running back home shouting to my mother that I was running away but I couldn't turn back now. I went on marching one-two-one-two down the center of the dusty, unknown road till I came to a tiny gingerbread house set on a steep grassy bank. My legs were wobbling but I marched up the stairs, stopping at the landing to mark time one-two-one-two in case anyone was watching. A lacy white trellis decorated the front porch and there I stopped in my tracks, for hanging from the ceiling was a shining bird cage with a beautiful golden bird in it, a real bird, singing. I could not take my eyes from it, but sank down on the stoop, my skirt of bill-posters crackling under me, filled with such rapture as I had never known. When the lady came out and spoke to me I burst into fierce sobs, not because she laughed at my paper dress or because she was taking me home to a certain spanking, but because I wanted to stay with the golden bird the rest of my life.

I had my own good reason for running away the next time, when I was eleven. We were on a farm with a new stepmother who didn't know what to do with us so she put us outdoors after breakfast and locked all the doors. But we couldn't go in the barn because she said it would bother the horses. We couldn't play in the orchard because we'd spoil the fruit. We couldn't go for a walk because we'd wear out our shoes. We couldn't sing our songs because the racket would keep the hens from laying. We couldn't read our old schoolbooks because we'd dirty them. However, unknown to her, we had discovered a pile of brown ledgers and colored pencils in a burned old cabin in the fields. My sister drew pictures and I wrote poems and stories. I must have knocked off a hundred poems and a dozen historical novels all romantically involving brave Colonial maidens and rich, titled Redcoats. Since our creative labors made no noise, we were happily undiscovered for a good fortnight.

Then one day the ledgers vanished from their hiding place under the kitchen porch.

"No use looking," our stepmother called out from the other side of the locked screen door. "I burned all that trash you were writing."

So I ran away. I didn't give her the money I made picking berries that week but used the whole ninety cents travelling to a startled aunt's house in the next county.

"But just what in the world did she do to you?" they all kept asking me. "Did she beat you?"

"She called my notebooks trash," I had to keep telling them over and over.

A person almost loses their patience trying to get some simple little thing through a grown-up's head.

My aunt's house was a fine place with a piano instead of a golden bird. I learned to play *Trés Moutarde* and decided that the next place I ran away to would be New York City, but it was eight years more before I made it. Even then it was by way of a farm that had paid my railroad fare and given me board in exchange for "farmeretting." There's something about farm life that gives you the strength to run anywhere in the world. Oh, there were always people to tell me I'd be sorry, strangers wouldn't make allowances for me the way my own folks would if I didn't make good; I'd be homesick. But whenever I left I shut the door on that place and was never sorry, nor did I ever miss anybody I left.

But you wait, you'll miss Ohio, they all said; it's in your blood, six generations of it. You'll see. They told me how real Ohioans can sense the instant they've crossed the State border. Maybe a person has been thousands of miles away, never thinking about old Richland County or Ashtabula or wherever. Comes a time he's on the Broadway Limited, fast asleep in his lower berth when suddenly he's wide awake, snaps his fingers and says, "We're in Ohio," and sure enough! Once it almost happened to me, at that. I was on a sleeper travelling west from New York when I woke up all of a sudden for no reason. I knew I was in Ohio. My heart began thumping with a kind of terror, the terror of discovering you're human which is worse than any fear of the supernatural. This is it, I thought, that Ohio feeling that is stronger than will-power or reason.

I yanked up the window shade and saw level fields stretching endlessly to a skimpy fringe of tall, long-legged trees far away against the pearly dawn sky. Hickory trees! Tears came to my eyes. Ohio hickories! So it was really true, I marvelled, there were unknown dimensions beyond logic, a blood-knowledge. How had I dared to doubt it! Then the station came into sight and I blinked hard. What angered me the most was the goofy readiness with which I had accepted the mystique of Ohio blood and the outraged incredulity with which I fought the simple scientific fact that we were in Erie, Pennsylvania.

You might argue that a little fact like Erie, Pennsylvania need not upset the essential truth of the theory. You could say I should not have looked out the window but should have been content to believe. If I'd just waited an hour longer before looking out it would have been Ohio all right. Nonetheless, I muttered bitterly, and after letting me down like this you won't catch me going back.

"You'll have to come back," my sister had warned me. "You can not fight it. Your family is your family."

"I'm not a family person," I said. "I'll never give them a thought."

That's where the joke was on me. Over the years this one died and that one, but I never went back to funerals. So they're dead, so the past is dead, and Ohio is gone. All right. Today is here. New York is here. Why go back to the dead?

Why indeed? The way it's turned out I haven't needed to. For the dead all come to me.

Do you know how some people's lives seem to stop like a clock at a certain mark? They go on living, get married, have families, save money, travel around the world, trade in their cars and houses and jobs, but all that is their dead life. Their life really stopped the year they were captain of the high school football team, the year they had the lead in the college play, the day they quit Paris or the army or the newspaper job. Other jobs and mates come and go, babies grow up and have babies, the exercise horse is mounted each day as if it was really going somewhere, but all the time the rider is transfixed in an old college song or in Tony's speakeasy or in that regiment.

You can run into one of these frozen riders on the street after twenty years and if you belong in that old picture he will pounce upon you with delight, cling to your hands for dear life, introduce you ecstatically to his companion. There is nobody in the world he's gladder to see, he shouts, and before you can open your mouth he's off telling anecdotes about I'll-never-forget-the-time, keeping you buttonholed on a windy corner for half an hour, a stage prop for his monologue.

When he gets home he can't wait to tell his wife guess-who-he-ran-into, of all people, and does she remember the time. . . . But before he can repeat all the same old stories, she interrupts to ask how you looked, what were you doing now, where were you living? Why, he doesn't know, he says, giving her a wounded look, hurt that she doesn't share his sentimental love of an old pal. The truth is he didn't even see you after the first flash of recognition; you could have been on crutches or rattling a tin cup, selling shoelaces for all he saw. What he was so glad to see was himself twenty years ago scoring that touchdown or being that crackerjack reporter. The only thing Old Softie is really soft about is Old Softie.

In a way something like that happened to me when I ran away from Ohio. People and places froze into position and nothing I've seen or heard of them since makes any impression on that original picture. It isn't that I'm crazy about the picture or even that I dislike it. It's just that I live in that picture, whether I want to or not, when I fall asleep at night.

It's as if the day I left Ohio I split in two at the crossroads, and went up both roads, half of me by day here in New York and the other half by night with the dead in long-ago Ohio. This has been going on so many years I wonder how I survive. How tired you can be in the morning after a night with the dead!

The dead never get tired. They always have to be on the go, and no matter how I beg to be let alone, the minute I close my eyes, there they are tugging at me, pulling me along on the picnic, my grandmother yanking one of my arms as if it was a chicken wing, my Aunt Dawn holding the other. Or else my sister and I are hanging onto an eternal picnic hamper, half carrying it and half carried along, for it almost floats by itself.

It's always a picnic or a shore dinner when you're out with the dead in my family. You would think they would have had enough chicken and potato salad and oyster pie after all those family reunions, and considering that their stomachs had killed most of them, but no, it's always the same. The basket's packed, here we go. Look, it's going to rain, I whimper; see how gray the sky is, do let me stay in bed. I'm so sleepy, so tired, and you all go so fast! But they pay no attention.

In dreams the sky is always gray, anyway, like the world seen through a chicken's eyes or so they say, and it's a very low sky, with hardly enough headroom even for us children. The grass is gray, too, as we run along just above it, feet not touching it, only I'm always stumbling because they hurry me along pell-mell. Always we have to be somewhere or we'll miss something; we must rush to catch the bus or the train that has no engine, or we must hitch up those horses I never see, and everything is whispering "Hurry, hurry, hurry." Everybody knows the plan, where we are going, and what we're to do—everybody but myself. Pilgrim Lake, Cooney's Grove, Put-in-Bay, Puritan Springs, Grange Park, all blend. Everybody knows which side of the trolley tracks to wait on except stupid me and which direction the car will come from. There is always a brass band in picnicland, although I never hear it. All I ever see is an empty bandstand (but it isn't empty, I know) with bunting draped around it. In one dream my sister let go my arm when we came to the bandstand and started painting her cheeks by wetting some of the red bunting (she always knew how to do things!)—a sure sign she was going to start flirting with the band boys.

"It's not nice for you to use rouge," I protested, shocked. "It doesn't look right for a dead girl."

Sometimes when I say the word "dead" the dream is over, but more often nobody pays any attention, we're in such a big hurry. My stockings fall down, my petticoat drops, my shoes are unlaced, my hair ribbon is lost, my side hurts from running; all I want is to lie down in the grass but no one will let me. The shore dinner, they whisper, hurry, hurry, hurry, hang onto the basket, pull up your stockings, pull down your dress, straighten your sash, the shore dinner, hurry, hurry, hurry. Stop being so bossy, I wail, don't you know I've run away from all of you, I don't belong to you any more, I've shut that door the way I always do, you needn't think you can take over my life, pushing me around in my sleep. Talk about Greenwich Village trash pestering me to whoop it up with them all night. What about dead trash forcing me to whoop it up all over hell and gone night after night? And while we're at it, why can't we go somewhere I want to, if we've got to go, and this time let's invite everybody, let it be my treat!

But it's always got to be their show. Sometimes my father shows up, eager to go. This I dread, for all the women start picking on him right away, and even though he's just as dead as they are he's never allowed to come along. He looks so disappointed that I want to cry out, "Never mind, Papa, the basket never gets opened up, we never really get there, and it's only a dream anyway."

Sometimes a new face appears, someone fresh from yesterday's obituary page, a New York friend, and this is a problem. It's hard to mix friends with family, live or dead, and I'm torn between them. Wait for me at the corner bar till I get rid of the folks, I whisper to Niles or La Touche or Gene or Jacques, I won't be forever. Wait for me and I'll tell you how I ran away from home.

But they fade away, smiling faintly. I don't hold it against them. Who wants to meet a 1910 Ohio child carrying a basket lunch in a dead man's saloon?

E. B. WHITE

ONCE MORE TO THE LAKE

One summer, along about 1904, my father rented a camp on a lake in Maine and took us all there for the month of August. We all got ringworm from some kittens and had to rub Pond's Extract on our arms and legs night and morning, and my father rolled over in a canoe with all his clothes on; but outside of that the vacation was a success and from then on none of us ever thought there was any place in the world like that lake in Maine. We returned summer after summer—always on August 1st for one month. I have since become a salt-water man, but sometimes in summer there are days when the restlessness of the tides and the fearful cold of the sea water and the incessant wind which blows across the afternoon and into the evening make me wish for the placidity of a lake in the woods. A few weeks ago this feeling got so strong I bought myself a couple of bass hooks and a spinner and returned to the lake where we used to go, for a week's fishing and to revisit old haunts.

I took along my son, who had never had any fresh water up his nose and who had seen lily pads only from train windows. On the journey over to the lake I began to wonder what it would be like. I wondered how time would have marred this unique, this holy spot—the coves and streams, the hills that the sun set behind, the camps and the paths behind the camps. I was sure the tarred road would have found it out and I wondered in what other ways it would be desolated. It is strange how much you can remember about places like that once you allow your mind to return into the grooves which lead back. You remember one thing, and that suddenly reminds you of another thing. I guess I remembered clearest of all the early mornings, when the lake was cool and motionless, remembered how the bedroom smelled of the lumber it was made of and of the wet woods whose scent entered through the screen. The partitions in the camp were thin and did not extend clear to the top of the rooms, and as I was always the first up I would dress softly so as not to wake the others, and sneak out into the sweet outdoors and start out in the canoe, keeping close along the shore in the long shadows of the pines. I remembered being very careful never to rub my paddle against the gunwale for fear of disturbing the stillness of the cathedral.

The lake had never been what you would call a wild lake. There were cottages sprinkled around the shores, and it was in farming country although the shores of the lake were quite heavily wooded. Some of the cottages were owned by nearby farmers, and you would live at the shore and eat your meals at the farmhouse. That's what our family did. But although it wasn't wild, it was a fairly large and undisturbed lake and there were places in it which, to a child at least, seemed infinitely remote and primeval.

I was right about the tar: it led to within half a mile of the shore. But when I got back there, with my boy, and we settled into a camp near a farmhouse and into the kind of summertime I had known, I could tell that it was going to be pretty much the same as it had been before—I knew it, lying in bed the first morning, smelling the bedroom, and hearing the boy sneak quietly out and go off along the shore in a boat. I began to sustain the illusion that he was I, and therefore, by simple transposition, that I was my father. This sensation persisted, kept cropping up all the time we were there. It was not an entirely new feeling, but in this setting it grew much stronger. I seemed to be living a dual existence. I would be in the middle of some simple act, I would be picking up a bait box or laying down a table fork, or I would be saying something, and suddenly it would be not I but my father who was saying the words or making the gesture. It gave me a creepy sensation.

We went fishing the first morning. I felt the same damp moss covering the worms in the bait can, and saw the dragonfly alight on the tip of my rod as it hovered a few inches from the surface of the water. It was the arrival of this fly that convinced me beyond any doubt that everything was as it always had been, that the years were a mirage and there had been no years. The small waves were the same, chucking the rowboat under the chin as we fished at anchor, and the boat was the same boat, the same color green and the ribs broken in the same places, and under the floor-boards the same fresh-water leavings and débris—the dead helgramite, the wisps of moss, the rusty discarded fishhook, the dried blood from yesterday's catch. We stared silently at the tips of our rods, at the dragonflies that came and went. I lowered the tip of mine into the water, tentatively, pensively dislodging the fly, which darted two feet away, poised, darted two feet back, and came to rest again a little farther up the rod. There had been no years between the ducking of this dragonfly and the other one—the one that was part of memory. I looked at the boy, who was silently watching his fly, and it was my hands that held his rod, my eyes watching. I felt dizzy and didn't know which rod I was at the end of.

We caught two bass, hauling them in briskly as though they were mackerel, pulling them over the side of the boat in a businesslike manner without any landing net, and stunning them with a blow on the back of the head. When we got back for a swim before lunch, the lake was exactly where we had left it, the same number of inches from the dock, and there was only the merest suggestion of a breeze. This seemed an utterly enchanted sea, this lake you could leave to its own devices for a few hours and come back to, and find that it had not stirred, this constant and trustworthy body of water. In the shallows, the dark, water-soaked sticks and twigs, smooth and old, were undulating in clusters on the bottom against the clean ribbed sand, and the track of the mussel was plain. A school of minnows swam by, each minnow with its small individual shadow, doubling the attendance, so clear and sharp in the sunlight. Some of the other campers were in swimming, along the shore, one of them with a cake of soap, and the water felt thin and clear and unsubstantial. Over the years there had been this person with the cake of soap, this cultist, and here he was. There had been no years.

Up to the farmhouse to dinner through the teeming, dusty

field, the road under our sneakers was only a two-track road. The middle track was missing, the one with the marks of the hooves and the splotches of dried, flaky manure. There had always been three tracks to choose from in choosing which track to walk in; now the choice was narrowed down to two. For a moment I missed terribly the middle alternative. But the way led past the tennis court, and something about the way it lay there in the sun reassured me; the tape had loosened along the backline, the alleys were green with plantains and other weeds, and the net (installed in June and removed in September) sagged in the dry noon, and the whole place steamed with midday heat and hunger and emptiness. There was a choice of pie for dessert, and one was blueberry and one was apple, and the waitresses were the same country girls, there having been no passage of time, only the illusion of it as in a dropped curtain—the waitresses were still fifteen; their hair had been washed, that was the only difference—they had been to the movies and seen the pretty girls with the clean hair.

Summertime, oh summertime, pattern of life indelible, the fade-proof lake, the woods unshatterable, the pasture with the sweetfern and the juniper forever and ever, summer without end; this was the background, and the life along the shore was the design, the cottagers with their innocent and tranquil design, their tiny docks with the flagpole and the American flag floating against the white clouds in the blue sky, the little paths over the roots of the trees leading from camp to camp and the paths leading back to the outhouses and the can of lime for sprinkling, and at the souvenir counters at the store the miniature birch-bark canoes and the post cards that showed things looking a little better than they looked. This was the American family at play, escaping the city heat, wondering whether the newcomers in the camp at the head of the cove were "common" or "nice," wondering whether it was true that the people who drove up for Sunday dinner at the farmhouse were turned away because there wasn't enough chicken.

It seemed to me, as I kept remembering all this, that those times and those summers had been infinitely precious and worth saving. There had been jollity and peace and goodness. The arriving (at the beginning of August) had been so big a business in itself, at the railway station the farm wagon drawn up, the first smell of the pine-laden air, the first glimpse of the smiling farmer, and the great importance of the trunks and your father's enormous authority in such matters, and the feel of the wagon under you for the long ten-mile haul, and at the top of the last long hill catching the first view of the lake after eleven months of not seeing this cherished body of water. The shouts and cries of the other campers when they saw you, and the trunks to be unpacked, to give up their rich burden. (Arriving was less exciting nowadays, when you sneaked up in your car and parked it under a tree near the camp and took out the bags and in five minutes it was all over, no fuss, no loud wonderful fuss about trunks.)

Peace and goodness and jollity. The only thing that was wrong now, really, was the sound of the place, an unfamiliar nervous sound of the outboard motors. This was the note that jarred, the one thing that would sometimes break the illusion and set the years moving. In those other summertimes all motors were inboard; and when they were at a little distance, the noise they made was a sedative, an ingredient of summer sleep. They were one-cylinder and two-cylinder engines, and some were make-and-break and some were jump-spark, but they all made a sleepy sound across the lake. The one-lungers throbbed and fluttered, and the twin-cylinder ones purred and purred, and that was a quiet sound too. But now the campers all had outboards. In the daytime, in the hot mornings, these motors made a petulant, irritable sound; at night, in the still evening when the afterglow lit the water, they whined about one's ears like mosquitoes. My boy loved our rented outboard, and his great desire was to achieve single-handed mastery over it, and authority, and he soon learned the trick of choking it a little (but not too much), and the adjustment of the needle valve. Watching him I would remember the things you could do with the old one-cylinder engine with the heavy flywheel, how you could have it eating out of your hand if you got really close to it spiritually. Motor boats in those days didn't have clutches, and you would make a landing by shutting off the motor at the proper time and coasting in with a dead rudder. But there was a way of reversing them, if you learned the trick, by cutting the switch and putting it on again exactly on the final dying revolution of the flywheel, so that it would kick back against compression and begin reversing. Approaching a dock in a strong following breeze, it was difficult to slow up sufficiently by the ordinary coasting method, and if a boy felt he had complete mastery over his motor, he was tempted to keep it running beyond its time and then reverse it a few feet from the dock. It took a cool nerve, because if you threw the switch a twentieth of a second too soon you would catch the flywheel when it still had speed enough to go up past center, and the boat would leap ahead, charging bull-fashion at the dock.

We had a good week at the camp. The bass were biting well and the sun shone endlessly, day after day. We would be tired at night and lie down in the accumulated heat of the little bedrooms after the long hot day and the breeze would stir almost imperceptibly outside and the smell of the swamp drift in through the rusty screens. Sleep would come easily and in the morning the red squirrel would be on the roof, tapping out his gay routine. I kept remembering everything, lying in bed in the mornings—the small steamboat that had a long rounded stern like the lip of a Ubangi, and how quietly she ran on the moonlight sails, when the older boys played their mandolins and the girls sang and we ate doughnuts dipped in sugar, and how sweet the music was on the water in the shining night, and what it had felt like to think about girls then. After breakfast we would go up to the store and the things were in the same place—the minnows in a bottle, the plugs and spinners disarranged and pawed over by the youngsters from the boys' camp, the fig newtons and the Beeman's gum. Outside, the road was tarred and cars stood in front of the store. Inside, all was just as it had always been, except there was more Coca-Cola and not so much Moxie and root beer and birch beer and sarsaparilla. We would walk out with a bottle of pop apiece and sometimes the pop would backfire up our noses and hurt. We explored the streams, quietly, where the turtles slid off the sunny logs and dug their way into the soft bottom; and we lay on the town wharf and fed worms to the tame bass. Everywhere we went I had trouble making out which was I, the one walking at my side, the one walking in my pants.

One afternoon while we were there at that lake a thunderstorm came up. It was like the revival of an old melodrama that I had seen long ago with childish awe. The second-act climax of the drama of the electrical disturbance over a lake in America had not changed in any important respect. This was the big scene, still the big scene. The whole thing was so familiar, the first feeling of oppression and heat and a general air around camp of not wanting to go very far away. In midafternoon (it was all the same) a curious darkening of the sky, and a lull in everything that had made life tick; and then the way the boats suddenly swung the other way at their moorings with the coming of a breeze out of the new quarter, and the premonitory rumble. Then the kettle drum, then the snare, then the bass drum and cymbals, then crackling light against the dark, and the gods grinning and licking their chops in the hills. Afterward the calm, the rain steadily rustling in the calm lake, the return of light and hope and spirits, and the campers running out in joy and relief to go swimming in the rain, their bright cries perpetuating the deathless joke about how they were getting simply drenched, and the children screaming with delight at the new sensation of bathing in the rain, and the joke about getting drenched linking the generations in a strong indestructible chain. And the comedian who waded in carrying an umbrella.

When the others went swimming my son said he was going in too. He pulled his dripping trunks from the line where they had hung all through the shower, and wrung them out. Languidly, and with no thought of going in, I watched him, his hard little body, skinny and bare, saw him wince slightly as he pulled up around his vitals the small, soggy, icy garment. As he buckled the swollen belt suddenly my groin felt the chill of death.

ZORA NEALE HURSTON

How It Feels to Be Colored Me

I am colored but I offer nothing in the way of extenuating circumstances except the fact that I am the only Negro in the United States whose grandfather on the mother's side was *not* an Indian chief.

I remember the very day that I became colored. Up to my thirteenth year I lived in the little Negro town of Eatonville, Florida. It is exclusively a colored town. The only white people I knew passed through the town going to or coming from Orlando. The native whites rode dusty horses, the Northern tourists chugged down the sandy village road in automobiles. The town knew the Southerners and never stopped cane chewing when they passed. But the Northerners were something else again. They were peered at cautiously from behind curtains by the timid. The more venturesome would come out on the porch to watch them go past and got just as much pleasure out of the tourists as the tourists got out of the village.

The front porch might seem a daring place for the rest of the town, but it was a gallery seat for me. My favorite place was atop the gate-post. Proscenium box for a born first-nighter. Not only did I enjoy the show, but I didn't mind the actors knowing that I liked it. I usually spoke to them in passing. I'd wave at them and when they returned my salute, I would say something like this: "Howdy-do-well-I-thank-you-where-you-goin'?" Usually automobile or the horse paused at this, and after a queer exchange of compliments, I would probably "go a piece of the way" with them, as we say in farthest Florida. If one of my family happened to come to the front in time to see me, of course negotiations would be rudely broken off. But even so, it is clear that I was the first "welcome-to-our-state" Floridian, and I hope the Miami Chamber of Commerce will please take notice.

During this period, white people differed from colored to me only in that they rode through town and never lived there. They liked to hear me "speak pieces" and sing and wanted to see me dance the parse-me-la, and gave me generously of their small silver for doing these things, which seemed strange to me for I wanted to do them so much that I needed bribing to stop. Only they didn't know it. The colored people gave no dimes. They deplored any joyful tendencies in me, but I was their Zora nevertheless. I belonged to them, to the nearby hotels, to the county—everybody's Zora.

But the changes came in the family when I was thirteen, and I was sent to school in Jacksonville. I left Eatonville, the town of the oleanders, as Zora. When I disembarked from the river-boat at Jacksonville, she was no more. It seemed that I had suffered a sea change. I was not Zora of Orange County anymore, I was now a little colored girl. I found it out in certain ways. In my heart as well as in the mirror, I became a fast brown—warranted not to rub nor run.

But I am not tragically colored. There is not great sorrow dammed up in my soul, nor lurking behind my eyes. I do not mind at all. I do not belong to the sobbing school of Negrohood who hold that nature somehow has given them a lowdown dirty deal and whose feelings are all hurt about it. Even in the helter-skelter skirmish that is my life, I have seen that the world is to the strong regardless of a little pigmentation more or less. No, I do not weep at the world—I am too busy sharpening my oyster knife.

Someone is always at my elbow reminding me that I am the granddaughter of slaves. It fails to register depression with me. Slavery is sixty years in the past. The operation was successful and the patient is doing well, thank you. The terrible struggle that made me an American out of a potential slave said "On the line!" The Reconstruction said "Get set!"; and the generation before said "Go!" I am off to a flying start and I must not halt in the stretch to look behind and weep. Slavery is the price I paid for civilization, and the choice was not with me. It is a bully adventure and worth all that I have paid through my ancestors for it. No one on earth ever had a greater chance for glory. The world to be won and nothing to be lost. It is thrilling to think— to know that for any act of mine, I shall get twice as much praise or twice as much blame. It is quite exciting to hold the center of the national stage, with the spectators not knowing whether to laugh or to weep.

The position of my white neighbor is much more difficult. No brown specter pulls up a chair beside me when I sit down to eat. No dark ghost thrusts its leg against mine in bed. The game of keeping what one has is never so exciting as the game of getting.

I do not always feel colored. Even now I often achieve the unconscious Zora of Eatonville before the Hegira. I feel most colored when I am thrown against a sharp white background.

For instance at Barnard. "Beside the waters of the Hudson" I feel my race. Among the thousand white persons, I am a dark rock surged upon, and overswept, but through it all, I remain myself. When covered by the waters, I am; and the ebb but reveals me again.

Sometimes it is the other way around. A white person set down in our midst, but the contrast is just as sharp for me. For instance, when I sit in the drafty basement that is The New World Cabaret with a white person, my color comes. We enter chatting about any little nothing that we have in common and are seated by the jazz waiters. In the abrupt way that jazz orchestras have, this one plunges into a number. It loses no time in circumlocutions, but gets right down to business. It constricts the thorax and splits the heart with its tempo and narcotic harmonies. This orchestra grows rambunctious, rears on its hind legs and attacks the tonal veil with primitive fury, rending it, clawing it until it breaks through to the jungle beyond. I follow those heathen—follow them exultingly. I dance wildly inside myself; I yell within, I whoop; I shake my assegai above my head, I hurl it true to the mark *yeeeeooww!* I am in the jungle and living in the jungle way.

My face is painted red and yellow and my body is painted blue. My pulse is throbbing like a war drum. I want to slaughter something—give pain, give death to what, I do not know. But the piece ends. The men of the orchestra wipe their lips and rest their fingers. I creep back slowly to the veneer we call civilization with the last tone and find the white friend sitting motionless in his seat, smoking calmly.

"Good music they have here," he remarks, drumming the table with his fingertips.

Music. The great blobs of purple and red emotion have not touched him. He has only heard what I felt. He is far away and I see him but dimly across the ocean and the continent that have fallen between us. He is so pale with his whiteness then and I am *so* colored.

At certain times I have no race, I am *me*. When I set my hat at a certain angle and saunter down Seventh Avenue, Harlem City, feeling as snooty as the lions in front of the Forty-Second Street Library, for instance. So far as my feelings are concerned, Peggy Hopkins Joyce on the Boule Mich with her gorgeous raiment, stately carriage, knees knocking together in a most aristocratic manner, has nothing on me. The cosmic Zora emerges. I belong to no race nor time. I am the eternal feminine with its string of beads.

I have no separate feeling about being an American citizen and colored. I am merely a fragment of the Great Soul that surges within the boundaries. My country, right or wrong.

Sometimes, I feel discriminated against, but it does not make me angry. It merely astonishes me. How *can* any deny themselves the pleasure of my company? It's beyond me.

But in the main, I feel like a brown bag of miscellany propped against a wall. Against a wall in company with other bags, white, red and yellow. Pour out the contents, and there is discovered a jumble of small things priceless and worthless. A first-water diamond, an empty spool, bits of broken glass, lengths of string, a key to a door long since crumbled away, a rusty knife-blade, old shoes saved for a road that never was and never will be, a nail bent under the weight of things too heavy for any nail, a dried flower or two still a little fragrant. In your hand is the brown bag. On the ground before you is the jumble it held—so much like the jumble in the bags, could they be emptied, that all might be dumped in a single heap and the bags refilled without altering the content of any greatly. A bit of colored glass more or less would not matter. Perhaps that is how the Great Stuffer of Bags filled them in the first place—who knows?

FRANK O'CONNOR

In Quest of Beer

It was a great relief to me when I took up the study of dreams to find that when I dreamed of an inn or a pub I was dreaming about a wife. I don't suppose the temperance societies go in much for dream language, but they would be well advised to remember that pubs and beer are as deeply rooted in a man's world as marriage itself. This goes back to the days when forests covered the earth, the roads were only tracks and the lighted alehouse was the very image of Life itself. All the great abbeys were inns as well, and if ever you find yourself on the road from Southampton to London, stop off at the hospital of St. Cross where, by a ritual that goes back to heaven knows what century, you are expected to ask for your "dole." The dole is now only a token piece of bread and a token nip of beer, and even the beer is brewed by a local brewery instead of on the premises, but it reminds you that there was a time when the custom might have meant the difference between life and death to you.

Now, I may as well confess that I am not by nature a drinker. That is partly because I had a father who was. I have written about him in various disguises, but temperance was never one of them. He drank in what I always think of as a peculiarly Irish way—in bouts. Between the bouts his behavior was admirable, so admirable indeed that he admired it himself, and the more he admired it, the greater grew the poor man's pride till, at last, he had to celebrate it. The result of the celebration was that inside a week he was again a wreck—moral, physical and financial. I remember once, during a slight argument, he opened my uncle's face with a poker. I felt deeply about these bouts, more particularly because I was frequently tagged on to him as a brake, but the only result of this was that I spent the entire day standing outside pubs receiving a lemonade or a penny every few hours to keep me content. Only twice did I manage to act like a brake. Once was very late at night when I was standing in the cold outside a pub miles from home and saw a woolly dog in the window of a shop. The toy dog cost sixpence, and sixpence was exactly what I had collected during the day, so I bought the dog for protection and walked home by myself. That almost cured Father of the drink. The second time was after a funeral when I drank Father's pint when he had his back turned and he, stone-cold sober, had to bring me home, drunk and with a cut over my eye, a sight that steadied him for months.

The result was that till I was thirty I hated the sight of pubs, and I'm still capable of feeling a shudder at the sight of some.

When an Irishman goes to a pub it is usually to get away from women. Drink is his escape from the emotional problems which, according to the best authorities, he now evades more successfully than any male in Europe. He wants nothing suggestive of love, family and home. Anything to do with sex is barred, and the risqué joke which keeps an English barroom happy for an hour is likely to provoke frowns. Conversation is generally serious; it may deal with sports, politics and the likelihood of war. The more intelligent customers may discuss what's wrong with the country, the church and the government. These are subjects which you cannot discuss with a woman, because she would be bound (a) to disagree and (b) to report the criticisms in quarters where they could do you damage.

At the same time, it must be understood that this Irish way of drinking is schizoid and, as such, leads to rows. Father's behavior with the poker was not exceptional. James Bridie, the Scottish dramatist, enthused endlessly over the fact that F. R. Higgins, the Irish poet, was knocked out in a Dublin bar during an argument about poetry. Except for a few intimate friends, I scarcely know a single Irishman who does not feel compelled at a certain stage of the proceedings to tell me exactly what he thinks of me, and I invariably find it astonishing. It is a tribute partly to the natural sweetness of the Irish character, partly to the repressive power of Irish society that it takes so much drink to bring Irishmen to the aggressive stage.

Mind, I do not resent it. The only type of Irishman I do resent is the kind that tells me what he thinks of me on less than half a bottle, and he is usually paranoic instead of schizoid and may safely be left to the psychiatrists, but all the same it creates problems. I once had a friend, a very gallant soldier with an intelligent and talented wife, and we visited a lot at each other's homes. One evening we were all at my apartment when an amateur musician called, and we played records and discussed music till late in the night. Apparently, my friend the officer was enjoying himself, but a few days later we met in town and went to my favorite pub for a drink. It was only then that I noticed he was slightly "high" and then only because of his unusual frankness.

He wasn't offensive, and I didn't resent it; on the contrary, I am always delighted to see what goes on behind that bland and gentle Irish mask. He merely asked me to admit that, whereas he was a very fine musician and would have had a most distinguished career as a violinist if only he'd continued his lessons, I knew nothing about music and was, in fact, forever chancing my arm by talking about things of which I knew nothing. In fact, he added, with an endearing smile, I was just a phony—pleasant enough, but a phony. I agreed to every single proposition: it may be some unconscious recollection of how Father used that poker, but I always do agree. And sometimes it takes an awful lot of agreeing, because the drinker himself is never so entirely submerged but that he notices something peculiar in his own behavior, so he keeps on reiterating his own propositions, usually in stronger and stronger terms, in the hope that they will begin to sound natural and familiar to himself.

Which they don't, of course, because we met again a few days later and had another drink, and this time he was apologetic, though he didn't know what about. He couldn't remember, and though I said at once that it wasn't worth remembering, he persisted and asked me to tell him frankly what he had said. "I'm quite sure I was offensive," he said, but when I tried to assure him that this was something he couldn't be even if he tried, he remained dissatisfied. He wanted to know his exact words, and I couldn't bring myself to repeat them, because if anybody were to repeat something I had said in that state, I should die of embarrassment. Of course, it did occur to me that he really wished to know because there were so many nasty things he might have said of me. At any rate, since then he has never been at ease with me. Again and again he has reproached me with my closeness; our friendship has lapsed, and it is all because a tiny fraction of his personality has broken loose and is drifting about the world under his name and out of his control. Psychologist friends look grave when I tell the story and imply that I may be causing him a severe trauma. Myself, I wouldn't be surprised if he gave up drink.

On the other hand, this schizoid attitude to drink produces a need for getting drunk that is almost pathological. Dissatisfaction with the climate, with the government, with the church, and above all with the women who fail to appreciate that there is anything to be dissatisfied about, grows in us till it projects itself in a thundering bout. I had an old friend who got his dissatisfaction musically. He was found lecturing a street musician, playing a penny whistle, on the subject of Italian music. "Can't you be joyous, man?" he snarled. "What's the use of playing that mournful stuff? Give us some Italian music with the sun in it! I'm a child of the sun." The child of the sun was one of the most popular men in town.

After all, serious drinking is not a crime; it is a visitation, "a good man's fault." We are not like the English. We do not drink to enjoy ourselves. We drink to forget, and the amount we drink corresponds roughly to the amount we have to forget, so nobody but a completely heartless man could expect us to assume responsibility for what we do under the influence. "Poor chap, poor chap! He had an awful lot of trouble. There was that brother of his, and the wife—you know about the wife, of course?" A drunk is like a blind man or an old person, to be helped across the road.

Accordingly there is no relation between the popular attitude to drink and the licensing laws, which anyhow are an inheritance from the English, who are always trying to regiment people into good behavior. It is true that we have modified them for the worse by the hour's closing in the afternoon, but there's a reason for that too. The hour's closing, known as "Kevin's Hour," is called after its author, Kevin O'Higgins, Minister of Justice. O'Higgins in his youth was, even by Irish standards, a remarkable drinker. After his reformation it dawned on him that if only some kind friend had brought him home each day at 2:30 P.M. he probably would never have had the energy to go back, thereby halving his problems. O'Higgins was later assassinated, but not by the drinkers. No word of reproach is ever heard against him. "Poor Kevin!" we say. "It was himself he was thinking of." We are a tolerant, gentle race. Why otherwise should we commemorate the Apostle of Temperance himself by naming a Limerick public house after him, and where but in Ireland could you drink yourself stupid in the Father Mathew Bar?

Between Kevin in heaven and the nonconformist English, we have a code of laws relating to licensing that bears as little relation to the facts as did Prohibition in America. But unlike Prohibition, this code has few enemies. It is regarded as something like an act of God rather than an act of Parliament. The last raid I saw was in the town of Clonmel on a Sunday morning. I was cycling through with a Limerick friend and a Harvard professor, and we had to undergo the ordeal of explaining in whispers to half a dozen suspicious townsmen that we were really strangers in search of a drink, not policemen in disguise. We were finally directed up an alleyway into a sort of back yard where a dozen or so unfortunates were waiting in groups of three or four. Significant whispers were passing from group to group, and the faces of the poor victims grew longer. 'Twas unknown if they'd open at all that morning. We were there ten minutes when another townsman whispered us away, then whisked us across the street to a door that opened and closed as if it were operated by an electric eye. No sooner did we start drinking—we were in Murphy's—than the word went round, "a raid," and a few of the customers vanished while Murphy and his wife stood watching the raid at the other pub, the one we had been lured away from. They weren't indignant, just shocked.

There are still things about it I don't understand. Why was

Murphy's not raided? Who directed the townsman who directed us? Those raids emanate from young superintendents in faraway towns who do not have to live with the consequences. Older policemen with pensions in view don't like to be mixed up in them; they are usually left to rookies. But even rookies wouldn't like to be caught investigating an American who might after all turn out to be a relation of the brother's boss in Brooklyn. If it had actually been known that he was a Harvard professor, even a District Justice wouldn't like to say a cross word to him, for a thing like that could damage a District Justice to the end of his days. My own view is that before the raid began, our townsman gave information at the barrack, and the guards grew pale and said, "But you couldn't let an American boy see a thing like that. For the love of God get him over the road to Murphy's and we won't raid Murphy's until late tonight!"

When a raid takes place in reality, it is governed by the same civilized attitude, and the legal and moral objections to perjury are politely overlooked by both sides. It always turns out that a funeral or a football match had taken place in the locality, and the policeman had entertained a numerous retinue of relatives and their friends; as to the man found in the outdoor toilet, and the one on the stable roof (one grasping a half empty bottle of whisky and the other using profane language), neither the publican nor his wife had ever seen either of them, or remembered admitting them—and the judge administers a stern warning and only a mild fine.

The Irish publican tends to be a man of charitable views. He can, of course, afford them, because, unlike his English proto-type who is merely an agent of the brewery, he usually owns his own premises. Besides, he has probably come through being a grocer's apprentice. The apprentice himself is an unusual type. In provincial towns he comes of an influential family and brings a lot of trade with him. In Dublin he almost invariably comes from Tipperary. He is never the wage slave you find in other countries, but an up-and-coming young businessman. In Tipperary they must, I think, have a lullaby that is sung over every male child who looks like a promising bartender and which warns him forever against the evils of drink. With this temptation forever hanging over them, they plunge with great violence into other activities. When they have saved enough to buy a pub for themselves they have usually mellowed into men of strong judgment and kind hearts.

Yet, though I know that the Irish publican is the real thing, I am a sucker for the English public house. I know all that is to be said against it. It is run by a brewery, a totalitarian organization that wants to leave nothing in the world original and strange, and produces beer that is quite indistinguishable from any other beer. God be with the few remaining small breweries of Ireland that make such wild beer and issue such strange advertisements: "Oh, what can ail thee, knight-at-arms, when one pint of Sweeney's XX will put you right again?" or, "He cometh not," she said, "having no doubt stopped for his usual pint of Sweeney's XX."

The English differ from the Irish in being steady drinkers, like my friend Mr. Franklin, who takes his two pints every Sunday morning regular; and even if the Queen, God bless her, were to come in and order drinks all round, Mr. Franklin would only beam, hold his hand over his glass and say, "No thanks, your Majesty, I've had mine."

Once in an English pub I heard a tragic story of an old regular who had just died, paralyzed, and had been deprived of his daily drinks by his wife and daughter, both teetotalers. The hero of the hour was another customer who had braved the two women the night before the sick man's death, with a quart of bitter hidden under his coat. I can still recall the emotion that spread through the pub as he described the scene in his modest, masculine English way. "When I took out the bottle 'is poor eyes lit up. Couldn't move, couldn't speak, but I shall never forget the way 'e looked. I 'ad to 'old 'is mouth open at the side and let it trickle down 'is throat. Next day 'e was dead, but 'e'd 'ad 'is drink."

The English like to drink in pleasant surroundings, and there is something in the tradition of the English publican that makes him a born museum director with a mania for antiques, pewter, copper and brass. "I don't know 'ow it is," one publican said to me. "I'm as fond of brass as anyone else, but I can't feel the same about it as I do about copper. Copper does something to me inside if you know what I mean." I did. I love to come out of the rain and dark into a low room whose black beams are studded with harness brasses, but it can never make up to me for the fiery glow of copper. Alas, I am a bad Irishman, for what is repressed in me is not the desire to tell my friends what skunks they are but how intelligent, sensitive and truehearted they are, and it is only in an English pub that I find a proper background for such sissified sentiments. "Good God!" said my oldest boozing companion the night I introduced him to an English pub. "Three hours' steady drinking and not one cross word!"

So this Sunday morning when I let my imagination stray, it flies not to any Irish pub but to a little hamlet in Buckinghamshire. My wife is back from church and I slip out quietly so she won't notice the time. The pub is next door, a plain, boxlike, red-brick house with benches outside the front door. Wendy, the cocker spaniel who is standing there, gives me a flick of her tail. She knows me. You enter a hallway, pass two or three tables and come to a narrow counter—all the bar there is, and a very drafty one, too, in spite of the electric heater. On the right is the room where they play darts, and on the left the parlor, dominated by a colored portrait of Queen Elizabeth, where strangers go when they have women with them. Jack, the proprietor, is not the owner, although his father and grandfather were publicans here before him, and in fact he only runs it not to break the tradition, for he makes his living in a motor works across the county.

Hilda, a Lancashire girl, has no respect for the tradition, though she keeps the pub clean as a battleship and always puts flowers on the counter. Hilda is desperate at arithmetic and has to do everything as a sum, chanting it and writing it out at the same time, but Gordon, one of the regulars, no matter where he may be on the premises, knows the meaning of the chant, and at the end of her list: "Six pints of the best bitter, two Woodbines, two Players, a chocolate bar and a packet of potato crisps," you hear his strong voice chime in, "Eight and tuppence ha'penny."

Hilda dreams of the day when she can have her own home near the motor works and her husband, Reggie, all to herself, evenings and weekdays, but Reggie knows the vanity of such dreams, for he, another excellent mechanic, has been a publican himself and would still be one if only he could make a living by it. Reggie tells me that the great secret of being a good publican is to "beat 'em at darts," but in his heart he knows that it's an art, just like music, at which he is expert.

"Lummy," he says, "the things you see in a pub. I remember one day a horse and cart drives up, and two men get off the cart with an old dog. The old dog lies on a bench, and they order two bitters. I serve them, and then the old dog lifts his head and yaps. 'Oh, sorry, old man,' one of them says. 'I'd quite forgotten about you. Another pint, please, for the dog.' 'For the dog?' I says. 'Yes,' he says, ' 'e likes a drink like the rest of us.' 'Excuse me,' I says, 'but what's his? Bitter or mild?' 'Oh, bitter,' he says, as if he was surprised. So I give the old dog a pint in a pewter and he just laps it up. And believe me, Frank, he drank pint for pint with those two men till they left. I can see it still. Under the cart, he was, between the wheels, rolling from side to side like a sailor. Oh, you do see funny things in a pub!"

And now it is two o'clock—closing time—and my wife has been on the phone to Hilda to tell her the roast is ruined, but anyway we have another, and I remember my Irish friend's cry: "Three hours' steady drinking and not one cross word!"

CYRIL CONNOLLY

Revisiting Greece

After examining a clutch of well-made travel books, I have sometimes wondered for how many pages one could keep it up by
setting out to tell the truth, not only about places but about the
inadequacy of our feelings. (I have known the Acropolis to
resemble a set of false teeth in a broken palate.) When at last we
take our long-wished-for holiday what really happens?

There is, first, the period of preparation (in a sense the only
time we are abroad); guidebooks are compared; experts are consulted; a mirage of a brown, lean summer self descending on an
obese island dances before our eyes and we are convincingly
importuned by the wrong clothes, the wrong books, the wrong
introductions. "Of course you will need a white dinner jacket
and a cummerbund"; "you must take the *whole* of Pausanias";
"an ultra-violet filter"; "stout walking shoes"; "the rubber flippers
should be made to measure."

At twenty we travel to discover ourselves, at thirty for love, at
forty out of greed and curiosity, at fifty for a revelation. Irresponsible, illiterate, shedding all ties and cares, we await the visitation,
the rebirth. Gradually the present dissolves, England becomes
totally unreal; we have in fact already left, not yet airborne but
anxiety-cradled; "if the flippers are not ready, they cannot possibly be sent on"; "you quite understand that these traveler's checks
are not negotiable on Mount Athos"; "don't go to the new hotel
but the other one"; "don't go to the old hotel"; "there are three
new hotels"; "Corfu is the place for you: it has everything"; "yes,
if you like a green island. I prefer Mikonos"; "it's never too hot
on Corfu"; "you would hate Corfu."

D-Day. Running in the new dark glasses in the car to the airport. Livid clouds, infra-red buses, a lurid day-of-judgment air about the hoardings along the clotted avenue. Signs of panic, cleverly concealed, as I board the plane, where I suffer from a private phobia, dispelled only by champagne, that the signal "Fasten your safety-belts" is staying on for the whole voyage.

Paris: the heat advances across the tarmac, our gaoler for the next six weeks. "Thick brown overcoat, stout walking shoes, whole of Pausanias," it mumbles; "Mr. Connolly? I think we can take care of all that." Inevitable contrast between London and Paris, the one muffled under its summer cloud-cap, all Wimbledon and roses, the other with a migraine of politics, bleached and persilled in the heat. The bookstall at London Airport for a nation of magazine readers — if that; at Le Bourget full of expensive works on art and philosophy. The paralysis of suburbia contrasted with the animation of the *banlieue* where a fair is in progress and a horse-drawn dray of children jingles under the catalpas.

How much of a holiday is spent lying gasping on one's back, in planes, trains, cabins, beaches, and hotel bedrooms, the guidebook held aloft like an awning? We really travel twice — as a physical object resembling a mummy or small wardrobe-trunk which is shuttled about at considerable expense; and as a mind married to a "Guide Bleu," always reading about the last place or the next one.

It is suddenly apparent that the heat permits no reading of any kind; whole areas of consciousness must be evacuated, the perimeter of sensation shortened; no past, no future. Only the guidebook survives and the other books we have brought sneak to the bottom of the suitcase. And now the Seven Indispensables perform their ghostly jig from pocket to pocket. The passport, the traveler's checks, the tickets, the dark glasses, the reading glasses, the pen, the comb. Where are they? I could have sworn I had them a moment ago.

A flying visit to Versailles to see the *petits appartements* rendered famous by the Pompadour, the Dubarry and Madame de Mitford. Intense disappointment; so much redecoration, and everywhere the milling multitudes, locusts of the postwar summer. Illumination: *The human eye deteriorates all it looks at.* Why is the decoration of the House of the Vettii at Pompeii so much less exciting than the new excavations? Because the human eye has faded the colors, vulgarized the painting. The camera also enfeebles its subject, and being photographed too often I believe to cause cancer of the soul.

And now, Venice, city of sore throats, frayed tempers, and leaking wallets; alas, never the same for me since I reviewed Hemingway's last novel but one. Much as I disliked the book I remain obsessed by his terrible colonel. I drink Valpolicella and take the fatal stroll to Harry's Bar, stopping on the little bridge where the colonel had a heart attack on his way from his wine to his martinis. How he would have hated the Biennale! So much painting that should never have come South of the Alps, North of the Po, West of Suez, or East of Saint Louis, all maltreated by the heat, the humidity, and the merciless light—except the paintings which have some secret poster quality, Delvaux's clustering cowlike nudes or Bacon's agonizing tycoons. Art is bottled sunshine and should never be exposed to it.

And everywhere art critics, never a painter; symbol of the age of culture-diffusion when publishers and village-explainers travel while authors have to stay at home, when painters in Maida Vale hear from their dealers in Mozambique or Mogador, when Byron would have received a postcard: "Dear B. London must be very hot. Just off to Ravenna to join the Galignanis and then to meet some Greek publishers at Missolonghi. Hope to be able to do something for you. How goes the Canto?—Yrs., John Murray."

Revisit the equestrian statue of Colleone in its dingy square. The base is too high. Better in a photograph. Failure to experience any emotion over Tintoretto. Horror of Surrealist masters in Biennale. Moved by nothing later than Pompeii. Great paintings should be kept under lock and key and shown as seldom as wonder working images. The real connoisseurs of art were the Pharaohs; they took it with them. Intoxication with Venetian gardens, the oleander drooping over the canal at some scabrous corner, the ubiquitous freshwater sea smell and the best drink in Europe, a tumbler of ice-cold peach juice in the colonel's bar. More hordes of milling tourists, squeaking *lederhosen*; Clapham Junction of the mechanized masses in the Piazza. Everybody is somebody. Nobody is anybody. Everyone is everywhere.

At last the boat: survival of an earlier form of travel, obeying the strange psychology of "on board ship." Whom we hate on the first day we shall love on the last, whom we greet on the first we shall not bid farewell; boredom will become its own reward and change suddenly to ecstasy. The *Achilleus* is a charmed vessel, trim, white, gay, its inmates friendly and delightful. The islands of the lagoon bob at their moorings as we churn through the warm night and the next blue day past Monte Gargano and Brindisi, with its lemon ices and Roman column, and across to Corfu where we stay for three hours instead of a week, just time to see the famous view at Canoni, so called because the tourist is fired at it like a cannonball.

That evening we are streaking through the Corinth Canal like mercury rising in a thermometer. The *Achilleus* has now gone completely Greek. The food is interesting and local, the crew sings, the married couples no longer flash their signals of distress, "save me, rescue me." The passengers crane over the rail to where the distant corona of Athens glows above the dark bulk of Salamis. We enter the sooty bustle of Piraeus as the last evening steamers beetle forth to fertilize the expectant islands and are extracted from our carefree cabin like ticks from a dog's ear. Nothing on shore will quite come up to it, even as Nice is never worthy of the Blue Train or New York of the *Queen Mary*. *Arriver, c'est déjà partir un peu.*

Great heat, like a smart doctor, begins every sentence "You'll have to cut out. . . ." With the temperature always around ninety, generalities alone can be appreciated, details and detours must be ignored; we are but fit for the simplest forms of sightseeing.

Air throbs, marble hisses, the sea glistens with malice, the exhausted landscape closes at lunchtime and does not reopen before six o'clock when the sun ceases its daily interrogation. We stagger across the grilled slabs of the Propylaea with only one idea—which is both idea and sensation—the juice of a lemon and an orange in equal proportions poured again and again over cubes of ice. After this postwar duty visit we flee the Parthenon and rush to take the first boat at the Piraeus. It is crowded and unbelievably noisy but there is a cool breeze as we round Sunium.

Bathed in lemon-yellow light like Rabat or Casablanca, Rhodes has some claim to be the perfect island. Neither too large nor too small, too hot nor too cold, fertile, hilly, legendary, and exotic, it lives in the present as well as the past. The medieval city of the knights has been so perfectly restored by the Italians as to outdo Carcassonne; it is a golden flypaper for tourists who are led to it like bombers to a dummy target, leaving the real town uninjured. Between the austerity of the medieval fortress and the flamboyant Fascist concrete outside the walls the old Turkish quarter sprawls in exquisite decay.

The few simple elements required by the Moslem conception of beauty, the dome and minaret, fountain, plane tree, and arcaded courtyard, are here combined into a dozen similar but never monotonous patterns . . . we are in a tiny Stamboul, a sixteenth and seventeenth century quarter of dignified exiles with their Persian tiles and Arabic inscriptions, their memories of fallen grandeur. No farther from the comfortable but hideous Hôtel des Roses than you can spit a pomegranate seed stands the little mosque of Murad-Reïz, its cemetery planted with mulberry and oleander. Few places are more soothing than a Turkish graveyard, where the turbaned tombs are jumbled like spillikins around the boles of cypresses and the cicadas zizz above the silent koubbas.

Here sleeps the commander who captured Tripoli, and probably the administrators who lost it, heroes and footlers together, the generals and admirals, the Beys and Pashas of that cruel, clean, pious, frugal horticultural community. The great admiral's grave is well kept-up and hung with Mecca-green cloth; otherwise the nodding conversation pieces are abandoned to shade and sun, each stone turban proudly proclaiming its owner's status or bearing a verse from the Koran by which we linger in bewilderment—even as one day in some far-flung graveyard a passing Chinese may halt, baffled by the enumeration of our meager virtues.

Mikonos by contrast is a rude stone altar erected to the stern god of summer. The town is a white African sneer arching brightly round the bay where a row of little restaurants vie with each other in disappointments. The heat swaggers through the spotless alleys where bearded Danish painters seal every exit with their easels.

To swim one must bump across the bay to some blinding cove or trudge the iron-hot mountain path, paved with mule-dung and brown thistle. The sun needles the brain cavity, desiccates the lung, and obtains a garnishee upon the liver. Doors bang, nerves jangle, little waves bristle and buffet through the afternoon and in our sleep fashionable voices cry "Mikonos for me," *"il y a toujours du vent à Mikonos."*

After this stony sanatorium its humble neighbor seems to flower with statues, tremendous in its exuberant and irretrievable collapse. Whereas Delphi's mountain womb remains one of the holy places of the human spirit, Delos is complex and baffling, irreverent even in its piety. With its swans and geese and cafeteria, the sacred lake where Apollo was born must have been not unlike the Round Pond in Kensington Gardens; the commercial Roman town survives in better shape than the Greek; the shrines of Isis and the phalloi of Dionysus have stood up better than Apollo's altars. In this center of the ancient slave trade, this eclectic battener on the world's religions whose moneylending priesthood were the Rothschilds of antiquity, the god of man's fulfilment in this world, the wielder of the lyre and the bow, is noticeably absent.

Yet Delos is magical. According to the admirable Greek usage, no fence surrounds the ruins nor is there an entrance fee; black with tourists and lizards, prostrate in the sunshine, the ancient stones are part of the world's daily life. Among the Roman pavements is the mysteriously haunting mosaic of anchor and dolphin which was found on the seals of the wine jars on the Greek ship salvaged outside Marseilles by M. Cousteau, and which aided him to identify his Sextius, owner of the vessel, with the proprietor of this sumptuous villa. By such means are we enabled to creep backward into time, liberated by significant detail such as the hand, in the museum, from that colossal archaic Apollo which was broken off by the fall of the sculptor Nikias's fabulous bronze palm tree.

Delphi remains sacred to Apollo while Delos had permission to exploit him; both became enormously rich, both tottered to destruction after Julian's reign in A.D. 363 with full treasuries, gold ceilings, and colonnades of marble statues (Delos had 3,000 intact under the opprobrium of the Christians). Abandoned to pirates through the Dark Ages, Delos must still have been one of the wonders of the world, a desert island carpeted with temples and matchless private buildings, a thousand years of sanctity still clinging to the shrines and avenues while Delphi, pillaged by Byzantium, issued its despairing last oracle and the bronze horses of St. Mark's, as I like to think, were reft from the impassive Charioteer.

We may walk across the sacred lake or stand on Apollo's temple at Delphi where the earth-dragon fumed and fretted and the priestess gave out incoherent moans for the priest to polish into the double meanings which answered our desire. But it is difficult to feel aware of the terrible god of youthful strength and intellectual beauty. He exists only in museums. For though Greek architecture has barely survived, and Greek music and painting not at all, we have at last learned how to display sculpture at its best.

In the new museum at Athens we no longer need to pretend to ourselves; here the chain of masterpieces signal to each other down the ages. This is how Greece was; this is what man can do. Apollo is manifest at last with his smile which seems instantly to annihilate all time and all suffering. Joy is under everything and if we feel pain it is our fault because we are not divine enough. Death has an appropriateness which transcends sorrow; the world belongs to the beautiful charm; is welded to courage, thought to action—even the serpent is a friend.

But humanity could not grow up without a religion of the mother; the world could not always belong to the graceful tactless hearties with red curls, bulging eyeballs, stocky behinds, a try-anything-once look below their waving helmets. Can one think of any archaic sculpture which takes even Zeus beyond early middle age? In this art "Hippocleides doesn't care" triumphs over the maxims of the seven sages. Irresponsible perfection went out about 475 B.C.; yet is it my imagination or are not the contemporary Greeks one of the happiest as well as the most friendly nations in the world?

GEORGE ORWELL

"The Moon under Water"

My favourite public house, "The Moon under Water", is only two minutes from a bus stop, but it is on a side-street, and drunks and rowdies never seem to find their way there, even on Saturday nights.

Its clientèle, though fairly large, consists mostly of "regulars" who occupy the same chair every evening and go there for conversation as much as for the beer.

If you are asked why you favour a particular public house, it would seem natural to put the beer first, but the thing that most appeals to me about "The Moon under Water" is what people call its "atmosphere".

To begin with, its whole architecture and fittings are uncompromisingly Victorian. It has no glass-topped tables or other modern miseries, and, on the other hand, no sham roof-beams, inglenooks or plastic panels masquerading as oak. The grained woodwork, the ornamental mirrors behind the bar, the cast-iron fireplaces, the florid ceiling stained dark yellow by tobacco-smoke, the stuffed bull's head over the mantelpiece—everything has the solid comfortable ugliness of the nineteenth century.

In winter there is generally a good fire burning in at least two of the bars, and the Victorian lay-out of the place gives one plenty of elbow-room. There are a public bar, a saloon bar, a ladies' bar, a bottle-and-jug for those who are too bashful to buy their supper beer publicly, and upstairs, a dining-room.

Games are only played in the public, so that in the other bars you can walk about without constantly ducking to avoid flying darts.

In "The Moon under Water" it is always quiet enough to talk. The house possesses neither a radio nor a piano, and even on Christmas Eve and such occasions the singing that happens is of a decorous kind.

The barmaids know most of their customers by name, and take a personal interest in everyone. They are all middle-aged women—two of them have their hair dyed in quite surprising shades—and they call everyone "dear", irrespective of age or sex. ("Dear", not "Ducky": pubs where the barmaid calls you "Ducky" always have a disagreeable raffish atmosphere.)

Unlike most pubs, "The Moon under Water" sells tobacco as well as cigarettes, and it also sells aspirins and stamps, and is obliging about letting you use the telephone.

You cannot get dinner at "The Moon under Water", but there is always the snack counter where you can get liver-sausage sandwiches, mussels (a specialty of the house), cheese, pickles and those large biscuits with caraway seeds in them which only seem to exist in public houses.

Upstairs, six days a week, you can get a good, solid lunch—for example, a cut off the joint, two vegetables and boiled jam roll—for about three shillings.

The special pleasure of this lunch is that you can have draught stout with it. I doubt whether as many as ten per cent of London pubs serve draught stout, but "The Moon under Water" is one of them. It is a soft, creamy sort of stout, and it goes better in a pewter pot.

They are particular about their drinking vessels at "The Moon under Water" and never, for example, make the mistake of serving a pint of beer in a handleless glass. Apart from glass and pewter mugs, they have some of those pleasant strawberry-pink china ones which are now seldom seen in London. China mugs went out about thirty years ago, because most people like their drink to be transparent, but in my opinion beer tastes better out of china.

The great surprise of "The Moon under Water" is its garden.

You go through a narrow passage leading out of the saloon, and find yourself in a fairly large garden with plane trees under which there are little green tables with iron chairs round them. Up at one end of the garden there are swings and a chute for the children.

On summer evenings there are family parties, and you sit under the plane trees having beer or draught cider to the tune of delighted squeals from children going down the chute. The prams with the younger children are parked near the gate.

Many as are the virtues of "The Moon under Water" I think that the garden is its best feature, because it allows whole families to go there instead of Mum having to stay at home and mind the baby while Dad goes out alone.

And though, strictly speaking, they are only allowed in the garden, the children tend to seep into the pub and even to fetch drinks for their parents. This, I believe, is against the law, but it is a law that deserves to be broken, for it is the puritanical non-sense of excluding children—and therefore to some extent, women—from pubs that has turned these places into mere booz-ing-shops instead of the family gathering-places that they ought to be.

"The Moon under Water" is my ideal of what a pub should be—at any rate, in the London area. (The qualities one expects of a country pub are slightly different.)

But now is the time to reveal something which the discerning and disillusioned reader will probably have guessed already. There is no such place as "The Moon under Water".

That is to say, there may well be a pub of that name, but I don't know of it, nor do I know any pub with just that combination of qualities.

I know pubs where the beer is good but you can't get meals, others where you can get meals but which are noisy and crowded, and others which are quiet but where the beer is gener-ally sour. As for gardens, offhand I can only think of three Lon-don pubs that possess them.

But, to be fair, I do know of a few pubs that almost come up to "The Moon under Water". I have mentioned above ten qualities that the perfect pub should have, and I know one pub that has eight of them. Even there, however, there is no draught stout and no china mugs.

And if anyone knows of a pub that has draught stout, open fires, cheap meals, a garden, motherly barmaids and no radio, I should be glad to hear of it, even though its name were something as prosaic as "The Red Lion" or "The Railway Arms".

A. J. LIEBLING

A GOOD APPETITE

The Proust *madeleine* phenomenon is now as firmly established in folklore as Newton's apple or Watt's steam kettle. The man ate a tea biscuit, the taste evoked memories, he wrote a book. This is capable of expression by the formula TMB, for Taste > Memory > Book. Some time ago, when I began to read a book called *The Food of France,* by Waverley Root, I had an inverse experience: BMT, for Book > Memory > Taste. Happily, the tastes that *The Food of France* re-created for me—small birds, stewed rabbit, stuffed tripe, Côte Rôtie, and Tavel—were more robust than that of the *madeleine,* which Larousse defines as "a light cake made with sugar, flour, lemon juice, brandy, and eggs." (The quantity of brandy in a *madeleine* would not furnish a gnat with an alcohol rub.) In the light of what Proust wrote with so mild a stimulus, it is the world's loss that he did not have a heartier appetite. On a dozen Gardiners Island oysters, a bowl of clam chowder, a peck of steamers, some bay scallops, three sautéed soft-shelled crabs, a few ears of fresh-picked corn, a thin swordfish steak of generous area, a pair of lobsters, and a Long Island duck, he might have written a masterpiece.

The primary requisite for writing well about food is a good appetite. Without this, it is impossible to accumulate, within the allotted span, enough experience of eating to have anything worth setting down. Each day brings only two opportunities for field work, and they are not to be wasted minimizing the intake of cholesterol. They are indispensable, like a prizefighter's hours on the road. (I have read that the late French professional gourmand Maurice Curnonsky ate but one meal a day—dinner. But that was late in his life, and I have always suspected his attainments anyway; so many mediocre witticisms are attributed to him that he could not have had much time for eating.) A good appetite gives an eater room to turn around in. For example, a non-professional eater I know went to the Restaurant Pierre, in the Place Gaillon, a couple of years ago, his mind set on a sensibly light meal: a dozen, or possibly eighteen, oysters, and a thick chunk of steak topped with beef marrow, which M. Pierre calls a *Délice de la Villette*—the equivalent of a "Stockyards' Delight." But as he arrived, he heard M. Pierre say to his headwaiter, "Here comes Monsieur L. Those two portions of *cassoulet* that are left—put them aside for him." A *cassoulet* is a substantial dish, of a complexity precluding its discussion here. (Mr. Root devotes three pages to the great controversy over what it should contain.) M. Pierre is the most amiable of restaurateurs, who prides himself on knowing in advance what his friends will like. A client of limited appetite would be obliged either to forgo his steak or to hurt M. Pierre's feelings. Monsieur L., however, was in no difficulty. He ate the two *cassoulets*, as was his normal practice; if he had consumed only one, his host would have feared that it wasn't up to standard. He then enjoyed his steak. The oysters offered no problem, since they present no bulk.

In the heroic age before the First World War, there were men and women who ate, in addition to a whacking lunch and a glorious dinner, a voluminous *souper* after the theater or the other amusements of the evening. I have known some of the survivors, octogenarians of unblemished appetite and unfailing good humor—spry, wry, and free of the ulcers that come from worrying about a balanced diet—but they have had no emulators in France since the doctors there discovered the existence of the human liver. From that time on, French life has been built to an increasing extent around that organ, and a niggling caution has replaced the old recklessness; the liver was the seat of the Maginot mentality. One of the last of the great around-the-clock gastronomes of France was Yves Mirande, a small, merry author of farces and musical-comedy books. In 1955, Mirande celebrated

his eightieth birthday with a speech before the curtain of the
Théâtre Antoine, in the management of which he was associated
with Mme. B., a protégée of his, forty years younger than himself.
But the theater was only half of his life. In addition, M. Mirande
was an unofficial director of a restaurant on the Rue Saint-
Augustin, which he had founded for another protégée, also forty
years younger than himself; this was Mme. G., a Gasconne and
a magnificent cook. In the restaurant on the Rue Saint-Augustin,
M. Mirande would dazzle his juniors, French and American, by
dispatching a lunch of raw Bayonne ham and fresh figs, a hot
sausage in crust, spindles of filleted pike in a rich rose *sauce
Nantua*, a leg of lamb larded with anchovies, artichokes on a
pedestal of foie gras, and four or five kinds of cheese, with a good
bottle of Bordeaux and one of champagne, after which he would
call for the Armagnac and remind Madame to have ready for
dinner the larks and ortolans she had promised him, with a few
langoustes and a turbot—and, of course, a fine *civet* made from
the *marcassin*, or young wild boar, that the lover of the leading
lady in his current production had sent up from his estate in the
Sologne. "And while I think of it," I once heard him say, "we
haven't had any woodcock for days, or truffles baked in the ashes,
and the cellar is becoming a disgrace—no more '34s and hardly
any '37s. Last week, I had to offer my publisher a bottle that was
far too good for him, simply because there was nothing between
the insulting and the superlative."

M. Mirande had to his credit a hundred produced plays,
including a number of great Paris hits, but he had just written
his first book for print, so he said "my publisher" in a special
mock-impressive tone. "An informal sketch for my definitive
autobiography," he would say of this production. The informal
sketch, which I cherish, begins with the most important decision
in Mirande's life. He was almost seventeen and living in the
small Breton port of Lannion—his offstage family name was Le
Querrec—when his father, a retired naval officer, said to him,
"It is time to decide your future career. Which will it be, the
Navy or the Church?" No other choice was conceivable in Lannion. At dawn, Yves ran away to Paris.

There, he had read a thousand times, all the famous wits and cocottes frequented the tables in front of the Café Napolitain, on the Boulevard des Capucines. He presented himself at the café at nine the next morning—late in the day for Lannion—and found that the place had not yet opened. Soon he became a newspaperman. It was a newspaper era as cynically animated as the corresponding period of the Bennett-Pulitzer-Hearst competition in New York, and in his second or third job he worked for a press lord who was as notional and niggardly as most press lords are; the publisher insisted that his reporters be well turned out, but did not pay them salaries that permitted cab fares when it rained. Mirande lived near the fashionable Montmartre cemetery and solved his rainy-day pants-crease problem by crashing funeral parties as they broke up and riding, gratis, in the carriages returning to the center of town. Early in his career, he became personal secretary to Clemenceau and then to Briand, but the gay theater attracted him more than politics, and he made the second great decision of his life after one of his political patrons had caused him to be appointed *sous-préfet* in a provincial city. A *sous-préfet* is the administrator of one of the districts into which each of the ninety *départements* of France is divided, and a young *sous-préfet* is often headed for a precocious rise to high positions of state. Mirande, attired in the magnificent uniform that was then de rigueur, went to his "capital," spent one night there, and then ran off to Paris again to direct a one-act farce. Nevertheless, his connections with the serious world remained cordial. In the restaurant on the Rue Saint-Augustin, he introduced me to Colette, by that time a national glory of letters.

The regimen fabricated by Mirande's culinary protégée, Mme. G., maintained him *en pleine forme*. When I first met him, in the restaurant, during the summer of the Liberation, he was a sprightly sixty-nine. In the spring of 1955, when we renewed a friendship that had begun in admiration of each other's appetite, he was as good as ever. On the occasion of our reunion, we began with a *truite au bleu*—a live trout simply done to death in hot water, like a Roman emperor in his bath. It was served up doused with enough melted butter to thrombose a regiment of Paul Dudley Whites, and accompanied, as was right, by an Alsatian wine—a Lacrimae Sanctae Odiliae, which once contributed slightly to my education. Long ago, when I was very young, I took out a woman in Strasbourg and, wishing to impress her with my knowledge of local customs, ordered a bottle of Ste. Odile. I was making the same mistake as if I had taken out a girl in Boston and offered her baked beans. "How quaint!" the woman in Strasbourg said. "I haven't drunk that for years." She excused herself to go to the telephone, and never came back.

After the trout, Mirande and I had two meat courses, since we could not decide in advance which we preferred. We had a magnificent *daube provençale*, because we were faithful to *la cuisine bourgeoise*, and then *pintadous*—young guinea hens, simply and tenderly roasted—with the first asparagus of the year, to show our fidelity to *la cuisine classique*. We had clarets with both courses—a Pétrus with the *daube*, a Cheval Blanc with the guineas. Mirande said that his doctor had discounseled Burgundies. It was the first time in our acquaintance that I had heard him admit he had a doctor, but I was reassured when he drank a bottle and a half of Krug after luncheon. We had three bottles between us—one to our loves, one to our countries, and one for symmetry, the last being on the house.

Mirande was a small, alert man with the face of a Celtic terrier—salient eyebrows and an upturned nose. He looked like an intelligent Lloyd George. That summer, in association with Mme. B., his theatrical protégée, he planned to produce a new play of Sartre's. His mind kept young by the theater of Mme. B., his metabolism protected by the restaurant of Mme. G., Mirande seemed fortified against all eventualities for at least another twenty years. Then, perhaps, he would have to recruit new protégées. The Sunday following our reunion, I encountered him at Longchamp, a racecourse where the restaurant does not face the horses, and diners can keep first things first. There he sat, radiant, surrounded by celebrities and champagne buckets, sending out a relay team of commissionaires to bet for him on the successive tips that the proprietors of stables were ravished to furnish him between races. He was the embodiment of a happy man. (I myself had a nice thing at 27-1.)

The first alteration in Mirande's fortunes affected me so directly that I did not at once sense its gravity for him. Six weeks later, I was again in Paris. (That year, I was shuttling frequently between there and London.) I was alone on the evening I arrived, and looked forward to a pleasant dinner at Mme. G.'s, which was within two hundred metres of the hotel, in the Square Louvois, where I always stop. Madame's was more than a place to eat, although one ate superbly there. Arriving, I would have a bit of talk with the proprietress, then with the waitresses—Germaine and Lucienne—who had composed the original staff. Waiters had been added as the house prospered, but they were of less marked personality. Madame was a bosomy woman—voluble, tawny, with a big nose and lank black hair—who made one think of a Saracen. (The Saracens reached Gascony in the eighth century.) Her conversation was a chronicle of letters and the theater—as good as a subscription to *Figaro Littéraire*, but more advanced. It was somewhere between the avant-garde and the main body, but within hailing distance of both and enriched with the names of the great people who had been in recently— M. Cocteau, Gene Kelly, la Comtesse de Vogüé. It was always well to give an appearance of listening, lest she someday fail to save for you the last order of larks *en brochette* and bestow them on a more attentive customer. With Germaine and Lucienne, whom I had known when we were all younger, in 1939, the year of the *drôle de guerre*, flirtation was now perfunctory, but the *carte du jour* was still the serious topic—for example, how the fat Belgian industrialist from Tournai had reacted to the *caille vendangeuse*, or quail potted with fresh grapes. "You know the man," Germaine would say. "If it isn't dazzling, he takes only two portions. But when he has three, then you can say to yourself . . ." She and Lucienne looked alike—compact little women, with high foreheads and cheekbones and solid, muscular legs, who walked like *chasseurs à pied*, a hundred and thirty steps to the minute. In 1939, and again in 1944, Germaine had been a brunette and Lucienne a blonde, but in 1955 Germaine had become a blonde, too, and I found it hard to tell them apart.

Among my fellow customers at Mme. G.'s I was always likely to see some friend out of the past. It is a risk to make an engagement for an entire evening with somebody you haven't seen for years. This is particularly true in France now. The almost embarrassingly pro-American acquaintance of the Liberation may be by now a Communist Party-line hack; the idealistic young Resistance journalist may have become an editorial writer for the reactionary newspaper of a textile magnate. The Vichy apologist you met in Washington in 1941, who called de Gaulle a traitor and the creation of the British Intelligence Service, may now tell you that the General is the best thing ever, while the fellow you knew as a de Gaulle aide in London may now compare him to Sulla destroying the Roman Republic. As for the women, who is to say which of them has resisted the years? But in a good restaurant that all have frequented, you are likely to meet any of them again, for good restaurants are not so many nowadays that a Frenchman will permanently desert one—unless, of course, he is broke, and in that case it would depress you to learn of his misfortunes. If you happen to encounter your old friends when they are already established at their tables, you have the opportunity to greet them cordially and to size them up. If you still like them, you can make a further engagement.

On the ghastly evening I speak of—a beautiful one in June—I perceived no change in the undistinguished exterior of Mme. G.'s restaurant. The name—something like Prospéria—was the same, and since the plate-glass windows were backed with scrim, it was impossible to see inside. Nor, indeed, did I notice any difference when I first entered. The bar, the tables, the banquettes covered with leatherette, the simple décor of mirrors and pink marble slabs were the same. The premises had been a business employees' bar-and-café before Mme. G., succeeding a long string of obscure proprietors, made it illustrious. She had changed the fare and the clientele but not the cadre. There are hundreds of identical fronts and interiors in Paris, turned out by some mass producer in the late twenties. I might have been warned by the fact that the room was empty, but it was only eight o'clock and still light outdoors. I had come unusually early because I was so hungry. A man whom I did not recognize came to meet me, rubbing his hands and hailing me as an old acquaintance. I thought he might be a waiter who had served me. (The waiters, as I have said, were not the marked personalities of the place.) He had me at a table before I sensed the trap.

"Madame goes well?" I asked politely.

"No, Madame is lightly ill," he said, with what I now realize was a guilty air.

He presented me with a *carte du jour* written in the familiar purple ink on the familiar wide sheet of paper with the name and telephone number of the restaurant at the top. The content of the menu, however, had become Italianized, the spelling had deteriorated, and the prices had diminished to a point where it would be a miracle if the food continued distinguished.

"Madame still conducts the restaurant?" I asked sharply.

I could now see that he was a Piedmontese of the most evasive description. From rubbing his hands he had switched to twisting them.

"Not exactly," he said, "but we make the same cuisine."

I could not descry anything in the smudged ink but misspelled noodles and unorthographical *"escaloppinis"*; Italians writing French by ear produce a regression to an unknown ancestor of both languages.

"Try us," my man pleaded, and, like a fool, I did. I was hungry. Forty minutes later, I stamped out into the street as purple as an *aubergine* with rage. The minestrone had been cabbage scraps in greasy water. I had chosen *côtes d'agneau* as the safest item in the mediocre catalogue that the Prospéria's prospectus of bliss had turned into overnight. They had been cut from a tired Alpine billy goat and seared in machine oil, and the *haricots verts* with which they were served resembled decomposed whiskers from a theatrical-costume beard.

"The same cuisine?" I thundered as I flung my money on the falsified *addition* that I was too angry to verify. "You take me for a jackass!"

I am sure that as soon as I turned my back the scoundrel nodded. The restaurant has changed hands at least once since then.

In the morning, I telephoned Mirande. He confirmed the disaster. Mme. G., ill, had closed the restaurant. Worse, she had sold the lease and the good will, and had definitely retired.

"What is the matter with her?" I asked in a tone appropriate to fatal disease.

"I think it was trying to read Simone de Beauvoir," he said. "A syncope."

Mme. G. still lives, but Mirande is dead. When I met him in Paris the following November, his appearance gave no hint of decline. It was the season for his sable-lined overcoat *à l'impresario*, and a hat that was a furry cross between a porkpie and a homburg. Since the restaurant on the Rue Saint-Augustin no longer existed, I had invited him to lunch with me at a very small place called the Gratin Dauphinois, on the Rue Chabanais, directly across from the building that once housed the most celebrated sporting house in Paris. The Rue Chabanais is a short street that runs from the Square Louvois to the Rue des Petits Champs—perhaps a hundred yards—but before the reform wave stimulated by a Municipal Councilor named Marthe Richard at the end of the Second World War, the name Chabanais had a cachet all its own. Mme. Richard will go down in history as the Carry Nation of sex. Now the house is closed, and the premises are devoted to some low commercial purpose. The walls of the midget Gratin Dauphinois are hung with cartoons that have a nostalgic reference to the past glories of the street.

Mirande, when he arrived, crackled with jokes about the locale. He taunted me with being a criminal who haunts the scene of his misdeeds. The fare at the Gratin is robust, as it is in Dauphiné, but it did not daunt Mirande. The wine card, similarly, is limited to the strong, rough wines of Arbois and the like, with a couple of Burgundies for clients who want to show off. There are no clarets; the proprietor hasn't heard of them. There are, of course, a few champagnes, for wedding parties or anniversaries, so Mirande, with Burgundies discounseled by his doctor, decided on champagne throughout the meal. This was a *drôle* combination with the mountain food, but I had forgotten about the lack of claret when I invited him.

We ordered a couple of dozen *escargots en pots de chambre* to begin with. These are snails baked and served, for the client's convenience, in individual earthenware crocks, instead of being forced back into shells. The snail, of course, has to be taken out of his shell to be prepared for cooking. The shell he is forced back into may not be his own. There is thus not even a sentimental justification for his reincarceration. The frankness of the service *en pot* does not improve the preparation of the snail, nor does it detract from it, but it does facilitate and accelerate his consumption. (The notion that the shell proves the snail's authenticity, like the head left on a woodcock, is invalid, as even a suburban housewife knows nowadays; you can buy a tin of snail shells in a supermarket and fill them with a mixture of nutted cream cheese and chopped olives.)

Mirande finished his dozen first, meticulously swabbing out the garlicky butter in each *pot* with a bit of bread that was fitted to the bore of the crock as precisely as a bullet to a rifle barrel. Tearing bread like that takes practice. We had emptied the first bottle of champagne when he placed his right hand delicately on the point of his waistcoat farthest removed from his spinal column.

"Liebling," he said, "I am not well."

It was like the moment when I first saw Joe Louis draped on the ropes. A great pity filled my heart. *"Maître,"* I said, "I will take you home."

The dismayed *patronne* waved to her husband in the kitchen (he could see her through the opening he pushed the dishes through) to suspend the preparation of the *gendarme de Morteau*—the great smoked sausage in its tough skin—that we had proposed to follow the snails with. ("Short and broad in shape, it is made of pure pork and . . . is likely to be accompanied . . . by hot potato salad."—Root, page 217.) We had decided to substitute for the *pommes à l'huile* the *gratin dauphinois* itself. ("Thinly sliced potatoes are moistened with boiled milk and beaten egg, seasoned with salt, pepper, and nutmeg, and mixed with grated cheese, of the Gruyère type. The potatoes are then put into an earthenware dish which has been rubbed with garlic and then buttered, spotted with little dabs of butter, and sprinkled with more grated cheese. It is then cooked slowly in not too hot an oven."—Root, page 228.) After that, we were going to have a fowl in cream with *morilles*—wild black mushrooms of the mountains. We abandoned all.

I led Mirande into the street and hailed a taxi.

"I am not well, Liebling," he said. "I grow old."

He lived far from the restaurant, beyond the Place de l'Etoile, in the Paris of the successful. From time to time on our way, he would say, "It is nothing. You must excuse me. I am not well."

The apartment house in which he and Mme. B. lived resembled one of the chic modern museums of the quarter, with entrance gained through a maze of garden patches sheathed in glass. Successive metal grilles swung open before us as I pushed buttons that Mirande indicated—in these modern palaces there are no visible flunkies—until we reached an elevator that smoothly shot us upward to his apartment, which was rather larger in area than the Square Louvois. The décor, with basalt columns and floors covered with the skin of jumbo Siberian tigers—a special strain force-fed to supply old-style movie stars—reminded me of the sets for *Belphégor*, a French serial of silent days that I enjoyed when I was a student at the Sorbonne in 1926. (It was, I think, about an ancient Egyptian high priest who came to life and set up bachelor quarters in Paris in the style of the Temple of Karnak.) Three or four maids rushed to relieve Mirande of his sable-lined coat, his hat, and his cane topped with the horn of an albino chamois. I helped him to a divan on which two Theda Baras could have defended their honor simultaneously against two villains of the silents without either couple's getting in the other's way. Most of the horizontal surfaces in the room were covered with sculpture and most of the vertical ones with large paintings. In pain though he was, Mirande called my attention to these works of art.

"All the sculptures are by Renoir," he said. "It was his hobby. And all the paintings are by Maillol. It was *his* hobby. If it were the other way around, I would be one of the richest chaps in France. Both men were my friends. But then, one doesn't give one's friends one's bread and butter. And, after all, it's less banal as it is."

After a minute, he asked me to help him to his bedroom, which was in a wing of the apartment all his own. When we got there, one of the maids came in and took his shoes off.

"I am in good hands now, Liebling," he said. "Farewell until next time. It is nothing."

I telephoned the next noon, and he said that his doctor, who was a fool, insisted that he was ill.

Again I left Paris, and when I returned, late the following January, I neglected Mirande. A Father William is a comforting companion for the middle-aged—he reminds you that the best is yet to be and that there's a dance in the old dame yet—but a sick old man is discouraging. My conscience stirred when I read in a gossip column in *France-Dimanche* that Toto Mirande was convalescing nicely and was devouring caviar at a great rate—with champagne, of course. (I had never thought of Mirande as Toto, which is baby slang for "little kid," but from then on I never referred to him in any other way; I didn't want anybody to think I wasn't in the know.) So the next day I sent him a pound of fresh caviar from Kaspia, in the Place de la Madeleine. It was the kind of medication I approved of.

I received a note from Mirande by tube next morning, reproaching me for spoiling him. He was going better, he wrote, and would telephone in a day or two to make an appointment for a return bout. When he called, he said that the idiotic doctor would not yet permit him to go out to a restaurant, and he invited me, instead, to a family dinner at Mme. B.'s. "Only a few old friends, and not the cuisine I hope to give you at Maxim's next time," he said. "But one makes out."

On the appointed evening, I arrived early—or on time, which amounts to the same thing—*chez* Mme. B.; you take taxis when you can get them in Paris at the rush hours. The handsome quarter overlooking the Seine above the Trocadéro is so dull that when my taxi deposited me before my host's door, I had no inclination to stroll to kill time. It is like Park Avenue or the near North Side of Chicago. So I was the first or second guest to arrive, and Mme. B.'s fourteen-year-old daughter, by a past marriage, received me in the Belphégor room, apologizing because her mother was still with Toto—she called him that. She need not have told me, for at that moment I heard Madame, who is famous for her determined voice, storming at an unmistakable someone: "You go too far, Toto. It's disgusting. People all over Paris are kind enough to send you caviar, and because you call it monotonous, you throw it at the maid! If you think servants are easy to come by . . ."

When they entered the room a few minutes later, my old friend was all smiles. "How did you know I adore caviar to such a point?" he asked me. But I was worried because of what I had heard; the Mirande I remembered would never have been irritated by the obligation to eat a few extra kilos of fresh caviar. The little girl, who hoped I had not heard, embraced Toto. "Don't be angry with *Maman!*" she implored him.

My fellow guests included the youngish new wife of an old former Premier, who was unavoidably detained in Lille at a congress of the party he now headed; it mustered four deputies, of whom two formed a Left Wing and two a Right Wing. ("If they had elected a fifth at the last election, or if, by good luck, one had been defeated, they could afford the luxury of a Center," Mirande told me in identifying the lady. "*C'est mal-heureux*, a party without a Center. It limits the possibilities of maneuver.") There was also an amiable couple in their advanced sixties or beginning seventies, of whom the husband was the grand manitou of Veuve Clicquot champagne. Mirande introduced them by their right name, which I forget, and during the rest of the evening addressed them as M. and Mme. Clicquot. There was a forceful, black-haired man from the Midi, in the youth of middle age—square-shouldered, stocky, decisive, blatantly virile—who, I was told, managed Mme. B.'s vinicultural enterprises in Provence. There were two guests of less decided individuality, whom I barely remember, and filling out the party were the young girl—shy, carefully unsophisticated and unadorned— Mme. B., Mirande, and me. Mme. B. had a strong triangular face on a strong triangular base—a strong chin, high cheekbones, and a wide, strong jaw, but full of stormy good nature. She was a woman who, if she had been a man, would have wanted to be called Honest John. She had a high color and an iron handgrip, and repeatedly affirmed that there was no affectation about her, that she was *sans façon*, that she called her shots as she saw them. "I won't apologize," she said to me. "I know you're a great feeder, like Toto here, but I won't offer you the sort of menu he used to get in that restaurant you know of, where he ruined his plumbing. Oh, that woman! I used to be so jealous. I can offer only a simple home dinner." And she waved us toward a marble table about twenty-two feet long. Unfortunately for me, she meant it. The dinner began with a kidney-and-mushroom mince served in a giant popover—the kind of thing you might get at a literary hotel in New York. The inner side of the pastry had the feeling of a baby's palm, in the true tearoom tradition.

"It is savory but healthy," Madame said firmly, setting an example by taking a large second helping before starting the dish on its second round. Mirande regarded the untouched doughy fabric on his plate with diaphanously veiled horror, but he had an excuse in the state of his health. "It's still a little rich for me, darling," he murmured. The others, including me, delivered salvos of compliments. I do not squander my moral courage on minor crises. M. Clicquot said, "Impossible to obtain anything like this *chez* Lapérouse!" Mme. Clicquot said, "Not even at the Tour d'Argent!"

"And what do you think of my little wine?" Mme. B. asked M. Clicquot. "I'm so anxious for your professional opinion—as a rival producer, you know."

The wine was a thin *rosé* in an Art Nouveau bottle with a label that was a triumph of lithography; it had spires and monks and troubadours and blondes in wimples on it, and the name of the *cru* was spelled out in letters with Gothic curlicues and pennons. The name was something like Château Guillaume d'Aquitaine, *grand vin*.

"What a madly gay little wine, my dear!" M. Clicquot said, repressing, but not soon enough, a grimace of pain.

"One would say a Tavel of a good year," I cried, "if one were a complete bloody fool." I did not say the second clause aloud.

My old friend looked at me with new respect. He was discovering in me a capacity for hypocrisy that he had never credited me with before.

The main course was a shoulder of mutton with white beans— the poor relation of a *gigot*, and an excellent dish in its way, when not too dry. This was.

For the second wine, the man from the Midi proudly produced a red, in a bottle without a label, which he offered to M. Clicquot with the air of a tomcat bringing a field mouse to its master's feet. "Tell me what you think of this," he said as he filled the champagne man's glass.

M. Clicquot—a veteran of such challenges, I could well imagine—held the glass against the light, dramatically inhaled the bouquet, and then drank, after a slight stiffening of the features that indicated to me that he knew what he was in for. Having emptied half the glass, he deliberated.

"It has a lovely color," he said.

"But what is it? What is it?" the man from the Midi insisted.

"There are things about it that remind me of a Beaujolais," M. Clicquot said (he must have meant that it was wet), "but on the whole I should compare it to a Bordeaux" (without doubt unfavorably).

Mme. B.'s agent was beside himself with triumph. "Not one or the other!" he crowed. "It's from the *domaine*—the Château Guillaume d'Aquitaine!"

The admirable M. Clicquot professed astonishment, and I, when I had emptied a glass, said that there would be a vast market for the wine in America if it could be properly presented. "Unfortunately," I said, "the cost of advertising . . ." and I rolled my eyes skyward.

"Ah, yes," Mme. B. cried sadly. "The cost of advertising!"

I caught Mirande looking at me again, and thought of the Pétrus and the Cheval Blanc of our last meal together *chez* Mme. G. He drank a glass of the red. After all, he wasn't going to die of thirst.

For dessert, we had a simple fruit tart with milk—just the thing for an invalid's stomach, although Mirande didn't eat it.

M. Clicquot retrieved the evening, oenologically, by producing two bottles of a wine "impossible to find in the cellars of any restaurant in France"—Veuve Clicquot '19. There is at present a great to-do among wine merchants in France and the United States about young wines, and an accompanying tendency to cry down the "legend" of the old. For that matter, hardware clerks, when you ask for a can opener with a wooden handle that is thick enough to give a grip and long enough for leverage, try to sell you complicated mechanical folderols. The motivation in both cases is the same—simple greed. To deal in wines of varied ages requires judgment, the sum of experience and flair. It involves the risk of money, because every lot of wine, like every human being, has a life span, and it is this that the good vintner must estimate. His object should be to sell his wine at its moment of maximum value—to the drinker as well as the merchant. The vintner who handles only young wines is like an insurance company that will write policies only on children; the unqualified dealer wants to risk nothing and at the same time to avoid tying up his money. The client misled by brochures warning him off clarets and champagnes that are over ten years old and assuring him that Beaujolais should be drunk green will miss the major pleasures of wine drinking. To deal wisely in wines and merely to sell them are things as different as being an expert in ancient coins and selling Indian-head pennies over a souvenir counter.

Despite these convictions of mine about wine, I should never have tried a thirty-seven-year-old champagne on the recommendation of a lesser authority than the blessed M. Clicquot. It is the oldest by far that I have ever drunk. (H. Warner Allen, in *The Wines of France*, published circa 1924, which is my personal wine bible, says, "In the matter of age, champagne is a capricious wine. As a general rule, it has passed its best between fifteen and twenty, yet a bottle thirty years old may prove excellent, though all its fellows may be quite undrinkable." He cites Saintsbury's note that "a Perrier Jouet of 1857 was still majestical in 1884," adding, "And all wine-drinkers know of such amazing discoveries." Mr. Root, whose book is not a foolish panegyric of everything French, is hard on champagne, in my opinion. He falls into a critical error more common among writers less intelligent: he attacks it for not being something else. Because its excellences are not those of Burgundy or Bordeaux, he underrates the peculiar qualities it does not share with them, as one who would chide Dickens for not being Stendhal, or Marciano for not being Benny Leonard.)

The Veuve Clicquot '19 was tart without brashness—a refined but effective understatement of younger champagnes, which run too much to rhetoric, at best. Even so, the force was all there, to judge from the two glasses that were a shade more than my share. The wine still had a discreet *cordon*—the ring of bubbles that forms inside the glass—and it had developed the color known as "partridge eye." I have never seen a partridge's eye, because the bird, unlike woodcock, is served without the head, but the color the term indicates is that of serous blood or a maple leaf on the turn.

"How nice it was, life in 1919, eh, M. Clicquot?" Mirande said as he sipped his second glass.

After we had finished M. Clicquot's offering, we played a game called lying poker for table stakes, each player being allowed a capital of five hundred francs, not to be replenished under any circumstances. When Mme. B. had won everybody's five hundred francs, the party broke up. Mirande promised me that he would be up and about soon, and would show me how men reveled in the heroic days of *la belle époque*, but I had a feeling that the bell was cracked.

I left Paris and came back to it seven times during the next year, but never saw him. Once, being in his quarter in the company of a remarkably pretty woman, I called him up, simply because I knew he would like to look at her, but he was too tired. I forget when I last talked to him on the telephone. During the next winter, while I was away in Egypt or Jordan or someplace where French papers don't circulate, he died, and I did not learn of it until I returned to Europe.

When Mirande first faltered, in the Rue Chabanais, I had failed to correlate cause and effect. I had even felt a certain selfish alarm. If eating well was beginning to affect Mirande at eighty, I thought, I had better begin taking in sail. After all, I was only thirty years his junior. But after the dinner at Mme. B.'s, and in the light of subsequent reflection, I saw that what had undermined his constitution was Mme. G.'s defection from the restaurant business. For years, he had been able to escape Mme. B.'s solicitude for his health by lunching and dining in the restaurant of Mme. G., the sight of whom Mme. B. could not support. Entranced by Mme. G.'s magnificent food, he had continued to live "like a cock in a pie"—eating as well, and very nearly as much, as when he was thirty. The organs of the interior—never very intelligent, in spite of what the psychosomatic quacks say— received each day the amount of pleasure to which they were accustomed, and never marked the passage of time; it was the indispensable roadwork of the prizefighter. When Mme. G., good soul, retired, moderation began its fatal inroads on his resistance. My old friend's appetite, insufficiently stimulated, started to loaf—the insidious result, no doubt, of the advice of the doctor whose existence he had revealed to me by that slip of the tongue about why he no longer drank Burgundy. Mirande commenced, perhaps, by omitting the fish course after the oysters, or the oysters before the fish, then began neglecting his cheeses and skipping the second bottle of wine on odd Wednesdays. What he called his pipes *("ma tuyauterie")*, being insufficiently exercised, lost their tone, like the leg muscles of a retired champion. When, in his kindly effort to please me, he challenged the *escargots en pots de chambre,* he was like an old fighter who tries a comeback without training for it. That, however, was only the revelation of the rot that had already taken place. What always happens happened. The damage was done, but it could so easily have been averted had he been warned against the fatal trap of abstinence.

NANCY MITFORD

CHIC—ENGLISH, FRENCH, AND AMERICAN

I really prefer the word elegance. "Chic" has lost value in its native country—"*Chic alors!*" cries the street urchin on finding ten francs in the gutter—and it never had much prestige in England. Roget in his *Thesaurus* lumps it together with "style, swank, swagger and showing off"; indeed, it represents everything that the English most dislike, a sort of bright up-to-date fashionableness they have never aspired to. For elegance in England is of such different stuff from that in any other country that it is not easy to make foreigners believe in it at all. (As regards the women, that is. English men and small children are universally admitted to be the model of good dressing; our Queen and Princess Margaret set the fashion for the world until they were ten.) It is based upon a contempt of the current mode and a limitless self-assurance.

When the Empress Eugénie paid a state visit to England she went with Queen Victoria to the opera. The Londoners sighed a little as the two ladies stood together in the Royal Box during the playing of the National Anthem; the beauty in her Paris clothes beside chubby little red-faced Victoria. Then the time came for them to take their seats. The Empress, with a graceful movement, looked round at her chair, but Queen Victoria dumped straight down, thus proving unmistakably that she was of Royal birth and upbringing. Had that chair not been in its place the skies would have fallen, and she knew it. The audience was proud of its Queen and never gave the parvenue Empress another thought—indeed, nobody in England was at all surprised when shortly afterwards the Second Empire collapsed.

Nearer our own time two English duchesses were turned away from Christian Dior. The people at the entrance considered them too dowdy to be admitted. In England, if you are a duchess you don't need to be well dressed—it would be thought quite eccentric. I cannot imagine why they ever had the idea of going to Dior, where they would certainly not have ordered anything. Perhaps they were tired after extensive sight-seeing and thought they would like to sit for a while, having a vision of Monsieur Worth's soothing empty salons in the days when their mothers dressed there. (In the days of their grandmothers Monsieur Worth came to the house like any other tradesman.) They had surely not envisaged the scented scramble at the top of the stairs, the enervating atmosphere of a salon where no window may ever be opened, the hideous trellis of crossed nylon legs round the room, and the all-in wrestling match for each and every chair. The duchesses went quietly, and if they did not quite realize what an escape they had had, they were probably rather happy to sit on a bench in the avenue Montaigne and watch the motors go by.

At the beginning of this century the English were rich and pleasure-loving; foreign currency was no problem; society women bought all their clothes in Paris. When the dresses were delivered they were put away for at least two years, since, in those days, nothing was considered so common as to be dressed in the height of fashion. Harlots and actresses could flaunt the current clothes, it was quite all right for them, and indeed a mark of their profession, but "one of us, dear child", never. Even the men would not think of wearing a new suit until it had spent one or two nights in the garden, making it look at least a year old.

Now this tradition continues in London. The dressmakers there slavishly follow the Paris fashion of two years before, while people in the streets lag another year, so that to anybody arriving from Paris the clothes have an odd and disproportioned look, skirts too long or short, waists too high or too low, and so on. Anyhow, the word elegant cannot truthfully be applied to the English by day. Ladylike is the most that can be said. They really have no idea of what day-clothes should be; and contrary to what is sometimes supposed, their sports and country clothes are deplorable. They are of tweed thick and hard as a board, in various shades of porridge, and made to last for ever. For the town English women have only one solution, a jacket and tight skirt with what the fashion papers call "a cunning slit up the back", which, when they walk, divides rather horribly over their calves.

Women seen about in London streets give a general appearance of tidy dreariness, but these same women at a ball are a surprise and a delight. In the evening they excel. With their beautiful jewels glittering on their beautiful skins, with their absolute unselfconsciousness, put them in any old satin skirt and deep décolleté and they are unbeatable. There is no more dazzling sight than a ball at Buckingham Palace.

French women, we are often told, are the most elegant. But where are they? Foreigners visiting Paris for the first time are often disappointed because they never see anybody well dressed. The fact is that elegance in Paris is confined to a small group of women who are seldom seen in public and never in the streets. They get into their own motors inside their own courtyards, rarely eat in restaurants or appear at the big dressmakers' (a selection of the clothes is sent for them to see at home), and in short it is an act of faith for the ordinary tourist to believe that they exist at all. They do, however, and are absolutely powerful in the world of elegance, since it is their taste which, in the end, everybody follows.

French dress designers, hairdressers, and cooks are admitted to be unbeatable, but they lose their eye, their hand, their skill after a few years in England or America. Why? Because they are no longer under the disciplinary control of *les femmes du monde*—that is to say, of a very few rich, ruthless, and savagely energetic women who know what they want and never spare anybody's feelings in their determination to get it. Back goes the dress, back goes the dish, back into the washtub goes the head, until the result is perfect—then and then only is heard the grudging *"Pas mal"*. Their vigilance extends to the smallest details. I once bought a suit in an expensive English shop and gave it to my Paris dressmaker for some minor alteration. She told me she had been obliged to take it home and do it herself, since she could not risk letting the girls in her workroom see how badly it was finished off. "But how could you have accepted it?" she kept saying. I didn't like to tell her that I had not turned it inside out, as any French woman would have done, so had no idea how the seams were sewn.

Anglo-Saxons do not quite understand French elegance and what it is. They have a vague romantic notion that any French woman can take any old bit of stuff, give it a clever twist, and look chic in it. This may be true of Italian peasants, but not of Parisians. Dressing, in Paris, is not a craft; it is an art not to be come by easily or cheaply; Parisians are not peasants, but citizens of the most civilized town in the world. When they cannot afford the time and money to be really well dressed, they abandon the idea of clothes and concentrate instead upon cooking and their children's education. Dresses with a cheaply fashionable air do not appeal to French women.

In writing about Americans I find myself at a disadvantage so great that perhaps I really should not attempt it. For I have never been to America. I study it, of course. I look at *Life* and *Time* and *The New Yorker,* I hang about behind Americans at cocktail parties and listen to what they are saying to each other. I read their books, in many of which they seem to behave oddly, nipping off their own breasts with garden shears and so on, but no more oddly I suppose than the English of *Wuthering Heights.* America is to me some great star observed through a telescope, and I never feel quite sure that it exists, now, or whether its light is not coming to me across centuries of time (future time, of course).

If I may venture then to speak about American elegance, as observed through my telescope during many a long wakeful night, I should say it is the elegance of adolescence. The bobby-soxers, the teen-agers, who seem to what we call "come out" so very young, are beautifully dressed. Their neat little clothes have more than an echo of Paris; the skirts are the right length, the waists in the right place, and they are, very suitably for children, understated. I imagine it would not do to turn them inside out and examine the seams. These young Americans do not care to have one good dress and wear it a whole season; they would rather have a quantity of cheap dresses and throw them away after two or three wearings. As I look through my telescope I see a charming flock of radiant little girls, in pretty dolls' clothes, clean, shining, with regular if rather big teeth, wonderful figures, and china skins. I also see a crowd of gracious ladies in canasta gowns, impeccable, not one blue hair out of place. But what happens to the intermediate ages? At what point do old little girls turn into young old ladies? Where are the grown-up women in the prime of life dressed as adults?

I think that the elegance of these three countries can be summed up by saying that in England the women are elegant until they are ten years old and perfect on grand occasions; in France a few women are entirely elegant always; in America most women are smart and impeccable, but with too much of an accent on immaturity for real elegance. The Latin American woman dressed in Paris is the very height of perfection, however.

GRAHAM GREENE

The Lost Childhood

Perhaps it is only in childhood that books have any deep influence on our lives. In later life we admire, we are entertained, we may modify some views we already hold, but we are more likely to find in books merely a confirmation of what is in our minds already: as in a love affair it is our own features that we see reflected flatteringly back.

But in childhood all books are books of divination, telling us about the future, and like the fortune-teller who sees a long journey in the cards or death by water they influence the future. I suppose that is why books excited us so much. What do we ever get nowadays from reading to equal the excitement and the revelation in those first fourteen years? Of course I should be interested to hear that a new novel by Mr E. M. Forster was going to appear this spring, but I could never compare that mild expectation of civilized pleasure with the missed heartbeat, the appalled glee I felt when I found on a library shelf a novel by Rider Haggard, Percy Westerman, Captain Brereton or Stanley Weyman which I had not read before. It is in those early years that I would look for the crisis, the moment when life took a new slant in its journey towards death.

I remember distinctly the suddenness with which a key turned in a lock and I found I could read—not just the sentences in a reading book with the syllables coupled like railway carriages, but a real book. It was paper-covered with the picture of a boy, bound and gagged, dangling at the end of a rope inside a well with the water rising above his waist—an adventure of Dixon

Brett, detective. All a long summer holiday I kept my secret, as I believed: I did not want anybody to know that I could read. I suppose I half consciously realized even then that this was the dangerous moment. I was safe so long as I could not read—the wheels had not begun to turn, but now the future stood around on bookshelves everywhere waiting for the child to choose—the life of a chartered accountant perhaps, a colonial civil servant, a planter in China, a steady job in a bank, happiness and misery, eventually one particular form of death, for surely we choose our death much as we choose our job. It grows out of our acts and our evasions, out of our fears and out of our moments of courage. I suppose my mother must have discovered my secret, for on the journey home I was presented for the train with another real book, a copy of Ballantyne's *Coral Island* with only a single picture to look at, a coloured frontispiece. But I would admit nothing. All the long journey I stared at the one picture and never opened the book.

But there on the shelves at home (so many shelves for we were a large family) the books waited—one book in particular, but before I reach that one down let me take a few others at random from the shelf. Each was a crystal in which the child dreamed that he saw life moving. Here in a cover stamped dramatically in several colours was Captain Gilson's *The Pirate Aeroplane*. I must have read that book six times at least—the story of a lost civilization in the Sahara and of a villainous Yankee pirate with an aeroplane like a box kite and bombs the size of tennis balls who held the golden city to ransom. It was saved by the hero, a young subaltern who crept up to the pirate camp to put the aeroplane out of action. He was captured and watched his enemies dig his grave. He was to be shot at dawn, and to pass the time and keep his mind from uncomfortable thoughts the amiable Yankee pirate played cards with him—the mild nursery game of Kuhn Kan. The memory of that nocturnal game on the edge of life haunted me for years, until I set it to rest at last in one of my own novels with a game of poker played in remotely similar circumstances.

And here is *Sophy of Kravonia* by Anthony Hope—the story of a kitchen-maid who became a queen. One of the first films I ever saw, about 1911, was made from that book, and I can hear still the rumble of the Queen's guns crossing the high Kravonian pass beaten hollowly out on a single piano. Then there was Stanley Weyman's *The Story of Francis Cludde*, and above all other books at that time of my life *King Solomon's Mines.*

This book did not perhaps provide the crisis, but it certainly influenced the future. If it had not been for that romantic tale of Allan Quatermain, Sir Henry Curtis, Captain Good, and, above all, the ancient witch Gagool, would I at nineteen have studied the appointments list of the Colonial Office and very nearly picked on the Nigerian Navy for a career? And later, when surely I ought to have known better, the odd African fixation remained. In 1935 I found myself sick with fever on a camp bed in a Liberian native's hut with a candle going out in an empty whisky bottle and a rat moving in the shadows. Wasn't it the incurable fascination of Gagool with her bare yellow skull, the wrinkled scalp that moved and contracted like the hood of a cobra, that led me to work all through 1942 in a little stuffy office in Freetown, Sierra Leone? There is not much in common between the land of the Kukuanas, behind the desert and the mountain range of Sheba's Breast, and a tin-roofed house on a bit of swamp where the vultures moved like domestic turkeys and the pi-dogs kept me awake on moonlit nights with their wailing, and the white women yellowed by atebrin drove by to the club; but the two belonged at any rate to the same continent, and, however distantly, to the same region of the imagination—the region of uncertainty, of not knowing the way about. Once I came a little nearer to Gagool and her witch-hunters, one night in Zigita on the Liberian side of the French Guinea border, when my servants sat in their shuttered hut with their hands over their eyes and someone beat a drum and a whole town stayed behind closed doors while the big bush devil—whom it would mean blindness to see—moved between the huts.

But *King Solomon's Mines* could not finally satisfy. It was not the right answer. The key did not quite fit. Gagool I could recognize—didn't she wait for me in dreams every night, in the passage by the linen cupboard, near the nursery door? and she continues to wait, when the mind is sick or tired, though now she is dressed in the theological garments of Despair and speaks in Spenser's accents:

> *The longer life, I wote the greater sin,*
> *The greater sin, the greater punishment.*

Gagool has remained a permanent part of the imagination, but Quatermain and Curtis—weren't they, even when I was only ten years old, a little too good to be true? They were men of such unyielding integrity (they would only admit to a fault in order to show how it might be overcome) that the wavering personality of a child could not rest for long against those monumental shoulders. A child, after all, knows most of the game—it is only an attitude to it that he lacks. He is quite well aware of cowardice, shame, deception, disappointment. Sir Henry Curtis perched upon a rock bleeding from a dozen wounds but fighting on with the remnant of the Greys against the hordes of Twala was too heroic. These men were like Platonic ideas: they were not life as one had already begun to know it.

But when—perhaps I was fourteen by that time—I took Miss Marjorie Bowen's *The Viper of Milan* from the library shelf, the future for better or worse really struck. From that moment I began to write. All the other possible futures slid away: the potential civil servant, the don, the clerk had to look for other incarnations. Imitation after imitation of Miss Bowen's magnificent novel went into exercise-books—stories of sixteenth-century Italy or twelfth-century England marked with enormous brutality and a despairing romanticism. It was as if I had been supplied once and for all with a subject.

Why? On the surface *The Viper of Milan* is only the story of a war between Gian Galeazzo Visconti, Duke of Milan, and Mastino della Scala, Duke of Verona, told with zest and cunning and an amazing pictorial sense. Why did it creep in and colour and explain the terrible living world of the stone stairs and the never quiet dormitory? It was no good in that real world to dream that one would ever be a Sir Henry Curtis, but della Scala who at last turned from an honesty that never paid and betrayed his friends and died dishonoured and a failure even at treachery—it was easier for a child to escape behind his mask. As for Visconti, with his beauty, his patience, and his genius for evil, I had watched him pass by many a time in his black Sunday suit smelling of mothballs. His name was Carter. He exercised terror from a distance like a snowcloud over the young fields. Goodness has only once found a perfect incarnation in a human body and never will again, but evil can always find a home there. Human nature is not black and white but black and grey. I read all that in *The Viper of Milan* and I looked round and I saw that it was so.

There was another theme I found there. At the end of *The Viper of Milan*—you will remember if you have once read it—comes the great scene of complete success—della Scala is dead, Ferrara, Verona, Novara, Mantua have all fallen, the messengers pour in with news of fresh victories, the whole world outside is cracking up, and Visconti sits and jokes in the wine-light. I was not on the classical side or I would have discovered, I suppose, in Greek literature instead of in Miss Bowen's novel the sense of doom that lies over success—the feeling that the pendulum is about to swing. That too made sense; one looked around and saw the doomed everywhere—the champion runner who one day would sag over the tape; the head of the school who would atone, poor devil, during forty dreary undistinguished years; the scholar . . . and when success began to touch oneself too, however mildly, one could only pray that failure would not be held off for too long.

One had lived for fourteen years in a wild jungle country without a map, but now the paths had been traced and naturally one had to follow them. But I think it was Miss Bowen's apparent zest that made me want to write. One could not read her without believing that to write was to live and to enjoy, and before one had discovered one's mistake it was too late—the first book one does enjoy. Anyway she had given me my pattern—religion might later explain it to me in other terms, but the pattern was already there—perfect evil walking the world where perfect good can never walk again, and only the pendulum ensures that after all in the end justice is done. Man is never satisfied, and often I have wished that my hand had not moved further than *King Solomon's Mines,* and that the future I had taken down from the nursery shelf had been a district office in Sierra Leone and twelve tours of malarial duty and a finishing dose of blackwater fever when the danger of retirement approached. What is the good of wishing? The books are always there, the moment of crisis waits, and now our children in their turn are taking down the future and opening the pages. In his poem "Germinal" A. E. wrote:

> *In ancient shadows and twilights*
> *Where childhood had strayed,*
> *The world's great sorrows were born*
> *And its heroes were made.*
> *In the lost boyhood of Judas*
> *Christ was betrayed.*

EMILY HAHN

THE STRANGER

Although she had been in New York at least a year and I was a newcomer, I had the feeling that it was my city rather than hers. In the first place she didn't seem to want New York. There are cities that I haven't wanted at all, cities that have let me pass through with a cold indifference on both sides, but she was the only person I had ever seen who really resisted New York.

We lived in the same boarding house and saw more of each other than we would otherwise have done, because we were the only denizens of our floor. It was an old house with big draughty rooms, and there was a smaller living-room that we used to lounge in. She had her job and I was looking for one. To me she was simply one of those enviable people who knew what to do at Ninety-sixth Street when they were on the wrong subway train. I heard her go out in the morning, always at the same time, and I heard her come back at night. She kept a large greasy jar of cold cream on her shelf of the medicine cabinet and on Sunday evening she fixed coffee in her room and bought sandwiches. Sometimes she would bring home a girl for the night, in which case they took more time in the bathroom than I approved of.

She wore quiet clothes with felt hats that were always a little wrong. She had a large pale face with blue eyes and light lashes; when she was quiet she looked as if she worried about money. At first I noticed all these things about her because she was there and I didn't have anything else to do. I think she was glad to have a new person to talk to. She told me where to get cream if I wanted breakfast in my room; she had a few words of advice about the job for which I was looking; she was full of information about transportation — buses, elevateds, street cars. Even now I'm sure I know only half of the things she used to have by heart.

Somehow I didn't want to talk to her. There was my city waiting for me; I had only just come and I was a little afraid. She had a job and didn't seem to worry about losing it, and didn't seem to have any hopes of improving it. She placidly went to work every day; every day she took the same route — in spite of knowing all about those other street cars and things — and worked all day and came home every night and put that cold cream on her face and went to bed. In New York! I thought that it might happen to me too. I began to avoid her. When I found a job and had worked for a week I discovered that I was walking down the same street every day and eating at the same restaurant, and I was badly frightened. I thought of her placid pale face and after that I took elaborate precautions to vary the road to the office. I made a rule never to eat lunch twice in succession at the same place.

Of course I was wrong about her. After a month or two, when the city and I were used to each other and I had other things to think about, she came running in one evening to show me a new dress. It wasn't a very nice dress — one of those very bright blue ones in the lower Broadway shops, with white lace and a short skirt. But she liked it, and of course I said I did. She was rather fluttered because she was going to a party with one of the girls who worked with her and occasionally went to a movie with her. She talked more than usual and smoked a cigarette; we sat for quite a while in my room and discussed movies, I remember. She was making vague plans to keep a cat; the landlady had said she could and she was wondering where to get it and how to take care of it. After she went away to get dressed I remembered how frightened I had been of her when I first came; for a minute I worried because I was not frightened of her any more.

Then something happened and I forgot. I got sick. For a week I was in bed, and then for a day or two I sat up in that little living-room, reading and thinking. I got acquainted with her again. She came in one Sunday while I had a headache and was lying down. She brought with her a cool damp cloth which she put on my forehead, and she sat down and began to sew. She was making handkerchiefs out of scraps of colored linen — drawing threads out and replacing them with threads of another color—and when she had made a pattern she rolled the edges of the linen and sewed them down. I was feeling lazy and peaceful and it fascinated me to watch her.

"They're for Christmas presents," she explained. "I've always made handkerchiefs all through the year for Christmas. The people at home like them. I make a lot for the church bazaars too."

"What church bazaars?"

"We have them every year at home. The money goes to the associated charities and all the girls turn in and help. They last for three days; there's a play the last night, and a dance afterwards. I remember the time I acted in 'The Servant in the House'—some of the boys who should have fixed the scenery forgot to prop up the door, and just at the last minute—"

Her voice was more animated than it had ever been. I was amazed. She was sewing faster now, and her cheeks were pink. She talked on, remembering other parties that they had had; remembering more stories about "the boys," remembering and describing her first real sleeveless dress—I have never heard anyone talk so much. I enjoyed it. She was being really friendly now; really off her guard. She wasn't looking at me; when the handkerchief was finished, she put it in her lap and looked at the wall as she talked; smiling a little. . . .

I wonder how many people are living in New York and not using it. You would think that the city would burst from so many people. You would think that all the houses would bulge with the thoughts in them about church bazaars and Christmas presents.

She started another handkerchief, a yellow one, and began another story about a dance in the next town to hers. A high-school dance with an imported orchestra, she said; four of them were going together in a car, and just as they were starting out . . .

The telephone rang. She started, and looked at me. The yellow linen dropped to her lap; the phone rang again. And her eyes, fixed on me now, were hating. For a minute her expression was dreadful. Her mouth had tightened. Then—

"You answer," she said, in her flat voice. "It's for you. It's always for you. . . ."

LOREN EISELEY

THE ANGRY WINTER

A time comes when creatures whose destinies have crossed somewhere in the remote past are forced to appraise each other as
though they were total strangers. I had been huddled beside the
fire one winter night, with the wind prowling outside and shaking the windows. The big shepherd dog on the hearth before me
occasionally glanced up affectionately, sighed, and slept. I was
working, actually, amidst the debris of a far greater winter. On
my desk lay the lance point of ice age hunters and the heavy leg
bone of a fossil bison. No remnants of flesh attached to these
relics. The deed lay more than ten thousand years remote. It was
represented here by naked flint and by bone so mineralized it
rang when struck. As I worked in my little circle of light, I
absently laid the bone beside me on the floor. The hour had
crept toward midnight. A grating noise, a heavy rasping of big
teeth diverted me. I looked down.

The dog had risen. That rock-hard fragment of a vanished
beast was in his jaws and he was mouthing it with a fierce intensity I had never seen exhibited by him before.

"Wolf," I exclaimed, and stretched out my hand. The dog
backed up but did not yield. A low and steady rumbling began
to rise in his chest, something out of a long-gone midnight.
There was nothing in that bone to taste, but ancient shapes were
moving in his mind and determining his utterance. Only fools
gave up bones. He was warning me.

"Wolf," I chided again.

As I advanced, his teeth showed and his mouth wrinkled to

strike. The rumbling rose to a direct snarl. His flat head swayed low and wickedly as a reptile's above the floor. I was the most loved object in his universe, but the past was fully alive in him now. Its shadows were whispering in his mind. I knew he was not bluffing. If I made another step he would strike.

Yet his eyes were strained and desperate. "Do not," something pleaded in the back of them, some affectionate thing that had followed at my heel all the days of his mortal life, "do not force me. I am what I am and cannot be otherwise because of the shadows. Do not reach out. You are a man, and my very god. I love you, but do not put out your hand. It is midnight. We are in another time, in the snow."

"The other time," the steady rumbling continued while I paused, "the other time in the snow, the big, the final, the terrible snow, when the shape of this thing I hold spelled life. I will not give it up. I cannot. The shadows will not permit me. Do not put out your hand."

I stood silent, looking into his eyes, and heard his whisper through. Slowly I drew back in understanding. The snarl diminished, ceased. As I retreated, the bone slumped to the floor. He placed a paw upon it, warningly.

And were there no shadows in my own mind, I wondered. Had I not for a moment, in the grip of that savage utterance, been about to respond, to hurl myself upon him over an invisible haunch ten thousand years removed? Even to me the shadows had whispered—to me, the scholar in his study.

"Wolf," I said, but this time, holding a familiar leash, I spoke from the door indifferently. "A walk in the snow." Instantly from his eyes that other visitant receded. The bone was left lying. He came eagerly to my side, accepting the leash and taking it in his mouth as always.

A blizzard was raging when we went out, but he paid no heed. On his thick fur the driving snow was soon clinging heavily. He frolicked a little—though usually he was a grave dog—making up to me for something still receding in his mind. I felt the snowflakes fall upon my face, and stood thinking of another time, and another time still, until I was moving from midnight to midnight under ever more remote and vaster snows. Wolf came to my side with a little whimper. It was he who was civilized now. "Come back to the fire," he nudged gently, "or you will be lost." Automatically I took the leash he offered. He led me safely home and into the house.

"We have been very far away," I told him solemnly. "I think there is something in us that we had both better try to forget." Sprawled on the rug, Wolf made no response except to thump his tail feebly out of courtesy. Already he was mostly asleep and dreaming. By the movement of his feet I could see he was running far upon some errand in which I played no part.

Softly I picked up his bone—our bone, rather—and replaced it high on a shelf in my cabinet. As I snapped off the light the white glow from the window seemed to augment itself and shine with a deep, glacial blue. As far as I could see, nothing moved in the long aisles of my neighbor's woods. There was no visible track, and certainly no sound from the living. The snow continued to fall steadily, but the wind, and the shadows it had brought, had vanished.

M. F. K. FISHER

The Flaw

There was a train, not a particularly good one, that stopped at Vevey about ten in the morning on the way to Italy. Chexbres and I used to take it to Milano.

It had a restaurant car, an old-fashioned one with the agreeable austerity of a third-class station café about it: brown wooden walls and seats, bare tables unless you ordered the highest-priced lunch, and a few faded advertisements for Aspirina Bayer and "*Visitez le Maroc*" permanently crooked above the windows.

There was one table, next to the galley, where the cooks and waiters sat. In the morning they would be talking and sorting greens for salad and cutting the tops off radishes for the *hors d'oeuvres,* and in the early afternoon they would eat enormously of some things that had been on the menu and some that certainly had not. There was always a big straw-wrapped flask of red wine with them.

Sometimes the head chef smoked while he drank, or read parts of a newspaper aloud, but usually he worked with his helpers. And if one of the two waiters sat there, he worked too.

We liked to go into the restaurant partly because of the cooks, who after a polite salute ignored us, and partly because of the waiters, who were always the same ones.

Of course, it is impossible that they were on every train that went to Milano through Vevey at ten in the morning. But they were on that train every time we took it, so that very soon they knew us and laughed and even patted Chexbres' shoulder delightedly when we appeared.

We always went into their car a few minutes after we started
. . . after we had been seen by the conductor and what few travelers there were on the unfashionable train. The restaurant would
be empty at that hour, of course, except for the table of amiably
chattering cooks.

We would order a large bottle of Asti Spumanti. That
delighted the waiters, whether it was the young smooth one or
the old sour withered one. We would sit drinking it, slightly
warm, from the thick train-goblets, talking and watching the flat
floor of the Valais grow narrower and wilder, waiting as always
with a kind of excited dread for the first plunge into the Simplon.

The champagne would stay us, in that familiar ordeal. We'd
drink gratefully, feeling the train sway, knowing a small taste of
death and rebirth, as all men do in swift passage through a
tunnel.

When we came out finally, into the light again and the high
mountains, we'd lift our glasses silently to each other, and feel
less foolish to see that the cooks too had known the same name-
less stress as we.

Then people would begin to come in for lunch, and we'd go
back to our compartment. The younger waiter would always call
us when there were only a few more people to serve, in an hour
or so.

Usually both waiters took care of us; they seemed to find us
strange, and interesting enough to crack their cosmic ennui, and
in some way fragile, so that they protected us. They would come
swaying down the aisle as we ate, crying to us, "There will be a
few bumps! Hold tight! Hold tight, M'sieu'-'dame! I will help
you!"

Then they would grasp the wine, and usually my arm, and we
would, it is true, make a few mild grating noises over some repairs
in the road. Then they would gasp with relief, and scuttle away
. . . one more crisis safely past.

It made us feel a little silly, as if we were imbeciles of royal
blood, or perhaps children who only *thought* they had gray hairs
and knew how to survive train trips alone. It was fun, too; almost
everyone likes to feel pampered by public servants.

The young waiter with the smooth almond face was more

given to the protective gestures, equally lavished on Chexbres or me to avoid any sexual misunderstandings, but the older one, whose body was bent and whose face was truly the most cynical I have ever seen, was the one who watched our eating.

He hovered like an evil-visaged hawk while we ordered, and we soon found that instead of advising changes then, he would simply substitute in the kitchen what he preferred to have us enjoy that day. After the first surprise it was fun, but we always kept up the bluff of looking at the menu and then watching him pretend to memorize our order.

One thing he permitted us: simplicity. The people who traveled on that train were the kind who liked plain food and plenty of it. The menu might or might not list meat or fish, but it always had *pasti* of some kind, and lentils or beans cooked with herbs, and of course fine honest garden salad. Then there would be one or two *antipasti*: the radishes we had watched being fixed, and butter for them in rather limp and sooty curls, and hardboiled eggs and sliced salami. There would be cheese for dessert, with fruit . . . fat cherries or peaches or grapes or oranges, according to the season, and always green almonds in the spring.

The people ate well, and even if they were very poor, and brought their own bread and wine into the restaurant, they ordered a plate of beans or a one-egg omelet with dignity which was no rebuke to the comparative prodigality around them. The two waiters served them with nonchalant skill, and everyone seemed to agree that Chexbres and I should be watched and fed and smiled at with extra care.

"Why are they like that? Why are they so good to us, all the people?" we would ask each other. I knew reasons for him, and he knew some for me, but for the two of us it was probably because we had a sort of palpable trust in each other.

Simple people are especially conscious of that. Sometimes it is called love, or good will. Whatever it was in us, the result was mysterious and warming, and we felt it very strongly in places like the restaurant car to Milano, always until the last time.

That was in the summer of 1939.

We were two ghosts, then. Our lives as normal living humans had ended in the winter, in Delaware, with Chexbres' illness.

And when we got word that we should go back to our old home in Switzerland and save what we could before war started, we went not so much for salvage, because possessions had no meaning any more to us, but because we were helpless to do anything else. We returned to the life that had been so real like fog, or smoke, caught in a current of air.

We were very live ghosts, and drank and ate and saw and felt and made love better than ever before, with an intensity that seemed to detach us utterly from life.

Everywhere there was a little of that feeling; the only difference was that we were safely dead, and all the other people, that summer, were laughing and singing and drinking wine in a kind of catalepsy, or like cancerous patients made happy with a magic combination of opiate before going into the operating theatre. We had finished with all that business, and they had it still to go through.

They looked at us with a kind of envious respect, knowing that war was coming to them, but that we were past it; and everywhere we went, except the one time on the Milano train, we moved beatifically incommunicado, archangels on leave. None could touch us, just as none could be harmed by our knowledge of pain yet to be felt.

The train was the same. By then we had grown almost used to miracles, and when the young almond-faced waiter stood in the door of the compartment and gaped helplessly at us, we laughed at him. He stammered and sputtered, all the time shaking our hands and laughing too, and it was plain that he had buried us long since.

When he saw what had happened to Chexbres, he turned very red, and then said quickly, trying not to stare, "But the Asti! At once! It will be very chic to drink it here!"

And before we could tell him how much we wanted to drink it in the old restaurant car, and look once more at the faded aspirin signs and listen to the cooks, he was gone. It was necessary for him to disappear; we were used by then to having people do impetuous things when they first saw us, ghosts come back so far. . . . We sighed, and laughed, because even that seemed funny.

The boy brought the champagne, wrapped elegantly in a red-checked napkin for the first time. He was suave and mischievous again, and it was plain that he felt like something in a paper-bound novel, serving fair wine that way at eleven in the morning in a first-class compartment. He swayed with exaggerated grace to the rocking of the car, and flicked soot from the little wall table like the headwaiter at the Café de la Paix, at least, with his flat black eyes dancing.

We saluted him with our first taste, hiding our regret at having to be "gentry" and drink where it was chic. The wine was the same, warm and almost sickish, and we looked quietly at each other, with delight . . . one more miracle.

But at Sion, before the tunnel, three Strength-through-Joyers got on, bulbous with knapsacks and a kind of sweaty health that had nothing to do with us. We huddled against the windows, not invisible enough, and I wondered how we could ever get past all those strong brown hairy legs to the corridor.

But there in the doorway, almost before the train started again, stood the little waiter. His face was impassive, but his eyes twinkled and yet were motherly.

"*Pardon, pardon*," he murmured. "*Entschuldigen Sie, bitte . . . bitte . . .*"

And before we knew it the German tourists were standing, trying to squeeze themselves small, and the boy was whisking us expertly, nonchalantly, out of the compartment, down the rocking aisle, and into our familiar hard brown seats in the restaurant.

It was all the same. We looked about us with a kind of wonder.

The old waiter saw us from the end of the car. His face did not change, but he put down his glass of wine and came to our table. The boy started to say something to him in an Italian dialect . . . it was like Niçois . . . but the old man motioned him brusquely aside.

His face was still the most cynical I had ever seen, but his eyes were over-full of tears. They ran slowly down his cheeks for a few minutes, into the evil old wrinkles, and he did not wipe them away. He stood by the table, flicking his napkin and asking crankily if we had made a good trip and if we planned to stay long in Milano. We answered the same way . . . things about traveling and the weather.

We were not embarrassed, any more than he was, by his tears; like all ghosts, I suppose, we had grown used to seeing them in other people's eyes, and along with them we saw almost always a kind of gratitude, as if people were thanking us for coming back and for being so trustful together. We seemed to reassure them, in a mysterious way . . . that summer more than ever.

While the old man was standing there, talking with his own gruff eagerness about crops and storms, flicking the table, he had to step in behind my chair for a minute while three men walked quickly through the car.

Two were big, not in uniform but with black shirts under their hot mussy coats, and stubble on their faces. The man between them was thinner and younger, and although they went single file and close together, we saw that he was handcuffed to each of them.

Before that summer such a thing would have shocked us, so that our faces would be paler and our eyes wider, but now we only looked up at the old waiter. He nodded, and his own eyes got very hot and dried all the tears.

"Political prisoner," he said, flicking the table, and his face was no more bitter than usual. "Escaped. They are bringing him back to Italy."

Then the chef with the highest bonnet saw us, and beamed and raised his glass, and the others turned around from their leafy table and saluted us too, and the door slammed behind the three dark men.

We got through the tunnel, that time, without feeling our palms grow sticky. It was the only difference: the train was the same, the people were the same. We were past the pain and travail, that was all. We were inviolate.

We drank the rest of the Asti, and as people began to come in to lunch, we made the signal to the suddenly active boy that we would be back later.

Just then there were shouts and thuds, and the sound of shattering glass. A kind of silence fell all about us, in spite of the steady rattle of the train. The old waiter ran down the car, not bumping a single table, and the door at the end closed sharply behind him. People looked strangely at one another.

Gradually the air settled, as if the motors inside all the travellers had started to hum again, and the young waiter took orders for lunch. When he got to us he said without looking at us, in his bad French, "I suggest that M'sieu'-'dame attend a moment . . . the restaurant is not crowded today."

As a suggestion it had the icy command of a policeman or a guardian angel about it, and we sat meekly. There was no more champagne. It did not really bother us.

Finally the old man came hurriedly back into the car. His face was furious, and he clutched his shoulder. The travellers stared at him, still chewing. He stopped for a minute by our table. He was panting, and his voice was very low.

"He tried to jump through the window," he said, and we knew he was talking about the refugee. "The bastards! They tore my coat! My only coat! The dirty bastards . . . look at that!"

He flapped the ripped shoulder of his greasy old black jacket at us, and then went madly down to the galley, muttering and trembling.

We stood up to go, and the smooth almond-faced waiter hurried toward us, swaying with the downhill rush of the train under a big tray of hot vegetables. "I am bringing M'sieu'-'dame's order at once," he called.

We sat down obediently. We were being bullied, but it was because he was trying to protect us, and it was kind of him. He brought two glasses of a dark vermouth, and as he put them in front of us he said confiding, "A special bottle we carry for the chef . . . very appetizing. There is a little muss on the platform. It will be swept up when M'sieu'-'dame have finished. *Santé!*"

As we lifted our glasses, willy-nilly, he cleared his throat, and then said in English, "Cheerio!" He smiled at us encouragingly, like an over-attentive nurse, and went back to serving the other people.

The vermouth was bitterer than any we had ever tasted, almost like a Swiss gentian-drink, but it tasted good after the insipid wine.

When we went through to our compartment, there was indeed a neat pile of broken glass on the platform between the cars, and the window of the door that opened when the train stopped was only half filled: the top part of the pane was gone, and the edge of the rest curved like ice in a smooth fine line, almost invisible.

The Strength-through Joyers leaped politely to attention when we got back to our compartment, and subsided in a series of small waves of questions in English . . . did smoke bother me, did we mind the door open, did we feel a draft. . . .

I forget the name of the town now where the train stops and the passport men come on. Is it Domodossola? How strange, not to know! It is as if I have deliberately wiped from my mind a great many names. Some of them I thought would stay there forever, whether I wanted them or not, like old telephone numbers that suddenly come between you and the sound of a new love's voice. I never thought to disremember this town, that man, such and such a river. Was it Domodossola?

That day we were there a long time. There seemed more policemen than usual, but it was always that way in Italy. We got the questions of visas and money straightened out; that used to upset me, and I'd feel like a blushing diamond-smuggler when the hard-eyed customs man would look at me. This time it was easy, unimportant.

I kept thinking it would be a good idea to walk back to the restaurant car while the train was quiet, but Chexbres said no, we should wait for the boy to call us.

Finally we started, very slowly. We went past a lot of roadwork. Men were building beds for new tracks with great blocks of gray stone, and the Germans looked at them with a grudging fascination, leaning over us to see better and exclaiming softly.

We were glad when the young waiter came to the door. "Your table is ready, M'sieu'-'dame," he announced loftily, and the men stood up hastily to let us out.

When we got to the end of the car, the boy turned back. "Take care, please," he said to Chexbres. "There is a little humidity on the platform."

And the place was wet, right enough. The curved piece of glass was still in the window, but it and the walls and the floor were literally dripping with water. We went carefully through it, and into the almost empty restaurant.

The chef rested at the end, reading a paper, but got up and

went back to the galley as we came in. Our table was nicely laid, with fresh linen, and there were two or three little square dishes of pickled onions and salami and butter. We felt very hungry, and quite gay.

The boy brought us some good wine, a fairly expensive red Chianti we always drank on that train, and we began to eat bread and salami with it. I remember there were some of those big white beans, the kind Italians peel and eat with salt when they are fresh and tender in the early summer. They tasted delicious, so fresh and cold. . . .

It was good to be eating and drinking there on that train, free forever from the trouble of life, surrounded with a kind of insulation of love. . . .

The old waiter came through the car. He was going to pass our table without looking at us. Chexbres spoke to him. "Stop a minute," he said. "Your coat . . . how is it?"

The man turned without answering, so that we could see the neat stitches that held his sleeve in place. I said something banal about the sewing . . . how good it was . . . and Chexbres asked quietly, "The man . . . the prisoner . . . did he get away?"

The old man suddenly looked at us, and his eyes were hateful, as if he loathed us. He said something foul, and then spat, "It's none of my business!" He hurried away, and we could not turn to watch him.

It was so shocking that we sat without any movement for quite a time. I could feel my heart beat heavily, and my throat was as if an iron collar hung around it, the way it used to be when Chexbres was first ill. Finally I looked at the few people still eating, and it seemed to me as if they met my eyes with a kind of hatred too, not as awful as the old man's but still crouching there. There was fear in it, and fear all around me.

Chexbres' face was full of pain. It was the first time it had come through for weeks, the first time since we started to drift like two happy ghosts along the old current of our lives together. The iron collar tightened, to see it there. I tried to drink some wine, but I couldn't swallow more than once.

The young waiter hurried past us without looking, and Chexbres stopped him firmly. "Please," he said. "What is wrong? What has happened?"

The boy looked impassively at us, and for a minute I thought he was going to be rude. Then he whispered, still protecting us, "Eat, M'sieu'-'dame. I will tell you in a minute." And he hurried off to the galley, bending supplely under the last great tray of emptied plates.

"Yes, you'd better eat something," Chexbres said coldly to me. "You've drunk rather a lot, you know." He picked up his fork, and I did too. The spaghetti was like ashes, because I felt myself coming to life again, and knew he did.

When we were the only ones left in the car, the boy came back. He stood leaning against the table across the aisle, still swaying with the motion of the train but now as if he were terribly tired, and talked to us so softly that we could hardly hear him. There was no friendliness in his voice, but not any hatred.

He said that when the train stopped at Domodossola, or wherever the border was, the political prisoner was being taken off, and suddenly he laughed and pressed his throat down on the edge of broken windowpane. The old waiter saw it.

"That was probably the plan in the first place," the boy said. "The poor bastard was chained to the cops. There was no escaping. It was a good job," he said. "The border police helped clean up the platform. That was why the train stopped so long.

"We're making up time now all right," the boy said, looking admiringly at the rocky valleys flash past us. "The old man keeps fussing about his coat. He's nuts anyway."

By the time we got to Milano everything was almost all right again, but for a few minutes the shell cracked. The world seeped in. We were not two ghosts, safe in our own immunity from the pain of living. Chexbres was a man with one leg gone, the other and the two arms soon to go . . . a small wracked man with snowy hair and eyes large with suffering. And I was a woman condemned, plucked at by demons, watching her true love die too slowly.

There in the train, hurrying across the ripe fields, feeling the tranced waiting of the people everywhere, we knew for a few minutes that we had not escaped. We knew no knife of glass, no distillate of hatred, could keep the pain of war outside.

I felt illimitably old, there in the train, knowing that escape was not peace, ever.

EUDORA WELTY

The Little Store

Two blocks away from the Mississippi State Capitol, and on the same street with it, where our house was when I was a child growing up in Jackson, it was possible to have a little pasture behind your backyard where you could keep a Jersey cow, which we did. My mother herself milked her. A thrifty homemaker, wife, mother of three, she also did all her own cooking. And as far as I can recall, she never set foot inside a grocery store. It wasn't necessary.

For her regular needs, she stood at the telephone in our front hall and consulted with Mr. Lemly, of Lemly's Market and Grocery downtown, who took her order and sent it out on his next delivery. And since Jackson at the heart of it was still within very near reach of the open country, the blackberry lady clanged on her bucket with a quart measure at your front door in June without fail, the watermelon man rolled up to your house exactly on time for the Fourth of July, and down through the summer, the quiet of the early-morning streets was pierced by the calls of farmers driving in with their plenty. One brought his with a song, so plaintive we would sing it with him:

> Milk, milk,
> Buttermilk,
> Snap beans—butterbeans—
> Tender okra—fresh greens . . .
> And buttermilk.

My mother considered herself pretty well prepared in her kitchen and pantry for any emergency that, in her words, might choose to present itself. But if she should, all of a sudden, need another lemon or find she was out of bread, all she had to do was call out, "Quick! Who'd like to run to the Little Store for me?"

I would.

She'd count out the change into my hand, and I was away. I'll bet the nickel that would be left over that all over the country, for those of my day, the neighborhood grocery played a similar part in our growing up.

Our store had its name — it was that of the grocer who owned it, whom I'll call Mr. Sessions — but "the Little Store" is what we called it at home. It was a block down our street toward the capitol and a half a block further, around the corner, toward the cemetery. I knew even the sidewalk to it as well as I knew my own skin. I'd skipped my jumping-rope up and down it, hopped its length through mazes of hopscotch, played jacks in its islands of shade, serpentined along it on my Princess bicycle, skated it backward and forward. In the twilight I had dragged my steamboat by its string (this was homemade out of every new shoebox, with candle in the bottom lighted and shining through colored tissue paper pasted over windows scissored out in the shapes of the sun, moon, and stars) across every crack of the walk without letting it bump or catch fire. I'd "played out" on that street after supper with my brothers and friends as long as "first-dark" lasted; I'd caught its lightning bugs. On the first Armistice Day (and this will set the time I'm speaking of) we made our own parade down that walk on a single velocipede — my brother pedaling, our little brother riding the handlebars, and myself standing on the back, all with arms wide, flying flags in each hand. (My father snapped that picture as we raced by. It came out blurred.)

As I set forth for the Little Store, a tune would float toward me from the house where there lived three sisters, girls in their teens, who ratted their hair over their ears, wore headbands like gladiators, and were considered to be very popular. They practiced for this in the daytime; they'd wind up the Victrola, leave the same record on they'd played before, and you'd see them bobbing past their dining-room windows while they danced with each other. Being three, they could go all day, cutting in:

> Everybody ought to know-oh
> How to do the Tickle-Toe
> (how to do the Tickle-Toe)—

they sang it and danced to it, and as I went by to the same song, I believed it.

A little further on, across the street, was the house where the principal of our grade school lived—lived on, even while we were having vacation. What if she would come out? She would halt me in my tracks—she had a very carrying and well-known voice in Jackson, where she'd taught almost everybody—saying "Eudora Alice Welty, spell OBLIGE." OBLIGE was the word that she of course knew had kept me from making 100 on my spelling exam. She'd make me miss it again now, by boring her eyes through me from across the street. This was my vacation fantasy, one good way to scare myself on the way to the store.

Down near the corner waited the house of a little boy named Lindsey. The sidewalk here was old brick, which the roots of a giant chinaberry tree had humped up and tilted this way and that. On skates, you took it fast, in a series of skittering hops, trying not to touch ground anywhere. If the chinaberries had fallen and rolled in the cracks, it was like skating through a whole shooting match of marbles. I crossed my fingers that Lindsey wouldn't be looking.

During the big flu epidemic he and I, as it happened, were being nursed through our sieges at the same time. I'd hear my father and mother murmuring to each other, at the end of a long day, "And I wonder how poor little *Lindsey* got along today?" Just as, down the street, he no doubt would have to hear his family saying, "And I wonder how is poor *Eudora* by now?" I got the idea that a choice was going to be made soon between poor little Lindsey and poor Eudora, and I came up with a funny poem. I wasn't prepared for it when my father told me it wasn't funny and my mother cried that if I couldn't be ashamed for myself, she'd have to be ashamed for me:

> There was a little boy and his name was Lindsey.
> He went to heaven with the influinzy.

He didn't, he survived it, poem and all, the same as I did. But his chinaberries could have brought me down in my skates in a flying act of contrition before his eyes, looking pretty funny myself, right in front of his house.

Setting out in this world, a child feels so indelible. He only comes to find out later that it's all the others along his way who are making themselves indelible to him.

Our Little Store rose right up from the sidewalk; standing in a street of family houses, it alone hadn't any yard in front, any tree or flowerbed. It was a plain frame building covered over with brick. Above the door, a little railed porch ran across on an upstairs level and four windows with shades were looking out. But I didn't catch on to those.

Running in out of the sun, you met what seemed total obscurity inside. There were almost tangible smells—licorice recently sucked in a child's cheek, dill-pickle brine that had leaked through a paper sack in a fresh trail across the wooden floor, ammonia-loaded ice that had been hoisted from wet croker sacks and slammed into the icebox with its sweet butter at the door, and perhaps the smell of still-untrapped mice.

Then through the motes of cracker dust, cornmeal dust, the Gold Dust of the Gold Dust Twins that the floor had been swept out with, the realities emerged. Shelves climbed to high reach all the way around, set out with not too much of any one thing but a lot of things—lard, molasses, vinegar, starch, matches, kerosene, Octagon soap (about a year's worth of octagon-shaped coupons cut out and saved brought a signet ring addressed to you in the mail. Furthermore, when the postman arrived at your door, he blew a whistle). It was up to you to remember what you came for, while your eye traveled from cans of sardines to ice cream salt to harmonicas to flypaper (over your head, batting around on a thread beneath the blades of the ceiling fan, stuck with its testimonial catch).

Its confusion may have been in the eye of its beholder. Enchantment is cast upon you by all those things you weren't supposed to have need for, it lures you close to wooden tops you'd outgrown, boy's marbles and agates in little net pouches, small rubber balls that wouldn't bounce straight, frazzly kite-string, clay bubble-pipes that would snap off in your teeth, the stiffest scissors. You could contemplate those long narrow boxes of sparklers gathering dust while you waited for it to be the Fourth of July or Christmas, and noisemakers in the shape of tin frogs for somebody's birthday party you hadn't been invited to yet, and see that they were all marvelous.

You might not have even looked for Mr. Sessions when he came around his store cheese (as big as a doll's house) and in front of the counter looking for you. When you'd finally asked him for, and received from him in its paper bag, whatever single thing it was that you had been sent for, the nickel that was left over was yours to spend.

Down at a child's eye level, inside those glass jars with mouths in their sides through which the grocer could run his scoop or a child's hand might be invited to reach for a choice, were wine-balls, all-day suckers, gumdrops, peppermints. Making a row under the glass of a counter were the Tootsie Rolls, Hershey Bars, Goo-Goo Clusters, Baby Ruths. And whatever was the name of those pastilles that came stacked in a cardboard cylinder with a cardboard lid? They were thin and dry, about the size of tiddly-winks, and in the shape of twisted rosettes. A kind of chocolate dust came out with them when you shook them out in your hand. Were they chocolate? I'd say rather they were brown. They didn't taste of anything at all, unless it was wood. Their attraction was the number you got for a nickel.

Making up your mind, you circled the store around and around, around the pickle barrel, around the tower of Cracker Jack boxes; Mr. Sessions had built it for us himself on top of a packing case, like a house of cards.

If it seemed too hot for Cracker Jacks, I might get a cold drink. Mr. Sessions might have already stationed himself by the cold-drinks barrel, like a mind reader. Deep in ice water that looked black as ink, murky shapes that would come up as Coca-Colas, Orange Crushes, and various flavors of pop were all swimming around together. When you gave the word, Mr. Sessions plunged his bare arm in to the elbow and fished out your choice, first try. I favored a locally bottled concoction called Lake's Celery. (What else could it be called? It was made by a Mr. Lake out of celery. It was a popular drink here for years but was not known universally, as I found out when I arrived in New York and ordered one in the Astor bar.) You drank on the premises, with feet set wide apart to miss the drip, and gave him back his bottle.

But he didn't hurry you off. A standing scales was by the door, with a stack of iron weights and a brass slide on the balance arm, that would weigh you up to three hundred pounds. Mr. Sessions, whose hands were gentle and smelled of carbolic, would lift you up and set your feet on the platform, hold your loaf of bread for you, and taking his time while you stood still for him, he would make certain of what you weighed today. He could even remember what you weighed last time, so you could subtract and announce how much you'd gained. That was goodbye.

Is there always a hard way to go home? From the Little Store, you could go partway through the sewer. If your brothers had called you a scarecat, then across the next street beyond the Little Store, it was possible to enter this sewer by passing through a private hedge, climbing down into the bed of a creek, and going into its mouth on your knees. The sewer—it might have been no more than a "storm sewer"—came out and emptied here, where Town Creek, a sandy, most often shallow little stream that ambled through Jackson on its way to the Pearl River, ran along the edge of the cemetery. You could go in darkness through this tunnel to where you next saw light (if you ever did) and climb out through the culvert at your own street corner.

I was a scarecat, all right, but I was a reader with my own refuge in storybooks. Making my way under the sidewalk, under the street and the street-car track, under the Little Store, down there in the wet dark by myself, I could be Persephone entering into my six-month sojourn underground—though I didn't suppose Persephone had to crawl, hanging onto a loaf of bread, and come out through the teeth of an iron grating. Mother Ceres would indeed be wondering where she could find me, and mad when she knew. "Now am I going to have to start marching to the Little Store for *myself*?"

I couldn't picture it. Indeed I'm unable today to picture the Little Store with a grown person in it, except for Mr. Sessions and the lady who helped him, who belonged there. We children thought it was ours. The happiness of errands was in part that of running for the moment away from home, a free spirit. I believed the Little Store to be a center of the outside world, and hence of happiness—as I believed what I found in the Cracker Jack box to be a genuine prize, which was as simply as I believed in the Golden Fleece.

But a day came when I ran to the store to discover, sitting on the front step, a grown person, after all—more than a grown person. It was the Monkey Man, together with his monkey. His grinding-organ was lowered to the step beside him. In my whole life so far, I must have laid eyes on the Monkey Man no more than five or six times. An itinerant of rare and wayward appearances, he was not punctual like the Gipsies, who every year with the first cool days of fall showed up in the aisles of Woolworth's. You never knew when the Monkey Man might decide to favor Jackson, or which way he'd go. Sometimes you heard him as close as the next street, and then he didn't come up yours.

But now I saw the Monkey Man at the Little Store, where I'd never seen him before. I'd never seen him sitting down. Low on that familiar doorstep, he was not the same any longer, and neither was his monkey. They looked just like an old man and an old friend of his that wore a fez, meeting quietly together, tired, and resting with their eyes fixed on some place far away, and not the same place. Yet their romance for me didn't have it in its power to waver. I wavered. I simply didn't know how to step around them, to proceed on into the Little Store for my mother's emergency as if nothing had happened. If I could have gone in there after it, whatever it was, I would have given it to them— putting it into the monkey's cool little fingers. I would have given them the Little Store itself.

In my memory they are still attached to the store—so are all the others. Everyone I saw on my way seemed to me then part of my errand, and in a way they were. As I myself, the free spirit, was part of it too.

All the years we lived in that house where we children were born, the same people lived in the other houses on our street too. People changed through the arithmetic of birth, marriage, and death, but not by going away. So families just accrued stories, which through the fullness of time, in those times, their own lives made. And I grew up in those.

But I didn't know there'd ever been a story at the Little Store, one that was going on while I was there. Of course, all the time the Sessions family had been living right overhead there, in the upstairs rooms behind the little railed porch and the shaded windows; but I think we children never thought of that. Did I fail to see them as a family because they weren't living in an ordinary house? Because I so seldom saw them close together, or having anything to say to each other? She sat in the back of the store, her pencil over a ledger, while he stood and waited on children to make up their minds. They worked in twin black eyeshades, held on their gray heads by elastic bands. It may be harder to recognize kindness—or unkindness either—in a face whose eyes are in shadow. His face underneath his shade was as round as the little wooden wheels in the Tinker Toy box. So was her face. I didn't know, perhaps didn't even wonder: were they husband and wife or brother and sister? Were they father and mother? There were a few other persons, of various ages, wandering singly in by the back door and out. But none of their relationships could I imagine, when I'd never seen them sitting down together around their own table.

The possibility that they had any other life at all, anything beyond what we could see within the four walls of the Little Store, occurred to me only when tragedy struck their family. There was some act of violence. The shock to the neighborhood traveled to the children, of course; but I couldn't find out from my parents what had happened. They held it back from me, as they'd already held back many things, "until the time comes for you to know."

You could find out some of these things by looking in the unabridged dictionary and the encyclopedia—kept to hand in our dining room—but you couldn't find out there what had happened to the family who for all the years of your life had lived upstairs over the Little Store, who had never been anything but patient and kind to you, who never once had sent you away. All I ever knew was its aftermath: they were the only people ever known to me who simply vanished. At the point where their life overlapped into ours, the story broke off.

We weren't being sent to the neighborhood grocery for facts of life, or death. But of course those are what we were on the track of, anyway. With the loaf of bread and the Cracker Jack prize, I was bringing home the intimations of pride and disgrace, and rumors and early news of people coming to hurt one another, while others practiced for joy—storing up a portion for myself of the human mystery.

BARBARA TUCHMAN

AN AUTHOR'S MAIL

Persons who address letters to the editor of a newspaper or other journal are usually angry at something that has appeared there and write to express their outrage or dissent, whereas those who write to the author of a book or article generally want to tell the writer of their enjoyment and approval. This is a happy difference, for it is gratifying how often the written word generates a strong emotion in the reader and moves him to express his or her satisfaction, or the reverse, to the unknown and unseen individual behind the pen. Although authors too receive their portion of hate mail, the receipt of letters is encouraging evidence that what they have written has reached into a reader's mind and caused it to take notice and consider the matter at hand or simply enjoy the unfolding of a tale—in short, evidence that the writer's business is performing its function and the product is not left to wither in sterility on a dead page.

Readers' letters can also serve as the visits of distant friends, as in the case of the melancholy ailing refugee, Alexander Lenard, translator of the much admired and wildly successful Latin version of Milne's *Winnie the Pooh:* "I gauge the amount of success by the names of the faraway friends who occasionally visit me with their letters," he wrote to a colleague, "and who saved me a dangerous journey into the outside world I prefer to know in their descriptions."

I, too, have rediscovered through my mail old friends lost along the path of years. A letter I received some time ago opened by reminding me, "We have had no communication for fifty years," which was putting it delicately, for in fact I had not laid eyes on the writer for those fifty years, not since a football game in the Yale Bowl round about 1934, and I was happy to meet him again, if only by mail.

The quality that I have found surprising is the feeling of affection and gratitude, almost, if I dare say so, of love that approving readers seem to feel for the author of a book they have enjoyed. One letter concluded simply with the salutation, "I love you," and another with, "love and gratitude for your essay," and a third with, "May God Bless you." Sometimes it happens in person. On the street the other day, in New York, I turned around at a voice speaking my name and saw a gentleman I did not recognize (doubtless because of my meager memory for names and faces) who told me that during a bout of insomnia last night he had read straight through *Bible and Sword* (my first book) and it had filled the night for him, and that his eighty-six-year-old bedridden father was enjoying himself reading steadily through *A Distant Mirror.* "I must give you a hug," he said, and did so on Vanderbilt Avenue. This affection that pleasure in a book can elicit is odd, but it makes an author feel happy that his book can evoke it.

Readers' own gems are another dividend of their letters. A line that appears in a reader's letter, which I wish I had written myself, is, "the shadow of nuclear war hangs over *The March of Folly* like a ghost from the future." Another good line came from, of all people, the very reactionary William Loeb, publisher of the New Hampshire *Union Leader.* Commenting on the notable lack of leaders in our time, he said that this was due largely to the fact that while we have many brilliant specialists in their own fields, they have "very narrow minds and no common sense."

Because I am subject to fits of discarding collected papers and documents in order to thin out overstuffed files, I am hampered in composing this survey, for there are letters that I remember that I can no longer locate. Reading over those that remain, I find they fall into several distinct categories—most frequent, I am happy to say, are the Pleased who want to tell me of the pleasure that I have given them or that they have taken in some work of mine they have read.

An active category is that of the Cranks who have schemes for saving the world through brotherhood or some form of ecumenism of one kind or another. Here too are the more substantial promoters of causes for saving endangered species, whether it be snail darters or whales or baby seals or national parks and wilderness areas, or for gun control or birth control, or for ensuring or defeating so-and-so's campaign for political office. Alternatively they have schemes for combating the world's iniquities in the form of nuclear warfare, vivisection, acid rain and toxic wastes, beach buggies and snowmobiles. I may be, indeed am, in deep sympathy with most of these goals, but four- to six-page letters that are typewritten and single-spaced, when the message could be stated in a paragraph, simply waste an author's or anyone's time and are destined for the wastebasket.

To a third category belong the Unfortunates, writing from prison or from an asylum for the insane, who insist they have been wrongfully committed or framed in some way as the object of persecution by some powerful hostile figure in the community. The author is asked to right the wrong by making the truth known to the authorities.

Prisoners are not generally protesting their incarceration so much as wanting communication and correspondence with the outside world, or else they want your letter of recommendation to the court or parole board for easing of sentence. As they are often very articulate persons with a record of studious accomplishment in prison, one would like to respond, were it not for husbands and lawyers and people like that who sternly warn against getting involved with prisoners, pointing out, reasonably enough, that one does not know what crime they have been committed for, and that correspondence will only draw one into all kinds of trouble. As I was brought up in a world that assumed that husbands and lawyers knew better than I about the wicked ways of the real world, I bow to their rule—except for once or twice when I have replied to prisoners' letters with quite harmless results.

The letters from Unfortunates reflect, I think, a belief that authors of books must be persons of status who can pull wires and exercise influence. One person with that belief did not write but telephoned to tell me a long story about her house and property that had been bequeathed by her deceased husband to their son, but was now, through some wicked machinations, being stolen from him by the executors of her husband's will. I don't know what she expected me—a writer of past history—to do about it or why she called me, and I would have hung up except that I could tell from her voice that she was very, very old and seemingly at the edge of her last effort. The tale, growing steadily more complex, went on and on until in futility I backed away and turned the phone over to my husband, a physician with long experience of wills and executors and practice in calming old ladies. The problem is, what is an author to do when invested in readers' fantasies with influence that she cannot exercise much less possess?

Others of the Unfortunates are victims of special circumstances, like the wife of a Vietnam veteran whose letter I found particularly heart-rending. She wrote that her husband, age thirty-five, was a combat veteran of Vietnam, now "suffering stress" in a VA hospital. "He feels guilt for having killed and for being alive while his buddies are dead. He volunteered for Vietnam out of a sense of patriotism and now has confused feelings. . . ." She had read a newspaper article quoting me as saying (in *The March of Folly*) that "America had lost its virtue" in Vietnam. "How are a Vietnam veteran and his family supposed to feel?" she continued. "Is society and history saying that the veteran himself was immoral or lost his virtue or is responsible for America losing its virtue? . . . My husband feels that in the eyes of the world he's a killer and a loser. Have you any words to put into a positive historical perspective for him to help him get on with his life? He is a great reader of history and has read most of your books (I give them to him for his birthdays)."

Feeling that I was under real obligation to this reader to put whatever I know to use, I took a great deal of thought in composing a reply that would be reassuring to the troubled veteran without excusing the war. I wrote to her that her husband could take satisfaction in having fulfilled his citizen's duty to act, as he had been told, in defense of his country and that at eighteen, as he must have been at the time, he was neither informed nor sophisticated enough to recognize the call as false; that he was caught in the old and insoluble dilemma of the private citizen who is ordered by higher authority or by a commanding officer to do wrong and that as he was in no position to solve a problem that has baffled philosophers and judges through the ages, he need feel no guilt; and finally that for the sake of herself—his wife—and future children, as well as himself, he should feel thankful, not guilty, to be alive. I am afraid I must have given no comfort and failed to hit the right note for I received no acknowledgment.

The sense that authors have powers to put things right need not come from people who have read one's books, but more likely from those who have seen one's name in the papers on the occasion of a speech or award or some public appearance. Indeed there is a class of people who are not readers at all but want only to identify with the author through some personal connection. The epitome of these was the driver of a telephone company repair truck, or maybe it was United Parcel—at any rate, someone who knew our house and neighborhood—who meeting me on the driveway stopped to say, "Oh! Mrs. Tuchman, I am one of your greatest fans." When I voiced the usual thanks for his kind words, he said quite honestly, "Of course, I haven't read any of your books, but I'm a fan." Though it was silly, I was touched by his declaration. It illustrates a curiosity of American life—that the mere condition of being a fan, fanship as one might call it, confers an identity in itself that is apparently craved by many people. It need not have any basis in real appreciation; simply declaring oneself a fan attaches one to a named personality and satisfies the search for a relationship. What is encouraging is that it now evidently reaches for its objects beyond sports figures and rock singers into the book world, even unto authors.

A persistent fan or identifier is a doctor in Texas who once invited me to speak to his club or organization for a Christian endeavor of some kind. I declined. Since then he sends me road maps of his region and periodically telephones long-distance to tell me I must positively take Geritol. I cannot say why he assumes I am anemic, unless that is his explanation for anyone who declines to come to Texas.

A single letter that I cannot place in any category, because—

fortunately — it had no fellows, was an anonymous envelope containing the cut-off cuff of a woman's coat of smooth flat fur with no message or letter attached. It was like receiving Van Gogh's ear and gave me a horrid feeling, as I suppose it was intended to, of some hidden animosity carrying a warning of more to come. We even consulted the police without of course their expressing any interest. I had no idea who sent it, although I had a vague suspicion impossible to verify, but that was the end of it. Nothing more followed.

To come unexpectedly on someone in the act of reading one's book, while it is outside the scope of letters, has the same effect as a letter. Once, coming to the window of a ski-lift ticket booth, I found the girl inside sitting hunched over reading *A Distant Mirror*. Since the staff at ski resorts is generally made up of college students, the ticket seller's readership was not particularly significant; still it was nice to find that rather ponderous book being actually read in a cold cabin on the slopes of Aspen. Less encouraging was the occasion in a bookstore when I saw a customer pick up a copy of *The Zimmerman Telegram* and start to read it. Ah, I thought, I shall actually see someone in the act of buying one of my books. The man read on and on, and just when I decided I couldn't wait any longer, he put the book back on the shelf, regretfully, I like to think, and moved away without buying.

Of unexpected readers, a recent experience occurred when I left a briefcase in a taxi. Told by the Taxi Commission to report place, time, and relevant details to the local precinct police station, I phoned, and on giving my name and address, the police officer said, "Are you the lady who writes those books?" On my admitting the fact, he said, "Those are great books. My Sergeant thinks so too." This time it was I who could have hugged him if we had not been separated by AT&T. Though not a letter, his verbal remark meant I had found readers who would not ordinarily read works of history at all. It was equal in satisfaction to half a dozen D. Litt.'s honoris causa, which is not to say that I do not appreciate those too, but "My Sergeant thinks so too" was something special.

Macaulay tells with relish how when he read his *History of*

England aloud to a club of workingmen, many of them wept at his most affecting scenes. I too felt I had reached through to a new audience. Chance remarks such as the police officer's, like letters, give authors the same sense that I suppose actors receive from contact with a live audience.

A sub-category of identifiers are illicit wooers who propose assignations. For some obscure reason these began to appear after the publication of *Stilwell and the American Experience in China, 1911–1945,* my book on General Stilwell. One such letter that I remember came from a man totally unknown to me, who named a particular cabin in the woods he knew of where we could meet for a romantic escapade. This type can hardly be called a category since there were only two or three of them, and I suspect they all came from the same person. I cannot give you any juicy quotes because their letters have vanished from my files, no doubt discreetly discarded to keep them from the prying eyes of some future doctoral candidate whose idea of literary criticism or biography is to turn up a scandal in the life of his subject. I have done my best to foil these voyeurs by throwing away all bundles of old correspondence that they might construe into love affairs, as is the style today. Not that my life has been crawling with misconduct, amorous or otherwise, but neither is it an open book. For all nosy investigators I would like to leave it a blank, apart from my published work, which is, after all, what counts.

A category of letters peculiar to historians is the "I was there" correspondent who writes to tell of his own experience on the scene of the author's book, in my case World War I or CBI (the China-Burma-India theater in World War II). Often these contain anecdotes and eyewitness scenes that I wish I had known when I wrote. Veterans of combat, English and American and a few French, write to tell what their fathers or uncles did in the war. One French officer sent me a medal the Germans had minted a trifle prematurely in 1914 to commemorate their expected entry into Paris. He had picked it up in the mud after the battle of the Marne and asked me to keep it as a token of his regard for *The Guns of August* and to leave it to his granddaughter on my death. When she came to see me on a visit to America some years ago, I was happy to be able to complete the transfer as the veteran of the Marne had wished. In England, survivors of the Old Contemptibles, who proudly maintained the name the Kaiser had scornfully applied, also a little prematurely, to the first contingent of the BEF (British Expeditionary Force) to land in France, wrote to me to make me an honorary member. Not so, a group of Merrill's Marauders, veterans of CBI, who threatened to sue for defamation because I had described them, for all their indomitable campaign in Burma, through mud, monsoon, and dysentery to the capture of Myitkyina, in harsh terms that I suppose I should not repeat here lest I be threatened with suit again. Since the words had been taken with accompanying quotation marks from a book by a doctor with Stilwell's troops that had been published by the U.S. Surgeon General's office, it was presumably authoritative. I thought the Marauders might have sued him, not me, but I gather the law works oddly in these matters: spreading rather than originating the objectionable phrase appears to be the offense. I never understood this, especially as the description was taken from an official source, but, as with other male-designed procedures that don't make sense, one should not seek logic.

The threat to sue faded because one of the Marauders turned out to be in civilian life a friend and hospital colleague of my husband and pleaded with him to persuade me to remove the offending phrases from the paperback edition. Though I do not like to surrender to pressure, I agreed because it was not essential to the story and I did not want a swarm of wrathful ex-Marauders circling around me like bees. The paperback, if it is yet to be published, is a convenient exit because one can always promise to remove the offense or revise it, which gives the opponent, who probably does not want to go to law anyway, a way out.

Of all my books, the Stilwell biography brought the most correspondence because so many of the participants of CBI were still alive and their letters tended to be lively and informative. One who, like the Marauders, felt maligned was General B., since deceased, a commander whom Stilwell considered incompetent and removed from his staff, recording pitilessly in his diary, "I sent B. to the showers today." I quoted this in my text because the incident fitted into the narrative and was so much Stilwell's style. This too raised a storm. After the war, B.'s incompetence carried him, in obedience to Parkinson's Law, straight up the Washington ladder to an important government post, whence emanated waves of agitation against my book. General B. eventually subsided, leaving a trail of denunciation of me in Far East studies, but he was smart enough, competent or not, to stop short of litigation.

Another category of letter writers is made up of those who feel they have been helped in some way by what they have read. Mostly these responses came from a reading of my essays, collected in *Practicing History*, which described to some extent my own reasons for, and methods of, writing. For a number of would-be authors, who had not known how to begin, these essays seem to unloose the impulse to get started that hitherto had been paralyzed. "It shook me up and brought me back to my senses," wrote a correspondent. "I needed that piece of writing and I keep re-reading parts of it." Another wrote that she had been so deeply embedded in writer's block as to be entirely static and unable to put a word on paper, but that the pieces in *Practicing History* had somehow started her going, and she felt that I had, through that book, "changed her life."

In the "I was there" category, everyone still alive who was caught in Europe in the summer of 1914 when war broke out, from schoolgirls traveling with their mothers to miscellaneous tourists and officials on business, must have written to tell me of his or her adventures. One party, recalled in a six-page, single-spaced typed letter, consisted of two sisters, aged nine and fifteen, who, with their mother, together with her maid and a pet fox terrier, were on their way to Baden-Baden in mid-July where the mother could go through her cure before the opening of the social season. They had with them a variety of trunks — one for hats, one for shoes, others for garments and such fashionable adornments as ostrich feather fans. On July 13, 1914, the last day of peace as it was to prove, they were picnicking on a hilltop in the Black Forest when "to our surprise we saw more than a dozen Zeppelins pass overhead across the sky." Supposing some special fiesta or military review must be the occasion, they found, down in the town, all kinds of parades, of soldiers, policemen, and firemen marching with brass bands, and much excitement in the streets. Back at the hotel they were told that all Americans and other foreigners had left the day before and they must try to leave by train at once. The subsequent adventures, with all train schedules disrupted because of mobilization, included departure on foot, without their trunks which they never saw again, and a ride in a peasant's hay wagon to a village from where a trolley took them to Lunéville. When the mother, given discouraging answers about the possibility of a train for Paris, asked what would happen "if we are unable to leave here," she was told with a bow and a French flourish, "Ah Madame, then you will have a front row box to view the war tomorrow!" The letter, written to me by the elder of the two sisters, continues with a vivid account of their exodus, full of real-life details that only an eyewitness could tell. At the railroad station they saw flatcars, loaded with the siege guns I described in my book, headed for Belgium; in Paris no one had any information, crowds besieging the American embassy blocked entry, the American Express was closed, food and cash were low, people overflowed the cafés and streets trying to pick up rumors, while through all the discomforts and troubles, "my mother remained without a spot on her clean suede gloves, not a wrinkle on her pale grey summer suit, not a hair deranged under her feathered toque hat. 'My children are gypsies!' she complained because we showed the wear and tear of sitting up all night in the train or sleeping stretched out on the floor of the corridor."

A built-in defect of these letters is that they only arrive after one's book has been written and published, so that they cannot be used for primary material as can a personal memoir or an oral interview or letters found in archives. This is awkward, especially when they correct one's published account, or fill in facts of critical importance I had not known. One of these came from a naval officer, now a captain, who had witnessed the sinking by the Japanese, on a pretense of error, of the American gunboat *Panay* on Yangtze patrol off Nanking in 1937. He tells how huge U.S. flags, made especially for the purpose, had been spread horizontally on large awnings. On December 12, he states, "the sun is approaching its maximum annual declination (south) and Nanking's latitude is 32° (north) so the attacking planes could approach their unsuspecting target in an easy shallow dive of about 35° while keeping the midday sun constantly behind the plane as viewed from the *Panay*. This is exactly what the pilots did. The movie reel of the attack (taken by Norman Soong) clearly showed the *Panay*'s chief gunner's mate manning one of the gunboat's six 50-caliber mounted machine guns and trying to shield his eyes from the sun with an extended hand. Anyone intelligent enough to pilot a plane knew he was attacking the American flag," my correspondent commented. "There is no room for doubt about this." I love the precise detail and absolute assurance of this letter. It could have made an indisputable statement in my text for the future sillies who like to claim that Roosevelt somehow manipulated the poor innocent Japanese into the war.

On that same subject, another letter came from one of the operators of "Purple," the decoding machine that broke the Japanese code. The writer reproved me for stating that the American fault at Pearl Harbor had been a failure of communication. "The high command," he wrote, "had ordered Admiral Kimmel and General Short in Hawaii to put their commands on 'war alert' which was all they could be told without betraying the priceless source of the intelligence. It was up to these officers to obey and this they did not do. Kimmel and Short were simply derelict in their duty. This was not a failure of communication. So much nonsense had appeared about FDR trying to get us into the war, that I wanted to add my bit."

Equally expert in his specialty was a gentleman in England who, jointly with two fellow specialists in the history of woodworking tools, questioned my reference in *A Distant Mirror* to the brace and bit as a development of the late thirteenth century. "The evolution of brace and bit," he explained, "is one of the major problems of our little specialty, the earliest evidence being an altarpiece of 1424." Goodness! All unwittingly I had stumbled into a major problem of medieval technology. The writer himself was, as he put it, the record holder, having traced an illustration of a brace back to a French wine-merchant's seal of 1407. In the

Barbara Tuchman

most polite way he asked for my reference to the thirteenth century, which "if it turns out to be based on a misapprehension," he kindly added, "will not affect the general point you are making in the broad sweep of your excellent narrative." As this was remarkably gentle for an Englishman addressing an American woman writer, a twice disadvantaged condition, I was determined to satisfy him, but I felt uneasy about that brace and bit. I went up to Cambridge where my research notes and manuscript for the book were deposited in the Houghton Library at Harvard and hunted through the notes until I found, to my dismay, although not to my surprise, that the book which had been my source had not in fact dated the tool's first appearance. I had read so much about the technological advances of the late thirteenth century that in listing some of them I must have mentally included the brace and bit without checking, as sometimes happens. I confessed to the English gentleman the "misapprehension" that he had already surmised. Now, when too ready to assume a fact without checking, I think of the brace and bit and take extra care.

CBI veterans wrote me numerous letters, many carrying distinguished names. General James Gavin sent me an anecdote of the Burma frontier—how Stilwell "dropped by a remote little post and after inspection, when the garrison fell in to hear the expected Speech always made by visiting generals about our Noble Cause, our Noble Allies and what a privilege it was to risk prickly heat and dhobi's itch for Democracy, Stilwell didn't. He just grinned at his sweaty and disheveled troops and remarked, 'I'm sure glad I'm not stuck way out here in the jungle like you poor dumb bastards.' Before dark the men had put up a sign rechristening their post Dumbastapur—a name the local tribesmen adopted thereafter." Actually I don't know how I missed that story in writing the book because it was a well-known incident, but I think General Gavin was on duty somewhere when I was doing the research and I failed to see him for an oral interview.

The late Senator Kenneth Keating of New York, subsequently American Ambassador in New Delhi, wrote several times saying the book "made me nostalgic about the days I used to fly over the Hump and arrive to be greeted by the smiling pick-pocketing

Chinese." He paid me the best compliment, when apropos of what he called my "insight into the events of the CBI theater," he said, "It is as if you had been here in person. My contact with some of the holy men of India leads me to believe you were here somewhere hiding in the bushes. I wish I had known it!" he added gallantly. The letters from CBI veterans were on the whole, except of course for Merrill's Marauders, very appreciative in saying that I had got it right and told it as it was, which is what a historian most wants to hear. When one correspondent wrote that he had been comparing the book to his own memories of his service in CBI and found it accurate in each case, I felt I was doing my job.

One also likes appreciation of one's prose, or at least I do because the art of writing concerns me as much as the subject matter. It was a CBI veteran, too, who wrote to say the Stilwell book was "a masterpiece and beautifully written," in what he called "the good old American idiom." I am not quite sure what he had in mind, but I took it as meaning what, in fact, I always try for—that is, clear easy-reading prose that avoids the Latinized language of academics with their endless succession of polysyllables, their deaf ear for sentence structure, and unconcern for clarity. A former Marine who classed himself as an Old China Hand told me that he had read the Stilwell book "right through in 36 hours," which I take also to be a tribute to clarity of prose, as it is when people write to say they have been reading one of my books aloud to each other. They are "pure pleasure to read" wrote a husband who had been reading *The March of Folly* aloud to his wife, "because you write like an angel." I am embarrassed to quote this kind of thing, but approval is what makes readers want to write letters. If this survey has become too unbearably self-congratulatory, I hope you will forgive and understand that, like ketchup on hamburgers, it comes with the subject.

Hate mail, on the contrary, in my experience comes, as might be expected, from Jewish issues. A flood of hostility descended in response to a piece I wrote under the title "They Poisoned the Wells," published in *Newsweek* as one of their series called "My Turn." It told how the Black Death in the Middle Ages was blamed on Jews who were alleged to have poisoned the wells,

although, as the Pope of the day pointed out, they died like everyone else. The point I was making—that in confused and fearful
times when people want to fix blame, the Jews will be the target—seemed to anger many in the Gentile community. Why, I
don't know, because the idea is hardly new or original and threat-
ens no one. The several score of letters I received, however—
virtually all unsigned, for people who vent their prejudices have
evidently neither the courage nor the conviction to sign their
names—gave me quite an experience of being hated rather than
admired or loved.

Students belong to a category of people who want help. For
purposes of a term paper or report for the school newspaper, they
always want to know, as a high-school boy wrote, "How you got
to writing books like *The Guns of August* and *The Zimmerman
Telegram*. Before I get this answered, how did you get started
writing books period?" My replies are probably inadequate. I just
tell them I started to write because I wanted to write; that was
what I wanted to do. I am sure this does not satisfy, but I do not
like to pose as an example. My feeling is that people whose urge
to do something is strong enough to make it worth doing will go
ahead and do it without need of an example.

One can make allowance for students, but I find it irritating
when adults write to ask the source of some piece of information
that plainly appears in my reference notes or who want me to list
books for them to read in pursuit of a given subject. Why can't
they find out for themselves? Have they never heard of libraries?
And why do they never consult my own bibliography, which,
from what I can tell, they never do? Are most people so passive
they want everything done for them? If one does not enter into
the research process oneself, one learns nothing.

Judging by letters, I think the greatest interest I ever aroused
was not by a book but by an article, "The Decline of Quality,"
published in the *New York Times Magazine* in November 1980.
"It was a tonic," in the words of one reader, "to those of us discouraged about America." Another who wrote that it "touched a
sensitive nerve" must have been right, for the letters kept coming
in every day's mail with the most extravagant compliments. "It
had the quality of a Turner painting," according to one. Though

I adore Turner, if there is one thing my writing is not, it is Turn-eresque. If it is to have comparison to a painter, I would like to think it might be Stubbs or perhaps Chardin—factual, straight-forward, and clear, with passages of poetry to add charm. "You belong," another writer wrote, happily paraphrasing Cole Porter's song "You're the Top," "with Gothic cathedrals, Matisse and Seattle Slew." A less enraptured correspondent stated calmly that the article "was above the average." A Harvard professor scolded because I had written that technological marvels like microchips and the electronic wonders of the computer, no matter how high in quality, belonged to a different order of things than the cre-ative works of the humanities. "I stopped reading right there," he announced. I cannot blame him because, although humanities is what I meant, I had in fact written, "the creative works of civilized society." It was one of those awful situations when one cannot think of the right word and in frustration one substitutes something unsuitable, which is *not* writing like an angel. Appearing at the time of Reagan's first election to the presidency, "The Decline of Quality" caused a Californian to write, "On election night I was very depressed and went to bed early picking up the *Times* magazine section on the way—what a relief to read your article. It immediately helped me out of my depression." What more could a writer want? "Gadflies," this correspondent added, "are never popular but they influence history and lift the spirits of the discouraged."

As opposed to correctors of error are the soul-mates, so to speak, who experience that special delight of finding the author agreeing with what they already think. "It so fits my own thoughts," wrote a veteran of Vietnam about *The March of Folly*, "that I believe totally your account of the Vietnam war. I will now," he concluded bravely, "read the rest of the book."

Similar to soul-mates are the propagators, readers so enthused by what you have written that they want to spread your words abroad. A mother wrote about "The Decline of Quality" that she had copied out my definition of quality and intended to inscribe it "on the walls of her children's bedrooms" and more important, she said, "force it on the attention of their school teachers." Of the same article the lawyer who wrote that it had "struck a sensitive nerve" added that it "impelled us to circulate a photocopy of it to our entire legal and paralegal staff." An executive of the Revlon Company took the opportunity "to pass it along to members of the merchandising staff," while another executive extracted several sentences from the piece, which he was going to put in poster form to use in his office. An even more active propagator was a magazine publisher who actually sent, or said he had, twelve hundred copies of *The March of Folly* to what he called "high echelon business people throughout America." A similar enthusiast wrote of that book, "What a wonderful service you have rendered the nation. Your new book influences our affairs more than anything written since *Uncle Tom's Cabin.*" While generously exaggerated, that was almost as good as comparison to Seattle Slew.

An article I wrote since then on responsibility for the Marines' deaths in Lebanon caused a propagator to send it to President Reagan and a senator to insert it in the Congressional Record. Commenting on the Lebanon piece, a friendly fan in Seattle wrote just to wish me "a beautiful autumn in Connecticut." A more recent piece entitled "Are We Smart Enough for Our Technology" was published in the *Christian Science Monitor,* whose editor revised the title, as editors will with their special talent for taking the punch out of authors' titles, into the bland heading "Reflections on Today's Scene." It carried nevertheless enough meaning to a reader for her to advise that it should be "required reading for all politicians, government officials, clergymen, teachers, students and citizens old enough to vote." That is quite inclusive, but no more so than the audience suggested for *The March of Folly* by a reader who thought it should be read by "everyone in the world." Modestly, that was my own opinion for I have always thought the theme of this book to be more important than the critics, who jumped on it with both feet, understood. In fact *The March of Folly* illustrates an interesting phenomenon of publishing—the discrepancy that often appears between critics and readers. The critics, as it seemed, had their tomahawks out in advance, because, according to my publisher, "you have just had too much success, Barbara, and that's when they want to pull you down." Readers, I am happy to say, evidently follow their own inclination with little attention to critics. They read and liked and bought the book sufficiently to circulate it by word of mouth and keep it on the best-seller list for six months, which, considering the reviews, was not bad, though not comparable to *A Distant Mirror*, which, curiously enough for a book on a subject no one would expect to be widely popular, sold the most of all my books, puncturing the axiom that a book's fortunes depend on the *New York Times*. The *New York Times* as it happened was on strike when that book came out and never published any review, yet *A Distant Mirror* took off like a sex manual or like a diet-and-fitness volume by Jane Fonda. The point about books is that you never can tell and even astute publishers cannot predict. Readers know best, which is just as well because it is they, after all, for whom we write, and their letters are the test.

LEWIS THOMAS

Notes on Punctuation

There are no precise rules about punctuation (Fowler lays out some general advice (as best he can under the complex circumstances of English prose (he points out, for example, that we possess only four stops (the comma, the semicolon, the colon and the period (the question mark and exclamation point are not, strictly speaking, stops; they are indicators of tone (oddly enough, the Greeks employed the semicolon for their question mark (it produces a strange sensation to read a Greek sentence which is a straightforward question: Why weepest thou; (instead of Why weepest thou? (and, of course, there are parentheses (which are surely a kind of punctuation making this whole matter much more complicated by having to count up the left-handed parentheses in order to be sure of closing with the right number (but if the parentheses were left out, with nothing to work with but the stops, we would have considerably more flexibility in the deploying of layers of meaning than if we tried to separate all the clauses by physical barriers (and in the latter case, while we might have more precision and exactitude for our meaning, we would lose the essential flavor of language, which is its wonderful ambiguity)))))))))))).

The commas are the most useful and usable of all the stops. It is highly important to put them in place as you go along. If you try to come back after doing a paragraph and stick them in the various spots that tempt you you will discover that they tend to swarm like minnows into all sorts of crevices whose existence you hadn't realized and before you know it the whole long sentence becomes immobilized and lashed up squirming in commas. Better to use them sparingly, and with affection, precisely when the need for each one arises, nicely, by itself.

I have grown fond of semicolons in recent years. The semicolon tells you that there is still some question about the preceding full sentence; something needs to be added; it reminds you sometimes of the Greek usage. It is almost always a greater pleasure to come across a semicolon than a period. The period tells you that that is that; if you didn't get all the meaning you wanted or expected, anyway you got all the writer intended to parcel out and now you have to move along. But with a semicolon there you get a pleasant little feeling of expectancy; there is more to come; read on; it will get clearer.

Colons are a lot less attractive, for several reasons: firstly, they give you the feeling of being rather ordered around, or at least having your nose pointed in a direction you might not be inclined to take if left to yourself, and, secondly, you suspect you're in for one of those sentences that will be labeling the points to be made: firstly, secondly and so forth, with the implication that you haven't sense enough to keep track of a sequence of notions without having them numbered. Also, many writers use this system loosely and incompletely, starting out with number one and number two as though counting off on their fingers but then going on and on without the succession of labels you've been led to expect, leaving you floundering about searching for the ninethly or seventeenthly that ought to be there but isn't.

Exclamation points are the most irritating of all. Look! they say, look at what I just said! How amazing is my thought! It is like being forced to watch someone else's small child jumping up and down crazily in the center of the living room shouting to attract attention. If a sentence really has something of importance to say, something quite remarkable, it doesn't need a mark to point it out. And if it is really, after all, a banal sentence needing more zing, the exclamation point simply emphasizes its banality!

Quotation marks should be used honestly and sparingly, when there is a genuine quotation at hand, and it is necessary to be very rigorous about the words enclosed by the marks. If something is to be quoted, the *exact* words must be used. If part of it must be left out because of space limitations, it is good manners to insert three dots to indicate the omission, but it is unethical to do this if it means connecting two thoughts which the original author did not intend to have tied together. Above all, quotation marks should not be used for ideas that you'd like to disown, things in the air so to speak. Nor should they be put in place around clichés; if you want to use a cliché you must take full responsibility for it yourself and not try to fob it off on anon., or on society. The most objectionable misuse of quotation marks, but one which illustrates the dangers of misuse in ordinary prose, is seen in advertising, especially in advertisements for small restaurants, for example "just around the corner," or "a good place to eat." No single, identifiable, citable person every really said, for the record, "just around the corner," much less "a good place to eat," least likely of all for restaurants of the type that use this type of prose.

The dash is a handy device, informal and essentially playful, telling you that you're about to take off on a different tack but still in some way connected with the present course—only you have to remember that the dash is there, and either put a second dash at the end of the notion to let the reader know that he's back on course, or else end the sentence, as here, with a period.

The greatest danger in punctuation is for poetry. Here it is necessary to be as economical and parsimonious with commas and periods as with the words themselves, and any marks that seem to carry their own subtle meanings, like dashes and little rows of periods, even semicolons and question marks, should be left out altogether rather than inserted to clog up the thing with ambiguity. A single exclamation point in a poem, no matter what else the poem has to say, is enough to destroy the whole work.

The things I like best in T. S. Eliot's poetry, especially in the *Four Quartets*, are the semicolons. You cannot hear them, but they are there, laying out the connections between the images and the ideas. Sometimes you get a glimpse of a semicolon coming, a few lines farther on, and it is like climbing a steep path through woods and seeing a wooden bench just at a bend in the road ahead, a place where you can expect to sit for a moment, catching your breath.

Commas can't do this sort of thing; they can only tell you how the different parts of a complicated thought are to be fitted together, but you can't sit, not even take a breath, just because of a comma,

RALPH ELLISON

Living with Music

In those days it was either live with music or die with noise, and we chose rather desperately to live. In the process our apartment—what with its booby-trappings of audio equipment, wires, discs and tapes—came to resemble the Collier mansion, but that was later. First there was the neighborhood, assorted drunks and a singer.

We were living at the time in a tiny ground-floor-rear apartment in which I was also trying to write. I say "trying" advisedly. To our right, separated by a thin wall, was a small restaurant with a juke box the size of the Roxy. To our left, a night-employed swing enthusiast who took his lullaby music so loud that every morning promptly at nine Basie's brasses started blasting my typewriter off its stand. Our living room looked out across a small back yard to a rough stone wall to an apartment building which, towering above, caught every passing thoroughfare sound and rifled it straight down to me. There were also howling cats and barking dogs, none capable of music worth living with, so we'll pass them by.

But the court behind the wall, which on the far side came knee-high to a short Iroquois, was a forum for various singing and / or preaching drunks who wandered back from the corner bar. From these you sometimes heard a fair barbershop style "Bill Bailey," free-wheeling versions of "The Bastard King of England," the saga of Uncle Bud, or a deeply felt rendition of Leroy Carr's "How Long Blues." The preaching drunks took on any topic that came to mind: current events, the fate of the long-sunk *Titanic* or the relative merits of the Giants and the Dodgers.

Naturally there was great argument and occasional fighting — none of it fatal but all of it loud.

I shouldn't complain, however, for these were rather entertaining drunks, who like the birds appeared in the spring and left with the first fall cold. A more dedicated fellow was there all the time, day and night, come rain, come shine. Up on the corner lived a drunk of legend, a true phenomenon, who could surely have qualified as the king of all the world's winos — not excluding the French. He was neither poetic like the others nor ambitious like the singer (to whom we'll presently come) but his drinking bouts were truly awe-inspiring and he was not without his sensitivity. In the throes of his passion he would shout to the whole wide world one concise command, "Shut up!" Which was disconcerting enough to all who heard (except, perhaps, the singer), but such were the labyrinthine acoustics of courtyards and areaways that he seemed to direct his command at me. The writer's block which this produced is indescribable. On one heroic occasion he yelled his obsessive command without one interruption longer than necessary to take another drink (and with no appreciable loss of volume, penetration or authority) for three long summer days and nights, and shortly afterwards he died. Just how many lines of agitated prose he cost me I'll never know, but in all that chaos of sound I sympathized with his obsession, for I, too, hungered and thirsted for quiet. Nor did he inspire me to a painful identification, and for that I was thankful. Identification, after all, involves feelings of guilt and responsibility, and since I could hardly hear my own typewriter keys I felt in no way accountable for his condition. We were simply fellow victims of the madding crowd. May he rest in peace.

No, these more involved feelings were aroused by a more intimate source of noise, one that got beneath the skin and worked into the very structure of one's consciousness — like the "fate" motif in Beethoven's Fifth or the knocking-at-the-gates scene in *Macbeth*. For at the top of our pyramid of noise there was a singer who lived directly above us; you might say we had a singer on our ceiling.

Now, I had learned from the jazz musicians I had known as a boy in Oklahoma City something of the discipline and devotion to his art required of the artist. Hence I knew something of what the singer faced. These jazzmen, many of them now world-famous, lived for and with music intensely. Their driving motivation was neither money nor fame, but the will to achieve the most eloquent expression of idea-emotions through the technical mastery of their instruments (which, incidentally, some of them wore as a priest wears the cross) and the give and take, the subtle rhythmical shaping and blending of idea, tone and imagination demanded of group improvisation. The delicate balance struck between strong individual personality and the group during those early jam sessions was a marvel of social organization. I had learned too that the end of all this discipline and technical mastery was the desire to express an affirmative way of life through its musical tradition and that this tradition insisted that each artist achieve his creativity within its frame. He must learn the best of the past, and add to it his personal vision. Life could be harsh, loud and wrong if it wished, but they lived it fully, and when they expressed their attitude toward the world it was with a fluid style that reduced the chaos of living to form.

The objectives of these jazzmen were not at all those of the singer on our ceiling, but though a purist committed to the mastery of the *bel canto* style, German *lieder*, modern French art songs and a few American slave songs sung as if *bel canto*, she was intensely devoted to her art. From morning to night she vocalized, regardless of the condition of her voice, the weather or my screaming nerves. There were times when her notes, sifting through her floor and my ceiling, bouncing down the walls and ricocheting off the building in the rear, whistled like tenpenny nails, buzzed like a saw, wheezed like the asthma of a Hercules, trumpeted like an enraged African elephant—and the squeaky pedal of her piano rested plumb center above my typing chair. After a year of non-cooperation from the neighbor on my left I became desperate enough to cool down the hot blast of his phonograph by calling the cops, but the singer presented a serious ethical problem: Could I, an aspiring artist, complain against the hard work and devotion to craft of another aspiring artist?

Then there was my sense of guilt. Each time I prepared to shatter the ceiling in protest I was restrained by the knowledge that I, too, during my boyhood, had tried to master a musical instrument and to the great distress of my neighbors—perhaps even greater than that which I now suffered. For while our singer was concerned basically with a single tradition and style, I had been caught actively between two: that of the Negro folk music, both sacred and profane, slave song and jazz, and that of Western classical music. It was most confusing; the folk tradition demanded that I play what I heard and felt around me, while those who were seeking to teach the classical tradition in the schools insisted that I play strictly according to the book and express that which I was *supposed* to feel. This sometimes led to heated clashes of wills. Once during a third-grade music appreciation class a friend of mine insisted that it was a large green snake he saw swimming down a quiet brook instead of the snowy bird the teacher felt that Saint-Saëns' *Carnival of the Animals* should evoke. The rest of us sat there and lied like little black, brown and yellow Trojans about that swan, but our stalwart classmate held firm to his snake. In the end he got himself spanked and reduced the teacher to tears, but truth, reality and our environment were redeemed. For we were all familiar with snakes, while a swan was simply something the Ugly Duckling of the story grew up to be. Fortunately some of us grew up with a genuine appreciation of classical music *despite* such teaching methods. But as an aspiring trumpeter I was to wallow in sin for years before being awakened to guilt by our singer.

Caught mid-range between my two traditions, where one attitude often clashed with the other and one technique of playing was by the other opposed, I caused whole blocks of people to suffer.

Indeed, I terrorized a good part of an entire city section. During summer vacation I blew sustained tones out of the window for hours, usually starting—especially on Sunday mornings—before breakfast. I sputtered whole days through M. Arban's (he's the great authority on the instrument) double- and triple-tonguing exercises—with an effect like that of a jackass hiccupping off a big meal of briars. During school-term mornings I practiced a truly exhibitionist "Reveille" before leaving for school, and in the evening I generously gave the ever-listening world a long, slow version of "Taps," ineptly played but throbbing with what I in my adolescent vagueness felt was a romantic sadness. For it was farewell to day and a love song to life and a peace-be-with-you to all the dead and dying.

On hot summer afternoons I tormented the ears of all not blessedly deaf with imitations of the latest hot solos of Hot Lips Paige (then a local hero), the leaping right hand of Earl "Fatha" Hines, or the rowdy poetic flights of Louis Armstrong. Naturally I rehearsed also such school-band standbys as the *Light Cavalry* Overture, Sousa's "Stars and Stripes Forever," the *William Tell* Overture, and "Tiger Rag." (Not even an after-school job as office boy to a dentist could stop my efforts. Frequently, by way of encouraging my development in the proper cultural direction, the dentist asked me proudly to render Schubert's *Serenade* for some poor devil with his jaw propped open in the dental chair. When the drill got going, or the forceps bit deep, I blew real strong.)

Sometimes, inspired by the even then considerable virtuosity of the late Charlie Christian (who during our school days played marvelous riffs on a cigar box banjo), I'd give whole summer afternoons and the evening hours after heavy suppers of black-eyed peas and turnip greens, cracklin' bread and buttermilk, lemonade and sweet potato cobbler, to practicing hard-driving blues. Such food oversupplied me with bursting energy, and from listening to Ma Rainey, Ida Cox and Clara Smith, who made regular appearances in our town, I knew exactly how I wanted my horn to sound. But in the effort to make it do so (I was no embryo Joe Smith or Tricky Sam Nanton) I sustained the curses of both Christian and infidel—along with the encouragement of those more sympathetic citizens who understood the profound satisfaction to be found in expressing oneself in the blues.

Despite those who complained and cried to heaven for Gabriel to blow a chorus so heavenly sweet and so hellishly hot that I'd forever put down my horn, there were more tolerant ones who were willing to pay in present pain for future pride.

For who knew what skinny kid with his chops wrapped around a trumpet mouthpiece and a faraway look in his eyes might become the next Armstrong? Yes, and send you, at some big dance a few years hence, into an ecstasy of rhythm and memory and brassy affirmation of the goodness of being alive and part of the community? Someone had to; for it was part of the group tradition—though that was not how they said it.

"Let that boy blow," they'd say to the protesting ones. "He's got to talk baby talk on that thing before he can preach on it. Next thing you know he's liable to be up there with Duke Ellington. Sure, plenty Oklahoma boys are up there with the big bands. Son, let's hear you try those 'Trouble in Mind Blues.' Now try and make it sound like ole Ida Cox sings it."

And I'd draw in my breath and do Miss Cox great violence.

Thus the crimes and aspirations of my youth. It had been years since I had played the trumpet or irritated a single ear with other than the spoken or written word, but as far as my singing neighbor was concerned I had to hold my peace. I was forced to listen, and in listening I soon became involved to the point of identification. If she sang badly I'd hear my own futility in the windy sound; if well, I'd stare at my typewriter and despair that I should ever make my prose so sing. She left me neither night nor day, this singer on our ceiling, and as my writing languished I became more and more upset. Thus one desperate morning I decided that since I seemed doomed to live within a shrieking chaos I might as well contribute my share; perhaps if I fought noise with noise I'd attain some small peace. Then a miracle: I turned on my radio (an old Philco AM set connected to a small Pilot FM tuner) and I heard the words

> *Art thou troubled?*
> *Music will calm thee . . .*

I stopped as though struck by the voice of an angel. It was Kathleen Ferrier, that loveliest of singers, giving voice to the aria from Handel's *Rodelinda*. The voice was so completely expressive of words and music that I accepted it without question—what lover of the vocal art could resist her?

Yet it was ironic, for after giving up my trumpet for the typewriter I had avoided too close a contact with the very art which she recommended as balm. For I had started music early and lived with it daily, and when I broke I tried to break clean. Now in this magical moment all the old love, the old fascination with music superbly rendered, flooded back. When she finished I realized that with such music in my own apartment, the chaotic sounds from without and above had sunk, if not into silence, then well below the level where they mattered. Here was a way out. If I was to live and write in that apartment, it would be only through the grace of music. I had tuned in a Ferrier recital, and when it ended I rushed out for several of her records, certain that now deliverance was mine.

But not yet. Between the hi-fi record and the ear, I learned, there was a new electronic world. In that realization our apartment was well on its way toward becoming an audio booby trap. It was 1949 and I rushed to the Audio Fair. I have, I confess, as much gadget-resistance as the next American of my age, weight and slight income; but little did I dream of the test to which it would be put. I had hardly entered the fair before I heard David Sarser's and Mel Sprinkle's Musician's Amplifier, took a look at its schematic and, recalling a boyhood acquaintance with such matters, decided that I could build one. I did, several times before it measured within specifications. And still our system was lacking. Fortunately my wife shared my passion for music, so we went on to buy, piece by piece, a fine speaker system, a first-rate AM-FM tuner, a transcription turntable and a speaker cabinet. I built half a dozen or more preamplifiers and record compensators before finding a commercial one that satisfied my ear, and, finally, we acquired an arm, a magnetic cartridge and—glory of the house—a tape recorder. All this plunge into electronics, mind you, had as its simple end the enjoyment of recorded music as it was intended to be heard. I was obsessed with the idea of reproducing sound with such fidelity that even when using music as a defense behind which I could write, it would reach the unconscious levels of the mind with the least distortion. And it didn't come easily. There were wires and pieces of equipment all over the tiny apartment (I became a compulsive experimenter) and it was worth your life to move about without first taking careful bearings. Once we were almost crushed in our sleep by the tape machine, for which there was space only on a shelf at the head of our bed. But it was worth it.

For now when we played a recording on our system even the drunks on the wall could recognize its quality. I'm ashamed to admit, however, that I did not always restrict its use to the demands of pleasure or defense. Indeed, with such marvels of science at my control I lost my humility. My ethical consideration for the singer up above shriveled like a plant in too much sunlight. For instead of soothing, music seemed to release the beast in me. Now when jarred from my writer's reveries by some especially enthusiastic flourish of our singer, I'd rush to my music system with blood in my eyes and burst a few decibels in her direction. If she defied me with a few more pounds of pressure against her diaphragm, then a war of decibels was declared.

If, let us say, she were singing *"Depuis le Jour"* from *Louise*, I'd put on a tape of Bidu Sayão performing the same aria, and let the rafters ring. If it was some song by Mahler, I'd match her spitefully with Marian Anderson or Kathleen Ferrier; if she offended with something from *Der Rosenkavalier*, I'd attack her flank with Lotte Lehmann. If she brought me up from my desk with art songs by Ravel or Rachmaninoff, I'd defend myself with Maggie Teyte or Jennie Tourel. If she polished a spiritual to a meaningless artiness I'd play Bessie Smith to remind her of the earth out of which we came. Once in a while I'd forget completely that I was supposed to be a gentleman and blast her with Strauss' *Zarathustra*, Bartók's *Concerto for Orchestra*, Ellington's "Flaming Sword," the famous crescendo from *The Pines of Rome*, or Satchmo scatting, "I'll be Glad When You're Dead" (you rascal you!). Oh, I was living with music with a sweet vengeance.

One might think that all this would have made me her most hated enemy, but not at all. When I met her on the stoop a few weeks after my rebellion, expecting her fully to slap my face, she astonished me by complimenting our music system. She even questioned me concerning the artists I had used against her. After that, on days when the acoustics were right, she'd stop singing until the piece was finished and then applaud—not always, I guessed, without a justifiable touch of sarcasm. And although I was now getting on with my writing, the unfairness of this business bore in upon me. Aware that I could not have withstood a similar comparison with literary artists of like caliber, I grew remorseful. I also came to admire the singer's courage and control, for she was neither intimidated into silence nor goaded into undisciplined screaming; she persevered, she marked the phrasing of the great singers I sent her way, she improved her style.

Better still, she vocalized more softly, and I, in turn, used music less and less as a weapon and more for its magic with mood and memory. After a while a simple twirl of the volume control up a few decibels and down again would bring a live-and-let-live reduction of her volume. We have long since moved from that apartment and that most interesting neighborhood and now the floors and walls of our present apartment are adequately thick and there is even a closet large enough to house the audio system; the only wire visible is that leading from the closet to the corner speaker system. Still we are indebted to the singer and the old environment for forcing us to discover one of the most deeply satisfying aspects of our living. Perhaps the enjoyment of music is always suffused with past experience; for me, at least, this is true.

It seems a long way and a long time from the glorious days of Oklahoma jazz dances, the jam sessions at Halley Richardson's place on Deep Second, from the phonographs shouting the blues in the back alleys I knew as a delivery boy, and from the days when watermelon men with voices like mellow bugles shouted their wares in time with the rhythm of their horses' hooves and farther still from the washerwomen singing slave songs as they stirred sooty tubs in sunny yards; and a long time, too, from those intense, conflicting days when the school music program of Oklahoma City was tuning our earthy young ears to classical accents—with music appreciation classes and free musical instruments and basic instruction for any child who cared to learn and uniforms for all who made the band. There was a mistaken notion on the part of some of the teachers that classical music had nothing to do with the rhythms, relaxed or hectic, of daily living, and that one should crook the little finger when listening to such refined strains. And the blues and the spirituals—jazz—? they would have destroyed them and scattered the pieces. Nevertheless, we learned some of it all, for in the United States when traditions are juxtaposed they tend, regardless of what we do to prevent it, irresistibly to merge. Thus musically at least each child in our town was an heir of all the ages. One learns by moving from the familiar to the unfamiliar, and while it might sound incongruous at first, the step from the spirituality of the spirituals to that of the Beethoven of the symphonies or the Bach of the chorales is not as vast as it seems. Nor is the romanticism of a Brahms or Chopin completely unrelated to that of Louis Armstrong. Those who know their native culture and love it unchauvinistically are never lost when encountering the unfamiliar.

Living with music today we find Mozart and Ellington, Kirsten Flagstad and Chippie Hill, William L. Dawson and Carl Orff all forming part of our regular fare. For all exalt life in rhythm and melody; all add to its significance. Perhaps in the swift change of American society in which the meanings of one's origin are so quickly lost, one of the chief values of living with music lies in its power to give us an orientation in time. In doing so, it gives significance to all those indefinable aspects of experience which nevertheless help to make us what we are. In the swift whirl of time music is a constant, reminding us of what we were and of that toward which we aspired. Art thou troubled? Music will not only calm, it will ennoble thee.

DORIS LESSING

My Father

We use our parents like recurring dreams, to be entered into when needed; they are always there for love or for hate; but it occurs to me that I was not always there for my father. I've written about him before, but novels, stories, don't have to be "true." Writing this article is difficult because it has to be "true." I knew him when his best years were over.

There are photographs of him. The largest is of an officer in the 1914–18 war. A new uniform—buttoned, badged, strapped, tabbed—confines a handsome, dark young man who holds himself stiffly to confront what he certainly thought of as his duty. His eyes are steady, serious, and responsible, and show no signs of what he became later. A photograph at sixteen is of a dark, introspective youth with the same intent eyes. But it is his mouth you notice—a heavily-jutting upper lip contradicts the rest of a regular face. His moustache was to hide it: "Had to do something—a damned fleshy mouth. Always made me uncomfortable, that mouth of mine."

Earlier a baby (eyes already alert) appears in a lace waterfall that cascades from the pillowy bosom of a fat, plain woman to her feet. It is the face of a head cook. "Lord, but my mother was a practical female—almost as bad as you!" as he used to say, or throw at my mother in moments of exasperation. Beside her stands, or droops, arms dangling, his father, the source of the dark, arresting eyes, but otherwise masked by a long beard.

The birth certificate says: Born 3rd August, 1886, Walton Villa, Creffield Road, S. Mary at the Wall, R.S.D. Name, Alfred Cook. Name and surname of Father: Alfred Cook Tayler. Name and maiden name of Mother: Caroline May Batley. Rank or Profession: Bank Clerk. Colchester, Essex.

They were very poor. Clothes and boots were a problem. They "made their own amusements." Books were mostly the Bible and *The Pilgrim's Progress.* Every Saturday night they bathed in a hip-bath in front of the kitchen fire. No servants. Church three times on Sundays. "Lord, when I think of those Sundays! I dreaded them all week, like a nightmare coming at you full tilt and no escape." But he rabbited with ferrets along the lanes and fields, bird-nested, stole fruit, picked nuts and mushrooms, paid visits to the blacksmith and the mill, and rode a farmer's carthorse.

They ate economically, but when he got diabetes in his forties and subsisted on lean meat and lettuce leaves, he remembered suet puddings, treacle puddings, raisin and currant puddings, steak and kidney puddings, bread and butter pudding, "batter cooked in the gravy with the meat," potato cake, plum cake, butter cake, porridge with treacle, fruit tarts and pies, brawn, pig's trotters and pig's cheek and home-smoked ham and sausages. And "lashings of fresh butter and cream and eggs." He wondered if this diet had produced the diabetes, but said it was worth it.

There was an elder brother described by my father as: "Too damned clever by half. One of those quick, clever brains. Now I've always had a slow brain, but I get there in the end, damn it!"

The brothers went to a local school and the elder did well, but my father was beaten for being slow. They both became bank clerks in, I think, the Westminster Bank, and one must have found it congenial, for he became a manager, the "rich brother," who had cars and even a yacht. But my father did not like it, though he was conscientious. For instance, he changed his writing, letter by letter, because a senior criticised it. I never saw his unregenerate hand, but the one he created was elegant, spiky, careful. Did this mean he created a new personality for himself, hiding one he did not like, as he hid his "damned fleshy mouth"? I don't know.

Nor do I know when he left home to live in Luton or why. He found family life too narrow? A safe guess—he found everything too narrow. His mother was too down-to-earth? He had to get away from his clever elder brother?

Being a young man in Luton was the best part of his life. It

ended in 1914, so he had a decade of happiness. His reminis-
cences of it were all of pleasure, the delight of physical movement, of dancing in particular. All his girls were "a beautiful
dancer, light as a feather." He played billiards and Ping-Pong
(both for his country); he swam, boated, played cricket and football, went to picnics and horse races, sang at musical evenings.
One family of a mother and two daughters treated him "like a
son only better. I didn't know whether I was in love with the
mother or the daughters, but oh I did love going there; we had
such good times." He was engaged to one daughter, then, for a
time, to the other. An engagement was broken off because she
was rude to a waiter. "I could not marry a woman who allowed
herself to insult someone who was defenceless." He used to say
to my wryly smiling mother: "Just as well I didn't marry either of
them; they would never have stuck it out the way you have, old
girl."

Just before he died he told me he had dreamed he was standing in a kitchen on a very high mountain holding X in his arms.
"Ah, yes, that's what I've missed in my life. Now don't you let
yourself be cheated out of life by the old dears. They take all the
colour out of everything if you let them."

But in that decade—"I'd walk 10, 15 miles to a dance two or
three times a week and think nothing of it. Then I'd dance every
dance and walk home again over the fields. Sometimes it was
moonlight, but I liked the snow best, all crisp and fresh. I loved
walking back and getting into my digs just as the sun was rising.
My little dog was so happy to see me, and I'd feed her, and make
myself porridge and tea, then I'd wash and shave and go off to
work."

The boy who was beaten at school, who went too much to
church, who carried the fear of poverty all his life, but who nevertheless was filled with the memories of country pleasures; the
young bank clerk who worked such long hours for so little
money, but who danced, sang, played, flirted—this naturally vigorous, sensuous being was killed in 1914, 1915, 1916. I think the
best of my father died in that war, that his spirit was crippled by
it. The people I've met, particularly the women, who knew him
young, speak of his high spirits, his energy, his enjoyment of life.

Also of his kindness, his compassion, and—a word that keeps recurring—his wisdom. "Even when he was just a boy he understood things that you'd think even an old man would find it easy to condemn." I do not think these people would have easily recognised the ill, irritable, abstracted, hypochondriac man I knew.

He "joined up" as an ordinary soldier out of a characteristically quirky scruple: it wasn't right to enjoy officers' privileges when the Tommies had such a bad time. But he could not stick the communal latrines, the obligatory drinking, the collective visits to brothels, the jokes about girls. So next time he was offered a commission he took it.

His childhood and young man's memories, kept fluid, were added to, grew, as living memories do. But his war memories were congealed in stories that he told again and again, with the same words and gestures, in stereotyped phrases. They were anonymous, general, as if they had come out of a communal war memoir. He met a German in no-man's-land, but both slowly lowered their rifles and smiled and walked away. The Tommies were the salt of the earth, the British fighting men the best in the world. He had never known such comradeship. A certain brutal officer was shot in a sortie by his men, but the other officers, recognising rough justice, said nothing. He had known men intimately who saw the Angels at Mons. He wished he could force all the generals on both sides into the trenches for just one day, to see what the common soldiers endured—*that* would have ended the war at once.

There was an undercurrent of memories, dreams, and emotions much deeper, more personal. This dark region in him, fate-ruled, where nothing was true but horror, was expressed inarticulately, in brief, bitter exclamations or phrases of rage, incredulity, betrayal. The men who went to fight in that war believed it when they said it was to end war. My father believed it. And he was never able to reconcile his belief in his country with his anger at the cynicism of its leaders. And the anger, the sense of betrayal, strengthened as he grew old and ill.

But in 1914 he was naive, the German atrocities in Belgium inflamed him, and he enlisted out of idealism, although he knew he would have a hard time. He knew because a fortuneteller told him. (He could be described as uncritically superstitious or as psychically gifted.) He would be in great danger twice, yet not die—he was being protected by a famous soldier who was his ancestor. "And sure enough, later I heard from the Little Aunties that the church records showed we were descended the back-stairs way from the Duke of Wellington, or was it Marlborough? Damn it, I forget. But one of them would be beside me all through the war, she said." (He was romantic, not only about this solicitous ghost, but also about being a descendant of the Huguenots, on the strength of the "e" in Tayler; and about "the wild blood" in his veins from a great uncle who, sent unjustly to prison for smuggling, came out of a ten-year sentence and earned it, very efficiently, along the coasts of Cornwall until he died.)

The luckiest thing that ever happened to my father, he said, was getting his leg shattered by shrapnel ten days before Passchendaele. His whole company was killed. He knew he was going to be wounded because of the fortuneteller, who had said he would know. "I did not understand what she meant, but both times in the trenches, first when my appendix burst and I nearly died, and then just before Passchendaele, I felt for some days as if a thick, black velvet pall was settled over me. I can't tell you what it was like. Oh, it was awful, awful, and the second time it was so bad I wrote to the old people and told them I was going to be killed."

His leg was cut off at mid-thigh, he was shell-shocked, he was very ill for many months, with a prolonged depression afterwards. "You should always remember that sometimes people are all seething underneath. You don't know what terrible things people have to fight against. You should look at a person's eyes, that's how you tell. . . . When I was like that, after I lost my leg, I went to a nice doctor man and said I was going mad, but he said, don't worry, everyone locks up things like that. You don't know— horrible, horrible, awful things. I was afraid of myself, of what I used to dream. I wasn't myself at all."

In the Royal Free Hospital was my mother, Sister McVeagh. He married his nurse which, as they both said often enough (though in different tones of voice), was just as well. That was 1919. He could not face being a bank clerk in England, he said, not after the trenches. Besides, England was too narrow and conventional. Besides, the civilians did not know what the soldiers had suffered, they didn't want to know, and now it wasn't done even to remember "The Great Unmentionable." He went off to the Imperial Bank of Persia, in which country I was born.

The house was beautiful, with great stone-floored high-ceilinged rooms whose windows showed ranges of snow-streaked mountains. The gardens were full of roses, jasmine, pomegranates, walnuts. Kermanshah he spoke of with liking, but soon they went to Teheran, populous with "Embassy people," and my gregarious mother created a lively social life about which he was irritable even in recollection.

Irritableness—that note was first struck here, about Persia. He did not like, he said, "the graft and the corruption." But here it is time to try and describe something difficult—how a man's good qualities can also be his bad ones, or if not bad, a danger to him.

My father was honourable—he always knew exactly what that word meant. He had integrity. His "one does not do that sort of thing," his "no, it is *not* right," sounded throughout my childhood and were final for all of us. I am sure it was true he wanted to leave Persia because of "the corruption." But it was also because he was already unconsciously longing for something freer, because as a bank official he could not let go into the dream-logged personality that was waiting for him. And later in Rhodesia, too, what was best in him was also what prevented him from shaking away the shadows: it was always in the name of honesty or decency that he refused to take this step or that out of the slow decay of the family's fortunes.

In 1925 there was leave from Persia. That year in London there was an Empire Exhibition, and on the Southern Rhodesian stand some very fine maize cobs and a poster saying that fortunes could be made on maize at 25 /- a bag. So on an impulse, turning his back forever on England, washing his hands of the corruption of the East, my father collected all his capital, £800, I think, while my mother packed curtains from Liberty's, clothes from Harrods, visiting cards, a piano, Persian rugs, a governess, and two small children.

Soon, there was my father in a cigar-shaped house of thatch

and mud on the top of a kopje that overlooked in all directions a great system of mountains, rivers, valleys, while overhead the sky arched from horizon to empty horizon. This was a couple of hundred miles south from the Zambesi, a hundred or so west from Mozambique, in the district of Banket, so called because certain of its reefs were of the same formation as those called *banket* on the Rand. Lomagundi—gold country, tobacco country, maize country—wild, almost empty. (The Africans had been turned off it into reserves.) Our neighbours were four, five, seven miles off. In front of the house . . . no neighbours, nothing; no farms, just wild bush with two rivers but no fences to the mountains seven miles away. And beyond these mountains and bush again to the Portuguese border, over which "our boys" used to escape when wanted by the police for pass or other offences.

And then? There was bad luck. For instance, the price of maize dropped from 25 / - to 9 / - a bag. The seasons were bad, prices bad, crops failed. This was the sort of thing that made it impossible for him ever to "get off the farm," which, he agreed with my mother, was what he most wanted to do.

It was an absurd country, he said. A man could "own" a farm for years that was totally mortgaged to the Government and run from the Land Bank, meanwhile employing half-a-hundred Africans at 12 / - a month and none of them knew how to do a day's work. Why, two farm labourers from Europe could do in a day what twenty of these ignorant black savages would take a week to do. (Yet he was proud that he had a name as a just employer, that he gave "a square deal.") Things got worse. A fortuneteller had told him that her heart ached when she saw the misery ahead for my father: this was the misery.

But it was my mother who suffered. After a period of neurotic illness, which was a protest against her situation, she became brave and resourceful. But she never saw that her husband was not living in a real world, that he had made a captive of her common sense. We were always about to "get off the farm." A miracle would do it—a sweepstake, a goldmine, a legacy. And then? What a question! We would go to England where life would be normal with people coming in for musical evenings and nice supper parties at the Trocadero after a show. Poor woman, for the twenty years we were on the farm, she waited for when life would begin for her and for her children, for she never understood that what was a calamity for her was for them a blessing.

Meanwhile my father sank towards his death (at 61). Everything changed in him. He had been a dandy and fastidious, now he hated to change out of shabby khaki. He had been sociable, now he was misanthropic. His body's disorders—soon diabetes and all kinds of stomach ailments—dominated him. He was brave about his wooden leg, and even went down mine shafts and climbed trees with it, but he walked clumsily and it irked him badly. He greyed fast, and slept more in the day, but would be awake half the night pondering about. . . .

It could be gold divining. For ten years he experimented on private theories to do with the attractions and repulsions of metals. His whole soul went into it but his theories were wrong or he was *unlucky*—after all, if he had found a mine he would have had to leave the farm. It could be the relation between the minerals of the earth and of the moon; his decision to make infusions of all the plants on the farm and drink them himself in the interests of science; the criminal folly of the British Government in not realising that the Germans and the Russians were conspiring as Anti-Christ to . . . the inevitability of war because no one would listen to Churchill, but it would be all right because God (by then he was a British Israelite) had destined Britain to rule the world; a prophecy said 10 million dead would surround Jerusalem—how would the corpses be cleared away?; people who wished to abolish flogging should be flogged; the natives understood nothing but a good beating; hanging must not be abolished because the Old Testament said "an eye for an eye and a tooth for a tooth. . . ."

Yet, as this side of him darkened, so that it seemed all his thoughts were of violence, illness, war, still no one dared to make an unkind comment in his presence or to gossip. Criticism of people, particularly of women, made him more and more uncomfortable till at last he burst out with: "It's all very well, but no one has the right to say that about another person."

In Africa, when the sun goes down, the stars spring up, all of

446446446446446.

them in their expected places, glittering and moving. In the rainy season, the sky flashed and thundered. In the dry season, the great dark hollow of night was lit by veld fires; the mountains burned through September and October in chains of red fire. Every night my father took out his chair to watch the sky and the mountains, smoking, silent, a thin shabby fly-away figure under the stars. "Makes you think—there are so many worlds up there, wouldn't really matter if we did blow ourselves up—plenty more where we came from."

The Second World War, so long foreseen by him, was a bad time. His son was in the Navy and in danger, and his daughter a sorrow to him. He became very ill. More and more often it was necessary to drive him into Salisbury with him in a coma, or in danger of one, on the back seat. My mother moved him into a pretty little suburban house in town near the hospitals, where he took to his bed and a couple of years later died. For the most part he was unconscious under drugs. When awake he talked obsessively (a tongue licking a nagging sore place) about "the old war." Or he remembered his youth. "I've been dreaming—Lord, to see those horses come lickety-split down the course with their necks stretched out and the sun on their coats and everyone shouting. . . . I've been dreaming how I walked along the river in the mist as the sun was rising. . . . Lord, lord, lord, what a time that was, what good times we all had then, before the old war."

WILLIAM ZINSSER

JURY DUTY

Jury duty again. I'm sitting in the "central jurors' room" of a courthouse in lower Manhattan, as I do every two years, waiting to be called for a jury, which I almost never am. It's an experience that all of us have known, in one form or another, as long as we can remember: organized solitude.

The chair that I sit in is a little island of apartness. I sit there alone, day after day, and I go out to lunch alone, a stranger in my own city. Strictly, of course, I'm not by myself. Several hundred other men and women sit on every side, as closely as in a movie theater, also waiting to be called for a jury, which they almost never are. Sometimes we break briefly into each other's lives, when we get up to stretch, offering fragments of talk to fill the emptiness. But in the end each of us is alone, withdrawn into our newspapers and our crossword puzzles and our sacred urban privacy.

The room intimidates us. It is a dreary place, done in thirties Bureaucratic, too dull to sustain more than a few minutes of mental effort. On the subconscious level, however, it exerts a strong and uncanny hold. It is the universal waiting room. It is the induction center and the clinic; it is the assembly hall and the office where forms are filled out. Thoughts come unbidden there, sneaking back from all the other moments—in the army, at camp, on the first day of school—when we were part of a crowd and therefore lonely.

The mere taking of roll call by a jury clerk will summon back the countless times when we have waited for our name to be yelled out—loud and just a little wrong. Like every person whose job is to read names aloud, the jury clerk can't read names aloud. Their shapes mystify him. They are odd and implausible names, as diverse as the countries that they came from, but surely the clerk has met them all before. *Hasn't* he? Isn't that what democracy—and the jury system—is all about? Evidently not.

We are shy enough, as we wait for our name, without the extra burden of wondering what form it will take. By now we know most of the variants that have been imposed on it by other clerks in other rooms like this, and we are ready to answer to any of them, or to some still different version. Actually we don't want to hear our name called at all in this vast public chamber. It is so private, so vulnerable. And yet we don't want to *not* hear it, for only then are we reassured of our identity, really certain that we are known, wanted, and in the right place. Dawn over Camp Upton, 1943: Weinberg, Wyzanski, Yanopoulos, Zapata, Zeccola, Zinsser. . . .

I don't begin my jury day in such a retrospective state. I start with high purpose and only gradually slide into mental disarray. I am punctual, even early, and so is everybody else. We are a conscientious lot—partly because we are so surrounded by the trappings of justice, but mainly because that is what we are there to be. I've never seen such conscientious-looking people. Observing them, I'm glad that American law rests on being judged by our peers. In fact, I'd almost rather be judged by my peers than judged by a judge.

Most of us start the day by reading. Jury duty is America's gift to her citizens of a chance to catch up on "good" books, and I always bring *War and Peace*. I remember to bring it every morning and I keep it handy on my lap. The only thing I don't do is read it. There's something about the room . . . the air is heavy with imminent roll calls, too heavy for tackling a novel that will require strict attention. Besides, it's important to read the newspaper first: sharpen up the old noggin on issues of the day. I'm just settling into my paper when the clerk comes in, around ten-twenty-five, and calls the roll ("Zissner?" "Here!"). Suddenly it is 1944 and I am at an army base near Algiers, hammering tin to make a hot shower for Colonel McCloskey. That sort of thing can shoot the whole morning.

If it doesn't, the newspaper will. Only a waiting juror knows how infinite the crannies of journalism can be. I read "Arrival of Buyers," though I don't know what they want to buy and have nothing to sell. I read "Soybean Futures," though I wouldn't know a soybean even in the present. I read classified ads for jobs that I didn't know were jobs, like "key-punch operators." What keys do they punch? I mentally buy 4bdrm 1½bth splt lvl homes w/fpl overlooking Long Island Sound and dream of taking ½ bath there. I read dog news and horoscopes ("bucking others could prove dangerous today") and medical columns on diseases I've never heard of, but whose symptoms I instantly feel.

It's an exhausting trip, and I emerge with eyes blurry and mind blank. I look around at my fellow jurors. Some of them are trying to work—to keep pace, pitifully, with the jobs that they left in order to come here and do nothing. They spread queer documents on their knees, full graphs and figures, and they scribble on yellow pads. But the papers don't seem quite real to them, or quite right, removed from the tidy world of filing cabinets and secretaries, and after a while the workers put the work away again.

Around twelve-forty-five the clerk comes in to make an announcement. We stir to attention: we are needed! "Go to lunch," he says. "Be back at two." We straggle out. By now the faces of all my fellow jurors are familiar (we've been here eight days), and I keep seeing them as we poke around the narrow streets of Chinatown looking for a restaurant that isn't the one where we ate yesterday. I smile tentatively, as New Yorkers do, and they smile tentatively back, and we go our separate ways. By one-fifty-five we are seated in the jurors' room again, drowsy with Chinese food and American boredom—too drowsy, certainly, to start *War and Peace*. Luckily, we all bought the afternoon paper while we were out. Talk about remote crannies of journalism!

Perhaps we are too hesitant to talk to each other, to invite ourselves into lives that would refresh us by being different from our own. We are scrupulous about privacy—it is one of the better gifts that the city can bestow, and we don't want to spoil it for somebody else. Yet within almost every New Yorker who thinks he wants to be left alone is a person desperate for human contact. Thus we may be as guilty as the jury system of not putting our time to good use.

What we want to do most, of course, is serve on a jury. We believe in the system. Besides, was there ever so outstanding a group of jurors as we, so intelligent and fair-minded? The clerks have told us all the reasons why jurors are called in such wasteful numbers: court schedules are unpredictable; trials end unexpectedly; cases are settled at the very moment when a jury is called; prisoners plead guilty to a lesser charge rather than wait years for a trial that might prove them innocent. All this we know, and in theory it makes sense.

In practice, however, somebody's arithmetic is wrong, and one of America's richest assets is being dribbled away. There must be a better way to get through the long and tragic list of cases awaiting a solution—and, incidentally, to get through *War and Peace.*

TRUMAN CAPOTE

TANGIER

Tangier? It is two days by boat from Marseille, a charming trip that takes you along the coast of Spain, and if you are someone escaping from the police, or merely someone escaping, then by all means come here: hemmed with hills, confronted by the sea, and looking like a white cape draped on the shores of Africa, it is an international city with an excellent climate eight months of the year, roughly March to November. There are magnificent beaches, really extraordinary stretches of sugar-soft sand and surf; and if you have a mind for that sort of thing, the nightlife, though neither particularly innocent nor especially varied, is dark to dawn, which, when you consider that most people nap all after-noon, and that very few dine before ten or eleven, is not too unusual. Almost everything else in Tangier is unusual, however, and before coming here you should do three things: be inocu-lated for typhoid, withdraw your savings from the bank, say good-bye to your friends — heaven knows you may never see them again. This advice is quite serious, for it is alarming, the number of travelers who have landed here on a brief holiday, then settled down and let the years go by. Because Tangier is a basin that holds you, a timeless place; the days slide by less noticed than foam in a waterfall; this, I imagine, is the way time passes in a monastery, unobtrusive and on slippered feet; for that matter, these two institutions, a monastery and Tangier, have another common denominator: self-containment. The average Arab, for example, thinks Europe and America are the same thing and in the same place, wherever that may be — in any event, he doesn't care; and frequently Europeans, hypnotized by the tinkling of an oud and the swarming drama around them, come to agree.

One spends a great lot of time sitting in the Petit Soko, a café-cluttered square at the foot of the Casbah. Offhand, it seems to be a miniature version of the Galleria in Naples, but on closer acquaintance it assumes a character so grotesquely individual you cannot fairly compare it with any other place in the world. At no hour of the day or night is the Petit Soko not crowded; Broadway, Piccadilly, all these places have their off moments, but the little Soko booms around the clock. Twenty steps away, and you are swallowed in the mists of the Casbah; the apparitions drifting out of these mists into the hurdy-gurdy clamor of the Soko make a lively show: it is a display ground for prostitutes, a depot for drug-peddlers, a spy center; it is also the place where some simpler folk drink their evening *apéritif.*

The Soko has its own celebrities, but it is a precarious honor, one is so likely at any second to be cut down and cast away, for the Soko audience, having seen just about everything, is excessively fickle. Currently, however, they are starring Estelle, a beautiful girl who walks like a rope unwinding. She is half-Chinese and half-Negro, and she works in a bordello called the Black Cat. Rumor has it that she once was a Paris model, and that she arrived here on a private yacht, planning, of course, to leave by the same means; but it appears that the gentleman to whom the yacht belonged sailed away one fine morning, leaving Estelle stranded. For a while there Maumi was giving her rather a race; the Soko appreciated Maumi's talents, both as a *flamenco* dancer and as a conversationalist: wherever he sat, there were always loud bursts of laughter. Alas, poor Maumi, an exotic young man given to cooling his face with a lacy fan, was stabbed in a bar the other night, and is now out of the running. Less heralded, but to me more intriguing, are Lady Warbanks and her two hangers-on, a curious trio that arrive each morning and have their breakfast at one of the sidewalk tables: this breakfast is unvarying—a bowl of fried octopus and a bottle of Pernod. Someone who ought really to know says that at one time the now very *déclassé* Lady Warbanks was considered the greatest beauty in London; probably it is true, her features are finely made and she has, despite the tight sailor suits she lumps herself into, a peculiar innate style. But her morals are not all they might be, and the same may be said of her companions. About these two: one is a sassy-faced, busy youth whose tongue is like a ladle stirring in a cauldron of scandal—he knows everything; and the other friend is a tough Spanish girl with brief, slippery hair and leather-colored eyes. She is called Sunny, and I am told that financed by Lady War-banks, she is on her way to becoming the only female in Morocco with an organized gang of smugglers: smuggling is a high-powered profession here, employing hundreds, and Sunny, it appears, has a boat and crew that nightly runs the Straits to Spain. The precise relation of these three to each other is not altogether printable; suffice to say that between them they combine every known vice. But this does not interest the Soko, for the Soko is concerned by quite another angle: how soon will Lady Warbanks be murdered, and which of the two will do it, the young man or Sunny? She is very rich, the Englishwoman, and if it is greed, as so obviously it is, that holds her companions, then clearly violence is indicated. Everyone is waiting. Meanwhile, Lady Warbanks sits innocently nibbling octopus and sipping her morning Pernod.

The Soko is also something of a fashion center, a proving ground for the latest fads. One innovation that has got off to a popular start among the flashier types are shoes with ribbon laces that wind right up to the knee. They are unbecoming, but not nearly so regrettable as the passion for dark glasses that has developed among Arab women, whose eyes, peering just above their veiling, have been always so provocative. Now all one sees are these great black lenses imbedded like coal-hunks in a snowball of cloth.

Of an evening at seven the Soko reaches its height. It is the crowded *apéritif* hour, some twenty nationalities are rubbing elbows in the tiny square, and the hum of their voices is like the singing of giant mosquitoes. Once, when we were sitting there, a sudden silence fell: an Arab orchestra, trumpeting in a gay style, moved along up the street past the bright cafés—it was the only cheerful Moorish music I've ever heard, all the rest sounds like a sad and fragmentary wailing. But death, it would seem, is not an unhappy event among Arabs, for this orchestra proved to be the vanguard of a funeral procession that then came joyfully winding through the throng. Presently the corpse, a half-naked man carried on an open litter, wobbled past, and a rhinestone lady, leaning from her table, sentimentally saluted him with a glass of Tio Pepe: a moment later she was laughing gold-toothed laughter, plotting, planning. And so was the little Soko.

"If you are going to write something about Tangier," said a person to whom I applied for certain information, "please leave out the riffraff; we have a lot of nice people here, and it's hard on us that the town has such a bad reputation."

Well, and though I'm not at all sure our definitions coincide, there are at least three people I think eminently nice. Jonny Winner, for instance. A sweet, funny girl, Jonny Winner. She is very young, very American, and you would never believe, looking at her clouded, wistful face, that she is able to take care of herself: to tell the truth, I don't think she is. Nevertheless, she has lived here two years, been across Morocco and to the Sahara alone. Why Jonny Winner wants to spend the rest of her life in Tangier is of course her own business; obviously she is in love: "But don't you love it, too? to wake up and know that you're here, and know that you can always be yourself, never be anyone that isn't you? And always to have flowers, and to look out your window and see the hills getting dark and the lights in the harbor? Don't you love it, too?" On the other hand, she and the town are always at war; whenever you meet her she is undergoing a new *crise:* "Have you heard? the most awful mess: some fool in the Casbah painted his house yellow, and now everybody's doing it—I'm just on my way to see if I can't put a stop to the whole thing."

The Casbah, traditionally blue and white, like snow at twilight, would be hideous painted yellow, and I hope Jonny gets her way—though certainly she has had no success in her campaign to keep them from clearing the Grand Soko, a heartrending business that has reduced her to prowling the streets, in tears. The Grand Soko is the great Arab market square: Berbers, down from the mountains with their goatskins and baskets, squat in circles under the trees listening to storytellers, flute players, magicians; cornucopia stalls spill over with flowers and fruit; hashish fume and the minty scent of *thé Arabe* cling to the air; vivid spices burn in the sun. All this is to be moved elsewhere, presumably to make way for a park, and Jonny is wringing her hands: "Why shouldn't I be upset? I feel as though Tangier were my house, and how would you like it if somebody came into your house and started moving the furniture around?"

So she has been out saving the Soko in four languages, French, Spanish, English and Arabic; though she speaks all of these exceedingly well, the closest she has come to official sympathy is the doorman at the Dutch consulate, and her only real emotional support has been an Arab taxi driver, who thinks her not the least mad and drives her around free of charge. One late afternoon a few days ago we saw Jonny dragging along through her beloved, dissolving Grand Soko; she looked absolutely done in, and she was carrying a mangy, sore-covered kitten. Jonny has a way of launching right into what she wants to say, and she said, "I was feeling just as though I couldn't go on living, and then I found Monroe. This is Monroe"—she patted the kitten—"and he's made me ashamed: he's so interested in living, and if he can be, why shouldn't I?"

Looking at them, Jonny and the kitten, both so bedraggled and bruised, you knew that somehow something would see them through: if not common sense, then their interest in life.

Ferida Green has plenty of common sense. When Jonny spoke to her about the situation in the Grand Soko, Miss Green said, "Oh, my dear, you mustn't worry. They are always tearing down the Soko, but it never really happens; I remember in 1906 they wanted to make it into a whaling center: imagine the odor!"

Miss Ferida is one of the three great Green ladies of Tangier, which includes her cousin, Miss Jessie, and her sister-in-law, Mrs. Ada Green; between them they manage more often than not to have the last say here. All three are past seventy: Mrs. Ada Green is famous for her chic, Miss Jessie for her wit, and Miss Ferida, the oldest, for her wisdom. She has not visited her native England in over fifty years; even so, observing the straw skimmer skewered to her hair and the black ribbon trailing from her pince-nez, one knows she goes out in the noonday sun and has never given up tea at five. Every Friday in her life there is a ritual known as Flour Morning. Seated at a table at the foot of her garden, and judging each case as it is presented, she rations flour to Arab applicants, usually old women who otherwise would starve: from the flour they make a paste which must last them until the next Friday. There is much joking and laughter, for the Arabs adore Miss Ferida, and for her, all these old women, such anonymous bundles of laundry to the rest of us, are friends whose personalities she comments on in a large ledger. "Fathma has a bad temper but is not bad," she writes of one, and of another: "Halima is a good girl. One can take her at face value."

And that, I suppose, is what you would have to say about Miss Ferida.

Anyone in Tangier longer than overnight is bound to hear about Nysa: how at the edge of twelve she was taken off the streets by an Australian who, in true Pygmalion fashion, created out of this raggedy Arab child an accomplished, extremely elegant personage. Nysa is, as far as I know, the only example in Tangier of a Europeanized Arab woman, a fact which, strangely, no one quite forgives her, neither the Europeans, nor the Arabs, who are avowedly bitter and who, because she lives in the Casbah, have constant opportunity to vent their malice: women send their children to scrawl obscenities on her door, men do not hesitate to spit at her on the street—for in their eyes she has committed the gravest sin possible: become a Christian. Such a situation must make for terrible resentment, but Nysa, at least as far as surface appearances go, never seems aware that there is anything to resent. She is a charming, calm girl of twenty-three; it is in itself an entertainment just to sit quietly and marvel over her beauty, the tilted eyes and the flowerlike hands. She does not see many people; like the princess in a storybook, she stays behind the walls and in the shade of her patio, reading, playing with her cats and a large white cockatoo who mimics whatever she does: sometimes the cockatoo flares forward and kisses her on the lips. The Australian lives with her; since he found her as a child she has never for a moment been separated from him; if something should happen to him, there really would be no way for Nysa to turn: she could not ever be an Arab again, and it isn't likely that she could pass completely into a European world. But the Australian is an old man now. One day I rang Nysa's bell; no one came to answer. There is a grillwork at the top of the door; peering, I saw her through a veil of vine and leaves standing in the shadows of her patio. When I rang again she remained dark and still as a statue. Later I heard that during the night the Australian had had a stroke.

At the end of June, and with the start of a new moon, *Ramadan* begins. For the Arabs, *Ramadan* is a month of abstinence. As dark comes on, a colored string is stretched in the air, and when the string grows invisible, conch horns signal the Arabs to the food and drink that during the day they cannot touch. These dark-night feasts emanate a festive spirit that lasts until dawn. From distant towers oboe players serenade before prayers; drums, hidden but heard, tom-tom behind closed doors, and the voices of men, singsonging the Koran, carry out of the mosques into the narrow, moon-bright streets. Even high on the mountain above Tangier you can hear the oboe player wailing in the far-off dark, a solemn thread of melody winding across Africa from here to Mecca and back.

Sidi Kacem is a limitless, Sahara-like beach bordered by olive groves; at the end of *Ramadan*, Arabs from all over Morocco arrive at Sidi Kacem in trucks, astride donkeys, on foot: for three days a city appears there, a fragile dream city of colored lights and cafés under lantern-lighted trees. We drove out there around midnight; the first glimpse of the city was like seeing a birthday cake blazing in a darkened room, and it filled you with the same exciting awe: you knew you could not blow out all the candles. Right away we got separated from the people we'd come with, but in the surge and sway it was impossible to stay together, and after the first few frightened moments we never bothered looking for them; the night caught us in its hand and there was nothing to do but become another of the masked, ecstatic faces flashing in the torch-flare. Everywhere little orchestras played. Voices, sweet and sultry as *kif* smoke, chanted over drums, and somewhere, stumbling through the silver, floating trees, we got smothered in a crowd of dancers: a circle of old bearded men beat the rhythm, and the dancers, so concentrated you could put a pin in them, rippled as though wind were moving them around. According to the Arab calendar this is the year 1370; seeing a shadow through the silk of a tent, watching a family fry honeycakes on a flat twig fire, moving among the dancers and hearing the trill of a lonely flute on the beach, it was simple to believe that one was living in 1370 and that time would never move forward.

Occasionally we had to rest; there were straw mats under the olive trees, and if you sat on one of these, a man would bring you a glass of hot mint tea. It was while we were drinking tea that we saw a curious line of men file past. They wore beautiful robes, and the man in front, old like a piece of ivory, carried a bowl of rose water which, to the accompaniment of bagpipes, he sprinkled from side to side. We got up to follow them, and they took us out of the grove onto the beach. The sand was as cold as the moon; humped dunes of it drifted toward the water, and flickers of light burst in the dark like fallen stars. At last the priest and his followers went into a temple which it was forbidden us to enter, and so we wandered down across the beach. J. said, "Look, a shooting star"; and then we counted the shooting stars, there were so many. Wind whispered on the sand like the sound of the seas; cutthroat figures outlined themselves against the kneeling orange moon, and the beach was as cold as a snowfield, but J. said, "Oh, I can't keep my eyes open any longer."

We woke up in a blue, almost dawn light. We were high on a dune, and there below us, spread along the shore, were all the celebrants, their brilliant clothes fluttering in the morning breeze. Just as the sun touched the horizon a great roar went up, and two horsemen, riding bareback, splashed through the surf and swept down the beach. Like a lifting curtain sunrise crept toward us across the sand, and we shuddered at its coming, knowing that when it reached us we would be back in our own century.

JAMES BALDWIN

STRANGER IN THE VILLAGE

From all available evidence no black man had ever set foot in this tiny Swiss village before I came. I was told before arriving that I would probably be a "sight" for the village; I took this to mean that people of my complexion were rarely seen in Switzerland, and also that city people are always something of a "sight" outside of the city. It did not occur to me—possibly because I am an American—that there could be people anywhere who had never seen a Negro.

It is a fact that cannot be explained on the basis of the inaccessibility of the village. The village is very high, but it is only four hours from Milan and three hours from Lausanne. It is true that it is virtually unknown. Few people making plans for a holiday would elect to come here. On the other hand, the villagers are able, presumably, to come and go as they please—which they do: to another town at the foot of the mountain, with a population of approximately five thousand, the nearest place to see a movie or go to the bank. In the village there is no movie house, no bank, no library, no theater; very few radios, one jeep, one station wagon; and, at the moment, one typewriter, mine, an invention which the woman next door to me here had never seen. There are about six hundred people living here, all Catholic—I conclude this from the fact that the Catholic church is open all year round, whereas the Protestant chapel, set off on a hill a little removed from the village, is open only in the summertime when the tourists arrive. There are four or five hotels, all closed now, and four or five *bistros*, of which, however, only two do any business during the winter. These two do not do a great deal, for life in the village seems to end around nine or ten o'clock. There are a few stores, butcher, baker, *épicerie*, a hardware store, and a money-changer—who cannot change travelers' checks, but must send them down to the bank, an operation which takes two or three days. There is something called the *Ballet Haus*, closed in the winter and used for God knows what, certainly not ballet, during the summer. There seems to be only one schoolhouse in the village, and this for the quite young children; I suppose this to mean that their older brothers and sisters at some point descend from these mountains in order to complete their education—possibly, again, to the town just below. The landscape is absolutely forbidding, mountains towering on all four sides, ice and snow as far as the eye can reach. In this white wilderness, men and women and children move all day, carrying washing, wood, buckets of milk or water, sometimes skiing on Sunday afternoons. All week long boys and young men are to be seen shoveling snow off the rooftops, or dragging wood down from the forest in sleds.

The village's only real attraction, which explains the tourist season, is the hot spring water. A disquietingly high proportion of these tourists are cripples, or semi-cripples, who come year after year—from other parts of Switzerland, usually—to take the waters. This lends the village, at the height of the season, a rather terrifying air of sanctity, as though it were a lesser Lourdes. There is often something beautiful, there is always something awful, in the spectacle of a person who has lost one of his faculties, a faculty he never questioned until it was gone, and who struggles to recover it. Yet people remain people, on crutches or indeed on deathbeds; and wherever I passed, the first summer I was here, among the native villagers or among the lame, a wind passed with me—of astonishment, curiosity, amusement, and outrage. That first summer I stayed two weeks and never intended to return. But I did return in the winter, to work; the village offers, obviously, no distractions whatever and has the further advantage of being extremely cheap. Now it is winter again, a year later, and I am here again. Everyone in the village knows my name, though they scarcely ever use it, knows that I come from America—though this, apparently, they will never really believe: black men come from Africa—and everyone knows that I am the friend of the son of a woman who was born here, and that I am staying in their chalet. But I remain as much a stranger today as I was the first day I arrived, and the children shout *Neger! Neger!* as I walk along the streets.

It must be admitted that in the beginning I was far too shocked to have any real reaction. In so far as I reacted at all, I reacted by trying to be pleasant—it being a great part of the American Negro's education (long before he goes to school) that he must make people "like" him. This smile-and-the-world-smiles-with-you routine worked about as well in this situation as it had in the situation for which it was designed, which is to say that it did not work at all. No one, after all, can be liked whose human weight and complexity cannot be, or has not been, admitted. My smile was simply another unheard-of phenomenon which allowed them to see my teeth—they did not, really, see my smile and I began to think that, should I take to snarling, no one would notice any difference. All of the physical characteristics of the Negro which had caused me, in America, a very different and almost forgotten pain were nothing less than miraculous—or infernal—in the eyes of the village people. Some thought my hair was the color of tar, that it had the texture of wire, or the texture of cotton. It was jocularly suggested that I might let it all grow long and make myself a winter coat. If I sat in the sun for more than five minutes some daring creature was certain to come along and gingerly put his fingers on my hair, as though he were afraid of an electric shock, or put his hand on my hand, astonished that the color did not rub off. In all of this, in which it must be conceded there was the charm of genuine wonder and in which there was certainly no element of intentional unkindness, there was yet no suggestion that I was human: I was simply a living wonder.

I knew that they did not mean to be unkind, and I know it now; it is necessary, nevertheless, for me to repeat this to myself each time that I walk out of the chalet. The children who shout *Neger!* have no way of knowing the echoes this sound raises in me. They are brimming with good humor and the more daring swell with pride when I stop to speak with them. Just the same, there are days when I cannot pause and smile, when I have no heart to play with them; when, indeed, I mutter sourly to myself, exactly as I muttered on the streets of a city these children have never seen, when I was no bigger than these children are now: *Your* mother *was a nigger.* Joyce is right about history being a nightmare—but it may be the nightmare from which no one *can* awaken. People are trapped in history and history is trapped in them.

There is a custom in the village—I am told it is repeated in many villages—of "buying" African natives for the purpose of converting them to Christianity. There stands in the church all year round a small box with a slot for money, decorated with a black figurine, and into this box the villagers drop their francs. During the *carnaval* which precedes Lent, two village children have their faces blackened—out of which bloodless darkness their blue eyes shine like ice—and fantastic horsehair wigs are placed on their blond heads; thus disguised, they solicit among the villagers for money for the missionaries in Africa. Between the box in the church and the blackened children, the village "bought" last year six or eight African natives. This was reported to me with pride by the wife of one of the *bistro* owners and I was careful to express astonishment and pleasure at the solicitude shown by the village for the souls of black folk. The *bistro* owner's wife beamed with a pleasure far more genuine than my own and seemed to feel that I might now breathe more easily concerning the souls of at least six of my kinsmen.

I tried not to think of these so lately baptized kinsmen, of the price paid for them, or the peculiar price they themselves would pay, and said nothing about my father, who having taken his own conversion too literally never, at bottom, forgave the white world (which he described as heathen) for having saddled him with a Christ in whom, to judge at least from their treatment of him, they themselves no longer believed. I thought of white men arriving for the first time in an African village, strangers there, as I am a stranger here, and tried to imagine the astounded populace touching their hair and marveling at the color of their skin. But there is a great difference between being the first white man to be seen by Africans and being the first black man to be seen by whites. The white man takes the astonishment as tribute, for he arrives to conquer and to convert the natives, whose inferiority in relation to himself is not even to be questioned; whereas I, without a thought of conquest, find myself among a people whose culture controls me, has even, in a sense, created me, people who have cost me more in anguish and rage than they will ever know, who yet do not even know of my existence. The astonishment with which I might have greeted them, should they have stumbled into my African village a few hundred years ago, might have rejoiced their hearts. But the astonishment with which they greet me today can only poison mine.

And this is so despite everything I may do to feel differently, despite my friendly conversations with the *bistro* owner's wife, despite their three-year-old son who has at last become my friend, despite the *saluts* and *bonsoirs* which I exchange with people as I walk, despite the fact that I know that no individual can be taken to task for what history is doing, or has done. I say that the culture of these people controls me—but they can scarcely be held responsible for European culture. America comes out of Europe, but these people have never seen America, nor have most of them seen more of Europe than the hamlet at the foot of their mountain. Yet they move with an authority which I shall never have; and they regard me, quite rightly, not only as a stranger in their village but as a suspect latecomer, bearing no credentials, to everything they have—however unconsciously— inherited.

For this village, even were it incomparably more remote and incredibly more primitive, is the West, the West onto which I have been so strangely grafted. These people cannot be, from the point of view of power, strangers anywhere in the world; they have made the modern world, in effect, even if they do not know it. The most illiterate among them is related, in a way that I am not, to Dante, Shakespeare, Michelangelo, Aeschylus, Da Vinci, Rembrandt, and Racine; the cathedral at Chartres says something to them which it cannot say to me, as indeed would New York's Empire State Building, should anyone here ever see it. Out of their hymns and dances come Beethoven and Bach. Go back a few centuries and they are in their full glory—but I am in Africa, watching the conquerors arrive.

The rage of the disesteemed is personally fruitless, but it is also absolutely inevitable; this rage, so generally discounted, so little understood even among the people whose daily bread it is, is one of the things that makes history. Rage can only with difficulty, and never entirely, be brought under the domination of the intelligence and is therefore not susceptible to any arguments whatever. This is a fact which ordinary representatives of the *Herrenvolk*, having never felt this rage and being unable to imagine it, quite fail to understand. Also, rage cannot be hidden, it can only be dissembled. This dissembling deludes the thoughtless, and strengthens rage and adds, to rage, contempt. There are, no doubt, as many ways of coping with the resulting complex of tensions as there are black men in the world, but no black man can hope ever to be entirely liberated from this internal warfare—rage, dissembling, and contempt having inevitably accompanied his first realization of the power of white men. What is crucial here is that, since white men represent in the black man's world so heavy a weight, white men have for black men a reality which is far from being reciprocal; and hence all black men have toward all white men an attitude which is designed, really, either to rob the white man of the jewel of his naïveté, or else to make it cost him dear.

The black man insists, by whatever means he finds at his disposal, that the white man cease to regard him as an exotic rarity and recognize him as a human being. This is a very charged and difficult moment, for there is a great deal of will power involved in the white man's naïveté. Most people are not naturally reflective any more than they are naturally malicious, and the white man prefers to keep the black man at a certain human remove because it is easier for him thus to preserve his simplicity and avoid being called to account for crimes committed by his forefathers, or his neighbors. He is inescapably aware, nevertheless, that he is in a better position in the world than black men are, nor can he quite put to death the suspicion that he is hated by black men therefore. He does not wish to be hated, neither does he wish to change places, and at this point in his uneasiness he can scarcely avoid having recourse to those legends which white men have created about black men, the most usual effect of which is that the white man finds himself enmeshed, so to speak, in his own language which describes hell, as well as the attributes which lead one to hell, as being as black as night.

Every legend, moreover, contains its residuum of truth, and the root function of language is to control the universe by describing it. It is of quite considerable significance that black men remain, in the imagination, and in overwhelming numbers in fact, beyond the disciplines of salvation; and this despite the fact that the West has been "buying" African natives for centuries. There is, I should hazard, an instantaneous necessity to be divorced from this so visibly unsaved stranger, in whose heart, moreover, one cannot guess what dreams of vengeance are being nourished; and, at the same time, there are few things on earth more attractive than the idea of the unspeakable liberty which is allowed the unredeemed. When, beneath the black mask, a human being begins to make himself felt one cannot escape a certain awful wonder as to what kind of human being it is. What one's imagination makes of other people is dictated, of course, by the laws of one's own personality and it is one of the ironies of black-white relations that, by means of what the white man imagines the black man to be, the black man is enabled to know who the white man is.

I have said, for example, that I am as much a stranger in this village today as I was the first summer I arrived, but this is not quite true. The villagers wonder less about the texture of my hair than they did then, and wonder rather more about me. And the fact that their wonder now exists on another level is reflected in their attitudes and in their eyes. There are the children who make those delightful, hilarious, sometimes astonishingly grave overtures of friendship in the unpredictable fashion of children; other children, having been taught that the devil is a black man, scream in genuine anguish as I approach. Some of the older women never pass without a friendly greeting, never pass, indeed, if it seems that they will be able to engage me in conversation; other women look down or look away or rather contemptuously smirk. Some of the men drink with me and suggest that

I learn how to ski—partly, I gather, because they cannot imagine what I would look like on skis—and want to know if I am married, and ask questions about my *métier*. But some of the men have accused *le sale nègre*—behind my back—of stealing wood and there is already in the eyes of some of them that peculiar, intent, paranoiac malevolence which one sometimes surprises in the eyes of American white men when, out walking with their Sunday girl, they see a Negro male approach.

There is a dreadful abyss between the streets of this village and the streets of the city in which I was born, between the children who shout *Neger!* today and those who shouted *Nigger!* yesterday—the abyss is experience, the American experience. The syllable hurled behind me today expresses, above all, wonder: I am a stranger here. But I am not a stranger in America and the same syllable riding on the American air expresses the war my presence has occasioned in the American soul.

For this village brings home to me this fact: that there was a day, and not really a very distant day, when Americans were scarcely Americans at all but discontented Europeans, facing a great unconquered continent and strolling, say, into a marketplace and seeing black men for the first time. The shock this spectacle afforded is suggested, surely, by the promptness with which they decided that these black men were not really men but cattle. It is true that the necessity on the part of the settlers of the New World of reconciling their moral assumptions with the fact—and the necessity—of slavery enhanced immensely the charm of this idea, and it is also true that this idea expresses, with a truly American bluntness, the attitude which to varying extents all masters have had toward all slaves.

But between all former slaves and slave-owners and the drama which begins for Americans over three hundred years ago at Jamestown, there are at least two differences to be observed. The American Negro slave could not suppose, for one thing, as slaves in past epochs had supposed and often done, that he would ever be able to wrest the power from his master's hands. This was a supposition which the modern era, which was to bring about such vast changes in the aims and dimensions of power, put to death; it only begins, in unprecedented fashion, and with dread-

ful implications, to be resurrected today. But even had this supposition persisted with undiminished force, the American Negro
slave could not have used it to lend his condition dignity, for the
reason that this supposition rests on another: that the slave in
exile yet remains related to his past, has some means—if only in
memory—of revering and sustaining the forms of his former life,
is able, in short, to maintain his identity.

This was not the case with the American Negro slave. He is
unique among the black men of the world in that his past was
taken from him, almost literally, at one blow. One wonders what
on earth the first slave found to say to the first dark child he bore.
I am told that there are Haitians able to trace their ancestry back
to African kings, but any American Negro wishing to go back so
far will find his journey through time abruptly arrested by the
signature on the bill of sale which served as the entrance paper
for his ancestor. At the time—to say nothing of the circumstances—of the enslavement of the captive black man who was
to become the American Negro, there was not the remotest possibility that he would ever take power from his master's hands.
There was no reason to suppose that his situation would ever
change, nor was there, shortly, anything to indicate that his situation had ever been different. It was his necessity, in the words of
E. Franklin Frazier, to find a "motive for living under American
culture or die." The identity of the American Negro comes out
of this extreme situation, and the evolution of this identity was a
source of the most intolerable anxiety in the minds and the lives
of his masters.

For the history of the American Negro is unique also in this:
that the question of his humanity, and of his rights therefore as a
human being, became a burning one for several generations of
Americans, so burning a question that it ultimately became one
of those used to divide the nation. It is out of this argument that
the venom of the epithet *Nigger!* is derived. It is an argument
which Europe has never had, and hence Europe quite sincerely
fails to understand how or why the argument arose in the first
place, why its effects are so frequently disastrous and always so
unpredictable, why it refuses until today to be entirely settled.
Europe's black possessions remained—and do remain—in

Europe's colonies, at which remove they represented no threat whatever to European identity. If they posed any problem at all for the European conscience, it was a problem which remained comfortingly abstract: in effect, the black man, *as a man,* did not exist for Europe. But in America, even as a slave, he was an inescapable part of the general social fabric and no American could escape having an attitude toward him. Americans attempt until today to make an abstraction of the Negro, but the very nature of these abstractions reveals the tremendous effects the presence of the Negro has had on the American character.

When one considers the history of the Negro in America it is of the greatest importance to recognize that the moral beliefs of a person, or a people, are never really as tenuous as life—which is not moral—very often causes them to appear; these create for them a frame of reference and a necessary hope, the hope being that when life has done its worst they will be enabled to rise above themselves and to triumph over life. Life would scarcely be bearable if this hope did not exist. Again, even when the worst has been said, to betray a belief is not by any means to have put oneself beyond its power; the betrayal of a belief is not the same thing as ceasing to believe. If this were not so there would be no moral standards in the world at all. Yet one must also recognize that morality is based on ideas and that all ideas are dangerous— dangerous because ideas can only lead to action and where the action leads no man can say. And dangerous in this respect: that confronted with the impossibility of remaining faithful to one's beliefs, and the equal impossibility of becoming free of them, one can be driven to the most inhuman excesses. The ideas on which American beliefs are based are not, though Americans often seem to think so, ideas which originated in America. They came out of Europe. And the establishment of democracy on the American continent was scarcely as radical a break with the past as was the necessity, which Americans faced, of broadening this concept to include black men.

This was, literally, a hard necessity. It was impossible, for one thing, for Americans to abandon their beliefs, not only because these beliefs alone seemed able to justify the sacrifices they had endured and the blood that they had spilled, but also because

these beliefs afforded them their only bulwark against a moral
chaos as absolute as the physical chaos of the continent it was
their destiny to conquer. But in the situation in which Americans
found themselves, these beliefs threatened an idea which,
whether or not one likes to think so, is the very warp and woof
of the heritage of the West, the idea of white supremacy.

Americans have made themselves notorious by the shrillness
and the brutality with which they have insisted on this idea, but
they did not invent it; and it has escaped the world's notice that
those very excesses of which Americans have been guilty imply
a certain, unprecedented uneasiness over the idea's life and
power, if not, indeed, the idea's validity. The idea of white
supremacy rests simply on the fact that white men are the cre-
ators of civilization (the present civilization, which is the only
one that matters; all previous civilizations are simply "contribu-
tions" to our own) and are therefore civilization's guardians and
defenders. Thus it was impossible for Americans to accept the
black man as one of themselves, for to do so was to jeopardize
their status as white men. But not so to accept him was to deny
his human reality, his human weight and complexity, and the
strain of denying the overwhelmingly undeniable forced Americans into rationalizations so fantastic that they approached the
pathological.

At the root of the American Negro problem is the necessity of
the American white man to find a way of living with the Negro
in order to be able to live with himself. And the history of this
problem can be reduced to the means used by Americans—
lynch law and law, segregation and legal acceptance, terrorization and concession—either to come to terms with this necessity,
or to find a way around it, or (most usually) to find a way of
doing both these things at once. The resulting spectacle, at once
foolish and dreadful, led someone to make the quite accurate
observation that "the Negro-in-America is a form of insanity
which overtakes white men."

In this long battle, a battle by no means finished, the unfore-
seeable effects of which will be felt by many future generations,
the white man's motive was the protection of his identity; the
black man's motive was the protection of his identity; the black

man was motivated by the need to establish an identity. And despite the terrorization which the Negro in America endured and endures sporadically until today, despite the cruel and totally inescapable ambivalence of his status in his country, the battle for his identity has long ago been won. He is not a visitor to the West, but a citizen there, an American; as American as the Americans who despise him, the Americans who fear him, the Americans who love him—the Americans who became less than themselves, or rose to be greater than themselves by virtue of the fact that the challenge he represented was inescapable. He is perhaps the only black man in the world whose relationship to white men is more terrible, more subtle, and more meaningful than the relationship of bitter possessed to uncertain possessor. His survival depended, and his development depends, on his ability to turn his peculiar status in the Western world to his own advantage and, it may be, to the very great advantage of that world. It remains for him to fashion out of his experience that which will give him sustenance, and a voice.

The cathedral at Chartres, I have said, says something to the people of this village which it cannot say to me; but it is important to understand that this cathedral says something to me which it cannot say to them. Perhaps they are struck by the power of the spires, the glory of the windows; but they have known God, after all, longer than I have known him, and in a different way, and I am terrified by the slippery bottomless well to be found in the crypt, down which heretics were hurled to death, and by the obscene, inescapable gargoyles jutting out of the stone and seeming to say that God and the devil can never be divorced. I doubt that the villagers think of the devil when they face a cathedral because they have never been identified with the devil. But I must accept the status which myth, if nothing else, gives me in the West before I can hope to change the myth.

Yet, if the American Negro has arrived at his identity by virtue of the absoluteness of his estrangement from his past, American white men still nourish the illusion that there is some means of recovering the European innocence, of returning to a state in which black men do not exist. This is one of the greatest errors Americans can make. The identity they fought so hard to protect has, by virtue of that battle, undergone a change: Americans are as unlike any other white people in the world as it is possible to be. I do not think, for example, that it is too much to suggest that the American vision of the world—which allows so little reality, generally speaking, for any of the darker forces in human life, which tends until today to paint moral issues in glaring black and white—owes a great deal to the battle waged by Americans to maintain between themselves and black men a human separation which could not be bridged. It is only now beginning to be borne in on us—very faintly, it must be admitted, very slowly, and very much against our will—that this vision of the world is dangerously inaccurate, and perfectly useless. For it protects our moral high-mindedness at the terrible expense of weakening our grasp of reality. People who shut their eyes to reality simply invite their own destruction, and anyone who insists on remaining in a state of innocence long after that innocence is dead turns himself into a monster.

The time has come to realize that the interracial drama acted out on the American continent has not only created a new black man, it has created a new white man, too. No road whatever will lead Americans back to the simplicity of this European village where white men still have the luxury of looking on me as a stranger. I am not, really, a stranger any longer for any American alive. One of the things that distinguishes Americans from other people is that no other people has ever been so deeply involved in the lives of black men, and vice versa. This fact faced, with all its implications, it can be seen that the history of the American Negro problem is not merely shameful, it is also something of an achievement. For even when the worst has been said, it must also be added that the perpetual challenge posed by this problem was always, somehow, perpetually met. It is precisely this black-white experience which may prove of indispensable value to us in the world we face today. This world is white no longer, and it will never be white again.

L. RUST HILLS

How to Eat an Ice-Cream Cone

Before you even get the cone, you have to do a lot of planning about it. We'll assume that you lost the argument in the car and that the family has decided to break the automobile journey and stop at an ice-cream stand for cones. Get things straight with them right from the start. Tell them that there will be an imaginary circle six feet away from the car, and that no one—man, woman, or especially child—will be allowed to cross the line and reenter the car until his ice-cream cone has been entirely consumed and he has cleaned himself up. Emphasize: Automobiles and ice-cream cones don't mix. Explain: Melted ice cream, children, is a fluid that is eternally sticky. One drop of it on a car-door handle spreads to the seat covers, to trousers, and thence to hands, and then to the steering wheel, the gear shift, the rearview mirror, all the knobs of the dashboard—spreads everywhere and lasts forever, spreads from a nice old car like this, which might have to be abandoned because of stickiness, right into a nasty new car, in secret ways that even scientists don't understand. If necessary, even make a joke: "The family that eats ice-cream cones together, sticks together." Then let their mother explain the joke and tell them you don't mean half of what you say, and no, we won't be getting a new car.

Blessed are the children who always eat the same flavor of ice cream or always know beforehand what kind they will want. Such good children should be quarantined from those who say "I want to wait and see what flavors there are." It's hard to just listen, while a beautiful young child who has always been perfectly happy with a plain vanilla ice-cream cone is subverted by a young schoolmate who has been invited along for the weekend, a pleasant and polite child, perhaps, but spoiled by permissive parents and flawed by an overactive imagination. This school-mate has a flair for contingency planning: "Well, I'll have banana, if they have banana, but if they don't have banana, then I'll have peach, if it's fresh peach, and if they don't have banana or fresh peach, I'll see what else they have that's like that, like maybe fresh strawberry or something, and if they don't have that or anything like that that's good, I'll just have chocolate marsh-mallow chip or chocolate ripple or something like that." Then— turning to one's own once simple and innocent child, now already corrupt and thinking fast—the schoolmate invites a simi-lar rigmarole: "What kind are *you* going to have?"

I'm a great believer in contingency planning. But none of this is realistic. Few adults, and even fewer children, are able to make up their mind beforehand what kind of ice-cream cone they'll want. It would be nice if they could be all lined up in front of the man who's making up the cones and just snap smartly, when their turn came, "Strawberry, please," "Vanilla, please," "Choco-late, please." But of course it never happens like that. There is always a great discussion, a great jostling and craning of necks and leaning over the counter to see down into the tubs of ice cream, and much consultation—"What kind are *you* having?"— back and forth, as if that should make any difference.

Humans are incorrigibly restless and dissatisfied, always in search of new experiences and sensations, seldom content with the familiar. It is this, I think, that accounts for others wanting to have a taste of your cone, and wanting you to have a taste of theirs. "Do have a taste of this fresh peach, it's delicious," my wife used to say to me, very much (I suppose) the way Eve wanted Adam to taste her delicious apple. An insinuating look of calculating curiosity would film my wife's eyes—the same look those beautiful, scary women in those depraved Italian films give a man they're interested in. "How's *yours?*" she would say. For this reason, I always order chocolate chip now. Down through the years, all those close enough to me to feel entitled to ask for a taste of my cone—namely wife and children—have learned what chocolate chip tastes like, so they have no legitimate reason to ask me for a taste. As for tasting other people's cones, never do it. The reasoning here is that if it tastes good, you'll wish you'd had it; if it tastes bad, you'll have had a taste of something that tastes bad; if it doesn't taste either good or bad, then you won't have missed anything. Of course no person in his right mind ever *would* want to taste anyone else's cone, but it is useful to have good, logical reasons for hating the thought of it.

Another important thing. Never let the man hand you the cones of others. Make him hand each one to each kid individually. That way you won't get disconcerting tastes of butter pecan and black raspberry on your own chocolate chip. And insist that he tell you how much it all costs and settle with him *before* he hands you your own cone. Make sure everyone has got paper napkins and everything *before* he hands you your own cone. Get *everything* straight before he hands you your own cone.

Then, when the moment finally comes, reach out and take it from him. Strange, magical, *dangerous* moment! Consider what it is that you are about to be handed: It is a huge irregular mass of ice cream, faintly domed at the top from the metal scoop that dug it out and then insecurely perched it on the uneven top edge of a hollow inverted cone made out of the most brittle and fragile of materials. Clumps of ice cream hang over the side, very loosely attached to the main body. There is always much more ice cream than the cone could hold, even if the ice cream were tamped down into the cone, which of course it isn't. And the essence of ice cream is that it melts. It doesn't just stay there teetering in this irregular, top-heavy mass, it also *melts*. And it melts fast. And it doesn't just melt, it melts into a stickiness that cannot be wiped off. The only thing one person could hand to another that might possibly be more dangerous is a live hand grenade on which the pin had been pulled five seconds earlier. And of course if anybody offered you that, you could say, "Oh. Uh, well—no thanks."

Ice-cream men handle cones routinely, and are inured. They are like professionals who are used to handling sticks of TNT, their movements quick and skillful. An ice-cream man may attempt to pass a cone to you casually, almost carelessly. Never accept a cone on this basis! Keep your hand at your side, over-coming the instinct by which everyone's hand goes out—almost automatically—whenever he is proffered something delicious and expected. The ice-cream man will look up at you, startled, questioning. Lock his eyes with your own, and *then*, slowly, calmly, and above all, deliberately, take the cone from him.

Grasp the cone firmly but gently between thumb and forefin-ger, two-thirds of the way up. Then dart swiftly away to an open area, away from the jostling crowd at the stand. Then take up the classic ice-cream-cone-eating stance: feet from one to two feet apart, body bent forward from the waist at a twenty-five-degree angle, right elbow well up, right forearm horizontal, at a level with your collarbone and about twelve inches from it. But don't start eating yet! Check first to see what emergency repairs may be necessary.

Immediate action is sometimes needed on three fronts at once. Frequently the ice cream will be mounted on the cone in a way that is perilously lopsided. This requires immediate corrective action to move it back into balance—a slight pressure downward with the teeth and lips to seat the ice cream more firmly in and on the cone—but not so hard, of course, as to break the cone. On other occasions, gobs of ice cream will be hanging loosely from the main body, about to fall to the ground (bad) or onto one's hand (far, far worse). This requires instant action too: snap-ping at the gobs with the split-second timing of a frog in a swarm of flies. But sometimes trickles of ice cream will already (already!) be running down the cone toward one's fingers, and one must quickly raise the cone, tilting one's face skyward, and lick with an upward motion to push the trickles away from the fingers and (as much as possible) into the mouth.

Which to do first? Every ice-cream cone is like every other ice-cream cone in that it has the potential to present all three prob-lems, but each ice-cream cone is paradoxically unique in that it will present the problems in a different order of emergency, and hence require a different order of solutions. And it is (thank God!) an unusual ice-cream cone that will present all three prob-lems in *exactly* the same degree of emergency. It is necessary to make an instantaneous judgment as to which of the basic three emergencies—lopsided mount, dangling gobs, already running trickles—presents the most immediate danger and then *act!* Otherwise the whole thing will be a mess before you've even tasted it.

In trying to make wise and correct decisions about the ice-cream cone in your hand, you should always try to keep your ultimate objective in mind. The first objective is to get the cone under control. Secondarily, one will want to eat the cone calmly and with pleasure. Real pleasure, of course, lies not simply in enjoying the taste of the ice-cream cone, but in eating it *right*, which is where the ultimate objective comes in.

Let us assume that you have darted to your open space and made your necessary emergency repairs. The cone is still dangerous, of course—still, so to speak, "live." But you can now proceed with it in an orderly fashion. First revolve the cone through the full 360 degrees, turning the cone by moving the thumb away from you and the forefinger toward you, so the cone moves counterclockwise. Snap at the loose gobs of ice cream as you do this. Then, with the cone still "wound," which will require the wrist to be bent at the full right angle toward you, apply pressure with the mouth and tongue to accomplish overall realignment, straightening and settling the whole mess. Then, unwinding the cone back through the full 360 degrees, remove any trickles of ice cream. Now, have a look at the cone. Some supplementary repairs may be necessary, but the cone is now defused.

At this point, you can risk a glance around you to see how badly the others are doing with their cones. Then, shaking your head with good-natured contempt for the mess they're making, you can settle down to eating yours. This is done by eating the ice cream off the top, at each bite pressing down cautiously, so that the ice cream settles farther and farther into the cone, being very careful not to break the cone.

If these procedures are followed correctly, you should shortly arrive at the ideal, your ultimate objective, the way an ice-cream cone is always pictured as being, but never actually is when it is handed to you. The ice cream should now form a small dome whose large circumference exactly coincides with the large circumference of the cone itself: a small skullcap that fits exactly on top of a larger, inverted dunce cap.

Like the artist, who makes order out of chaos, you have taken an unnatural, abhorrent, irregular, chaotic form like this:

and from it you have sculpted an ordered, ideal shape that might be envied by Praxiteles or even Euclid:

Now at last you can begin to take little nibbles of the cone itself, being very careful not to crack it. Revolve the cone so that its rim remains level as it descends, while you eat both ice cream and cone. Because it is in the geometrical nature of things, the inverted cone shape, as you keep nibbling the top off it, still remains a cone *shape*; and because you are constantly reforming with your tongue the little dome of ice cream on top, it follows in logic—and in actual practice, if you are skillful and careful— that as you eat the cone on down it continues to look exactly the same, so that at the very end you will hold between your thumb and forefinger a tiny, idealized replica of an ice-cream cone, a harmless thing perhaps an inch high.

Then, while the others are licking their sticky fingers, prepara- tory to wiping them on their clothes, or going back to the ice- cream stand for more paper napkins to try to clean themselves up—*then* you can hold the miniature cone up for everyone to see, and pop it gently into your mouth.

FLANNERY O'CONNOR

The King of the Birds

When I was five, I had an experience that marked me for life. Pathé News sent a photographer from New York to Savannah to take a picture of a chicken of mine. This chicken, a buff Cochin Bantam, had the distinction of being able to walk either forward or backward. Her fame had spread through the press, and by the time she reached the attention of Pathé News, I suppose there was nowhere left for her to go—forward or backward. Shortly after that she died, as now seems fitting.

If I put this information in the beginning of an article on peacocks, it is because I am always being asked why I raise them, and I have no short or reasonable answer.

From that day with the Pathé man I began to collect chickens. What had been only a mild interest became a passion, a quest. I had to have more and more chickens. I favored those with one green eye and one orange or with overlong necks and crooked combs. I wanted one with three legs or three wings but nothing in that line turned up. I pondered over the picture in Robert Ripley's book, *Believe It or Not*, of a rooster that had survived for thirty days without his head; but I did not have a scientific temperament. I could sew in a fashion and I began to make clothes for chickens. A gray bantam named Colonel Eggbert wore a white piqué coat with a lace collar and two buttons in the back. Apparently Pathé News never heard of any of these other chickens of mine; it never sent another photographer.

My quest, whatever it was actually for, ended with peacocks. Instinct, not knowledge, led me to them. I had never seen or heard one. Although I had a pen of pheasants and a pen of quail, a flock of turkeys, seventeen geese, a tribe of mallard ducks, three Japanese silky bantams, two Polish Crested ones, and several chickens of a cross between these last and the Rhode Island Red, I felt a lack. I knew that the peacock had been the bird of Hera, the wife of Zeus, but since that time it had probably come down in the world—the Florida *Market Bulletin* advertised three-year-old peafowl at sixty-five dollars a pair. I had been quietly reading these ads for some years when one day, seized, I circled an ad in the *Bulletin* and passed it to my mother. The ad was for a peacock and hen with four seven-week-old peabiddies. "I'm going to order me those," I said.

My mother read the ad. "Don't those things eat flowers?" she asked.

"They'll eat Startena like the rest of them," I said.

The peafowl arrived by Railway Express from Eustis, Florida, on a mild day in October. When my mother and I arrived at the station, the crate was on the platform and from one end of it protruded a long, royal-blue neck and crested head. A white line above and below each eye gave the investigating head an expression of alert composure. I wondered if this bird, accustomed to parade about in a Florida orange grove, would readily adjust himself to a Georgia dairy farm. I jumped out of the car and bounded forward. The head withdrew.

At home we uncrated the party in a pen with a top on it. The man who sold me the birds had written that I should keep them penned up for a week or ten days and then let them out at dusk at the spot where I wanted them to roost; thereafter, they would return every night to the same roosting place. He had also warned me that the cock would not have his full complement of tail feathers when he arrived; the peacock sheds his tail in late summer and does not regain it fully until after Christmas.

As soon as the birds were out of the crate, I sat down on it and began to look at them. I have been looking at them ever since, from one station or another, and always with the same awe as on that first occasion; though I have always, I feel, been able to keep a balanced view and an impartial attitude. The peacock I had bought had nothing whatsoever in the way of a tail, but he car-

ried himself as if he not only had a train behind him but a retinue to attend it. On that first occasion, my problem was so greatly
what to look at first that my gaze moved constantly from the cock
to the hen to the four young peachickens, while they, except that
they gave me as wide a berth as possible, did nothing to indicate
they knew I was in the pen.

Over the years their attitude toward me has not grown more
generous. If I appear with food, they condescend, when no other
way can be found, to eat it from my hand; if I appear without
food, I am just another object. If I refer to them as "my" peafowl,
the pronoun is legal, nothing more. I am the menial, at the beck
and squawk of any feathered worthy who wants service. When I
first uncrated these birds, in my frenzy I said, "I want so many of
them that every time I go out the door, I'll run into one." Now
every time I go out the door, four or five run into me—and give
me only the faintest recognition. Nine years have passed since
my first peafowl arrived. I have forty beaks to feed. Necessity is
the mother of several other things besides invention.

For a chicken that grows up to have such exceptional good looks,
the peacock starts life with an inauspicious appearance. The pea-
biddy is the color of those large objectionable moths that flutter
about light bulbs on summer nights. Its only distinguished features are its eyes, a luminous gray, and a brown crest which
begins to sprout from the back of its head when it is ten days old.
This looks at first like a bug's antennae and later like the head
feathers of an Indian. In six weeks green flecks appear in its neck,
and in a few more weeks a cock can be distinguished from a hen
by the speckles on his back. The hen's back gradually fades to an
even gray and her appearance becomes shortly what it will always
be. I have never thought the peahen unattractive, even though
she lacks a long tail and any significant decoration. I have even
once or twice thought her more attractive than the cock, more
subtle and refined; but these moments of boldness pass.

The cock's plumage requires two years to attain its pattern,
and for the rest of his life this chicken will act as though he
designed it himself. For his first two years he might have been
put together out of a rag bag by an unimaginative hand. During

his first year he has a buff breast, a speckled back, a green neck like his mother's, and a short gray tail. During his second year he has a black breast, his sire's blue neck, a back which is slowly turning the green and gold it will remain; but still no long tail. In his third year he reaches his majority and acquires his tail. For the rest of his life—and a peachicken may live to be thirty-five—he will have nothing better to do than manicure it, furl and unfurl it, dance forward *and backward* with it spread, scream when it is stepped upon, and arch it carefully when he steps through a puddle.

Not every part of the peacock is striking to look at, even when he is full-grown. His upper wing feathers are a striated black and white and might have been borrowed from a Barred Rock fryer; his end wing feathers are the color of clay; his legs are long, thin, and iron-colored; his feet are big; and he appears to be wearing the short pants now so much in favor with playboys in the summer. These extend downward, buff-colored and sleek, from what might be a blue-black waistcoat. One would not be disturbed to find a watch chain hanging from this, but none does. Analyzing the appearance of the peacock as he stands with his tail folded, I find the parts incommensurate with the whole. The fact is that with his tail folded, nothing but his bearing saves this bird from being a laughingstock. With his tail spread, he inspires a range of emotions, but I have yet to hear laughter.

The usual reaction is silence, at least for a time. The cock opens his tail by shaking himself violently until it is gradually lifted in an arch around him. Then, before anyone has had a chance to see it, he swings around so that his back faces the spectator. This has been taken by some to be insult and by others to be whimsey. I suggest it means only that the peacock is equally well satisfied with either view of himself. Since I have been keeping peafowl, I have been visited at least once a year by first-grade schoolchildren, who learn by living. I am used to hearing this group chorus as the peacock swings around, "Oh, look at his underwear!" This "underwear" is a stiff gray tail, raised to support the larger one, and beneath it a puff of black feathers that would be suitable for some really regal woman—a Cleopatra or a Clytemnestra—to use to powder her nose.

When the peacock has presented his back, the spectator will usually begin to walk around him to get a front view; but the peacock will continue to turn so that no front view is possible. The thing to do then is to stand still and wait until it pleases him to turn. When it suits him, the peacock will face you. Then you will see in a green-bronze arch around him a galaxy of gazing, haloed suns. This is the moment when most people are silent.

"Amen! Amen!" an old Negro woman once cried when this happened, and I have heard many similar remarks at this moment that show the inadequacy of human speech. Some people whistle; a few, for once, are silent. A truck driver who was driving up with a load of hay and found a peacock turning before him in the middle of the road shouted, "Get a load of that bastard!" and braked his truck to a shattering halt. I have never known a strutting peacock to budge a fraction of an inch for truck or tractor or automobile. It is up to the vehicle to get out of the way. No peafowl of mine has ever been run over, though one year one of them lost a foot in the mowing machine.

Many people, I have found, are congenitally unable to appreciate the sight of a peacock. Once or twice I have been asked what the peacock is "good for"—a question which gets no answer from me because it deserves none. The telephone company sent a lineman out one day to repair our telephone. After the job was finished, the man, a large fellow with a suspicious expression half hidden by a yellow helmet, continued to idle about, trying to coax a cock that had been watching him to strut. He wished to add this experience to a large number of others he had apparently had. "Come on now, bud," he said, "get the show on the road, upsy-daisy, come on now, snap it up, snap it up."

The peacock, of course, paid no attention to this.

"What ails him?" the man asked.

"Nothing ails him," I said. "He'll put it up terreckly. All you have to do is wait."

The man trailed about after the cock for another fifteen minutes or so; then, in disgust, he got back in his truck and started off. The bird shook himself and his tail rose around him.

"He's doing it!" I screamed. "Hey, wait! He's doing it!"

The man swerved the truck back around again just as the cock

turned and faced him with the spread tail. The display was perfect. The bird turned slightly to the right and the little planets
above him hung in bronze, then he turned slightly to the left
and they were hung in green. I went up to the truck to see how
the man was affected by the sight.

He was staring at the peacock with rigid concentration, as if
he were trying to read fine print at a distance. In a second the
cock lowered his tail and stalked off.

"Well, what did you think of that?" I asked.

"Never saw such long ugly legs," the man said. "I bet that
rascal could outrun a bus."

Some people are genuinely affected by the sight of a peacock,
even with his tail lowered, but do not care to admit it; others
appear to be incensed by it. Perhaps they have the suspicion that
the bird has formed some unfavorable opinion of them. The peacock himself is a careful and dignified investigator. Visitors to
our place, instead of being barked at by dogs rushing from under
the porch, are squalled at by peacocks whose blue necks and
crested heads pop up from behind tufts of grass, peer out of
bushes, and crane downward from the roof of the house, where
the bird has flown, perhaps for the view. One of mine stepped
from under the shrubbery one day and came forward to inspect
a carful of people who had driven up to buy a calf. An old man
and five or six white-haired, bare-footed children were piling out
the back of the automobile as the bird approached. Catching
sight of him they stopped in their tracks and stared, plainly
hacked to find this superior figure blocking their path. There was
silence as the bird regarded them, his head drawn back at its
most majestic angle, his folded train glittering behind him in the
sunlight.

"Whut is thet thang?" one of the small boys asked finally in a
sullen voice.

The old man had got out of the car and was gazing at the
peacock with an astounded look of recognition. "I ain't seen one
of them since my grandaddy's day," he said, respectfully remov-
ing his hat. "Folks used to have 'em, but they don't no more."

"Whut is it?" the child asked again in the same tone he had
used before.

"Churren," the old man said, "that's the king of the birds!"

The children received this information in silence. After a minute they climbed back into the car and continued from there to stare at the peacock, their expressions annoyed, as if they disliked catching the old man in the truth.

The peacock does most of his serious strutting in the spring and summer when he has a full tail to do it with. Usually he begins shortly after breakfast, struts for several hours, desists in the heat of the day, and begins again in the late afternoon. Each cock has a favorite station where he performs every day in the hope of attracting some passing hen; but if I have found anyone indifferent to the peacock's display, besides the telephone lineman, it is the peahen. She seldom casts an eye at it. The cock, his tail raised in a shimmering arch around him, will turn this way and that, and with his clay-colored wing feathers touching the ground, will dance forward and backward, his neck curved, his beak parted, his eyes glittering. Meanwhile the hen goes about her business, diligently searching the ground as if any bug in the grass were of more importance than the unfurled map of the universe which floats nearby.

Some people have the notion that only the peacock spreads his tail and that he does it only when the hen is present. This is not so. A peafowl only a few hours hatched will raise what tail he has—it will be about the size of a thumbnail—and will strut and turn and back and bow exactly as if he were three years old and had some reason to be doing it. The hens will raise their tails when they see an object on the ground which alarms them, or sometimes when they have nothing better to do and the air is brisk. Brisk air goes at once to the peafowl's head and inclines him to be sportive. A group of birds will dance together, or four or five will chase one another around a bush or tree. Sometimes one will chase himself, end his frenzy with a spirited leap into the air, and then stalk off as if he had never been involved in the spectacle.

Frequently the cock combines the lifting of his tail with the raising of his voice. He appears to receive through his feet some shock from the center of the earth, which travels upward through him and is released: *Eee-ooo-ii! Eee-ooo-ii!* To the melancholy this sound is melancholy and to the hysterical it is hysterical. To me it has always sounded like a cheer for an invisible parade.

The hen is not given to these outbursts. She makes a noise like a mule's bray—*heehaw, heehaw, aa-aawww*—and makes it only when necessary. In the fall and winter, peafowl are usually silent unless some racket disturbs them; but in the spring and summer, at short intervals during the day and night, the cock, lowering his neck and throwing back his head, will give out with seven or eight screams in succession as if this message were the one on earth which needed most urgently to be heard.

At night these calls take on a minor key and the air for miles around is charged with them. It has been a long time since I let my first peafowl out at dusk to roost in the cedar trees behind the house. Now fifteen or twenty still roost there; but the original old cock from Eustis, Florida, stations himself on top of the barn, the bird who lost his foot in the mowing machine sits on a flat shed near the horse stall, there are others in the trees by the pond, several in the oaks at the side of the house, and one that cannot be dissuaded from roosting on the water tower. From all these stations calls and answers echo through the night. The peacock perhaps has violent dreams. Often he wakes and screams "Help! Help!" and then from the pond and the barn and the trees around the house a chorus of adjuration begins:

> Lee-yon lee-yon,
> Mee-yon mee-yon!
> Eee-e-yoy eee-e-yoy!
> Eee-e-yoy eee-e-yoy!

The restless sleeper may wonder if he wakes or dreams.

It is hard to tell the truth about this bird. The habits of any peachicken left to himself would hardly be noticeable, but multiplied by forty, they become a situation. I was correct that my peachickens would all eat Startena; they also eat everything else. Particularly they eat flowers. My mother's fears were all borne out. Peacocks not only eat flowers, they eat them systematically, beginning at the head of a row and going down it. If they are not hungry, they will pick the flower anyway, if it is attractive, and let it drop. For general eating they prefer chrysanthemums and roses. When they are not eating flowers, they enjoy sitting on top of them, and where the peacock sits he will eventually fashion a dusting hole. Any chicken's dusting hole is out of place in a flower bed, but the peafowl's hole, being the size of a small crater, is more so. When he dusts he all but obliterates the sight of himself with sand. Usually when someone arrives at full gallop with the leveled broom, he can see nothing through the cloud of dirt and flying flowers but a few green feathers and a beady, pleasure-taking eye.

From the beginning, relations between these birds and my mother were strained. She was forced, at first, to get up early in the morning and go out with her clippers to reach the Lady Bankshire and the Herbert Hoover roses before some peafowl had breakfasted upon them; now she has halfway solved her problem by erecting hundreds of feet of twenty-four-inch-high wire to fence the flower beds. She contends that peachickens do not have enough sense to jump over a low fence. "If it were a high wire," she says, "they would jump onto it and over, but they don't have sense enough to jump over a low wire."

It is useless to argue with her on this matter. "It's not a challenge," I say to her; but she has made up her mind.

In addition to eating flowers, peafowl also eat fruit, a habit which has created a lack of cordiality toward them on the part of my uncle, who had the fig trees planted about the place because he has an appetite for figs himself. "Get that scoundrel out of that fig bush!" he will roar, rising from his chair at the sound of a limb breaking, and someone will have to be dispatched with a broom to the fig trees.

Peafowl also enjoy flying into barn lofts and eating peanuts off peanut hay; this has not endeared them to our dairyman. And as they have a taste for fresh garden vegetables, they have often run afoul of the dairyman's wife.

The peacock likes to sit on gates or fence posts and allow his tail to hang down. A peacock on a fence post is a superb sight. Six or seven peacocks on a gate are beyond description; but it is not very good for the gate. Our fence posts tend to lean in one direction or another and all our gates open diagonally.

In short, I am the only person on the place who is willing to underwrite, with something more than tolerance, the presence of peafowl. In return, I am blessed with their rapid multiplication. The population figure I give out is forty, but for some time now I have not felt it wise to take a census. I had been told before I bought my birds that peafowl are difficult to raise. It is not so, alas. In May the peahen finds a nest in some fence corner and lays five or six large buff-colored eggs. Once a day, thereafter, she gives an abrupt *hee-haa-awww!* and shoots like a rocket from her nest. Then for half an hour, her neck ruffled and stretched forward, she parades around the premises, announcing what she is about. I listen with mixed emotions.

In twenty-eight days the hen comes off with five or six moth-like, murmuring peachicks. The cock ignores these unless one gets under his feet (then he pecks it over the head until it gets elsewhere), but the hen is a watchful mother and every year a good many of the young survive. Those that withstand illnesses and predators (the hawk, the fox, and the opossum) over the winter seem impossible to destroy, except by violence.

A man selling fence posts tarried at our place one day and told me that he had once had eighty peafowl on his farm. He cast a nervous eye at two of mine standing nearby. "In the spring, we couldn't hear ourselves think," he said. "As soon as you lifted your voice, they lifted their'n, if not before. All our fence posts wobbled. In the summer they ate all the tomatoes off the vines. Scuppernongs went the same way. My wife said she raised her flowers for herself and she was not going to have them eat up by a chicken no matter how long his tail was. And in the fall they shed them feathers all over the place anyway and it was a job to clean up. My old grandmother was living with us then and she was eighty-five. She said, 'Either they go, or I go.' "

"Who went?" I asked.

"We still got twenty of them in the freezer," he said.

"And how," I asked, looking significantly at the two standing nearby, "did they taste?"

"No better than any other chicken," he said, "but I'd a heap rather eat them than hear them."

I have tried imagining that the single peacock I see before me is the only one I have, but then one comes to join him; another flies off the roof, four or five crash out of the crêpe-myrtle hedge; from the pond one screams and from the barn I hear the dairyman denouncing another that has got into the cowfeed. My kin are given to such phrases as, "Let's face it."

I do not like to let my thoughts linger in morbid channels, but there are times when such facts as the price of wire fencing and the price of Startena and the yearly gain in peafowl all run uncontrolled through my head. Lately I have had a recurrent dream: I am five years old and a peacock. A photographer has been sent from New York and a long table is laid in celebration. The meal is to be an exceptional one: myself. I scream, "Help! Help!" and awaken. Then from the pond and the barn and the trees around the house, I hear that chorus of jubilation begin:

> *Lee-yon lee-yon,*
> *Mee-yon mee-yon!*
> *Eee-e-yoy eee-e-yoy!*
> *Eee-e-yoy eee-e-yoy!*

I intend to stand firm and let the peacocks multiply, for I am sure that, in the end, the last word will be theirs.

CYNTHIA OZICK

THE LESSON OF THE MASTER

There was a period in my life—to purloin a famous Jamesian title, "The Middle Years"—when I used to say, with as much ferocity as I could muster, "I hate Henry James and I wish he was dead."

I was not to have my disgruntled way. The dislike did not last and turned once again to adoration, ecstasy, and awe; and no one is more alive than Henry James, or more likely to sustain literary immortality. He is among the angels, as he meant to be.

But in earlier days I felt I had been betrayed by Henry James. I was like the youthful writer in "The Lesson of the Master" who believed in the Master's call to live immaculately, unspoiled by what we mean when we say "life"—relationship, family mess, distraction, exhaustion, anxiety, above all disappointment. Here is the Master, St. George, speaking to his young disciple, Paul Overt:

> "One has no business to have any children," St. George placidly declared. "I mean, of course, if one wants to do anything good."
> "But aren't they an inspiration—an incentive?"
> "An incentive to damnation, artistically speaking."

And later Paul inquires:

> "Is it deceptive that I find you living with every appearance of domestic felicity—blest with a devoted, accomplished wife, with children whose acquaintance I haven't yet had the pleasure of making, but who *must* be delightful young people, from what I know of their parents?"

St. George smiled as for the candour of his question. "It's all excellent, my dear fellow—heaven forbid I should deny it. . . . I've got a loaf on the shelf; I've got everything in fact but the great thing."

"And the great thing?" Paul kept echoing.

"The sense of having done the best—the sense which is the real life of the artist and the absence of which is his death, of having drawn from his intellectual instrument the finest music that nature had hidden in it, of having played it as it should be played. He either does that or he doesn't—and if he doesn't he isn't worth speaking of."

Paul pursues:

"Then what did you mean . . . by saying that children are a curse?"

"My dear youth, on what basis are we talking?" and St. George dropped upon the sofa at a short distance from him. . . . "On the supposition that a certain perfection's possible and even desirable—isn't it so? Well, all I say is that one's children interfere with perfection. One's wife interferes. Marriage interferes."

"You think, then, the artist shouldn't marry?"

"He does so at his peril—he does so at his cost."

Yet the Master who declares all this is himself profoundly, inextricably, married; and when his wife dies, he hastens to marry again, choosing Life over Art. Very properly James sees marriage as symbol and summary of the passion for ordinary human entanglement, as experience of the most commonplace, most fated kind.

But we are also given to understand, in the desolation of this comic tale, that the young artist, the Master's trusting disciple, is left both perplexed and bereft: the Master's second wife is the young artist's first love, and the Master has stolen away his disciple's chance for ordinary human entanglement.

So the Lesson of the Master is a double one: choose ordinary human entanglement, and live; or choose Art, and give up the vitality of life's passions and panics and endurances. What I am going to tell now is a stupidity, a misunderstanding, a great Jamesian life-mistake: an embarrassment and a life-shame. (Imagine that we are in one of those lavishly adorned Jamesian chambers where intimate confessions not accidentally but suspensefully take place.) As I have said, I felt myself betrayed by a Jamesian trickery. Trusting in James, believing, like Paul Overt, in the overtness of the Jamesian lesson, I chose Art, and ended by blaming Henry James. It seemed to me James had left out the one important thing I ought to have known, even though he was saying it again and again. The trouble was that I was listening to the Lesson of the Master at the wrong time, paying powerful and excessive attention at the wrong time; and this cost me my youth.

I suppose a case can be made that it is certainly inappropriate for anyone to moan about the loss of youth and how it is all Henry James's fault. All of us will lose our youth, and some of us, alas, have lost it already; but not all of us will pin the loss on Henry James.

I, however, do. I blame Henry James.

Never mind the sublime position of Henry James in American letters. Never mind the Jamesian prose style—never mind that it too is sublime, nuanced, imbricated with a thousand distinctions and observations (the reason H. G. Wells mocked it), and as idiosyncratically and ecstatically redolent of the spirals of past and future as a garlic clove. Set aside also the Jamesian impatience with idols, the moral seriousness active in both the work and the life. (I am thinking, for example, of Edith Wharton's compliance in the face of their mutual friend Paul Bourget's anti-Semitism, and James's noble and definitive dissent.) Neglect all this, including every other beam that flies out from the stupendous Jamesian lantern to keep generations reading in rapture (which is all right), or else scribbling away at dissertation after dissertation (which is not so good). I myself, after all, committed a Master's thesis, long ago, called "Parable in Henry James," in which I tried to catch up all of James in the net of a single idea. Before that, I lived many months in the black hole of a microfilm cell, transcribing every letter James ever wrote to Mr. Pinker, his London agent, for a professorial book; but the professor drank, and died, and after thirty years the letters still lie in the dark.

All that while I sat cramped in that black bleak microfilm cell, and all that while I was writing that thesis, James was sinking me and despoiling my youth, and I did not know it.

I want, parenthetically, to recommend to the Henry James

Society—there is such an assemblage—that membership be limited: no one under age forty-two and three-quarters need apply. Proof of age via birth certificate should be mandatory; otherwise the consequences may be harsh and horrible. I offer myself as an Extreme and Hideous Example of Premature Exposure to Henry James. I was about seventeen, I recall, when my brother brought home from the public library a science-fiction anthology, which, through an odd perspective that perplexes me still, included "The Beast in the Jungle." It was in this anthology, and at that age, that I first read James—fell, I should say, into the jaws of James. I had never heard of him before. I read "The Beast in the Jungle" and creepily thought: Here, here is my autobiography.

From that time forward, gradually but compellingly—and now I yield my scary confession—I became Henry James. Leaving graduate school at the age of twenty-two, disdaining the Ph.D. as an acquisition surely beneath the concerns of literary seriousness, I was already Henry James. When I say I "became" Henry James, you must understand this: though I was a near-sighted twenty-two-year-old young woman infected with the commonplace intention of writing a novel, I was *also* the elderly bald-headed Henry James. Even without close examination, you could see the light glancing off my pate; you could see my heavy chin, my watch chain, my walking stick, my tender paunch.

I had become Henry James, and for years and years I remained Henry James. There was no doubt about it: it was my own clear and faithful truth. Of course, there were some small differences: for one thing, I was not a genius. For another, even in my own insignificant scribbler class, I was not prolific. But I carried the Jamesian idea, I was of his cult, I was a worshiper of literature, literature was my single altar; I was, like the elderly bald-headed James, a priest at that altar; and that altar was all of my life. Like John Marcher in "The Beast in the Jungle," I let everything pass me by for the sake of waiting for the Beast to spring—but unlike John Marcher, I knew what the Beast was, I knew exactly, I even knew the Beast's name: the Beast was literature itself, the sinewy grand undulations of some unraveling fiction, meticulously dreamed out in a language of masterly resplendence, which was to pounce on me and turn me into an enchanted and glorious

Being, as enchanted and glorious as the elderly bald-headed Henry James himself.

But though the years spent themselves extravagantly, that ambush never occurred: the ambush of Sacred and Sublime Literature. The great shining Beast of Sacred and Sublime Literature did not pounce. Instead, other beasts, lesser ones, unseemly and misshapen, sprang out—all the beasts of ordinary life: sorrow, disease, death, guilt, responsibility, envy, grievance, grief, disillusionment—the beasts that are chained to human experience, and have nothing to do with Art except to interrupt and impede it, exactly according to the Lesson of the Master.

It was not until I read a certain vast and subtle book that I understood what had happened to me. The book was not by Henry James, but about him. Nowadays we give this sort of work a special name: we call it a nonfiction novel. I am referring, of course, to Leon Edel's ingenious and beautiful biography of Henry James, which is as much the possession of Edel's imagination as it is of the exhilaratingly reported facts of James's life. In Edel's rendering, I learned what I had never before taken in— but the knowledge came, in the Jamesian way, too late. What I learned was that Henry James himself had not always been the elderly bald-headed Henry James—that he too had once been twenty-two years old.

This terrible and secret knowledge instantly set me against James. From that point forward I was determined to eradicate him. And for a long while I succeeded.

What had happened was this: in early young-womanhood I believed, with all the rigor and force and stunned ardor of religious belief, in the old Henry James, in his scepter and his authority. I believed that what *he* knew at sixty I was to encompass at twenty-two; at twenty-two I lived like the elderly bald-headed Henry James. I thought it was necessary—it was imperative, there was no other path!—to be, all at once, with no progression or evolution, the author of the equivalent of *The Ambassadors* or *The Wings of the Dove*, just as if "A Bundle of Letters," or "Four Meetings," or the golden little "The Europeans" had never preceded the great late Master.

For me, the Lesson of the Master was a horror, a Jamesian tale of a life of mishap and mistake and misconceiving. Though the Master himself was saying, in *The Ambassadors*, in Gloriani's garden, to Little Bilham, through the urgent cry of Strether, "Live, live!"—and though the Master himself was saying, in "The Beast in the Jungle," through May Bartram, how ghastly, how ghostly, it is to eschew, to evade, to turn from, to miss absolutely and irrevocably what is all the time there for you to seize—I mistook him, I misheard him, I missed, absolutely and irrevocably, his essential note. What I heard instead was: *Become a Master*.

Now the truth is it could not have been done, even by a writer of genius; and what a pitiful flicker of the flame of high ambition for a writer who is no more than the ordinary article! No one—not even James himself—springs all at once in early youth into full Mastery, and no writer, whether robustly gifted, or only little and pale, should hope for this implausible fate.

All this, I suppose, is not at all a "secret" knowledge, as I have characterized it, but is, rather, as James named it in the very person of his naïve young artist, most emphatically *overt*—so obvious that it is a mere access of foolishness even to talk about it. Still, I offer the implausible and preposterous model of myself to demonstrate the proposition that the Lesson of the Master is not a lesson about genius, or even about immense ambition; it is a lesson about misreading—about what happens when we misread the great voices of Art, and suppose that, because they speak of Art, they *mean* Art. The great voices of Art never mean *only* Art; they also mean Life, they always mean Life, and Henry James, when he evolved into the Master we revere, finally meant nothing else.

The true Lesson of the Master, then, is, simply, never to venerate what is complete, burnished, whole, in its grand organic flowering or finish—never to look toward the admirable and dazzling end; never to be ravished by the goal; never to worship ripe Art or the ripened artist; but instead to seek to be young while young, primitive while primitive, ungainly when ungainly—to look for crudeness and rudeness, to husband one's own stupidity or ungenius.

There *is* this mix-up most of us have between ourselves and what we admire or triumphantly cherish. We see this mix-up, this mishap, this mishmash, most often in writers: the writer of a new generation ravished by the genius writer of a classical generation, who begins to dream herself, or himself, as powerful, vigorous, and original—as if being filled up by the genius writer's images, scenes, and stratagems were the same as having the capacity to pull off the identical magic. To be any sort of competent writer one must keep one's psychological distance from the supreme artists.

If I were twenty-two now, I would not undertake a cannibalistically ambitious Jamesian novel to begin with; I would look into the eyes of Henry James at twenty-two, and see the diffident hope, the uncertainty, the marveling tentativeness, the dream that is still only a dream; the young man still learning to fashion the Scene. Or I would go back still further, to the boy of seventeen, misplaced in a Swiss Polytechnic School, who recalled in old age that "I so feared and abhorred mathematics that the simplest arithmetical operation had always found and kept me helpless and blank." It is not to the Master in his fullness I would give my awed, stricken, desperate fealty, but to the faltering, imperfect, dreaming youth.

If these words should happen to reach the ears of any young writer dumbstruck by the elderly bald-headed Henry James, one who has hungrily heard and ambitiously assimilated the voluptuous cathedral-tones of the developed organ-master, I would say to her or him: put out your lean and clumsy forefinger and strike your paltry, oafish, feeble, simple, skeletal, single note. Try for what Henry James at sixty would scorn—just as he scorned the work of his own earliness, and revised it and revised it in the manner of his later pen in that grand chastisement of youth known as the New York Edition. Trying, in youth, for what the Master in his mastery would condemn—that is the only road to modest mastery. Rapture and homage are not the way. Influence is perdition.

JEAN HOLLANDER

COPS AND WRITERS

Two years ago the chairman of the English department at Trenton State College asked me to take over a class in the short story for policemen in Plainfield. I agreed, not quite certain whether or not I really wanted to. Although I had taught adult classes before, I had for the last few years been teaching mainly college freshmen. Now the thought of confronting a class of policemen was enough to shake my accustomed sense of authority. Getting lost on my way to Plainfield and thus arriving late for the first class did not help to calm me. Even more disturbing than the roomful of bulging, brawny cops (and they do loom large in the small seats of classrooms) that I had envisioned was the handful of seven resentful men waiting for me. To make things more awkward, they were expecting the male teacher listed in the catalogue, not the floundering, nervous female who entered. Fortunately, I had come prepared with copies of Kafka's "The Judgment," a difficult text at best. While they read, I had time to regain my breath and my bearing. And they, struck by the strange plot and confusing details, realized that they required help to solve the riddles posed by such an unfamiliar piece of writing. When I had previously tried to teach the story to freshmen at Trenton State College, they had been both baffled and bored by it. Although Princeton University students had been more interested in the story, many found the principal theme of universal guilt unconvincing. But here the class went well. By the time the policemen and I were finished asking many questions and supplying some answers, it seemed to me that we had covered the major aspects of Kafka's enigmatic tale.

Afterward I thought about the reasons for the success of that first class. Perhaps these policemen's much-discussed need for authority was reflected in the basic structure of the Kafka story: the victory of the father figure symbolized by the son's obedience to his father's death sentence upon him. But in the story the father's fall, even as the sentence is being carried out, is hardly a triumph of authority. Surely their understanding of the son's subtle guilt, which is unrelated to the real or imagined neglect of his father, speaks for a more sensitive understanding of moral responsibility than cops are usually given credit for. Interestingly, they also had a much more immediate grasp of the humor in Kafka's writing than most students do. Having themselves often been involved in events that entail so much terror or horror, these men had learned how to use irony to make those situations bearable. Being unable to respond emotionally to the ugliness of some scenes which they were forced to confront had taught them distance. They knew that one way to bear the unbearable is to laugh at it. Kafka's mixture of the grotesque and the serious, of surreal events described with minute realistic details and seemingly mundane realities that suddenly refuse to obey the rules of existence did not surprise them. They could laugh at the father hopping about on the bed flipping up the ends of his dressing gown. They readily understood the macabre complexity involved in his judgment, its wild parody of Jehovah and its simultaneous psychological necessity. Later in the term, they had no problem appreciating both the pathos and the humor in the scene in which a charwoman throws away the dried-out beetle that once was Gregor, the protagonist, in Kafka's "Metamorphosis."

My task that term was to make them understand some of the subtler ways writers communicate their meanings. For their part, they tried, sometimes quite vehemently, to explain some of the crudities of experience which they found in the reading. There is no way of gauging how well I learned their lessons—but they were impressive in their quickness to use whatever clues for interpretation I gave them. Each man's eye and memory for detail was remarkable. Their understanding of human behavior and motivation, of the various reactions possible to any given situation, made every class an unpredictable but always interesting experience. Although they soon allowed me a superior knowledge of the technical aspects of literature, in the interpretation of characters or the experiential meaning of a story they were less likely to yield; they felt that in the understanding of human nature they were more qualified than I.

It was, then, with eagerness that I accepted another assignment in the same police program a year later to teach a course called "Experiencing Literature." This time I knew what to expect. The syllabus I devised was much longer and more difficult than the one usually given at the college, although it followed the general outline of the introductory course. During eleven three-hour meetings we studied twenty short stories, fifty-eight poems, and five plays. Some of the stories were not easy to understand, nor did they all even qualify as short. They included Hawthorne's "Young Goodman Brown," Faulkner's "The Bear" and "A Rose for Emily," Hemingway's "The Short Happy Life of Francis Macomber," Flannery O'Connor's "A Good Man Is Hard to Find," James Joyce's "Araby," and Franz Kafka's "The Metamorphosis." The poets we read began with "Anonymous" (ballads), through Shakespeare's sonnets, Donne, Herrick, Marvell, Keats, Shelley, Coleridge, Blake, Browning, Whitman, Dickinson, and continued to Yeats, Hopkins, Eliot, Dylan Thomas, Frost, Anthony Hecht, and Allen Ginsberg. In the weeks devoted to the drama, we read *Oedipus Rex* and *Antigone*, a short medieval play called *Quem Quaeritis*, John Millington Synge's *Riders to the Sea*, Ionesco's *The Gap*, and ended with Shakespeare's *Othello*. Although I told them that I had made the course more difficult than the equivalent class at the college, they never complained. In fact, they took it as a matter of pride, feeling that this heavier reading load proved that they had more mettle than the other students. Despite the long hours and nervous strain of their police work, they were usually well prepared and attended classes regularly except when they were on duty or had to appear in court.

I decided to begin the term's work with the short story since that form would be the easiest for them, not only because most of their reading up to then had probably been in that genre, but also because a study of the reaction of people to various situations was something they relied on in their daily work. For instance, they had to be able to predict how others would react to their directives and interventions before deciding on their own form of action; they had to be able to take in the details of a situation quickly and correctly before intervening. No matter how factual and sparse police reports may seem to us, they must make use of a selection of vital detail, similar to that which a writer of a short story has to make.

This was taught to me by one of my students, a captain, at the end of the term. I had begun the study of the short story by stressing the differences between a factual report, such as a scientist's or a policeman's report, and the presentation of a creative writer. While a selection of necessary details is involved in both, the officer must remain neutral and clearly try to present a picture of the facts, while the artist usually begins with a preconceived message or attitude which is then transmitted through the use of carefully selected details of action described in words intended to provoke associations and emotional reactions in the reader. Only at the end of the term did the captain point out to me that he and his men also try to evaluate the events they describe and that their description of a sequence of events must of necessity be structured and colored by their understanding of what has taken place.

The policemen's reactions to events and characters in the stories were surprisingly unprejudiced. Forms of behavior that most of us—in our narrow-mindedness—expect policemen to object to were accepted without hesitation. They did not object to writers whose stories had to do with their protagonist's rebellion against society's accepted values. Nor did stories in which the strong father becomes the villain and in which our usual ideals of manhood are turned around offend them. The many hunters among my students readily granted the message in those hunting tales in which sensitivity triumphs over male aggressiveness, stories that show the boy becoming a man because he *fails* to shoot the deer, goose, or catbird. The only characters they did object to were those they thought unrealistic. As the previous class had done, this one also excelled in interpreting the ways in which characters reveal themselves, subtly manipulate and influence each other; they, too, understood how the story usually saves its insight, its revelation, for the end.

This almost instinctive grasp of the writing of fiction was

revealed when the policemen volunteered to write their own short stories. Although warned that this assignment would have very little bearing on their term grades, they put obvious effort into the task, and some wrote stories of ten or fifteen pages. They not only took great pains with plot and character, but with style and language. The stories were surprisingly well written, revealing an understanding of what a solid short story must contain: the revelation of character, the use of background description and language to create atmosphere and mood, the need to sustain suspense and yet make each event as it occurs seem natural, the insight achieved either by the characters in the story or the reader or both. They tended to favor surprise endings. Some stories were sheer fantasies, or derived from previous reading, films, or television shows. Most wrote stories, obviously based on their own experiences, that revealed the amazing distance they must put between their personal lives and their work, which is part of the training for being a good cop. These stories, as well as their discussions of them, showed how coolly they judged their own weaknesses as well as the humor with which they accepted some of the difficulties or injustices of existence. Despite their authors' unmistakable sense of irony and awareness of corruption, these stories demonstrated how clearly, almost naively, these policemen wanted to continue to believe in some of the so-called American virtues—that courage is worth the effort and will be admired; that hard work will be rewarded; that life is somehow good; and that, despite the weariness, boredom, and occasional ugliness and danger, despite all their dislike of most of their routine and despite their own occasional grousing and complaints, they somehow did like being cops; that life, even in a chaotic and violent world, is worth it after all.

The stories also revealed varieties of unexpected sympathies and understanding. An officer who had recently arrested a sexual offender wrote a sympathetic account of the events and emotions leading up to the offense from the arrested man's point of view. Another officer, who had been incensed when called upon in a particularly sad case of child neglect and abuse—about which he was unable to do anything in real life—had his protagonist policeman, with deliberate wish fulfillment, shoot the mother because she reminded him of his own mother. One man wrote of a heroic arrest by a rookie who gets the admiration of all bystanders for this deed and affirms how good it feels to have done the "right thing" even at risk to one's life. (I later learned that this new man had indeed been present at a similar situation, but had acted in the routine, prescribed manner—that is, without any unnecessary risks or heroics.) Another described a boring day in the life of a cop, which begins with his not wanting to go on duty and counting the days to retirement, but ends with his realization that he likes his job after all. A student whom I knew to be an avid hunter had his hunter protagonist suddenly see the beauty and sacredness of all life as he lies dying in the woods.

These stories revealed an impressive willingness to see the other side, even while taking a firm stand on one side. Aware that the big man who goes berserk in a bar will be sorry he has hurt anyone the next morning, they, the cops, must cope with that awareness even as they go in to stop him. They must somehow use a minimum of force to subdue him, knowing him to be twice as strong as anybody else and not very reasonable at that moment. When they answer the call to a family feud involving a wife beating, policemen know that the moment they intervene and try to arrest the man, the very victim will become protective of him and turn on the arresting officer, frequently with a weapon. Their stories made me realize that most of them chose their profession, not out of a need to bully, but out of a sincere respect for order, a conviction that there is a right way to behave and that law and order are valid components of the good life. Most denied at least the frequency of police brutality. Those that did admit to the temptation of such illegal abuse explained the stress of these situations.

The segment of the course devoted to the study of poetry proved for them the most trying part of our reading list. For most students in regular programs, the challenge in learning to read poetry is to discover that interpretation is not a free-floating exercise in fantasy. That was not the problem in this class. Their training had prepared them for the fact that all interpretations and conclusions must be based on details taken from the text. But they resented having to rely on the verbal implications, the delicacies of tone, the unreliable shadings through which poetry communicates. I began this section of the course with narrative poetry, since I thought that the story line and revelation of character found in such poetry would yield more readily to the methods of investigation with which they were already familiar from our study of the short story. Perhaps the change in form was too abrupt, or the dialects used in the early ballads too strange. The diction in Browning's "My Last Duchess" seemed stilted and obscure to them. The archaic, ornate vocabulary of Shelley and Keats confused and displeased them. Some had trouble hearing the rhythms, the stressed and unstressed beats of a line.

But even here, frustrated by what they considered a lack of clear details, they underestimated their own understanding. I was continually amazed and impressed by their ability to understand the literal meaning of the most difficult poems. Donne's "The Flea" was quickly seen to be a poem about seduction. They easily understood that in the sonnet "Batter My Heart" the speaker wishes to reform, to get closer to God. Their difficulty, as for most students, lay in accepting Donne's metaphysical forcing of two opposing ideas into one image or word. Either their religious beliefs or a narrower sense of what is fitting made Donne's forced fusion of religious and sexual passion offensive to them. While they might not all have been regular churchgoers, most of the men seem to have had some faith in God or a belief in an afterlife, and this merging of sex and salvation surprised and even shocked them.

To test whether the policemen had learned a method of approaching poetry rather than merely repeating given explanations, I asked them, as part of an examination, to interpret a very difficult poem, "God's Grandeur" by Gerard Manley Hopkins. They had no trouble deciding on the basic message of the poem. They also did well in discovering the complexities in some of Hopkins's metaphors. I had asked them to focus on certain key words—for example, the word *charged* in the opening line, "The world is charged with the grandeur of God." They did well in rendering the varieties of meaning that word gives the statement, citing references to debts, electricity, command, and power. But they had trouble seeing how metaphors structure a poem. They did not, for instance, go on to say that in the line "And for all this, nature is never spent," the word *spent* continues the idea of debt and power introduced in the earlier image. Despite their complaints about how difficult the language and metaphors in most of the poems were, they all decided that Matthew Arnold's "Dover Beach" was a better poem than Anthony Hecht's parody "The Dover Bitch," although Hecht's came closer to their own speech patterns.

In the drama selections, they again surprised me by rejecting Synge's modern, rather easily understood *Riders to the Sea* as uninteresting. Perhaps the play's message of failure and despair, against which Synge holds us all to be helpless, displeased them. Perhaps a universe in which nature and the sea are deemed enemies was alien to their own experience. On the other hand, the ancient dilemmas found in *Oedipus Rex*—character versus fate, man against the gods, crime and the acceptance of guilt—did interest them. There were the usual discussions of justice. Was Oedipus's punishment too great for a crime committed in ignorance? Although the law they themselves enforced clearly differentiates between accident and intention, between involuntary manslaughter and a planned murder, their conclusions were by no means uniform. For despite our commonly held stereotypes of law enforcement officers, their views on most political and legal issues were broad. The range of their attitudes was even more apparent in our discussion of the play *Antigone*. Antigone's rebellion against Creon's rule, her need to uphold a higher moral order against his edict, aroused surprising sympathy and agreement. A group of cops seemed a strange assembly in which to find such strong feelings against authority and such admiration for this symbolic forerunner of women's liberation. Although Creon's view was very well presented by one of the more voluble and witty students in the class, the majority of the group favored Antigone, choosing an unwritten code over the law of the land and a higher moral plane over that of political expediency.

Despite the difficulty in language that reading Shakespeare's *Othello* represented, the mystery of Iago's motivation and his success in manipulating Othello led to some of our most interesting discussions. As in the study of the short story, the students' understanding of personality, of how people react to given situations was forceful and exciting. They judged Shakespeare's play a more worthy subject of study than Ionesco's *The Gap*, which puzzled and bored them. While their comments showed that they largely understood what Ionesco was trying to say, that message of such poems as Don L. Lee's "But He Was Cool or; he even stopped for green lights" and of X. J. Kennedy's "In a Prominent Bar in Secaucus One Day," this was not the sort of thing they came to class for after a full day on the job.

Tired from the day's work, with barely time to eat before class began, leaving wives, children, loves, friends, television, and beer behind them, these policemen did not come to class to rehearse the familiar. They came to learn something new, to learn new ways of thinking and observing that were generally lacking in their daily lives. Yet somehow their own daily involvement with the harsher realities of life made it even more necessary for them to hold on to certain ideals. I would sometimes sense a kind of wonder and gratitude coming from them that their wives were not like some of the women they must deal with in the performance of their duties, and an irrational insistence that this be so. The artificial barrier between the kind of women they arrested and the others must be the more defended the more intangible and fragile it was. In this connection, there was a strange courtliness in the language they used to address me, so different from the way they would speak among themselves.

The classes not only taught me greater respect for the intelligence and integrity of these men, but they also gave me insight into the complexities which they must encounter and survive each day. I came to see how their own rebelliousness fights against fitting into the immediate authoritarian structure of their superiors, how they resent, even while they obey, foolish rules and frivolous expectations. They must control and hide their own objections to discipline when they confront these same needs in others. They must understand and predict the resistance others feel against obeying their orders, while at the same time denying that understanding in order to elicit the proper response from those around them. Confronting violence, they must somehow strive to respond without violence. Feeling fear, they are not allowed to behave as though they were afraid. Seeing madness, they may not set their own fantasies free. Exposed to repeated evidence of corruption in others, they may not take corruption as natural. Confronted during their working hours with the horrors men and women inflict on each other and on their children, they must come home and erase these visions from their minds. Once they remove their uniforms, they must somehow resume connubial habits, renew their faith in the general goodness of their wives and children. I do not know whether divorce statistics for policemen and criminal records of their offspring differ from those of other families, but one could not be with them for long without appreciating how much harder it must be for a policeman to come home and be willing to suspend his disbelief, to not disturb the smiling surfaces of family relationships or see the potential corruption in those around him.

I saw them practice a similar control every time the class gathered. Some men were still in uniform, some had a gun bulging here or there, some were very tired, having just put in hours of testifying in court or on extra duty. I would overhear them discussing a recent suicide, a particularly bloody murder scene, an ugly family brawl, a case of child neglect, and then put all such thoughts aside as the class began. All the corruption they confronted daily did not keep them from being interested in why Iago does what he does. Is he innately evil as Satan is and cannot help himself? Does he get pleasure out of hurting others? Is he a practical man expressing his resentment at being passed over for promotion? Does he enjoy the sense of power that his manipulation of others gives him? Did he mean to commit only one act that forces him to worse deeds to cover his tracks? Is he a man caught in his own web? Another time, they would put their immediate experience of violence, danger, and hostility aside to puzzle over the speaker in Frost's poem "Stopping by Woods on a Snowy Evening." Is he only a tired man who still has work to do? Or do Frost's images signify other meanings? What do the miles he still must go stand for, and just what sort of sleep is the poet referring to? Do the woods symbolize larger themes of morality? Of mortality?

Like Frost's poem, many of the works we studied offered the

revelation and acceptance of mortality as a major insight. For the young students in most literature classes, this theme of our universal fate needs to be developed slowly and pursued gingerly, since to most college students the possibility of their own death is still something of an academic abstraction. In this particular class, although these students never objected to its presence, I became aware of the cruelty of that persistent message. They were too disciplined and too polite to point out how common-place the vulnerability of the flesh was in their daily routine. But perhaps these discussions were one reason why they enjoyed the classes. Here they could escape to a situation where violent deeds became part of a formal system we could all discuss, reason about, and justify. If most of us, who are only rarely forced to confront our own mortality, need the catharsis that art provides, how much more must policemen, who live amid the chaos of unpredictable violence, need it. In the literary setting we were safe and could calmly evaluate and consider the violent events in which characters condemn each other to death, take their own lives, put out their own eyes, and accept guilts, vague and specific. In the classroom we could make judgments that might the next moment be undone without a trace, without harm to anyone, without the tightened throat and the accelerated heart-beat. Antigone or Creon? What are their motivations? Whose actions are higher in the scale of morality? Soothing inquiry, this, after walking or driving their "beat" in the uniform that leaves men naked.

Perhaps the great frequency and variety of class response was the result of this emotional and intellectual need. Perhaps shar-ing the same profession, the same concerns and frustrations, made these men feel more at ease with one another, made them more willing to respond even when they were unsure of the cor-rectness of an answer. True, being older and more accustomed to being listened to, they didn't suffer the agonies of shyness fighting against the need for self-assertion that so often trouble the young student. Perhaps the very personality traits that made them choose their profession—a willingness to assume authority, to tell others what to do, and, to some extent, what to think—enabled them to take a more aggressive part in class. Whatever the reasons, discussions tended to be more exciting, with many different views being offered by more people than in most college classes. The only silent students were those who, pressed by job or family problems, had not done a particular assignment. Even the generally shy students (and to my surprise I found that there are shy policemen) would be suddenly forced by conviction or disagreement to speak up.

Another interesting aspect of our special situation was the obliteration of rank in the classroom. Different interpretations and impressions were argued out, with only my greater knowledge of the "facts" and more years of having studied these matters counting occasionally and convincingly in my favor. All term long, my only discriminations among them as individuals involved questions of who was prepared more thoroughly, or had greater insight, or could express himself better or more frequently. It was not until we gathered at my house to celebrate the end of term, not until we were in a social setting in which the discussion ranged to more personal attitudes and experiences, that I became aware of their ranks—there were a sergeant and a captain in the group—obviously very important distinctions in their professional lives.

The Law Enforcement Education Program at Trenton State College, in which I was involved, was instituted about eight years ago at the request of the Plainfield Police Department. Unlike so many foundering adult education programs these days, this one is self-supporting and succeeds because of the interest, dedication, and energy of the participants. Although most of the men attend classes four evenings a week, it usually takes them almost eight years to obtain a degree. Since most of the courses offered are in the area of their special interest, criminal justice, rather than the humanities, I have not been involved in the program for the past semester. But a recent Steiner cartoon in *The New Yorker* reminded me what fun it had been to teach literature to the cops of Piscataway and Plainfield. The cartoon shows two burly policemen about to arrest a sorry-looking criminal. The caption has one of the officers, who is holding a book in his hand, saying, "First I'm going to read you your rights, then I'm

going to read you a brief passage from *The Merchant of Venice*."
I doubt whether any of my former students are now going about
their duties reciting *Othello*. But I do think that some of what we
have read and discussed remains with them. And I, too, have
learned and remember.

DAN JACOBSON

THE VANISHING ACT

We expect our children's childhood to pass as slowly as we remember our own to have done. And so it does—*to them*. To them a week or a month or a year can appear ocean-like in its expanses of sameness or changeableness. To us, however, to the parents we have become, the childhood of our children passes as swiftly as everything else in adult years. From moment to moment, we feel, we are left vainly grasping after people who are no longer there. They have vanished even while we were looking at them. How can we recall the six-week-old infant when he has been shouldered out of his own life and out of our minds by someone of the same name and with something of the same features who is now six months old; and how can we recall the six-month-old infant when another infant aged two years or three years or five years has taken his place? And the fifteen-year-old who replaces that five-year-old will in turn be swiftly replaced by an adult with whom our relationship is bound to be quite different from the other, provisional relationships we had before with all his or her other, provisional selves.

True, we change as adults too; we change more rapidly than we are willing to acknowledge, whether in looking at ourselves or others. But the speed and extent of those changes cannot be compared with the metamorphoses our children pass through. Where have they gone, those earlier avatars of their selfhood, those forms they assumed for this moment or that? Into photograph albums, it seems, and anecdote; if anywhere. ("Do you remember that time . . . ?" "Well, when she was about three she

313

used to . . .") But photographs and anecdotes are a poor exchange for living recollections, recollections of figures so full of life they seem substantial enough to blot out the light behind them. Other loves, other acquaintances, people older than ourselves or contemporary with ourselves, we can remember in that fashion, even after a lapse of years, even when such people may have meant little to us. Of our children, of our children's younger selves, virtually nothing remains. When we try to think of them as they once were (perhaps a few months ago!) we have to be content, all too often, with unexpected, unanchored fragments. A forgotten item of clothing seen by chance in a drawer, for example, will perhaps produce not so much a visual image as some sort of tactile reawakening within the self, a "feel" of having handled the small body which the garment once covered. Revisiting, on our own, a place we have been to with our children, we may find them suddenly revisiting us: not as individuals who were then of this height or whose hair was cut in that way, but as urgent *presences* merely, beings whose hands were in our own or slipping away from them, whose voices were raised or silent. What those presences also bring back is not so much a recollection of our emotions as of theirs: their eagerness, their curiosity, their anxiety, their readiness to run ahead or to retreat, their imperious hungers or uncurtailable rages, their collapses into sleepiness or indifference. Only in that context can we recall the sensation, private to us, unknown to them, of having been in charge, of having been under pressure, of having once been parents.

That is all. We can hardly blame ourselves for feeling that it isn't enough. The children have gone and have taken with them the emotions they aroused, as if into an abyss deeper than that into which every other passion from the past eventually falls. Passions of sexual love, or of fear, or of ambition, or of the shame or pride we felt as children in the parents we once had—those in some sense are still with us; they remain accessible in the memory, attached to particular scenes or experiences. But the physical and moral passions of parenthood, which any parent knows to be as deep, as startling, as much a remaking of the whole self as any other, turn out also to be as evanescent as the constantly self-transforming bodies which had aroused them.

Protectiveness and wonder; a sense of being nakedly needed and of needing to be needed; infatuations with shades and textures of skin and hair, with knees and fingernails, with flawless eyes and hollow napes of necks, with lips moister and more delicate than any others we have kissed; pleasures of touching, stroking, smelling, gazing, encompassing; fatigues, irritations, bewilderments, clenched anxieties over illnesses and unexplained absences; incredulity at the responsibilities we have assumed and the half-ashamed delight in finding our way back to much of what we had lost from the time of our own infancy—all once there, and all gone. Gone, leaving so few particular, individual, moment-attached tracings or scorings in the mind.

No wonder, then, that there should be so many works of literature which deal with family relationships from the child's point of view and so few which deal with those relationships from that of the parent. The absence of literature on the subject—I am not speaking of child-rearing manuals—is in fact one of the reasons why succeeding generations of parents are so surprised at what they find themselves going through. No one has warned them! Like the rest of us, writers can recall, sometimes all too clearly or fondly, what it was like to be a child. But to know what it is to be a parent, or to recall what it was to have been a parent, is a much more elusive and problematical business. Think of all those books about children and their parents, or parent-figures, to be found among the literary classics (and think of the movies, or of the novels with other names, which are derived at a greater or lesser remove from them)—*The Mill on the Floss* and *David Copperfield*, *Mansfield Park* and *Jane Eyre*, *Tom Jones* and *War and Peace*, *Sons and Lovers* and *Portrait of the Artist as a Young Man*. All are in effect novels about being a child and having a parent or parents, and about growing out of them, not about being a parent and having a child and having it grow out of you. So are plays like *The Oresteia* or *Romeo and Juliet* or *Hamlet*. (How much we are given of Hamlet's feelings about his mother and stepfather; what ugly, truncated glimpses we are given of their feelings about him.) And so one could go on, almost indefinitely. *The Metamorphosis*, *Swann's Way*, *Great Expectations*, *The Brothers Karamazov*, *The Tin Drum* ... And on the other side? One has to struggle to think of them. *Silas Marner*,

Dombey and Son perhaps, Turgenev's *Fathers and Sons*, and indubitably the greatest of all such works, and great partly because it adopts with such passion the parental point of view, *King Lear*. (Think how easy it would have been to present sympathetically, from their perspective, the problems of the two daughters, Goneril and Regan, confronted as they are with an aged father who has nothing to do with his time and energy but disrupt their domestic arrangements. If only either woman had had a "granny flat" in her castle!) The Bible, interestingly enough, also gives us more of King David's dealings with his errant sons from David's point of view than from theirs; he is the one who really matters, whose hurts and hopes really count; not they and theirs. And that's about all.

None of this (which we take so much for granted that I have never seen it remarked on elsewhere) is accidental. The drama of parenthood from within—and the loss of it, which is part of its drama—remains the great unexplored subject of imaginative writing; in comparison with it, supposedly taxing subjects like the end of the world or the inner life of a mad dictator can appear positively banal. The trouble is, though, that the subject is unexplored because it is largely unexplorable. The emotions of parenthood are experienced in a way and at a level distinctive to themselves, and then they vanish, along with the children who occasion them, to whom they are devoted, and who never rest from carrying out their task of transforming themselves, moment by moment, into other beings.

Until at last they succeed to such an extent that they cease to be children. "Have you any children?" a well-known Scottish poet was once asked. "No," he replied, in grimly humorous, Scottish fashion, "I have a man and a woman." It goes without saying that his relationship with "his" man and woman, and theirs with him, will be forever affected by the fact that they were once his children; in some respects which will be obvious to both sides, and in others which will be hidden from them, they will continue to respond to one another according to patterns laid down in their earliest years together. But what will also become increasingly obvious to both sides is that the balance of responsibility and dependence between them has begun to swing slowly but inexorably in the other direction.

Just as the parents of young children feel bound to protect and help them, to shield them from the ugliness of life and its dangers, so grown children begin to feel that they have this obligation towards their parents. When they keep silent about events or emotions in their own lives, it is not because they are afraid of their parents' anger or disapproval, as before, but because they are indifferent to them, or because their parents have begun to acquire in their eyes something of the innocence of children, the pathos of their ignorance; like children they seem to have become especially vulnerable to mental and physical injury. And indeed, if parents live long enough, and suffer the illnesses and deprivations which age inevitably brings, they will revert to being children, wrinkled children, impossible children; beings whom their children will care for out of affection, out of pity, out of piety, out of exasperation, out of regard for the past; hardly out of passion.

Well, one can see the sense of it, if it is not our wills or individual circumstances but the continuation of the race which ultimately determines such matters. Children are lovable, and are loved, precisely because and to the degree that they are vulnerable. Their vulnerability is signalled in every possible fashion: in their stature, in the shape of their heads, their halting speech, the softness of their skins, their eager movements. If we were not moved to cherish them by such manifestations of weakness, the race would not survive. The vulnerability of old people, on the other hand, has no such appeal; they have exhausted their usefulness, racially speaking, and nature has no compunction in making this fact as evident to everyone around them as it makes the charm and vitality of children. However, only megalomaniacs are given to thinking of themselves as representatives of the race or of nature. The rest of us, parents of children and children of parents, are kept busy enough trying to cope, as best we can, with all the vicissitudes of role, with all the plaitings together and unravellings of relationships, which are forced in such remorseless succession and simultaneity upon us.

Now, an anecdote. A story of the kind which Coleridge, in "The Nightingale", describing how he held up his infant to the moon, so that the tears in the baby's eyes glittered in the moonlight, calls "a father's tale." In other words, an episode treasured not because of its weight but precisely because of its smallness or fragility, its transience, its everydayness—these being the very qualities out of which and into which the intense emotions of parenthood grow. The child who appears in the tale, and who has since been transformed into a young man driving around London in a battered yellow van, selling "whole foods" from door to door, has of course no recollection of the incident. But then, I am pretty sure that if I had not made a note of it at the time, it would have slipped out of my memory like innumerable other incidents or perceptions, some no doubt even smaller, some which must have seemed more weighty, which in their turn clutched quite as fiercely at my heart. The occasions of feeling once lost, all that remains is the conviction that the feeling was once there.

Soon after my son's third birthday a departing neighbour foisted a pet budgerigar on our household. *Faute de mieux* we accepted it, and hung up the cage in the hall. The bird was male; it was canary-yellow all over, except for its head and neck which were stippled blue. Sometimes, when it stretched out a wing, a wave of iridiscent light, which was neither blue nor yellow, or was both at once, would pass from its neck along its wing. Then it would stretch out a leg, too, sideways under the wing, as if to hold it up, like the spar of an umbrella. Having completed the movement, it would regain its balance before solemnly repeating the step on the other side, in ballet-dancer fashion. Its eyes were bright and never gave anything away; its beak was tiny and so fiercely bent over itself you couldn't help feeling its breath must have been as stertorous as an old man's, if only your ears had been sharp enough to hear it. It never sang or chirped much, this budgie, and talked not at all, but it climbed up and down its toy ladder, and gazed with cocked head at itself in the little, plastic-backed looking-glass that was suspended in the corner of the cage; occasionally it swung itself back and forth on a kind of trapeze provided for it, and bit languidly at the bars which kept it imprisoned. It ate in little flurries, and drank with a haughty, connoisseur-like deliberation at the water in its bowl.

That was when it was well. Some weeks after we had taken

charge of it, however, it fell ill. One day it moped, the next day its feathers no longer lay smoothly over and under each other; on the morning of the third day my son called me urgently to come to the cage to see what had happened. The bird lay in a queerly uncomfortable position; one that no living creature would have been able to sustain. Its shoulders were hunched up, its beak rested on the floor of the cage and was turned to one side, its tail pointed upwards. The rest of it was nothing: some feathers one could blow away with a breath, a foot like a barbed grass-seed. Death had not had to make much of an effort to carry it off.

It was hard to say, though, what it was about the bird that had so roused my son's misgiving. Its immobility? Its hunched posture? The fact that it lay on the floor of the cage? An instinctive alarm aroused by all of these? Anyway, just as the condition of the bird had somehow spoken to him of death, so everything about him, as he stood beneath the cage, looking up at it, spoke to me of life: his stillness as much as his movement, his silence as much as his speech, the light that came off him and the light that seemed to be within him. His hair gleamed, his eyes flashed green, his skin was suffused with its own glow; there were stars, white stars and dark stars, in his open mouth. I could hardly bear it, somehow that his eyelids were paler than the skin around them. He was wearing a green knitted jersey with a stand-up collar and buttons at its neck, and a pair of orange pants of a coarsely woven material that seemed to come no more than about two inches down his thighs.

"The bird's dead," I told him.

The word itself seemed to mean little to him. "What does he do when he's dead?"

"Nothing. We must bury it."

"Berry? What means *berry*?"

"We put it in the ground."

"Why?"

"Because it's dead."

"Are you going to do it now?"

"Yes."

"Can I watch?"

"Yes."

I took the cage off its hook and went with it to the garden at the back of the house. The day was pale, the sky was high, the air cold: one of those days in early spring when it is hard to believe that the sunlight will ever have enough warmth to start the whole business of the year afresh. I picked up a trowel and the two of us knelt at the edge of a flower bed. When I opened the door of the cage and tried to get at the bird with my fingers, I found that the aperture was too small; my fingers could hardly get in. So, holding up the cage, I removed the sliding tray beneath it which made up its floor. The bird fell stiffly, straight downwards, its tiny length revolving vertically once in the air before it hit the ground. As it fell my son cried out in amazement, with an unmistakeable note of pity and fear in his voice, "Ah the budgie's *all* dead!"

It took me only a moment to dig a hole and flick the bird into it. This produced a cry of dismay: "Don't do that! You'll hurt the budgie!" It was already almost out of sight. Only a few feathers were showing. Another trowelful and they were gone. I tamped down the earth and got to my feet. My son had risen first. His body was framed by the matted, pallid oblong of lawn behind him. From below he fixed on me a look of outrage and disbelief.

"How's the budgie going to get out now?" he demanded.

"It doesn't want to get out," I replied. The inappropriateness of the phrase was apparent to me the moment it was out of my mouth. Wanting? Not wanting? That stiff, befeathered morsel, crushed beneath some lumps of earth? We were the one who had wants: he to protect the bird from its death; I to protect him from his; both of us to do what we could not.

JEREMY BERNSTEIN

TAKE THE "A" TRAIN

Last spring I came across an obituary notice in the *New York Times* that brought back all sorts of memories. It read:

> William Alonzo (Cat) Anderson, a trumpet player best remembered for recordings of "Take the A Train" with Duke Ellington's orchestra, died of cancer yesterday. He was sixty-four years old.
>
> Mr. Anderson, who learned trumpet as a boy in a home for orphans in Charleston, S.C., patterned himself after Louis Armstrong but soon developed the powerful high-note mastery that became the trademark of his fifty-year career.
>
> He was born in Greenville, S.C. Mr. Anderson toured first with the Carolina Cottonpickers, in 1932–36, with the Sunset Royal Orchestra, 1936–41, and joined Ellington in 1944.
>
> His sound helped shape the smooth cosmopolitan Ellington style of the 1940s. For a time he struck out on his own, touring with his own band after 1947, but he went back to Ellington in 1950.
>
> The piercing sound of the high-register lead trumpet in Ellington's signature song, Billy Strayhorn's "Take the A Train," belonged to Cat Anderson.
>
> Recently, Mr. Anderson had played with his own quartet and did studio recording sessions in Los Angeles.
>
> Surviving is his wife, Dorothy.

For a few years, while I was in high school, Cat Anderson — the name came from the remarkable feline appearance of his broad open face (he looked like a large tiger) — was one of my closest friends. Considering the way in which my life has evolved, this part of it seems difficult now to fathom — even to me — and I would like to explain how all of it came about.

In the 1940s, when I was growing up in New York City, middle-class families felt that it was desirable, if not essential, to send their children to private schools. The public schools were alleged to be both overcrowded and dangerous. *La plus ça change. . . .* Unknown to me, at that very time there were two New York public schools, the Bronx High School of Science and Peter Stuyvesant High School, where I could have gotten a first-rate scientific education instead of the unbelievably mediocre hodge-podge I did get. But our school did have some sort of psycholo-gist — she was known as a "guidance counselor" — to whom we were obliged to report for periodic visits. My last visit with her took place in the spring of 1947, and there are two things I remember clearly about it. The first was that, according to her, the intelligence in our family was distributed inversely with age — my younger brother was smarter than I was, and my still younger sister was the brightest of all. Why she felt that I should be informed of this, I haven't the foggiest idea. Her other observa-tion was that I appeared to suffer from an excessive preoccupa-tion — a fascination for celebrated people (celebrities) — which she thought might indicate a sense of insecurity. At the time I had no idea of what to make of this either, but I did understand how she might have come to her conclusions about celebrities.

I wrote a weekly column for my high school newspaper, which I called "Seeing Stars." I think that, even then, I was already addicted to *The New Yorker,* and I wrote a "Talk of the Town"-like column for our newspaper, which consisted of interviews I had somehow obtained with people like Edgar Bergen, Henry Morgan, Tommy Dorsey, Benny Goodman, and Duke Ellington. Furthermore, on a questionnaire that I filled out preceding my interview, at the place where I was to put down my future career goals, I wrote, "radio announcer or jazz trumpet player" — both of which careers then appealed to me greatly. In fact, I had even gone for an announcer's audition at WQXR, the classical music station. It was given by Duncan Pirnie, now the dean of that station's announcers. After I had read for him, he said, "Son, can you take it?" I nodded a weak affirmative, and he said, "Frankly, you were terrible." If I really wanted to become a radio announcer, he said, I should practice reading newspaper columns aloud and then come back. I did that for awhile and then lost interest.

My trumpet playing lasted a good deal longer. It began in the late 1930s and went on for some twenty years. At the time about which I am writing, I was studying the trumpet at a music school that was run by the Ninety-second Street Young Men's Hebrew Association. I studied classical trumpet but spent most of my practice hours trying, without much success, to imitate the jazz trumpet solos that I had heard on records. I had a large collection of sheet music on which some of these solos had been written down, and I tried to read them as faithfully as I could. During much of this period I still had the idea of becoming a radio announcer. I had made the wonderful discovery that if one looked like one knew what one was doing, it was possible to sneak past the guards at the NBC studios in Radio City and to wander around the place unmolested. The networks—there were actually two, NBC "red" and NBC "blue"—offered guided tours, and for this purpose glass "bubbles" were in place overlooking the studios. From them I would watch, hour after hour, many of my favorite radio programs being produced. Those were still the days of the sound-effects man, and the studios used to be filled with squeaking doors, sheet metal that sounded like rain when it was rattled, and boxes full of cornstarch that, when stepped on, sounded like footsteps in the snow. Many days after school—and always on Saturdays—I used to take the A train (the Eighth Avenue express subway) down to Radio City and immerse myself in that absolutely marvelous and peculiar world. It was on one of those Saturday afternoon forays that I "discovered" the Duke Ellington Orchestra.

It might be imagined that, because of my interest in jazz, I would have known about Duke Ellington. In fact, I did not. My idea of great jazz at that time was Harry James, mainly because of his uncanny ability to play the trumpet. For me, then, the ne plus ultra of jazz was to listen to James play "Carnival of Venice" or "The Flight of the Bumblebee" on the trumpet. Notes cascaded in great clumps. The triplets appeared to be impeccable, and the scales, all played at incredible velocity, almost unbelievable. Much later, when I got to know Cat Anderson, who also admired James, he told me that if one slowed down the old seventy-eight RPM records with one's thumb, one could actually hear a few clinkers in these solos. I never had the heart to try. In any case, one Saturday afternoon as I was wandering around Radio City, I came to a large studio that appeared to be set up for a musical broadcast. Ellington used to broadcast Saturday afternoons on NBC "blue." There was a large number of men—black—seated around the studio in various stages of relaxation. Some were reading, a few were fiddling with instruments, and in a corner I spotted what appeared to be a chess game. I mention that the musicians were black because all of the musicians I had interviewed—Benny Goodman, Tommy Dorsey, and the rest—were white, and it was very rare then to see a racially mixed jazz orchestra. I knew in some vague way that jazz had begun as a black art form, but I had never seen a black musician play, let alone had a black friend. There were no blacks in our school. In any event, I seated myself in an obscure corner of the studio to wait to see what would happen. Just before whatever hour it was that the orchestra was to play, Duke Ellington went to the piano and began playing the opening chords of "Take the A Train." As if by magic the orchestra gathered itself together, and as the program went on the air, "A Train" was resounding throughout the studio with some of the musicians playing while walking to take their seats on the platform. I was overwhelmed by the music, and I decided then and there that, as far as jazz was concerned, Harry James was not the True Jacob and that I wanted very much to get to know and understand these marvelous musicians.

For several Saturdays I snuck into these concerts without finding a way to open up a conversation with anyone. Finally I found an entrée, and this, oddly enough, turned out to be through chess. The lead tenor saxophone player at that time was a man named Al Sears. (The great Ben Webster had departed the orchestra not long before.) Sears had a sort of dual personality. While playing, and especially in front of an audience, he was a veritable tornado, given to a great deal of foot stomping and general gymnastics with his saxophone. In fact, the other members of the orchestra used to kid Sears about these theatrics—sometimes while he was playing one of his more outré solos, they would pass around one of the hat-shaped metal mutes that the trumpet section used when playing choruses in numbers like "It Don't Mean a Thing If It Ain't Got That Swing." Change would be put into the hat with a clanking noise that was audible to Sears but not to the audience. (Sears was also a composer. During the time I knew him, he wrote a rather successful song called "Castle Rock." I once asked him what the title meant, thinking it might have some arcane literary significance. "Jerry," he said kindly, "a rock is an [Anglo-Saxon], and a castle rock is a great big [Anglo-Saxon].") Offstage, on the other hand, he was a quiet, studious man. He had worked his way through college by playing the saxophone and, after graduation, not finding any comparable job opportunities open to him, had continued, I think somewhat reluctantly, with his music. While in school, Sears became interested in chess, and he used to bring a pocket-sized set with him on Saturdays to pass the time before the broadcasts began. Chess was then one of my other loves, so sensing an opportunity, I asked Sears if he would like to play. In this way we began a series of chess games that took place every Saturday.

The games aroused a great deal of interest among the rest of the orchestra, and before long I had gotten to know most of the players, including Cat Anderson and the Duke himself. I simply became part of the scene. If the orchestra played in Harlem, I used to take the A train up to 125th Street where either Al Sears or Cat Anderson would meet me and then make sure I got back on the subway to go home afterward. I was then fifteen, and I guess they were worried that I might get into trouble wandering around late at night by myself. When Cat Anderson learned that I played the trumpet, he asked me to bring it with me so he could hear me play. In truth, I was pretty bad. I had a big round tone, a small technique, and very little musical sense. Cat listened, refrained from stating the obvious, and gave me a few pointers—something he continued to do whenever the orchestra was in town. On one memorable occasion, with the collusion of the rest of the trumpet section, and no doubt with the Duke himself, I was allowed to sit in and blow a few notes when the orchestra played in what was then Dave Wolper's Hurricane Club on Broadway. I doubt if anyone in the audience noticed.

When I went to Harvard, my trumpet went with me, and I played in the Harvard-Radcliffe Orchestra. When Duke Ellington came to Boston, I always went to see him and to have dinner with members of the group. My parents by then had moved back to Rochester from New York City, and during one of my school vacations, Duke Ellington played Batavia, which was nearby. Sears stayed in our house, and later my father drove the three of us to Batavia. My father is a rabbi, and knowing the Duke's interest in religion, Sears arranged for all of us to have lunch in the Berry Patch in Batavia. During lunch the Duke said to my father that if he could take only two things to a desert island, one of them would be the Bible and the other would be Lena Horne. I forget what my father's reply was.

Early in my sophomore year at Harvard—the fall of 1948—I got the inspired notion of inviting the Duke Ellington Orchestra to play at Harvard. To this end I organized, with a few friends, something called the New Friends of Jazz. As I write this I have in front of me a sere, brownish document, dated October 3, 1948, that reads:

Sirs:

The interest in jazz, expressed by most Americans, [I have preserved the original punctuation. I do not know what the commas are doing there.] is as pronounced at Harvard as elsewhere. [I am not sure there *was* much interest in jazz at Harvard in 1948.] However, in the recent past there has been no group at the college which was willing to take the initiative in organizing, sponsoring and presenting the best in modern jazz via the concert stage. We of the New Friends of Jazz hope to fill this gap. [There was once a review of a book in mathematics that contained the sentence: "This book fills a well-needed gap."]

The New Friends proposes to present a series of four concerts in Sander's Theatre during the following year. The first of these is tentatively planned for November 12, and will feature Duke Ellington and his orchestra. We plan to charge an admission sufficiently great so that Mr. Ellington and his successors will be able to play the date without financial loss to themselves. Further, we wish to make sufficient money to enable us to run our organization in the future on a sound basis. [I also thought we might make a killing.]

As the New Friends is purely a promotional unit, the ordinary mechanism of club government is unnecessary. [We were filing to become a club like the Harvard Lampoon or the Porcellian.] The members have been selected for particular talents [one of which was to put up the initiation fee] and will each have an area of responsibility in which he will have complete charge. Policy decisions will be made by simple majority vote and for the time being Jerry Bernstein and Sidney Stires [now a successful New York investment banker] have assumed the offices of president and vice president.

I signed the letter and appended to it a brief constitution and a list of members that numbered ten, not including Stires and myself. We must have gotten some sort of preliminary go-ahead from the university, because I have a copy of an ad that offers tickets at "College Prices"—a $2.40 maximum—to a "Carnegie Hall Attraction." We sold a few tickets before the university decided that we were not a proper club and put us out of business. I have a copy of a small ad that appeared in the *Harvard Crimson* noting that the Duke Ellington concert had been "postponed" and offering a refund to anyone who had purchased a ticket. That was the end of the New Friends of Jazz.

The last time I saw Sears was in my senior year. The orchestra had come to Boston, and I invited Sears to Sunday lunch at Eliot House, where I was then living. I remember that the lunch was rather painful. By this time I was deeply committed to studying mathematics and physics and was no longer the fifteen-year-old boy who used to come up to Harlem at night to follow the band. Sears must have sensed this without my saying anything, because when we parted he mentioned it, and I could not deny it. I had gone on to become something else and had turned a page in my life. Sears did not stay with the orchestra too much longer. He went into music publishing and died a few years ago.

When I was still in high school, I tried to help Cat Anderson with his project of starting his own orchestra. That had been his ambition for many years. One of my "Seeing Stars" columns was an interview with the singer Nat "King" Cole, which took place backstage in the old Paramount Theater in New York. During this interview I told Cole about Cat Anderson's project and that Cat was looking for help with it. I have no idea if anything came of that, but Cat's orchestra was not a success, because, as his obituary notes, a few years later he was back with Duke Ellington. The last time I saw him and also spoke with the Duke was sometime in the late 1960s. The orchestra had an engagement at the Empire Room of the Waldorf Astoria, and I went to see it. I had not seen Cat for many years, but he looked unchanged and told me that he had moved to California, where he spent his final years.

The trumpet went with me from Harvard to the Institute for Advanced Study in Princeton, where I played in a little group that gave a concert of ancient music. (Someone made a record of it, and when I went to Princeton to teach a couple of years ago, I was told that it had been played on the local radio station.) I remember that after our concert, one of my colleagues thought of a remark that Niels Bohr was supposed to have made about a lady musician: "She plays divinely bad."

Speaking of Bohr, the last time that I played my trumpet in public was at a New Year's Eve party in 1957. Marvin Goldberger, who was a physics professor at Princeton—he is now the president of Caltech—and his wife, Mildred, gave famous parties at Princeton. On this occasion he and Mildred outdid themselves. They hired the local firehouse and served roast suckling pig. I was to usher in the New Year at midnight by playing "Auld Lange Syne." Just before midnight I took out my horn and went into a corner to warm up. At midnight, as I began to play, the door of the firehouse opened and in walked Niels Bohr and Robert Oppenheimer. Oppenheimer gave me a very odd look, and I decided right then and there that the last thing I needed at the Institute was the reputation of being a minstrel. In any case, it was difficult to find a place to practice. So I sort of gave it up. Somehow the mouthpiece of the old Conn trumpet, which I had had since I first began playing in Rochester in the 1930s, froze to the rest of the instrument and could no longer be detached. This made it impossible to put the horn into its case, and I have no idea where it is now. A few years ago someone gave me a French army bugle to try, and I discovered that I no longer had any embouchure at all. Try as I would, not a single note came out.

JOHN GREGORY DUNNE

QUINTANA

Quintana will be eleven this week. She approaches adolescence with what I can only describe as panache, but then watching her journey from infancy has always been like watching Sandy Koufax pitch or Bill Russell play basketball. There is the same casual arrogance, the implicit sense that no one has ever done it any better. And yet it is difficult for a father to watch a daughter grow up. With each birthday she becomes more like us, an adult, and what we cling to is the memory of the child. I remember the first time I saw her in the nursery at Saint John's Hospital. It was after visiting hours and my wife and I stood staring through the soundproof glass partition at the infants in their cribs, wondering which was ours. Then a nurse in a surgical mask appeared from a back room carrying a fierce, black-haired baby with a bow in her hair. She was just seventeen hours old and her face was still wrinkled and red and the identification beads on her wrist had not our name but only the letters "NI." "NI" stood for "No Information," the hospital's code for an infant to be placed for adoption. Quintana is adopted.

It has never been an effort to say those three words, even when they occasion the well-meaning but insensitive compliment, "You couldn't love her more if she were your own." At moments like that, my wife and I say nothing and smile through gritted teeth. And yet we are not unaware that sometime in the not too distant future we face a moment that only those of us who are adoptive parents will ever have to face—our daughter's decision to search or not to search for her natural parents.

I remember that when I was growing up a staple of radio drama was the show built around adoption. Usually the dilemma involved a child who had just learned by accident that it was adopted. This information could only come accidentally, because in those days it was considered a radical departure from the norm to inform your son or daughter that he or she was not your own flesh and blood. If such information had to be revealed, it was often followed by the specious addendum that the natural parents had died when the child was an infant. An automobile accident was viewed as the most expeditious and efficient way to get rid of both parents at once. One of my contemporaries, then a young actress, was not told that she was adopted until she was twenty-two and the beneficiary of a small inheritance from her natural father's will. Her adoptive mother could not bring herself to tell her daughter the reason behind the bequest and entrusted the task to an agent from the William Morris office.

Today we are more enlightened, aware of the psychological evidence that such barbaric secrecy can only inflict hurt. When Quintana was born, she was offered to us privately by the gynecologist who delivered her. In California, such private adoptions are not only legal but in the mid-sixties, before legalized abortion and before the sexual revolution made it acceptable for an unwed mother to keep her child, were quite common. The night we went to see Quintana for the first time at Saint John's, there was a tacit agreement between us that "No Information" was only a bracelet. It was quite easy to congratulate ourselves for agreeing to be so open when the only information we had about her mother was her age, where she was from and a certified record of her good health. What we did not realize was that through one bureaucratic slipup we would learn her mother's name and that through another she would learn ours, and Quintana's.

From the day we brought Quintana home from the hospital, we tried never to equivocate. When she was little, we always had Spanish-speaking help and one of the first words she learned, long before she understood its import, was *adoptada*. As she grew older, she never tired of asking us how we happened to adopt her. We told her that we went to the hospital and were given our choice of any baby in the nursery. "No, not that baby," we had said, "not that baby, not that baby . . ." All this with full gestures of inspection, until finally: "That baby!" Her face would always light up and she would say: "Quintana." When she asked a question about her adoption, we answered, never volunteering more than she requested, convinced that as she grew her questions would become more searching and complicated. In terms I hoped she would understand, I tried to explain that adoption offered to a parent the possibility of escaping the prison of the genes, that no matter how perfect the natural child, the parent could not help acknowledging in black moments that some of his or her bad blood was bubbling around in the offspring; with an *adoptada*, we were innocent of any knowledge of bad blood.

In time Quintana began to intuit that our simple parable of free choice in the hospital nursery was somewhat more complex than we had indicated. She now knew that being adopted meant being born of another mother, and that person she began referring to as "my other mommy." How old, she asked, was my other mommy when I was born? Eighteen, we answered, and on her stubby little fingers she added on her own age, and with each birthday her other mommy became twenty-three, then twenty-five and twenty-eight. There was no obsessive interest, just occasional queries, some more difficult to answer than others. Why had her other mother given her up? We said that we did not know—which was true—and could only assume that it was because she was little more than a child herself, alone and without the resources to bring up a baby. The answer seemed to satisfy, at least until we became close friends with a young woman, unmarried, with a small child of her own. The contradiction was, of course, apparent to Quintana, and yet she seemed to understand, in the way that children do, that there had been a millennium's worth of social change in the years since her birth, that the pressures on a young unmarried mother were far more in 1966 than they were in 1973. (She did, after all, invariably refer to the man in the White House as President Nixon Vietnam Watergate, almost as if he had a three-tiered name like John Quincy Adams.) We were sure that she viewed her status with equanimity, but how much so we did not realize until her eighth birthday party. There were twenty little girls at the party, and as little girls do, they were discussing things gynecological, specifically the orifice in their mothers' bodies from which they had emerged at birth. "I didn't," Quintana said matter-of-factly. She was sitting in a large wicker fan chair and her pronouncement impelled the other children to silence. "I was adopted." We had often wondered how she would handle this moment with her peers, and we froze, but she pulled it off with such élan and aplomb that in moments the other children were bemoaning their own misfortune in not being adopted, one even claiming, "Well, I was almost adopted."

Because my wife and I both work at home, Quintana has never had any confusion about how we make our living. Our mindless staring at our respective typewriters means food on the table in a way the mysterious phrase "going to the office" never can. From the time she could walk, we have taken her to meetings whenever we were without help, and she has been a quick study on the nuances of our life. "She's remarkably well adjusted," my brother once said about her. "Considering that every time I see her she's in a different city." I think she could pick an agent out of a police lineup, and out of the blue one night at dinner she offered that all young movie directors were short and had frizzy hair and wore Ditto pants and wire glasses and shirts with three buttons opened. (As far as I know, she had never laid eyes on Bogdanovich, Spielberg or Scorsese.) Not long ago an actress received an award for a picture we had written for her. The actress's acceptance speech at the televised award ceremony drove Quintana into an absolute fury. "She never," Quintana reported, "thanked *us*." Since she not only identifies with our work but at times even considers herself an equal partner, I of course discussed this piece with her before I began working on it. I told her what it was about and said I would drop it if she would be embarrassed or if she thought the subject too private. She gave it some thought and finally said she wanted me to write it.

I must, however, try to explain and perhaps even try to justify my own motives. The week after *Roots* was televised, each child in Quintana's fifth-grade class was asked to trace a family tree. On my side Quintana went back to her great-grandfather Burns, who arrived from Ireland shortly after the Civil War, a ten-year-old refugee from the potato famine, and on her mother's side to her great-great-great-great-grandmother Cornwall, who came west in a wagon train in 1846. As it happens, I have little interest in family beyond my immediate living relatives. (I can never remember the given names of my paternal grandparents and have never known my paternal grandmother's maiden name. This lack of interest mystifies my wife.) Yet I wanted Quintana to understand that if she wished, there were blood choices other than Dominick Burns and Nancy Hardin Cornwall. Over the past few years, there has been a growing body of literature about adoptees seeking their own roots. I am in general sympathetic to this quest, although not always to the dogged absolutism of the more militant seekers. But I would be remiss if I did not say that I am more than a little sensitive to the way the literature presents adoptive parents. We are usually shown as frozen in the postures of radio drama, untouched by the changes in attitudes of the last several generations. In point of fact we accept that our children might seek out their roots, even encourage it; we accept it as an adventure like life itself—perhaps painful, one hopes enriching. I know not one adoptive parent who does not feel this way. Yet in the literature there is the implicit assumption that we are threatened by the possibility of search, that we would consider it an act of disloyalty on the part of our children. The patronizing nature of this assumption is never noted in the literature. It is as if we were Hudson and Mrs. Bridges, below-stairs surrogates taking care of the wee one, and I don't like it one damn bit.

Often these days I find myself thinking of Quintana's natural mother. Both my wife and I admit more than a passing interest in the woman who produced this extraordinary child. (As far as we know, she never named the father, and even more interesting, Quintana has never asked about him.) When Quintana was small, and before the legalities of adoption were complete, we imagined her mother everywhere, a wraithlike presence staring through the chain-link fence at the blond infant sunbathing in the crib. Occasionally today we see a photograph of a young woman in a magazine—the mother as we imagine her to look—

and we pass it to each other without comment. Once we even checked the name of a model in *Vogue* through her modeling agency; she turned out to be a Finn. I often wonder if she thinks of Quintana, or of us. (Remember, we know each other's names.) There is the possibility that having endured the twin traumas of birth and the giving up of a child, she blocked out the names the caseworker gave her, but I don't really believe it. I consider it more likely that she has followed the fairly well-documented passage of Quintana through childhood into adolescence. Writers are at least semipublic figures, and in the interest of commerce or selling a book or a movie, or even out of simple vanity, we allow interviews and photo layouts and look into television cameras; we even write about ourselves, and our children. I recall wondering how this sentient young woman of our imagination had reacted to four pages in *People*. It is possible, even likely, that she will read this piece. I know that it is an almost intolerable invasion of her privacy. I think it probable, however, that in the dark reaches of night she has considered the possibility of a further incursion, of opening a door one day and seeing a young woman who says, "Hello, Mother, I am your daughter."

Perhaps this is romantic fantasy. We know none of the circumstances of the woman's life, or even if she is still alive. We once suggested to our lawyer that we make a discreet inquiry and he quite firmly said that this was a quest that belonged only to Quintana, if she wished to make it, and not to us. What is not fantasy is that for the past year, Quintana has known the name of her natural mother. It was at dinner and she said that she would like to meet her one day, but that it would be hard, not knowing her name. There finally was the moment: we had never equivocated; did we begin now? We took a deep breath and told Quintana, then age ten, her mother's name. We also said that if she decided to search her out, we would help her in any way we could. (I must allow, however, that we would prefer she wait to make this decision until the Sturm and Drang of adolescence is past.) We then considered the possibility that her mother, for whatever good or circumstantial reasons of her own, might prefer not to see her. I am personally troubled by the militant contention that the natural mother has no right of choice in this matter. "I did not ask to be born," an adoptee once was quoted in a news story I read. "She has to see me." If only life were so simple, if only pain did not hurt. Yet we would never try to influence Quintana on this point. How important it is to know her parentage is a question only she can answer; it is her decision to make.

All parents realize, or should realize, that children are not possessions, but are only lent to us, angel boarders, as it were. Adoptive parents realize this earlier and perhaps more poignantly than others. I do not know the end of this story. It is possible that Quintana will find more reality in family commitment and cousins across the continent and heirloom orange spoons and pictures in an album and faded letters from Dominick Burns and diary entries from Nancy Hardin Cornwall than in the uncertainties of blood. It is equally possible that she will venture into the unknown. I once asked her what she would do if she met her natural mother. "I'd put one arm around Mom," she said, "and one arm around my other mommy, and I'd say, 'Hello, Mommies.' "

If that's the way it turns out, that is what she will do.

V. S. NAIPAUL

IN THE MIDDLE OF THE JOURNEY

Coming from a small island—Trinidad is no bigger than Goa—
I had always been fascinated by size. To see the wide river, the
high mountain, to take the twenty-four-hour train journey: these
were some of the delights the outside world offered. But now
after six months in India my fascination with the big is tinged
with disquiet. For here is a vastness beyond imagination, a sky so
wide and deep that sunsets cannot be taken in at a glance but
have to be studied section by section, a landscape made monotonous by its size and frightening by its very simplicity and its special quality of exhaustion: poor choked crops in small crooked
fields, undersized people, undernourished animals, crumbling
villages and towns which, even while they develop, have an air
of decay. Dawn comes, night falls; railway stations, undistin-
guishable one from the other, their name-boards cunningly concealed, are arrived at and departed from, abrupt and puzzling
interludes of populousness and noise; and still the journey goes
on, until the vastness, ceasing to have a meaning, becomes insup-
portable, and from this endless repetition of exhaustion and
decay one wishes to escape.

To state this is to state the obvious. But in India the obvious is
overwhelming, and often during these past six months I have
known moments of near-hysteria, when I have wished to forget
India, when I have escaped to the first-class waiting room or
sleeper not so much for privacy and comfort as for protection, to
shut out the sight of the thin bodies prostrate on railway platforms, the starved dogs licking the food-leaves clean, and to shut

out the whine of the playfully assaulted dog. Such a moment I knew in Bombay, on the day of my arrival, when I felt India only as an assault on the senses. Such a moment I knew five months later, at Jammu, where the simple, frightening geography of the country becomes plain—to the north the hills, rising in range after ascending range; to the south, beyond the temple spires, the plains whose vastness, already experienced, excited only unease.

Yet between these recurring moments there have been so many others, when fear and impatience have been replaced by enthusiasm and delight, when the town, explored beyond what one sees from the train, reveals that the air of exhaustion is only apparent, that in India, more than in any other country I have visited, things are happening. To hear the sounds of hammer on metal in a small Punjab town, to visit a chemical plant in Hyderabad where much of the equipment is Indian-designed and manufactured, is to realize that one is in the middle of an industrial revolution, in which, perhaps because of faulty publicity, one had never really seriously believed. To see the new housing colonies in towns all over India is to realize that, separate from the talk of India's ancient culture (which invariably has me reaching for my *lathi*), the Indian aesthetic sense has revived and is now capable of creating, out of materials which are international, something which is essentially Indian. (India's ancient culture, defiantly paraded, has made the Ashoka Hotel one of New Delhi's most ridiculous buildings, outmatched in absurdity only by the Pakistan High Commission, which defiantly asserts the Faith.)

I have been to unpublicized villages, semi-developed and undeveloped. And where before I would have sensed only despair, now I feel that the despair lies more with the observer than the people. I have learned to see beyond the dirt and the recumbent figures on string beds, and to look for the signs of improvement and hope, however faint: the brick-topped road, covered though it might be with filth; the rice planted in rows and not scattered broadcast; the degree of ease with which the villager faces the official or the visitor. For such small things I have learned to look: over the months my eye has been adjusted.

Yet always the obvious is overwhelming. One is a traveller and as soon as the dread of a particular district has been lessened by familiarity, it is time to move on again, through vast tracts which will never become familiar, which will sadden; and the urge to escape will return.

Yet in so many ways the size of the country is only a physical fact. For, perhaps because of the very size, Indians appear to feel the need to categorize minutely, delimit, to reduce to manageable proportions.

"Where do you come from?" It is the Indian question, and to people who think in terms of the village, the district, the province, the community, the caste, my answer that I am a Trinidadian is only puzzling.

"But you look Indian."

"Well, I am Indian. But we have been living for several generations in Trinidad."

"But you look Indian."

Three or four times a day the dialogue occurs, and now I often abandon explanation. "I am a Mexican, really."

"Ah." Great satisfaction. Pause. "What do you do?"

"I write."

"Journalism or books?"

"Books."

"Westerns, crime, romance? How many books do you write a year? How much do you make?"

So now I invent: "I am a teacher."

"What are your qualifications?"

"I am a BA."

"Only a BA? What do you teach?"

"Chemistry. And a little history."

"How interesting!" said the man on the Pathankot–Srinagar bus. "I am a teacher of chemistry too."

He was sitting across the aisle from me, and several hours remained of our journey.

In this vast land of India it is necessary to explain yourself, to define your function and status in the universe. It is very difficult.

If I thought in terms of race or community, this experience of India would surely have dispelled it. An Indian, I have never before been in streets where everyone is Indian, where I blend unremarkably into the crowd. This has been curiously deflating, for all my life I have expected some recognition of my difference; and it is only in India that I have recognized how necessary this stimulus is to me, how conditioned I have been by the multiracial society of Trinidad and then by my life as an outsider in England. To be a member of a minority community has always seemed to me attractive. To be one of four hundred and thirty-nine million Indians is terrifying.

A colonial, in the double sense of one who had grown up in a Crown colony and one who had been cut off from the metropolis, be it either England or India, I came to India expecting to find metropolitan attitudes. I had imagined that in some ways the largeness of the land would be reflected in the attitudes of the people. I have found, as I have said, the psychology of the cell and the hive. And I have been surprised by similarities. In India, as in tiny Trinidad, I have found the feeling that the metropolis is elsewhere, in Europe or America. Where I had expected largeness, rootedness and confidence, I have found all the colonial attitudes of self-distrust.

"I am craze phor phoreign," the wife of a too-successful contractor said. And this craze extended from foreign food to German sanitary fittings to a possible European wife for her son, who sought to establish his claim further by announcing at the lunch table, "Oh, by the way, did I tell you we spend three thousand rupees a month?"

"You are a tourist, you don't know," the chemistry teacher on the Srinagar bus said. "But this is a terrible country. Give me a chance and I leave it tomorrow."

For among a certain class of Indians, usually more prosperous than their fellows, there is a passionate urge to explain to the visitor that they must not be considered part of poor, dirty India, that their values and standards are higher, and they live perpetually outraged by the country which gives them their livelihood. For them the second-rate foreign product, either people or manufactures, is preferable to the Indian. They suggest that for them, as much as for the European "technician", India is only a country to be temporarily exploited. How strange to find, in free India, this attitude of the conqueror, this attitude of plundering—a frenzied attitude, as though the opportunity might at any moment be withdrawn—in those very people to whom the developing society has given so many opportunities.

This attitude of plundering is that of the immigrant colonial society. It has bred, as in Trinidad, the pathetic philistinism of the *renonçant* (an excellent French word that describes the native who renounces his own culture and strives towards the French). And in India this philistinism, a blending of the vulgarity of East and West—those sad dance floors, those sad "western" cabarets, those transistor radios tuned to Radio Ceylon, those Don Juans with letter jackets or check tweed jackets—is peculiarly frightening. A certain glamour attaches to this philistinism, as glamour attaches to those Indians who, after two or three years in a foreign country, proclaim that they are neither of the East nor of the West.

The observer, it must be confessed, seldom sees the difficulty. The contractor's wife, so anxious to demonstrate her Westernness, regularly consulted her astrologer and made daily trips to the temple to ensure the continuance of her good fortune. The schoolteacher, who complained with feeling about the indiscipline and crudity of Indians, proceeded, as soon as we got to the bus station at Srinagar, to change his clothes in public.

The Trinidadian, whatever his race, is a genuine colonial. The Indian, whatever his claim, is rooted in India. But while the Trinidadian, a colonial, strives towards the metropolitan, the Indian of whom I have been speaking, metropolitan by virtue of the uniqueness of his country, its achievements in the past and its manifold achievements in the last decade or so, is striving towards the colonial.

Where one had expected pride, then, one finds the spirit of plunder. Where one had expected the metropolitan one finds the colonial. Where one had expected largeness one finds narrowness. Goa, scarcely liberated, is the subject of an unseemly inter-State squabble. Fifteen years after Independence the politician as national leader appears to have been replaced by the politician as village headman (a type I had thought peculiar to the colonial Indian community of Trinidad, for whom politics was a game where little more than PWD contracts was at stake).

To the village headman India is only a multiplicity of villages. So that the vision of India as a great country appears to be something imposed from without and the vastness of the country turns out to be oddly fraudulent.

Yet there remains a concept of India—as what? Something more than the urban middle class, the politicians, the industrialists, the separate villages. Neither this nor that, we are so often told, is the "real" India. And how well one begins to understand why this word is used! Perhaps India is only a word, a mystical idea that embraces all those vast plains and rivers through which the train moves, all those anonymous figures asleep on railway platforms and the footpaths of Bombay, all those poor fields and stunted animals, all this exhausted plundered land. Perhaps it is this, this vastness which no one can ever get to know: India as an ache, for which one has a great tenderness, but from which at length one always wishes to separate oneself.

OLIVER SACKS

The Bull on the Mountain

Saturday the 24th of August started overcast and sullen in the Norwegian village where I was staying a few years ago, but there was promise of fine weather later in the day. I could start my climb early, through the low-lying orchards and woods, and by noon, I reckoned, reach the top of the mountain. By then, perhaps, the weather would have cleared, and there would be a magnificent view from the summit—the lower mountains all around me, sweeping down into Hardanger Fiord, and the great fiord itself visible in its entirety. "Climb" suggests scaling rocks, and ropes. But it was not that sort of climb, simply a steep mountain path. I foresaw no particular problems or difficulties. I was as strong as a bull, in the prime, the pride, the high noon of life. I looked forward to the walk with assurance and pleasure.

I soon got into my stride—a supple swinging stride, which covers ground fast. I had started before dawn, and by half past seven had ascended, perhaps, to two thousand feet. Already the early mists were beginning to clear. Now came a dark and piney wood, where the going was slower, partly because of knotted roots in the path and partly because I was enchanted by the world of tiny vegetation which sheltered in the wood, and was often stopping to examine a new fern, a moss, a lichen. Even so, I was through the woods by a little after nine, and had come to the great cone that formed the mountain proper and towered above the fiord to six thousand feet. To my surprise there was a fence and a gate at this point, and the gate bore a still more surprising notice: BEWARE OF THE BULL! in Norwegian, and for those who might not be able to read the words, a rather droll picture of a man being tossed.

I stopped, and scrutinized the picture and scratched my head. A *bull? Up here?* What would a bull be doing up here? I had not seen even sheep in the pastures and farms down below. Perhaps it was some sort of joke, tacked there by the villagers, or by some previous hiker with an odd sense of humor. Or perhaps there *was* a bull, summering amid a vast mountain pasture, subsisting on the spare grass and scrubby vegetation. Well, enough of speculation! Onward to the top!

The terrain had changed again. It was now very stony, with enormous boulders here and there; but there was also a light topsoil, muddy in places because it had rained in the night, but with plenty of grass and a few scanty shrubs—fodder enough for an animal that had the whole mountain to graze.

The path was much steeper and fairly well marked, though, I felt, not much used. It was not exactly a populous part of the world. I had seen no visitors apart from myself, and the villagers, I imagined, were too busy with farming and fishing, and other activities, to go jaunting up the local mountains. All the better. I had the mountain to myself. Onward, upward—though I could not see the top, I had already ascended, I judged, three thousand feet, and if the path ahead was simply steep, but not tricky, I could make the top by noon, as I had planned.

And so I forged ahead, keeping up a brisk pace despite the gradient, blessing my energy and stamina, and especially my strong legs, trained by years of hard exercise and hard lifting in the gym. Strong quadriceps muscles in the thighs, strong body, good wind, good stamina—I was grateful to Nature for endowing me well. And if I drove myself to feats of strength, and long swims, and long climbs, it was a way of saying "Thank you" to Nature and using to the full the good body she had given me.

Around eleven o'clock, when the shifting mists allowed, I had my first glimpses of the mountain top—not so far above me. I *would* make it by noon. There was still a light mist clinging here and there, sometimes shrouding the boulders so that they were difficult to make out. Occasionally a boulder, half seen through the mist, looked almost like a vast crouching animal, and would reveal its true nature only when I came closer. There were ambiguous moments when I would stop in uncertainty, while I descried the shrouded shapes before me. . . . But when it happened, it was not at all ambiguous!

The real reality was not such a moment, not touched in the least by ambiguity or illusion. I had, indeed, just emerged from the mist, and was walking around a boulder big as a house, the path curving around it so that I could not see ahead, and it was this inability to see ahead that permitted the meeting. I practically trod on what lay before me—an enormous animal sitting in the path, and indeed wholly occupying the path, whose presence had been hidden by the rounded bulk of the rock. It had a huge horned head, a stupendous white body, and an enormous, mild, milk-white face. It sat unmoved by my appearance, exceedingly calm, except that it turned its vast white face up toward me. And in that moment it changed before my eyes, becoming transformed from magnificent to utterly monstrous. The huge white face seemed to swell and swell, and the great bulbous eyes became radiant with malignance. The face grew huger and huger all the time, until I thought it would blot out the universe. The bull became hideous—hideous beyond belief, hideous in strength, malevolence, and cunning. It seemed now to be stamped with the infernal in every feature. It became first a monster, and now the Devil.

I retained my composure, or a semblance of composure, for a minute in which, perfectly "naturally," as if turning about at the end of a stroll, I swung in mid-stride through 180 degrees, and deftly, daintily, began my descent. But then—oh horrible!—my nerve suddenly broke, dread overwhelmed me, and I ran for dear life—ran madly, blindly, down the steep, muddy, slippery path, lost here and there in patches of mist. Blind, mad panic!—there is nothing worse in the world, nothing worse—and nothing more dangerous.

I cannot say exactly what happened. In my plunging flight down the treacherous path I must have misstepped—stepped onto a loose rock, or into midair. It is as if there is a moment missing from my memory—there is "before" and "after," but no "in-between." One moment I was running like a madman, conscious of heavy panting and heavy thudding footsteps, unsure whether they came from the bull or from me, and the next I was lying at the bottom of a short sharp cliff of rock, with my left leg twisted grotesquely beneath me and in my knee such a pain as I had never, ever known before. To be full of strength and vigor one moment and virtually helpless the next, in the pink and pride of health one moment and a cripple the next, with all one's powers and faculties one moment and without them the next—such a change, such suddenness, is difficult to comprehend, and the mind casts about for explanations.

I had encountered this phenomenon in others—in my patients who had been suddenly stricken or injured, and now I was to encounter it in myself. My first thought was this: that there had been an accident, and that someone I knew had been seriously injured. Later, it dawned on me that the victim was myself; but with this came the feeling that it was not really serious. To show that it was not serious, I got to my feet, or rather I *tried* to, but I collapsed in the process, because the left leg was completely limp and floppy, and gave way beneath me like a piece of spaghetti. It could not support any weight at all, but just buckled beneath me, buckled backward at the knee, making me yell with pain. But it was much less the pain that so horribly frightened me than the flimsy, toneless giving-way of the knee and my absolute impotence to prevent or control it—and the apparent paralysis of the leg. And then, the horror, so overwhelming for a moment, disappeared in face of a "professional attitude."

"OK, Doctor," I said to myself. "Would you kindly examine the leg?"

Very professionally, and impersonally, and not at all tenderly, as if I were a surgeon examining "a case," I took the leg and examined it—feeling it, moving it this way and that. I murmured my findings aloud as I did so, as if for a class of students: "No movement at the knee, gentlemen, no movement at the hip. . . . You will observe that the entire quadriceps has been torn from the patella. But though it has torn loose, it has not retracted—it is wholly toneless, which might suggest nerve injury as well. The patella has lost its major attachment, and can be flipped around—so!—like a ball-bearing. It is readily dislocated—there is nothing to hold it.

"As for the knee itself"—and here I illustrated each point as I made it—"we find abnormal motility, a quite pathological range of motion. It can be flexed without any resistance at all"—here I manually flexed the heel to the buttock—"and can also be hyper-extended, with apparent dislocation." Both movements, which I illustrated, caused me to scream. "Yes, gentlemen," I concluded, summarizing my findings, "a fascinating case! A complete rupture of the quadriceps tendon. Muscle paralyzed and atonic—probably nerve injury. Unstable knee joint—seems to dislocate backward. Probably ripped out the cruciate ligaments. Can't really tell about bone injury—but there could easily be one or more fractures. Considerable swelling, probably tissue and joint fluid, but tearing of blood vessels can't be excluded."

I turned with a pleased smile to my invisible audience, as if awaiting a round of applause. And then, suddenly, the "professional" attitude and persona broke down, and I realized that this "fascinating case" was *me—me myself*, fearfully disabled, and quite likely to die. The leg was utterly useless—far more so than if it had been broken. I was entirely alone, near the top of a mountain, in a desolate and sparsely populated part of the world. My whereabouts were known to nobody. This frightened me more than anything else. I could die where I lay, and nobody would know it.

Never had I felt so alone, so lost, so forlorn, so utterly beyond the pale of help. It hadn't occurred to me until then how terrifying and seriously alone I was. I had not felt "alone" when I was romping up the mountain (I never do when I am enjoying myself). I had not felt alone when I was examining my injury (I saw now what a comfort the imagined "class" was). But now, all of a sudden, the fearful sense of my aloneness rushed in upon me. I remembered that someone had told me, a few days before, of "a fool of an Englishman" who had climbed this very mountain, alone, two years before, and had been found a week later dead from exposure, having broken both his legs. It was at an altitude, and latitude, where the temperature sinks well below freezing at night, even in August. I had to be found by nightfall or I should never survive. I had to get lower, if I possibly could, because then at least there was a chance of my being seen. I even entertained hopes, now I came to consider things, that I might be able to descend the entire mountain, with a bum leg, by myself; and it was not until much later that I realized how this, above all, was a comforting delusion. Yet if I pulled myself together, did what I could, there was a sporting chance that I would make it yet.

I suddenly found myself very calm. First of all, I had to address myself to the leg. I had discovered that while any movement at the knee was agonizing, and indeed, literally, physiologically shocking, I was fairly comfortable when the leg lay flat and supported on the ground. But having no bone or "inner structure" to hold it, it had no protection against helpless passive movements at the knee, as might be caused by any unevenness in the ground. So, clearly, it needed an outer structure, or splint.

And here one of my idiosyncrasies came to my aid. Habit, more than anything else, made me carry an umbrella under practically all conditions, and it seemed natural enough, or purely automatic, that when I went for a walk in bad weather (even up a mountain more than a mile), I should take my stout and trusty umbrella with me. Besides, it had been useful as a walking stick on the way up. And now it found its finest moment—in splinting my leg. Without such a splint I could scarcely have moved. I snapped off the handle and tore my anorak in two. The length of the umbrella was just right—the heavy shaft almost matched the length of my leg—and I lashed it in place with strong strips of anorak, sufficiently firmly to prevent a helpless flailing of the knee, but not so tightly as to impede circulation.

By now about twenty minutes had elapsed since my injury, or possibly less. Could all this have occurred in so short a time? I looked at my watch to see if it had stopped, but the second hand was going around with perfect regularity. *Its* time, abstract, impersonal, chronological, had no relation to my time—*my* time which consisted solely of personal moments, life moments, crucial moments. As I looked at the dial, I matched, in imagination, the movement of the hands, going steadily round and round—the relentless regularity of the sun in the heavens—with my own uncertain descent of the mountain. I could not think of hurrying—that would exhaust me. I could not think of dawdling—that would be worse. I had to find the right pace, and steadily keep it up.

I found myself now gratefully taking note of my assets and resources, where before I could only take note of the injury. Mercifully, then, I had not torn an artery, or major vessel, internally, for there was only a little swelling around the knee and no real coolness or discoloration of the leg. The quadriceps was apparently paralyzed, it was true—but I made no further neurological examination. I had not fractured my spine or my skull in my fall. And—God be praised!—I had three good limbs, and the energy and strength to put up a good fight. And, by God, I would! This would be the fight of my life—the fight of one's life which is the fight *for* life.

I could not hurry—I could only hope. But my hopes would be extinguished if I were not found by nightfall. Again I looked at my watch, as I was to do many anxious times again in the hours that followed. At these latitudes it would be a rather lengthy evening and dusk, starting around 6 and gradually getting darker and cooler. By 7:30 it would be quite cool, and difficult to see. I had to be found by about 8, at the latest. By 8:30 it would be pitch-black—impossible to see and impossible to proceed. And though by strenuous exercise I might, just conceivably, last through the night, the chances were distinctly, indeed heavily, against it. I thought, for a moment, of Tolstoy's "Master and Man"—but there were not two of us to keep each other warm. If only I had a companion with me! The thought suddenly came to me once again, in the words from the Bible not read since childhood, and not consciously recollected, or brought to mind, at all: "Two are better than one . . . for if they fall, the one will lift up his fellow; but woe to him that is alone when he falleth, for he hath not another to help him up." And, following immediately upon this, came a sudden memory, eidetically clear, of a small animal I had seen in the road, with a broken back, hoisting its paralyzed hind legs along. Now I felt exactly like that creature. The sense of my humanity as something apart, something above animality and morality—this too disappeared at that moment, and again the words of Ecclesiastes came to my mind: "For that which befalleth the sons of men befalleth beasts; as the one dieth, so dieth the other . . . so that a man hath no preeminence above a beast."

While splinting my leg, and keeping myself busy, I had again "forgotten" that death lay in wait. Now, once again, it took the Preacher to remind me. "But," I cried inside myself, "the instinct of life is strong within me. I want to live—and, with luck, I may still do so. I don't think it is yet my time to die." Again the Preacher answered, neutral, noncommittal: "To everything there is a season, and a time to every purpose under the heaven. A time to be born, and a time to die; a time. . . ." This strange, deep, emotionless clarity, neither cold nor warm, neither severe nor indulgent, but utterly truthful, I had encountered in others, especially in patients who were facing death and did not conceal the truth from themselves; I had marveled, though in a way uncomprehendingly, at the simple ending of *Hadji Murad*—how, when Murad has been fatally shot, "images without feelings" stream through his mind; but now, for the first time, I encountered this—in myself.

These images, and words, and passionless feelings did not, as they say, go through my head "in a flash." They took their time—several minutes at least—the time they would have taken in reality, not in a dream; they were meditations, which did not hurry at all—but neither did they distract me in the least from my tasks. Nobody looking on (so to speak) would have seen me "musing," would have seen any pause. On the contrary, they would have been impressed by my brisk and workmanlike appearance and behavior, by the quick and efficient way in which I splinted my leg, made a brief check of everything, and set off downhill.

And so I proceeded, using a mode of travel I had never used before—roughly speaking, gluteal and tripedal. That is to say, I slid down on my backside, heaving or rowing myself with my arms and using my good leg for steering and, when needed, for braking, with the splintered leg hanging nervelessly before me. I did not have to think out this unusual, unprecedented, and — one might think — unnatural way of moving. I did it without thinking, and very soon got accustomed to it. And anyone seeing me rowing swiftly and powerfully down the slopes would have said, "Ah, he's an old hand at it. It's second nature to him."

The legless don't need to be *taught* to use crutches: it comes "unthinkingly" and "naturally," as if the person had been practicing it, in secret, all his life. The organism, the nervous system, has an immense repertoire of "trick movements" and "backups" of every kind — completely automatic strategies, which are held "in reserve." We would have no idea of the resources that exist *in potentia* if we did not see them called forth as needed.

So it happened with me. It was a reasonably efficient mode of progress, as long as the path descended continually, and evenly, and not too steeply. If it was not even, the left leg would tend to catch on irregularities of all sorts — it seemed curiously inept at avoiding these — and I cursed it several times for being "stupid" or "senseless." I found, indeed, that whenever the terrain became difficult, I had to keep an eye on this not only powerless but stupid leg. Most frightening of all were those sections of the path which were too slippery or too steep, because it was difficult not to slide down almost uncontrollably, ending with a lurch or a crash which agonizingly buckled the knee and exposed the limitations of my improvised splint.

It occurred to me at one point, after a particularly sickening crash, to cry for help, and I did so, lustily, with Gargantuan yells, which seemed to echo and resound from one peak to another. The sudden sound in the silence startled and scared me; and then I had a sudden fear that it might startle the bull, which I had completely forgotten. I had a frightened vision of the animal, now furiously rearoused, charging down the path to toss or crush me. Trembling with terror, and with immense effort and pain, I managed to heave myself off the path until I was hidden behind a boulder. Here I remained for about ten minutes, until the continuing silence reassured me and I was able to crawl out and continue my descent.

I could not decide whether it had been foolish and provocative to yell, or whether my folly lay rather in fearing to yell. I decided, in any event, not to yell again; and whenever the impulse seized me I held my tongue, remembering that I was still in the bull's domain, where perhaps he maintained a sharp-eared dominion; and I would further say to myself, for good measure, "Why shout? Save your breath. You're the only human being in hundreds of square miles." And so I descended in absolute silence, not even daring to whistle aloud, for everywhere now I felt the bull listening. I even tried to mute the sound of my breathing. And so the hours passed, silently, slithering. . . .

At about 1:30—I had been traveling two hours—I came again to the swollen stream with stepping-stones that I had hesitated to cross even when climbing up, with both legs. Clearly, I could not "row" myself through this. I had therefore to turn over and "walk" on rigidly outstretched arms—and even so my head was only just out of the water. The water was fast-flowing, turbulent, and glacially cold, and my left leg, dropping downward, unsupported, out of control, was violently jarred by stones on the bottom, and sometimes blown like a flag sideways at a right angle to my trunk. My hip seemed almost as loose as my knee, but it caused me no pain—unlike my knee, which, excruciatingly, was buckled and dislocated as I crossed the stream. Several times I felt my consciousness ebbing and feared I would faint and drown in the stream; and I ordered myself to hold on, with strong language and threats.

"Hold on, you fool! Hold on for dear life! I'll *kill* you if you let go—and don't you forget it!"

I half collapsed when finally I made the other side, shuddering with cold, and pain, and shock. I felt exhausted, prostrated, at the end of my strength, and I lay stunned, motionless, for a couple of minutes. Then, somehow my exhaustion became a sort of tiredness, an extraordinarily comfortable, delicious languor.

"How nice it is here," I thought to myself. "Why not a little rest—a nap maybe?"

The apparent sound of this soft, insinuating, inner voice suddenly woke me, sobered me, and filled me with alarm. It was not "a nice place" to rest and nap. The suggestion was lethal and filled me with horror, but I was lulled by its soft, seductive tones.

"No," I said fiercely to myself. "This is Death speaking—and in its sweetest, deadliest Siren-voice. Don't listen to it now! Don't listen to it ever! You've got to go on whether you like it or not. You can't rest here—you can't rest anywhere. You must find a pace you can keep up, and go on steadily."

This good voice, this "Life" voice, braced and resolved me. My trembling stopped and my faltering too. I got going once more, and didn't falter again.

There came to my aid now melody, rhythm, and music (what Kant calls the "quickening" art). Before crossing the stream, I had *muscled* myself along—moving by main force, with my very strong arms. Now, so to speak, I was *musicked* along. I did not contrive this. It happened to me. I fell into a rhythm, guided by a sort of marching or rowing song, sometimes the Volga Boatmen's Song, sometimes a monotonous chant of my own, accompanied by the words "*Ohne Hast, ohne Rast! Ohne Hast, ohne Rast!*" ("Without haste, without rest"), with a strong heave on every *Hast* and *Rast.* Never had Goethe's words been put to better use! Now I no longer had to think about going too fast or too slow. I got into the music, got into the swing, and this ensured that my tempo was right. I found myself perfectly coordinated by the rhythm—or perhaps subordinated would be a better term: the musical beat was generated within me, and all my muscles responded obediently—all save those in my left leg, which seemed silent—or mute? Does not Nietzsche say that when listening to music, we "listen with our muscles"? I was reminded of my rowing days in college, how the eight of us would respond as one man to the beat, a sort of muscle orchestra conducted by the cox.

Somehow, with this "music," it felt much less like a grim anxious struggle. There was even a certain primitive exuberance, such as Pavlov called "muscular gladness." And now, further, to gladden me more, the sun burst from behind the clouds, massaged me with warmth and soon dried me off. And with all this, and perhaps other things, I found my internal weather was most happily changed.

It was only after chanting the song in a resonant and resounding bass for some time that I suddenly realized that I had forgotten the bull. Or, more accurately, I had forgotten my fear—partly seeing that it was no longer appropriate, partly that it had been absurd in the first place. I had no room now for this fear, or for any other fear, because I was filled to the brim with music. And even when it was not literally (audibly) music, there was the music of my muscle orchestra playing—"the silent music of the body," in Harvey's lovely phrase. With this playing, the musicality of my motion, I myself became the music—"You are the music, while the music lasts." A creature of muscle, motion, and music, all inseparable and in unison with one another—except for that unstrung part of me, that poor broken instrument which could not join in and lay motionless and mute without tone or tune.

I had once, as a child, had a violin which got brutally smashed in an accident. I felt for my leg, now, as I felt long ago for that poor broken fiddle. Mixed with my happiness and renewal of spirit, with the quickening music I felt in myself, was a new and sharper and most poignant sense of loss for that broken musical instrument that had once been my leg. When will it recover, I thought to myself? When will it sound its own tune again? When will it rejoin the joyous music of the body?

By two o'clock the clouds had cleared sufficiently for me to get a magnificent view of the fiord beneath me, and of the tiny village I had left nine hours before. I could see the old church, where I had heard Mozart's great Mass in C minor the previous evening. I could almost see—no, I *could* see—individual figures in the street. Was the air abnormally, uncannily, clear? Or was there some abnormal clarity in my perceptions?

I thought of a dream related by Leibniz, in which he found himself at a great height overlooking the world—with provinces, towns, lakes, fields, villages, hamlets, all spread beneath him. If he wished to see a single person—a peasant tilling, an old woman washing clothes—he had only to direct and concentrate his gaze: "I needed no telescope except my attention." And so it was with me: an anguish of yearning sharpened my eyes, a violent need to see my fellow men and, even more, to be seen by them. Never had they seemed dearer, or more remote. I felt so close, watching them as through a powerful telescope, and yet utterly removed, not part of their world. If only I had a flag or a flare—a rifle, a carrier pigeon, a radio transmitter! If only I could give a truly Gargantuan yell—one that would be heard ten miles away! For how could they know that here was a fellow creature, a crippled human being, fighting for his life five thousand feet above them? I was within sight of my rescuers, and yet I would probably die. There was something impersonal, or universal, in my feeling. I would not have cried, "Save *me*, Oliver Sacks!" but "Save this hurt living creature! Save *Life!*" the mute plea I know so well from my patients—the plea of *all* life facing the abyss, if it be strongly, vividly, rightly alive.

An hour passed, and another and another, under a glorious cloudless sky, the sun blazing pale-golden with a pure Arctic light. It was an afternoon of peculiar splendor, earth and air conspiring in beauty, radiant, suffused in serenity. As the blue and golden hours passed, I continued steadily on my downward trek, which had become so smooth, so void of difficulties, that my mind could move free of the ties of the present. My mood changed again, although I was to realize this only later. Long-forgotten memories, all happy, came unbidden to my mind: memories, first, of summer afternoons, tinged with a sunniness that was also happiness and blessedness—sun-warmed afternoons with my family and friends, summer afternoons going back and back into earliest childhood. Hundreds of memories would pass through my mind, in the space between one boulder and the next, and yet each was rich, simple, ample, and conveyed no sense of being hurried through.

Nor was it a flitting of faces and voices. Entire scenes were relived, entire conversations replayed, without the least abbreviation. The very earliest memories were all of our garden—our big old garden in London, as it used to be before the war. I cried with joy and tears as I saw it—our garden with its dear old iron railings intact, the lawn vast and smooth, just cut and rolled (the huge old roller there in a corner); the orange-striped hammock with cushions bigger than myself, in which I loved to roll and swing for hours; and—joy of my heart—the enormous sunflowers, whose vast inflorescence fascinated me endlessly and showed me at five the Pythagorean mystery of the world. (For it was then, in the summer of 1938, that I discovered that the whorled florets were multiples of prime numbers, and I had such a vision of the order and beauty of the world as was to be a prototype of every scientific wonder and joy I was later to experience.) All of these thoughts and images, involuntarily summoned and streaming through my mind, were essentially happy, and essentially grateful. And it was only later that I said to myself, "What is this mood?" and realized that it was a preparation for death. "Let your last thinks be all thanks," as Auden says.

At about six, rather suddenly, I noticed that the shadows were longer, and that the sun was lower in the heavens. Some part of me, Joshua-like, had thought to hold the sun in mid-course, to prolong to eternity the gold and azure afternoon. Now, abruptly, I saw that it was evening, and that in an hour, more or less, the sun would set.

Not long after this I came to a long transverse ridge commanding an unobstructed view of the village and fiord. I had attained this ridge at about ten in the morning: it had been about halfway between the gate and the point where I fell. Thus what had taken me little more than an hour to climb had taken me, crippled, nearly seven hours to descend. I saw how grossly, how optimistically, I had miscalculated everything—comparing my "rowing" to striding, when it was, I could now see, six times as slow. How could I have imagined that one was half as fast as the other, and that the ascent from the relatively warm and populous low-lying farmland, which had taken four hours or so, could be retraced in just twice that time, bringing me within range of the highest farmhouse by dusk or nightfall. I had hugged to myself, like a warm comforter, in the long hours of my journey—interspersed with my exalted but not cozy thoughts—a warm, sweet vision of the waiting farmhouse, glowing softly like a Dutch interior, with a dumpy, motherly farmwife who would feed me and revive me with love and warm milk, while her husband, a dour giant, went to the village for help. I had been secretly sustained by this vision throughout the interminable hours of my descent, and now it vanished, suddenly, like a candle blown out, on the chill clarity of that high transverse ridge.

I could see now, what had been shrouded in mists on the way up in the morning, how far away, unattainably far, the village still was. And yet, though hope had just expired and died, I took comfort from seeing the village, and especially the church, gilded, or rather crimsoned now, in the long evening light. I could see straggling worshipers on their way to evening service and had the strangest persuasion that the service was for me. It came to me once more, and overwhelmingly, how I had sat in that church only the evening before, and heard the C-minor Mass, and so powerful was the memory that I could actually hear it in my ears—hear it with such vividness that I wondered, for a long second, whether it was again being sung below, and wafted up to me, miraculously, by some trick of the air. As I listened, profoundly moved, with tears on my face, I suddenly realized that it was not the Mass that I was hearing—no, not the Mass, but the Requiem instead. My mind, my unconscious, had switched one for the other. Or was it—again that uncanny acoustic illusion—was it that they *were* singing the Requiem, down there for me?

Shortly after seven the sun disappeared, seeming to draw, as it did so, all color and warmth from the world. There were none of the lingering effulgences of a more temperate sunset—this was a simpler, sterner, more Arctic phenomenon. The air was suddenly grayer, and colder, and the grayness and coldness seemed to penetrate right to my marrow.

The silence had become intense. I could no longer hear any sounds about me. *I could no longer hear myself.* Everything seemed embedded in silence. There were odd periods when I thought I was dead, when the immense calm became the calm of death. Things had ceased to happen. There was no happening any more. This must be the beginning of the end.

Suddenly, incredibly, I heard a shout, a long yodeling call which seemed very close to me. I turned, and saw a man and a boy standing on a rock, a little above me, and not ten yards from the path, their figures silhouetted against the darkening dusk. I never even saw my rescuers before they saw me. I think, in those last dark minutes, that my eyes had been fixed on the dim path before me, or had perhaps been staring unseeing into space—they had ceased to be on the lookout, constantly roving and scanning, as they had been at all times in the course of the day. I think, indeed, that I had become almost completely unaware of the environment, having, at some level, given up all thoughts of rescue and life, so that rescue, when it came, came from nowhere, a miracle, a grace, at the very last moment.

In another few minutes it would have been too dark to see. The man who yodeled was just lowering a gun, and the youth by his side was similarly armed. They ran down toward me. I needed no words to explain my condition. I hugged them both, I kissed them—these bearers of life. I stammered out, in broken Norwegian, what had happened on the heights, and what I could not put into words I drew in the dust.

The two of them laughed at my picture of the bull. They were full of humor, these two, and as they laughed I laughed too— and suddenly, with the laughter, the tragic tension exploded, and I felt vividly, so to speak, comically alive once again. I thought I had had every emotion on the heights, but—it now occurred to me—I hadn't laughed once. Now I couldn't stop laughing—the laughter of relief, and the laughter of love, that deep-down laughter that comes from the center of one's being. The silence was exploded, the quite deathly silence that had seized me, as in a spell, those last minutes.

The men were reindeer hunters, father and son, who had pitched camp nearby. Hearing a noise outside, a movement in the undergrowth, they had come out cautiously with their rifles at the ready, their minds on the game they might bag, and when they peered over the rock they saw that their game was me.

The huntsman gave me some aquavit from a flask—the burning fluid was indeed the "water of life." "Don't worry," he said, "I will go down to the village. I will be back within two hours. My son will stay with you. You're safe and sound—and the bull won't come here!"

From the moment of my rescue my memories become less vivid, less charged. I was in others' hands now and had no more responsibility to act, or feel. I said very little to the boy, but though we hardly spoke I found great comfort in his presence. Occasionally he would light me a cigarette—or pass me the aquavit his father had left. I had the deepest sense of security and warmth. I fell asleep.

It was less than two hours before a posse of stout villagers arrived carrying a litter—onto which they loaded me, with considerable difficulty. The flailing leg, which had lain silent and unnoticed for so long, objected loudly, but they carried me gently, rhythmically, down the steep mountain trail. At the gate—the gate, whose warning sign I had ignored!—I was transferred onto a sort of mountain tractor. As it jogged slowly downhill—first through woods, and then through orchards and farms—the men sang softly among themselves, and passed the aquavit around. One of them gave me a pipe to smoke. I was back—God be praised!—in the good world of men.

JOAN DIDION

ON KEEPING A NOTEBOOK

" 'That woman Estelle,' " the note reads, " 'is partly the reason why George Sharp and I are separated today.' *Dirty crepe-de-Chine wrapper, hotel bar, Wilmington RR, 9:45 A.M. August Monday morning.*"

Since the note is in my notebook, it presumably has some meaning to me. I study it for a long while. At first I have only the most general notion of what I was doing on an August Monday morning in the bar of the hotel across from the Pennsylvania Railroad station in Wilmington, Delaware (waiting for a train? missing one? 1960? 1961? why Wilmington?), but I do remember being there. The woman in the dirty crepe-de-Chine wrapper had come down from her room for a beer, and the bartender had heard before the reason why George Sharp and she were separated today. "Sure," he said, and went on mopping the floor. "You told me." At the other end of the bar is a girl. She is talking, pointedly, not to the man beside her but to a cat lying in the triangle of sunlight cast through the open door. She is wearing a plaid silk dress from Peck & Peck, and the hem is coming down.

Here is what it is: the girl has been on the Eastern Shore, and now she is going back to the city, leaving the man beside her, and all she can see ahead are the viscous summer sidewalks and the 3 A.M. long-distance calls that will make her lie awake and then sleep drugged through all the steaming mornings left in August (1960? 1961?). Because she must go directly from the train to lunch in New York, she wishes that she had a safety pin for the hem of the plaid silk dress, and she also wishes that she could forget about the hem and the lunch and stay in the cool bar that smells of disinfectant and malt and make friends with the woman in the crepe-de-Chine wrapper. She is afflicted by a little self-pity, and she wants to compare Estelles. That is what that was all about.

Why did I write it down? In order to remember, of course, but exactly what was it I wanted to remember? How much of it actually happened? Did any of it? Why do I keep a notebook at all? It is easy to deceive oneself on all those scores. The impulse to write things down is a peculiarly compulsive one, inexplicable to those who do not share it, useful only accidentally, only secondarily, in the way that any compulsion tries to justify itself. I suppose that it begins or does not begin in the cradle. Although I have felt compelled to write things down since I was five years old, I doubt that my daughter ever will, for she is a singularly blessed and accepting child, delighted with life exactly as life presents itself to her, unafraid to go to sleep and unafraid to wake up. Keepers of private notebooks are a different breed altogether, lonely and resistant rearrangers of things, anxious malcontents, children afflicted apparently at birth with some presentiment of loss.

My first notebook was a Big Five tablet, given to me by my mother with the sensible suggestion that I stop whining and learn to amuse myself by writing down my thoughts. She returned the tablet to me a few years ago; the first entry is an account of a woman who believed herself to be freezing to death in the Arctic night, only to find, when day broke, that she had stumbled onto the Sahara Desert, where she would die of the heat before lunch. I have no idea what turn of a five-year-old's mind could have prompted so insistently "ironic" and exotic a story, but it does reveal a certain predilection for the extreme which has dogged me into adult life; perhaps if I were analytically inclined I would find it a truer story than any I might have told about Donald Johnson's birthday party or the day my cousin Brenda put Kitty Litter in the aquarium.

So the point of my keeping a notebook has never been, nor is it now, to have an accurate factual record of what I have been doing or thinking. That would be a different impulse entirely, an instinct for reality which I sometimes envy but do not possess. At no point have I ever been able successfully to keep a diary; my approach to daily life ranges from the grossly negligent to the merely absent, and on those few occasions when I have tried dutifully to record a day's events, boredom has so overcome me that the results are mysterious at best. What is this business about "shopping, typing piece, dinner with E, depressed"? Shopping for what? Typing what piece? Who is E? Was this "E" depressed, or was I depressed? Who cares?

In fact I have abandoned altogether that kind of pointless entry; instead I tell what some would call lies. "That's simply not true," the members of my family frequently tell me when they come up against my memory of a shared event. "The party was *not* for you, the spider was *not* a black widow, *it wasn't that way at all.*" Very likely they are right, for not only have I always had trouble distinguishing between what happened and what merely might have happened, but I remain unconvinced that the distinction, for my purposes, matters. The cracked crab that I recall having for lunch the day my father came home from Detroit in 1945 must certainly be embroidery, worked into the day's pattern to lend verisimilitude; I was ten years old and would not now remember the cracked crab. The day's events did not turn on cracked crab. And yet it is precisely that fictitious crab that makes me see the afternoon all over again, a home movie run all too often, the father bearing gifts, the child weeping, an exercise in family love and guilt. Or that is what it was to me. Similarly, perhaps it never did snow that August in Vermont; perhaps there never were flurries in the night wind, and maybe no one else felt the ground hardening and summer already dead even as we pretended to bask in it, but that was how it felt to me, and it might as well have snowed, could have snowed, did snow.

How it felt to me: that is getting closer to the truth about a notebook. I sometimes delude myself about why I keep a notebook, imagine that some thrifty virtue derives from preserving everything observed. See enough and write it down, I tell myself, and then some morning when the world seems drained of wonder, some day when I am only going through the motions of doing what I am supposed to do, which is write—on that bankrupt morning I will simply open my notebook and there it will all be, a forgotten account with accumulated interest, paid passage back to the world out there: dialogue overheard in hotels and elevators and at the hat-check counter in Pavillon (one middle-aged man shows his hat check to another and says,"That's my old football number"); impressions of Bettina Aptheker and Benjamin Sonnenberg and Teddy ("Mr. Acapulco") Stauffer; careful *aperçus* about tennis bums and failed fashion models and Greek shipping heiresses, one of whom taught me a significant lesson (a lesson I could have learned from F. Scott Fitzgerald, but perhaps we all must meet the very rich for ourselves) by asking, when I arrived to interview her in her orchid-filled sitting room on the second day of a paralyzing New York blizzard, whether it was snowing outside.

I imagine, in other words, that the notebook is about other people. But of course it is not. I have no real business with what one stranger said to another at the hat-check counter in Pavillon; in fact I suspect that the line "That's my old football number" touched not my own imagination at all, but merely some memory of something once read, probably "The Eighty-Yard Run." Nor is my concern with a woman in a dirty crepe-de-Chine wrapper in a Wilmington bar. My stake is always, of course, in the unmentioned girl in the plaid silk dress. *Remember what it was to be me:* that is always the point.

It is a difficult point to admit. We are brought up in the ethic that others, any others, all others, are by definition more interesting than ourselves; taught to be diffident, just this side of self-effacing. ("You're the least important person in the room and don't forget it," Jessica Mitford's governess would hiss in her ear on the advent of any social occasion; I copied that into my notebook because it is only recently that I have been able to enter a room without hearing some such phrase in my inner ear.) Only the very young and the very old may recount their dreams at breakfast, dwell upon self, interrupt with memories of beach picnics and favorite Liberty lawn dresses and the rainbow trout in a creek near Colorado Springs. The rest of us are expected, rightly, to affect absorption in other people's favorite dresses, other people's trout.

And so we do. But our notebooks give us away, for however dutifully we record what we see around us, the common denominator of all we see is always, transparently, shamelessly, the implacable "I." We are not talking here about the kind of notebook that is patently for public consumption, a structural conceit for binding together a series of graceful *pensées*; we are talking about something private, about bits of the mind's string too short to use, an indiscriminate and erratic assemblage with meaning only for its maker.

And sometimes even the maker has difficulty with the meaning. There does not seem to be, for example, any point in my knowing for the rest of my life that, during 1964, 720 tons of soot fell on every square mile of New York City, yet there it is in my notebook, labeled "FACT." Nor do I really need to remember that Ambrose Bierce liked to spell Leland Stanford's name "£eland $tanford" or that "smart women almost always wear black in Cuba," a fashion hint without much potential for practical application. And does not the relevance of these notes seem marginal at best?:

> In the basement museum of the Inyo County Courthouse in Independence, California, sign pinned to a mandarin coat: "This MANDARIN COAT was often worn by Mrs. Minnie S. Brooks when giving lectures on her TEAPOT COLLECTION."

> Redhead getting out of car in front of Beverly Wilshire Hotel, chinchilla stole, Vuitton bags with tags reading:

> > MRS LOU FOX
> > HOTEL SAHARA
> > VEGAS

Well, perhaps not entirely marginal. As a matter of fact, Mrs. Minnie S. Brooks and her MANDARIN COAT pull me back into my own childhood, for although I never knew Mrs. Brooks and did not visit Inyo County until I was thirty, I grew up in just such a world, in houses cluttered with Indian relics and bits of gold ore and ambergris and the souvenirs my Aunt Mercy Farnsworth brought back from the Orient. It is a long way from that world to Mrs. Lou Fox's world, where we all live now, and is it not just as well to remember that? Might not Mrs. Minnie S. Brooks help me to remember what I am? Might not Mrs. Lou Fox help me to remember what I am not?

But sometimes the point is harder to discern. What exactly did I have in mind when I noted down that it cost the father of someone I know $650 a month to light the place on the Hudson in which he lived before the Crash? What use was I planning to make of this line by Jimmy Hoffa: "I may have my faults, but being wrong ain't one of them"? And although I think it interesting to know where the girls who travel with the Syndicate have their hair done when they find themselves on the West Coast, will I ever make suitable use of it? Might I not be better off just passing it on to John O'Hara? What is a recipe for sauerkraut doing in my notebook? What kind of magpie keeps this notebook? *"He was born the night the Titanic went down."* That seems a nice enough line, and I even recall who said it, but is it not really a better line in life than it could ever be in fiction?

But of course that is exactly it: not that I should ever use the line, but that I should remember the woman who said it and the afternoon I heard it. We were on her terrace by the sea, and we were finishing the wine left from lunch, trying to get what sun there was, a California winter sun. The woman whose husband was born the night the *Titanic* went down wanted to rent her house, wanted to go back to her children in Paris. I remember wishing that I could afford the house, which cost $1,000 a month. "Someday you will," she said lazily. "Someday it all comes." There in the sun on her terrace it seemed easy to believe in someday, but later I had a low-grade afternoon hangover and ran over a black snake on the way to the supermarket and was flooded with inexplicable fear when I heard the checkout clerk explaining to the man ahead of me why she was finally divorcing her husband. "He left me no choice," she said over and over as she punched the register. "He has a little seven-month-old baby by her, he left me no choice." I would like to believe that my dread then was for the human condition, but of course it was for me, because I wanted a baby and did not then have one and because I wanted to own the house that cost $1,000 a month to rent and because I had a hangover.

It all comes back. Perhaps it is difficult to see the value in having one's self back in that kind of mood, but I do see it; I think we are well advised to keep on nodding terms with the people we used to be, whether we find them attractive company or not. Otherwise they turn up unannounced and surprise us, come hammering on the mind's door at 4 A.M. of a bad night and demand to know who deserted them, who betrayed them, who is going to make amends. We forget all too soon the things we thought we could never forget. We forget the loves and the betrayals alike, forget what we whispered and what we screamed, forget who we were. I have already lost touch with a couple of people I used to be; one of them, a seventeen-year-old, presents little threat, although it would be of some interest to me to know again what it feels like to sit on a river levee drinking vodka-and-orange-juice and listening to Les Paul and Mary Ford and their echoes sing "How High the Moon" on the car radio. (You see I still have the scenes, but I no longer perceive myself among those present, no longer could even improvise the dialogue.) The other one, a twenty-three-year-old, bothers me more. She was always a good deal of trouble, and I suspect she will reappear when I least want to see her, skirts too long, shy to the point of aggravation, always the injured party, full of recriminations and little hurts and stories I do not want to hear again, at once saddening me and angering me with her vulnerability and ignorance, an apparition all the more insistent for being so long banished.

It is a good idea, then, to keep in touch, and I suppose that keeping in touch is what notebooks are all about. And we are all on our own when it comes to keeping those lines open to ourselves: your notebook will never help me, nor mine you. "*So what's new in the whiskey business?*" What could that possibly mean to you? To me it means a blonde in a Pucci bathing suit sitting with a couple of fat men by the pool at the Beverly Hills Hotel. Another man approaches, and they all regard one another in silence for a while. "So what's new in the whiskey business?" one of the fat men finally says by way of welcome, and the blonde stands up, arches one foot and dips it in the pool, looking all the while at the cabaña where Baby Pignatari is talking on the telephone. That is all there is to that, except that several years later I saw the blonde coming out of Saks Fifth Avenue in New York with her California complexion and a voluminous mink coat. In the harsh wind that day she looked old and irrevocably tired to me, and even the skins in the mink coat were not worked the way they were doing them that year, not the way she would have wanted them done, and there is the point of the story. For a while after that I did not like to look in the mirror, and my eyes would skim the newspapers and pick out only the deaths, the cancer victims, the premature coronaries, the suicides, and I stopped riding the Lexington Avenue IRT because I noticed for the first time that all the strangers I had seen for years—the man with the seeing-eye dog, the spinster who read the classified pages every day, the fat girl who always got off with me at Grand Central—looked older than they once had.

It all comes back. Even that recipe for sauerkraut: even that brings it back. I was on Fire Island when I first made that sauerkraut, and it was raining, and we drank a lot of bourbon and ate the sauerkraut and went to bed at ten, and I listened to the rain and the Atlantic and felt safe. I made the sauerkraut again last night and it did not make me feel any safer, but that is, as they say, another story.

JOSEPH EPSTEIN

I Like a Gershwin Tune

You may not have caught my act at the old Pratt-Lane Hotel. Brilliant stuff. A knockout, take my word for it. I came on and sang one number, and one number only: "Any Bonds Today?" Maybe you'll recall the song's most powerful line, which—modesty won't do here—I belted out gloriously: "Bonds of freedom, that's what I'm selling, any bonds today?" The crowd—my parents and their friends—went wild. The year was 1942, the war was on, and I was five. I retired as a singer later that same year, when I was told in nursery school not to sing so loudly, especially since I sang off-key. Knowing when to quit—that, I'd say, is the name of the game.

I admire people who know when to quit, especially singers, many of whom go on much too long. "I always wanted to sing as well as Frank Sinatra," someone I know reported recently of the great crooner, "and now I can." Julie London, the torch singer, must have recognized that, beyond a certain age, carrying that torch can only singe a woman's no-longer-lush eyelashes. Another singer whose retirement I regret is Tom Lehrer, whose musical parodies, though much dated, still amuse. A friend tells me that he asked Lehrer why he stopped writing and performing his comic songs. "Since Henry Kissinger won the Nobel Peace Prize," Lehrer replied, "nothing seems funny anymore."

In the America of the 1940s and 1950s, when I was growing up, popular music was everywhere; and it was not of interest only to the young, as popular music is today. Singers were great heroes, bandleaders famous personages. At a neighborhood delicatessen in Rogers Park called Ashkenaz, there was a sandwich called The Lou Breese, named after the bandleader at the Chicago Theater. I don't recall the contents of that sandwich, but I feel confident it must, by today's standards, have been powerfully life-threatening: chopped liver and pastrami, perhaps. I do know, though, that I would rather have a sandwich named after me than receive an honorary degree from any university in the Western world.

Radio shows not only featured singers, but many had a singer as part of the regular cast—Jack Benny had Dennis Day and Bob Hope had Frances Langford. A bandleader named Kay Kyser had a radio show that he called, in a kind of subtitle, "The Kollege of Musical Knowledge." Ozzie Nelson, of *The Adventures of Ozzie and Harriet*, was another bandleader. Jokes about the drunkenness of musicians, a specialty of Phil Harris, who was also on *The Jack Benny Program*, were also endemic. In the early years of television, singers of popular songs were still thought necessary: Arthur Godfrey had Julius LaRosa, Steve Allen had Steve Lawrence and Eydie Gorme. Any singer who had a big hit song was certain to be booked on *The Ed Sullivan Show*. Bing Crosby and Frank Sinatra were more widely known than any American athlete or politician except the president. Popular music was part of the national (as opposed to teen) culture in a way that it has not come close to being ever again.

Mine was far from a musical family. No one played an instrument, and the phonograph, as it was then called when it wasn't called the Victrola (after the firm RCA Victor), was not at the center of our family life. The only records I remember being played in our apartment were an album of 78s of Stephen Foster songs sung by Bing Crosby that my father liked to nap to and an album of fast-talking Danny Kaye songs, "Minnie the Moocher" prominent among them. My father would occasionally hum a tune while shaving—"Anybody Here Seen Kelly?" was in his extremely limited repertoire—but my mother never sang in my hearing. I probably got my off-key singing voice from her.

But even in this relatively unmusical home I could not avoid the sheer musicality of life. Singing was part of grade-school life; every year in grammar school, one's class would prepare programs to sing at semi-annual assemblies. Music lessons as well as tap dancing lessons were offered through the public school system at very low rates. In high school, one had to take a course in music, which, along with art, was known as a minor subject. Our music teacher was a lovely woman: a spinster more than six feet tall who dressed in tailored suits, Miss Adele Burke played great rolling arpeggios on the piano while singing Jerome Kern and Rodgers and Hart songs in a florid style. Every other movie seemed to have singing in it; José Iturbi or Oscar Levant was regularly seated at a piano near a swimming pool or in a marvelously suave Manhattan apartment; and it was not uncommon for the male lead in these movies to croon into the ear of his inamorata, which, in reality, couldn't have been all that pleasant from the standpoint of the inamorata.

So pervasive was song in middle-class American life, and so tied up with the notion of romance, that a regular activity of Middle Western college fraternities was serenading sororities. When a member of a fraternity gave his pin to a member of a sorority, not only was a serenade called for, but during the serenade the boy was expected to step forth and sing, solo, directly to the girl. I spent a semester in such a fraternity, and I still remember the serenade of a boy named Ronald Kaplan to Janey Weinstein, an heiress to a funeral-parlor fortune. Ronnie Kaplan, large and rather lumpy, was a boy with the gift of perpetual middle age — how easy growing older must have been for him! At the appropriate moment during the serenade, he stepped forth to allow, in a quavering voice, that yes, Janey, though both the Rockies and Gibraltar might crumble and all the rest of it, his love, hey! no question about it, his love was here to stay. It turned out he was right, for they later married and, as far as I know, lived happily ever after.

I don't mean to imply that I grew up in a limitlessly rich era of songwriting. Throughout my boyhood a regular flow of entirely junky novelty songs kept popping up, among them "Mairzy Doats," "I Like Chewing Gum," "Chickery-Chick, Cha-la, Cha-la," "Come On-a My House," "Mañana," "The Doggie in the Window," "Behind the Green Door," and the immemorial "Purple People Eater." As a kid, I was swept up by these songs quite as much as so many of my countrymen. I have a painful memory of standing before a mirror caressing into shape an ambitious pompadour I wore at fourteen and singing a little number titled "Cincinnati Dancing Pig" (we were, I seem to recall, invoked to witness him do "the barnyard jig"), when my learned and immensely dignified grandfather walked into the room. At that moment, gazing upon his idiot grandson, he must have felt that his leaving Bialystok fifty-odd years before had been a grave mistake.

A number of the famous male singers of my youth were notably cheesy and tended to sing songs about their quite hopeless enthrallment by love. Such singers as Don Cornell, Al Martino, Tony Martin (whose real claim to fame was his marriage to the beautiful dancer Cyd Charisse), and particularly Frankie Laine specialized in the big heartbreak numbers. The torment caused Frankie Laine by a woman named "Jezebel" (whose "eyes promised paradise") was almost more than one could bear to contemplate.

Laine, a Chicagoan of Italian ancestry, had some of the greatest record hits of my adolescence. Along with "Jezebel," he scored with two western songs—"Mule Train" and "The Cry of the Wild Goose." This was before television, and so one had to imagine what Laine looked like. Whips cracked while this man sang, rhythms pounded like the heart of a miser in a French restaurant in New York, and I imagined Frankie Laine to be a darker and perhaps more muscular Gary Cooper. When he appeared at the Chicago Theater, which in those days—the late 1940s and early 1950s—had stage shows as well as movies, I betook myself there to see him in person. A profound letdown doesn't begin to describe what happened. Frankie Laine was a thickset man with rather a large nose who wore a pretty obvious toupee. This "brother of the old wild goose," as he styled himself in one of his songs, seemed more fit to own a Buick agency or a State Street jewelry store than to drive the mule train that he kept screaming about in his hit song. Not the last of life's little disappointments, I fear.

The Chicago Theater was something of a hangover from vaudeville days, and the headliners of its stage shows were almost always singers. I saw there a flash-in-the-pan singer named Johnnie Ray, who after two big hits, "Cry" and "The Little White Cloud That Cried," disappeared. On its stage I saw the elegant Billy Eckstine, wearing one of his famous high Mr. B. shirt collars and singing "Everything I Have Is Yours." Joni James, a singer who had had a hit during my high school days called "Let Me Go Lover," stopped off to play the Chicago Theater on her way to obscurity.

The Four Aces, my favorite group in those years, also appeared at the Chicago Theater, singing their immensely stylized songs, which contained such lines as "as we danced the night away, my heart said she's for me." They wore gold-colored tuxedo jackets and their hairdos made them look as if they came straight from the Exxon Valdes oil spill. The Crew Cuts, another foursome, this one from Toronto, sang at one of our high school dances at the Edgewater Beach Hotel; they, surely it cannot so soon have been forgotten, gave the English language the phrase "sh-boom, sh-boom."

By the time I saw Nat King Cole—again at the Chicago Theater—he had already entered his hit-record and therefore high-popularity phase. I heard him sing his signature songs from this period, which included "Mona Lisa," "Dance, Ballerina, Dance," and "Walkin' My Baby Back Home." Melodramatic and a little foolish as these songs are, Nat Cole lent them some of his own immense dignity. He was a very elegant man, with a diction and timbre, if I am using that word correctly, that were like no one else's. Because he sang love songs without seeming to want your girl, he was the first black singer to break through and find himself in the empyrean of popularity wherein dwelt such singers as Bing Crosby, Perry Como, and Frank Sinatra. For a time in the 1950s, he had his own television show.

I came a little late for the young Frank Sinatra, who drove bobby-soxers bonkers, but I do remember that the movie *From Here to Eternity* put him back in business as a big-time draw. He was a marvelous singer who was not without a flaw or two as a human being. He was known for flares of terrible temper, during which he might do something humiliating to a studio musician; later, to make it up to him, he might, big-hearted guy that he is, buy the musician's parents, say, the town of Kenosha, Wisconsin.

My own sense is that the late-night hours Frank kept may have made him cranky. This is a man, after all (if we are to believe the evidence of his songs), who was regularly out in the wee small hours of the morning, when it was a quarter to three, no one in the place but the bartender and he; and even when he went to bed he kept imagining some girl dancing on his ceiling, from "underneath his counterpane." (Go figure people's taste in bedding. You don't suppose Frank slept in a canopy bed, do you?) Doubtless, these bad habits were reinforced by the mood indigo that he suffered, which first came upon him when his baby said good-bye. But he, Frank, could sing, no doubt about that. In a novel by Willie Morris, the hero thanks Frank Sinatra and Nat King Cole for what little sexual success he had in high school.

Fred Astaire, whose singing I have come to like more and more (and for whom Irving Berlin said he enjoyed writing more than for any other singer), hadn't Sinatra's problems. His songs, like his movies, are pure, sweet fantasy, and on the whole charmingly upbeat. Apart from having to undergo the mild depression of a foggy day in London town, when even the British Museum appears to have lost its charm, most of the difficulties Astaire encountered took place on the dance floor, as when a woman he admired danced every dance with "that same fortunate man"—not him. Yet Astaire did log more than his share of time dancing cheek to cheek, which, you might say—actually he did say it—is nice work if you can get it, which he did. As made plain, in another song, he was dancing and he couldn't be bothered now.

Fred Astaire's indomitably cheerful songs, implying days spent in ascots and buttery cashmere jackets and nights spent in white ties and tails, always suggested urbanity and suavity, with only occasional dips into self-pity ("A Fine Romance," "Let's Call the Whole Thing Off"). In this, Astaire was anomalous. Self-pity has been the keynote emotion in much of American popular music. You have either lost or cannot obtain the affection of the one you love; your innate qualities of sensitivity, constancy, and profound affection are not appreciated. Songs pledging undying affection—"I'll Never Stop Loving You" is one that comes to mind—were big. George S. Kaufman was probably closer to capturing the truth of the matter when he said that he would have preferred it if Irving Berlin's song "Always" had been instead titled "Thursday," so that its clincher line would go, "I'll be loving you, Thursday."

Self-pity is probably the only authentic emotion that adolescent boys and girls feel, which partly explains the pre-eminence of popular music in my era. I know I felt self-pity myself, though I'm not sure that I didn't have to whip myself into it artificially. Even though I must have felt young love—"They tried to tell us we're too young" was a line in a hit song of my adolescence— my youthful existence lacked genuine romantic drama. As a boy, I surely yearned, but never can it be said that I pined—I didn't really have the attention span for extended pining. I should have liked to have been the kind of fellow who could drive women mad with longing, even the worthless kind that stimulates certain women. But I soon enough sensed that these were not the roles central casting had put me on earth to play.

In 1953, when I was sixteen, Raymond Chandler, complaining about the low quality of public education in America, wrote to a friend that "about all they teach there is the increasingly simple art of seduction." I for one could have used that course, but— damn—it wasn't offered at my school. I left no string of broken hearts, paternity suits, or attempted suicides in my wake. As a youth, I was, not to put too fine a point on it, a less than fully convincing seducer.

In my lifetime I have felt jealousy and I have known sexual envy, but even as an adolescent, I never felt the need to devote myself, full-time, to the great sex chase. The world, in Ira Gershwin's rather mortal phrase, never had to "pardon my mush," though, as a boy and young man, I had many a crush. Yet I don't believe I ever made an entire fool of myself in pursuit of a woman—perhaps only a third or half a fool. This left a fair amount of free time for reading, sports, and popular music.

Popular music is, of course, almost entirely about the sex wars: about yearning and love unrequited, about betrayal and consummations left at the stage of devout wishing. It is music to fantasize by. None of this is to say that popular music didn't stir me—or doesn't stir me still. When Louis Armstrong asks for "a kiss to build a dream on," allowing how his imagination will build upon that kiss, I do believe I understand him. But perhaps the last time I took this music altogether seriously was in high school, in the age of sexual awakening.

A friend at dinner not long ago claimed that he considered most fish as no more than a vehicle on which to convey sauce to the mouth. In a similar vein, when I was in high school, music was, through dancing, a way to get close to girls. Mine was the last generation that went in for what is now called slow, but would more accurately be called close, dancing. Our dancing came just after the jitterbug, danced to swing music, and before the twist—the first of the non-touching dances that began in the early 1960s—and all the autoerotic solo dancing that followed.

Every so often at a wedding or other large party where a band has been hired, a couple in their late fifties or early sixties will hit the dance floor to do a jitterbug. What great fun it looks! The last jitterbugging couple I remember from high school days was Frankie Sommers and Nancy Shaffner. Frankie, a couple of years older than I, was one of the golden boys of my youth. He could throw a football sixty yards, and nothing ever got past him in his position in left field. His voice had a charming rasp, and his smile could light up an alley in a terrifying neighborhood.

Nancy, like Frankie, was small. She wore braces and had a slight lisp. Frankie and Nancy—they seemed a perfect couple, and they went on to marry. I gather that they, too, stayed married. They were a smash on the dance floor, bopping away to a Count Basie or Duke Ellington tune. So good were they that, once they began, everyone else left the dance floor the way dancing couples cleared the floor for Fred Astaire and Ginger Rogers in the movies. Frankie, who had the build of a gymnast, would toss Nancy in the air, or dip her across his hips, or swing her between his legs. Fantastic stuff!

The rest of us, more earthbound, slogged away at our slow dancing. "Graduation's almost here, my love," with the preceding line, "should the teacher stand so near, my love," was the kind of lyric to which we vibrated. "I wanna be loved with inspiration" was a line in a song in which the singers—the Andrews

Sisters—went on to make plain that they were in "no mood for turtledoving." Neither, let me say here, was I, who was ready at all times to get "On a Slow Boat to China," firm in my belief that "Love Is a Many Splendored Thing."

Intellectuals don't dance. Or so, accused of acting out of character, I was told as I came off the dance floor with my wife a few years ago in San Francisco. Clearly I am an exception to an entertaining, but less than entirely sound, generalization. I have always thought dancing a fine thing, wish I were better at it, and admire those who can beautifully glide around a dance floor.

In my last year of grade school, at the age of thirteen, I was sent to something called Fortnightly—though I could swear it met every Saturday afternoon—where some of my classmates and I were taught dance-floor etiquette and many intricate dance steps, almost all of which I have long since forgotten. I have retained the handy, all-purpose box step, the basis of the waltz and other dances, which has kept me from being the otherwise perfect wallflower. For a time in high school, I fancied myself a rumba king (also based on the box step) and doubtless made a considerable jackass of myself. In the 1950s, Latin American dances were big stuff: even the sedate Perry Como sang a hopeless tune called "Papa Loves Mambo." All I wish to say in my own defense is that, in a life marred by many sins, large and small, of commission and omission, at least I never danced the cha-cha. I hope this will be recalled in my favor on Judgment Day.

Social life at my high school, Nicholas Senn, was organized around dancing. Not only were there school and club dances, but records were played during the three lunch periods in our large assembly hall, and kids could dance there if they wished. There was even a goofy little jog step called the Senn Walk, in which the boy held his left hand far away from his body, making dancing couples look slightly contorted.

Disc jockeys were important figures in the Chicago of those years. One among them, a man named Howard Miller, who died not long ago, was a towering figure. He was said to be able to launch a song into popularity through main force—main force being the playing of a song over and over, which is to say plugging it ruthlessly, on his own show. He was married to a singer named June Valli, who had a weepy hit titled "Crying in the Chapel," now justly forgotten. Miller was also notable for giving optimistic weather reports, falsifying the temperature by as much as ten degrees—this in the undramatic days before the advent of wind-chill factors—so that, after getting his rosy report, one would step out on a winter's day and be blown off the sidewalk. When rock 'n' roll came on the scene, Miller himself was blown away as a disc jockey and began a rather blustery political talk show.

But the great disc jockey for young pseudo-sophisticates like me was a man named Jay Andres. He played light classics—such as "The Story of Three Loves," taken from the powerful theme of Rachmaninoff's "Rhapsody on a Theme of Paganini"—along with much Sarah Vaughan, Ella Fitzgerald, Mel Tormé, Nat Cole, Dick Haymes, and other, cooler, more understated singers. His show was on at night, late-ish. The highlight of many a date came when an adolescent boy, driving his father's clunky Buick northward on the wonderful Outer Drive, turned to his date and, his hand hovering over the radio dial, asked, "A little Jay Andres?" The question retains its magic for me even now. "A little Jay Andres?" ranks up there with "A little champagne?"

The next stage in my popular-music life came at the University of Chicago, where the music of choice seemed to be folk music. I gave this a shot, went to a concert or two, and heard an impressive woman named Odetta, a young man named Bob Gibson, and a number of others whose names are now lost to me. The charms of a folk music hootenanny did not entirely escape me, though, if the truth be told, I had a bit of trouble "identifying," as the kids say, with John Henry. Whenever I heard the song, I replaced the name John Henry, a steel-driving man, with that of Al Rabinowitz, a cab-driving man among my contemporaries. But it was no go.

Two albums dominate the musical recollections I have of my days at college. One was Harry Belafonte's calypso album, with its red background and picture of the devastatingly handsome Belafonte in a green shirt on its cover. "Day O," "Jamaica Farewell," "Brown Skin Girl," and "Come Back Liza" were some of the songs on the album, and no greater music for singing in the shower was ever devised ("Come Mr. Tally Man, and tally me banana"). I later saw Belafonte in performance, and, unlike Frankie Laine, he was in no wise disappointing but rather one of those extraordinary performers who you still don't want to leave the stage, even after a two-hour show.

The other album that I listened to over and over was "The Misty Miss Christy," torch songs by June Christy, who sang for the Stan Kenton band. Her songs about loneliness, desertion, betrayal, and general mistreatment at the hands of men made Ovid, in the *Heroides*, seem, in the crying-the-blues department, strictly bush-league. The cumulative impression the album conveyed was of a beautiful woman alone at a bar—smoking a cigarette and two drinks ahead of everyone else in the room—who had gotten a very raw deal. The fantasy that it allowed to college boys was that, with a bit of luck, one might meet such a woman and make her—and oneself—well. The questions about her— why had so many men left her in the lurch and was there something fundamentally wrong with so habitually unhappy a woman—were, of course, best left unanswered. In musical romance, only the unexamined life is worth living.

At twenty and twenty-one, I spent a bit of time in Rush Street nightclubs hoping to meet such a woman. I heard the beautiful Fran Jeffries, who was married to Dick Haymes, sing at the smart (as it would then have been called) club called Mr. Kelly's. At the old Black Orchid, I heard Peggy Lee, whose marriage to an alcoholic musician gave her sufficient reason to sing her own sad songs, which she did exceedingly well. I would occasionally drop in at the lounge at the Maryland Hotel, also on Rush Street; and, on the city's south side, I heard Miles Davis at the Sutherland Lounge.

Sad to report, I never met either June Christy or the June Christy-like woman, who might have called me Baby, or implored me to drink up and order anything I like, or asked me to come to the party and leave my blues behind. Instead, one day at Mr. Kelly's, I began a conversation with Mort Sahl, who invited me to walk back with him to his hotel. Along the way, we traded jokes, and one that he told me—the year was 1956—was that President Eisenhower and Adlai Stevenson were supposed to meet to discuss the state of the country before the election, but the meeting had to be canceled because Eisenhower's interpreter never showed up.

Music pervaded even the military. One of the first things a number of soldiers did with their first army paycheck was buy a portable radio. I remember the barracks in basic training at Fort Leonard Wood, in Missouri, flooded with music. The hit song of the time was "Tom Dooley," sung by the Kingston Trio. A bit of a downer, that song—Tom, you may recall, was invoked to hang down his head, poor boy he was going to die. Jukeboxes at the PX blared lots of Elvis. The year was 1958, and Elvis himself was then a private at Fort Hood, Texas. Two bunks down from mine, an Appalachian fellow named Bobby Flowers, who was drafted because his wife turned him in for failing to make alimony payments, used to sing about flying over these prison walls but for the want of angel's wings, and he made lots of jokes about his wife, while rather menacingly cleaning his M1 rifle.

For the *clichémeisters*, the decade of the 1950s is musically lashed to Elvis Presley. Not quite true. First, the King, as his fans now call the old boy, came rather late in the decade; and, second, you had to be an adolescent when he came along to get worked up about him. For those of us who came of age earlier in the decade, popular music meant an elegant club singer such as Julie London, with whom every man must have been in love (I know I was); it meant an immensely rich period for jazz; and it meant the end of the great era of musical comedy. For us, the fifties had nothing whatsoever to do with hound dogs, heartbreak hotels, and blue suede shoes.

Presley was many things, not least among them a southerner. As everyone now acknowledges, his songs combined black rhythms with a country-western outlook. In the army and later, while living in the South, I heard vast quantities of country-western music, and I came to like it, though I always, perhaps I should confess, felt rather superior to it. My pedantry seemed to get in the way. A song such as "Everybody's Somebody's Fool" seemed to me badly in need of qualification; and that God made honky-tonk angels seemed to me, as a reader of Thomas Aquinas, theologically dubious. Still, as a young man, I put in my hours in a few Arkansas and Texas honky-tonks (no angels sighted), where the atmosphere seemed to bristle with potential bottle-breaking violence every time the band took a break.

I don't remember when *The Hit Parade*—which was first on the radio, then on television, and always, I believe, sponsored by Lucky Strike, L(ucky) S(trike) M(eans) F(ine) T(obacco)—ceased broadcasting, but over the years, in the back of my mind, I have kept a little list of songs that are on my Hate Parade. On this list appear "Begin the Beguine" (Desi Arnaz), "My Way" (Frank Sinatra), "I Gotta Be Me" (Sammy Davis, Jr.), "I Left My Heart in San Francisco" (Tony Bennett), "Oh My Papa" (Eddie Fisher), "People" (Barbra Streisand), "Leaving on a Jet Plane" (Peter, Paul, & Mary), and "There's No Business Like Show Business" (by anyone). If there is a jukebox in hell, these will be the only songs it plays, relentlessly.

At the same time, there are some songs less than Schubertian in quality that, when I hear them, continue to give pleasure. Vaughn Monroe's "Ghost Riders in the Sky," which I haven't heard in years, is such a song. I find a good many of Dean Martin's songs—"Goin' to Houston," "That's Amore"—always make me laugh, perhaps owing to the utter casualness with which he seemed to sing them. I like "You've Got to See Momma Every Night" both for itself and because it reminds me of an old Groucho Marx story, the punch line of which is, "You've got to order sea bass every night, or you can't order sea bass at all." I adore Jimmy Durante singing "September Song" and George Burns singing the Lennon/McCartney song "When I'm Sixty-Four." Sometimes a wildly goofy line or two can put a song permanently in my mind, such as the song that, inquiring into the name change of Constantinople to Istanbul, asks why the former name "got the works" and then responds that this is "nobody's business but the Turks'."

Some songs stir up memories more surely than M. Proust's petite madeleine. Sarah Vaughan singing "Make Yourself Comfortable" takes me back to lengthy necking (what a funny word!) sessions in a living room on a shady street named Mozart, but pronounced in Chicago *Moe-zart.* The song "Fascination" recalls Gary Cooper, in the Billy Wilder movie *Love in the Afternoon,* sweating it out in a steam bath in Paris, while four violinists, in tuxedos in the steam bath with him, schmaltzily play that tune to comfort him in his sadness about losing the love of Audrey Hepburn. Every time I hear "Send in the Clowns," I think of taking my father-in-law, a very elegant man then dying of cancer, to a matinee performance of *A Little Night Music*. "Imagination," as another song says, "is funny."

Reading an article in *Esquire* about David Letterman, I learn that "he prefers music to stoke him, never to soothe." The music of Letterman's choice, it shouldn't surprise us, is rock 'n' roll. The comedian is, musically, of the rock generation. B.R. or A.R., Before Rock or After Rock, is one of the great, perhaps uncrossable, divisions of humankind. Those of us who came before cannot hope—and, let us speak candidly, do not all that much wish—to understand the musical tastes of those who came after. I, unlike David Letterman, prefer music that soothes me, for the world stokes me rather more than I like as it is, thank you very much.

Listening to Louis Armstrong sing almost anything makes me happy and reminds me of life's vibrant possibilities. Armstrong was, I think, a musical genius, a wonderful singer, and the best jazz trumpeter the world has known. "A man blowing a trumpet successfully," wrote the Welsh writer Rhys Davies, "is a rousing spectacle." But it's Louie the singer who really knocks me out. When he sings, in the divine rasp that was his voice, that it's not the pale moon that excites him, I almost have to leave my chair, so ready am I for bopping around the room. I wish I could do what I do one-twentieth as well as he did what he did. But even if I could, I shall, in my line of work, never be able to say, as he did: "Take it, Ella. Swing it!"

Certain phrases from the songs I love still send me: "the very thought of you"; "see the jungle when it's wet with rain"; "it never entered my mind"; "Argentines without means do it"; "no kick from champagne"; "hates California, it's cold and it's damp"; "diamond bracelets Woolworth doesn't sell, baby"; "see the pyramids along the Nile"; "the world will always welcome lovers"; "still I can't get started with you"; "that's the story of, that's the glory of love"; "nights were sour spent with Schopenhauer." I admire the general culture and wit that allowed Ira Gershwin to write that last phrase. Sad to think there is no one around today likely to write anything to equal it. "Oh, baby, say you'll be mine / we'll acquire a cozy cottage / and I'll read you Wittgenstein." Not, this attempt of my own, nearly so fine.

Many of those phrases were written fifty and more years ago. During the first three decades of this century, a remarkable generation of songwriters arose—what other verb can one use to explain the presence of even minor genius—most of them Jewish guys with names such as Irving, Ira, Larry, Harold, Gus, Oscar, Sammy, and a few brilliant non-tribesmen named Cole, Noel, Harry, Johnny, and Hoagy. (My favorite songwriting name is Irving Caesar; he wrote the lyrics for "Tea for Two" when woken by Vincent Youmans in the middle of the night and claimed that most of his songs were written in fewer than fifteen minutes.)

S. N. Behrman, in a fine memoir titled *People in a Diary*, claimed that the figure in Manhattan and Hollywood during the 1920s who seemed to outshine everyone else in sheer vitality and effulgence of talent was George Gershwin. Gershwin possessed, according to Behrman, "the quality of joy"—joy unimpeded, as he points out, by modesty. Of his mother, Gershwin once remarked: "You know the extraordinary thing about her—she's so modest about me." Behrman recounts having to bring Gershwin the bad news that a woman he claimed to love was secretly married. "Do you know," he said, "if I weren't so busy, I'd feel terrible."

Ira Gershwin, the younger brother and generally thought the junior partner, was, in his quiet way, quite as impressive. He was intensely, though unpretentiously, literary, and in his late adolescence, as he reports in his autobiography, he "fooled around with French verse forms, such as the triolet, villanelle, and especially the rondeau." He had an interest in etymology and was a reader of the *Oxford English Dictionary*. Fred Astaire said of George Gershwin that "he wrote for feet," while Ira wrote for the head. "You reading Heine, I somewhere in China," appears in the same song, "Isn't It a Pity?," as the Schopenhauer allusion.

George Gershwin died at age thirty-nine. "He lived all his life in youth," Behrman notes, adding that "his rhythms were the pulsations of youth; he reanimated them in those much older than he was. He reanimates them still." George had the gorgeous vitality, Ira the splendid sophistication, and together they gave people who could spare a few moments to listen a sense of what lies behind the phrase *joie de vivre*. Gershwin's last word, on his deathbed, was "Astaire."

But if the Gershwins and others wrote songs that had about them the spirit of youth, it was youth of a different kind than we have come to associate with being young. It was youth untroubled, full of promise, agonizing over nothing greater than winning that boy or girl. "Moon and June and roses and rainbow's end" runs a phrase in a Blossom Dearie song titled "Down with Love." Ah, all those lovely, lilting rhymes: caressing / blessing, breeze / memories, arms / charms, sighing / crying, tree / bees . . . do it, even chimpanzees do it.

Why do so many of these lyrics remain in my mind when I worry that the four numbers I need to use the cash machine at my bank won't stay in my memory? They are more amusing, for one thing; but, more pertinently, they are also part of my own youth. I'm glad I grew up in a time when "writers who knew better words" had not begun to use four- or even no-letter words. I feel a debt, a positive obligation, to remember some of those words, just as I owe all those female singers—"vocalists," as they were then called—a letter of thanks for all those daydreams. "So here's to the ladies, God bless 'em," as the Victorians used to say. Thanks, Billie, Ella, Sarah, Peggy, Julie, June, Judy, Jo, Lena, Lee, Rosie, Anita, Chris, Dinahs (Washington and Shore), Doris, Keely, Eartha, and Blossom. Thanks, I wish I could say, for the memories, but let me say instead, thanks for the sweet fantasies.

I find myself listening more and more to the best of this music. The pleasure, far from decreasing, seems greater than ever. A few months ago I memorized, for my own diversion, the lyrics to "Stars Fell on Alabama" and "Softly, as in a Morning Sunrise," which I now retain as mantras. I suppose I ought to be grateful that I can neither play the piano nor sing, else I should spend most of my waking hours sitting at the piano playing and singing this music. Instead, I walk around with all these tunes in my head. At my stage in life, where mild depression would seem only to make good sense, they provide a regular and by no means artificial boost.

BRUCE CHATWIN

THE BEY

Among my first jobs at Sotheby's was that of porter in the Department of Greek and Roman Antiquities. Whenever there was a sale I would put on my grey porter's uniform and stand behind the glass vitrines, making sure that prospective buyers didn't sticky the objects with their fingers.

One morning there appeared an elderly and anachronistic gentleman in a black Astrakhan-collared coat, carrying a black silver-tipped cane. His syrupy eyes and brushed-up moustache announced him as a relic of the Ottoman Empire.

"Can you show me something beautiful?" he asked. "Greek, *not* Roman!"

"I think I can," I said.

I showed him a fragment of an Attic white-ground lekythos by the Achilles Painter which had the most refined drawing, in golden-sepia, of a naked boy. It had come from the collection of Lord Elgin.

"Ha!" said the old gentleman. "I see you have The Eye. I too have The Eye. We shall be friends."

He handed me his card. I watched the black coat recede into the gallery:

Paul A— — — F — — — Bey
Grand Chamberlain du Cour du Roi des Albanis

"So," I said to myself. "Zog's Chamberlain."

He was true to his word. We became friends. He would turn up in London on some business of Albanians in exile. He fretted about Queen Geraldine in Estoril. He regretted that King Leka in Madrid had to earn his living in real-estate.

He spoke of the works of art that had been his. He had sold his Fauve Braques and paintings by Juan Gris *en bloc* to the Australian art collector, Douglas Cooper. He spoke of the excellent pheasant shooting in his ancestral domain. He had never been to Albania but had spent his life between Switzerland and Alexandria. Did I know, he once asked, that the government of Enver Hoxha was a homosexual cabal?

"At least, that's what they tell me."

I soon realised that the Bey was not a buyer but a seller. His straitened circumstances forced him from time to time to dispense with a work of art. Would I, he enquired rather sheepishly, be interested in acquiring some odds and ends from his collection?

"I certainly would," I said.

"Perhaps I could show you a few things at the Ritz?"

I had next to no money. The Directors at Sotheby's assumed that people like myself had private incomes to supplement our wretched salaries. What was I to do? Exist on air? I earned myself a little extra by trafficking in antiquities—until the Chairman told me to stop. It was wrong for members of the staff to deal in works of art because they actively hindered a possible sale at auction.

I felt this was unfair. Almost everyone in the art business seemed to be at it.

But with the Bey my conscience was clear. He refused to sell anything at auction. I don't think he could bear the idea of his things being handled on viewing day by the hoi polloi, by people who did *not* have The Eye. Besides, he gave me everything as a present. Spread out over his bed at the Ritz would be a cluster of exquisite objects: an Archaic Greek bronze, a fragment of a Mosan chasse, a Byzantine cameo, an Egyptian green slate palette of pre-dynastic period, and many others.

"Would you like them?" he asked anxiously.

"I would."

"In that case I give them to you! Between two friends who have The Eye there can be no question of money."

I would wrap the treasures in tissue paper and, taking them to a dealer friend, find out how much I could get for them. I always tried to keep one or two for myself.

A day later the phone would ring. "Chatwin, could you spare a few moments to have a drink with me?"

"Of course I could, Bey."

We would meet in the Ritz Bar.

"Chatwin, I've one or two little favours to ask you. You know how tiresome it is to move funds around Europe. Banks are so unobliging these days. I find I've overspent on this visit. I wonder if you could settle a few things for me."

"Of course, Bey."

"I've been a bit extravagant at the tailor. Three or four suits. Four pairs of shoes at Lobb's. And there's the poor old Bentley! She had to have a new radiator."

"I'll see what I can do," I said.

I went to the tailor and asked for the Bey's bill. I went to Lobb. I discovered from Jack Barclay the cost of the radiator. The Bey's prices were never excessive; but, in the best Oriental tradition, we always had a haggle at the end. Otherwise, the deal would not be a deal.

"Chatwin, I wonder if you could have a word with the Ritz cashier? I thought of leaving for Switzerland on Saturday week."

"Out of the question, Bey. I suggest this Monday."

"Alas, that cannot be. On Tuesday Lady Turnbull is giving a cocktail for the Anglo-Albanian Society. As Chamberlain, I have to attend."

"Wednesday then?"

"Wednesday it shall be."

"And no more phone calls after today?"

This went on for two or three years. Nowadays, I sometimes thumb through the catalogues of an American museum, or an exhibition of ancient art, and there, illustrated full-plate, will be an object or a painting that passed from the Bey to myself: "A unique Cycladic marble vessel . . .", "A Pentellic marble head of a youth from a late fifth-century Attic stele . . .", "A white marble head of a Putto, attributed to Desiderio di Settignano . . .", "A painting of Christ Mocked, in tempera on linen, by a follower of Mantegna, possibly by Melozzo da Forli . . ."

We have one object left from the Bey's collection: my wife's

engagement ring. It is a Greek electrum ring of the late fifth
century B.C. The Bey bought it in 1947 from a Cairo dealer called
Tano. I believe it comes from the Tell-el Mashkuta Treasure,
most of which is now in the Brooklyn Museum.

The intaglio has a wounded lioness levering with her mouth
and forepaw the hunter's spear from her flank. Not entirely suitable as an engagement present, but I think it the loveliest Greek
ring I ever saw.

I write about the Bey because people of his kind will never
come again. His life, I suspect, was a bit of a sham. The Eye was
always young and pure.

PHYLLIS ROSE

Tools of Torture:
An Essay on Beauty and Pain

In a gallery off the rue Dauphine, near the *parfumerie* where I get my massage, I happened upon an exhibit of medieval torture instruments. It made me think that pain must be as great a challenge to the human imagination as pleasure. Otherwise there's no accounting for the number of torture instruments. One would be quite enough. The simple pincer, let's say, which rips out flesh. Or the head crusher, which breaks first your tooth sockets, then your skull. But in addition I saw tongs, thumbscrews, a rack, a ladder, ropes and pulleys, a grill, a garrote, a Spanish horse, a Judas cradle, an iron maiden, a cage, a gag, a strappado, a stretching table, a saw, a wheel, a twisting stork, an inquisitor's chair, a breast breaker, and a scourge. You don't need complicated machinery to cause incredible pain. If you want to saw your victim down the middle, for example, all you need is a slightly bigger than usual saw. If you hold the victim upside down so the blood stays in his head, hold his legs apart, and start sawing at the groin, you can get as far as the navel before he loses consciousness.

Even in the Middle Ages, before electricity, there were many things you could do to torment a person. You could tie him up in an iron belt that held the arms and legs up to the chest and left no point of rest, so that all his muscles went into spasm within minutes and he was driven mad within hours. This was the twisting stork, a benign-looking object. You could stretch him out backward over a thin piece of wood so that his whole body weight rested on his spine, which pressed against the sharp wood. Then you could stop up his nostrils and force water into his stomach through his mouth. Then, if you wanted to finish him off, you and your helper could jump on his stomach, causing internal hemorrhage. This torture was called the rack. If you wanted to burn someone to death without hearing him scream, you could use a tongue lock, a metal rod between the jaw and collarbone that prevented him from opening his mouth. You could put a person in a chair with spikes on the seat and arms, tie him down against the spikes, and beat him, so that every time he flinched from the beating he drove his own flesh deeper onto the spikes. This was the inquisitor's chair. If you wanted to make it worse, you could heat the spikes. You could suspend a person over a pointed wooden pyramid and whenever he started to fall asleep, you could drop him onto the point. If you were Ippolito Marsili, the inventor of this torture, known as the Judas cradle, you could tell yourself you had invented something humane, a torture that worked without burning flesh or breaking bones. For the torture here was supposed to be sleep deprivation.

The secret of torture, like the secret of French cuisine, is that nothing is unthinkable. The human body is like a foodstuff, to be grilled, pounded, filleted. Every opening exists to be stuffed, all flesh to be carved off the bone. You take an ordinary wheel, a heavy wooden wheel with spokes. You lay the victim on the ground with blocks of wood at strategic points under his shoulders, legs, and arms. You use the wheel to break every bone in his body. Next you tie his body onto the wheel. With all its bones broken, it will be pliable. However, the victim will not be dead. If you want to kill him, you hoist the wheel aloft on the end of a pole and leave him to starve. Who would have thought to do this with a man and a wheel? But, then, who would have thought to take the disgusting snail, force it to render its ooze, stuff it in its own shell with garlic butter, bake it, and eat it?

Not long ago I had a facial—only in part because I thought I needed one. It was research into the nature and function of pleasure. In a dark booth at the back of the beauty salon, the aesthetician put me on a table and applied a series of ointments to my face, some cool, some warmed. After a while she put something into my hand, cold and metallic. "Don't be afraid, madame," she said. "It is an electrode. It will not hurt you. The other end is attached to two metal cylinders, which I roll over your face. They break down the electricity barrier on your skin and allow the moisturizers to penetrate deeply." I didn't believe this hocus-pocus. I didn't believe in the electricity barrier or in the ability of these rollers to break it down. But it all felt very good. The cold metal on my face was a pleasant change from the soft warmth of the aesthetician's fingers. Still, since Algeria it's hard to hear the word "electrode" without fear. So when she left me for a few minutes with a moist, refreshing cheesecloth over my face, I thought, What if the goal of her expertise had been pain, not moisture? What if the electrodes had been electrodes in the Algerian sense? What if the cheesecloth mask were dipped in acid?

In Paris, where the body is so pampered, torture seems particularly sinister, not because it's hard to understand but because — as the dark side of sensuality — it seems so easy. Beauty care is among the glories of Paris. *Soins esthétiques* include makeup, facials, massages (both relaxing and reducing), depilations (partial and complete), manicures, pedicures, and tanning, in addition to the usual run of *soins* for the hair: cutting, brushing, setting, waving, styling, blowing, coloring, and streaking. In Paris the state of your skin, hair, and nerves is taken seriously, and there is little of the puritanical thinking that tries to persuade us that beauty comes from within. Nor do the French think, as Americans do, that beauty should be offhand and low-maintenance. Spending time and money on *soins esthéthiques* is appropriate and necessary, not self-indulgent. Should that loving attention to the body turn malevolent, you have torture. You have the procedure — the aesthetic, as it were — of torture, the explanation for the rich diversity of torture instruments, but you do not have the cause.

Historically torture has been a tool of legal systems, used to get information needed for a trial or, more directly, to determine guilt or innocence. In the Middle Ages confession was considered the best of all proofs, and torture was the way to produce a confession. In other words, torture didn't come into existence to give vent to human sadism. It is not always private and perverse but sometimes social and institutional, vetted by the government and, of course, the Church. (There have been few bigger fans of torture than Christianity and Islam.) Righteousness, as much as viciousness, produces torture. There aren't squads of sadists beating down the doors to the torture chambers begging for jobs. Rather, as a recent book on torture by Edward Peters says, the institution of torture creates sadists; the weight of a culture, Peters suggests, is necessary to recruit torturers. You have to convince people that they are working for a great goal in order to get them to overcome their repugnance to the task of causing physical pain to another person. Usually the great goal is the preservation of society, and the victim is presented to the torturer as being in some way out to destroy it.

From another point of view, what's horrifying is how easily you can persuade someone that he is working for the common good. Perhaps the most appalling psychological experiment of modern times, by Stanley Milgram, showed that ordinary, decent people in New Haven, Connecticut, could be brought to the point of inflicting (as they thought) severe electric shocks on other people in obedience to an authority and in pursuit of a goal, the advancement of knowledge, of which they approved. Milgram used—some would say abused—the prestige of science and the university to make his point, but his point is chilling nonetheless. We can cluck over torture, but the evidence at least suggests that with intelligent handling most of us could be brought to do it ourselves.

In the Middle Ages, Milgram's experiment would have had no point. It would have shocked no one that people were capable of cruelty in the interest of something they believed in. That was as it should be. Only recently in the history of human thought has the avoidance of cruelty moved to the forefront of ethics. "Putting cruelty first," as Judith Shklar says in *Ordinary Vices*, is comparatively new. The belief that the "pursuit of happiness" is one of man's inalienable rights, the idea that "cruel and unusual punishment" is an evil in itself, the Benthamite notion that behavior should be guided by what will produce the greatest happiness for the greatest number—all these principles are only two centuries old. They were born with the eighteenth-century democratic revolutions. And in two hundred years they have not been universally accepted. Wherever people believe strongly in some cause, they will justify torture—not just the Nazis, but the French in Algeria.

Many people who wouldn't hurt a fly have annexed to fashion the imagery of torture—the thongs and spikes and metal studs—hence reducing it to the frivolous and transitory. Because torture has been in the mainstream and not on the margins of history, nothing could be healthier. For torture to be merely kinky would be a big advance. Exhibitions like the one I saw in Paris, which presented itself as educational, may be guilty of pandering to the tastes they deplore. Solemnity may be the wrong tone. If taking one's goals too seriously is the danger, the best discouragement of torture may be a radical hedonism that denies that any goal is worth the means, that refuses to allow the nobly abstract to seduce us from the sweetness of the concrete. Give people a good croissant and a good cup of coffee in the morning. Give them an occasional facial and a plate of escargots. Marie Antoinette picked a bad moment to say "Let them eat cake," but I've often thought she was on the right track.

All of which brings me back to Paris, for Paris exists in the imagination of much of the world as the capital of pleasure—of fun, food, art, folly, seduction, gallantry, and beauty. Paris is civilization's reminder to itself that nothing leads you less wrong than your awareness of your own pleasure and a genial desire to spread it around. In that sense the myth of Paris constitutes a moral touchstone, standing for the selfish frivolity that helps keep priorities straight.

NANCY MAIRS

Ron Her Son

"Bye, Grandma," says Chris, who is not quite two, raising his round, wide-eyed face and pouting to meet my lips. "Bye, Grandma," echoes Alex, who suddenly, after a week of spurning all advances, raises his face too for a kiss. Angel is crying as I give her a hug. Ron is characteristically stiff and taciturn in the face of feeling, but he lets me put my arms around him and kiss him, and he even hugs me back a little. Then, in a swirl of arms and legs, a bobbing of heads, they are in their huge, battered station wagon, which must somehow convey them—blankets and bottles, clothes and thermos jugs and trinkets from Mexico and disposable diapers—from here to Texas and then on to Key West. The early morning is grayish and humid, unusual for Tucson in September. I stand on the porch in my nightgown and wave even after they've pulled out of sight.

What has just happened should be that commonplace of American family life, the visit of a son and his wife and their two children to Grandma and Grandpa's house. But it's not. What has just happened is, in many small ways, a miracle.

Ron is not, in fact, my son. Although biologically I am old enough to be his mother, his birth would have put a severe crimp in my high-school style—more, would have been a miracle indeed, since I remained a virgin for several years after Ron was born. Not for seven years after his birth would I actually take on motherhood, and even then people thought me (with some reason) too young. And yet he's more my son than anyone else's. George and I have owned ourselves his parents for longer than anyone else has been willing to do. He may be ours by default, but he is ours. He told me so himself, years ago, in a ragged typewritten note I find now in a file of odd documents that account piecemeal for his life with us:

To Nancy

To the one who took me in. Who give me food the one who cared for me the one who helped me in my hour of need. Who loved me. Here is to a wonder person. On her day, Mother's day.
HAPPY MOTHER'S DAY

Love,
Ron her son

Last comer, eldest child: orphan, waif, bad boy: survivor: son.

George found Ron at the Chazen Institute, a school for emotionally disturbed children where he taught during our first year in Tucson. It was, I imagine, fairly typical of such a place: the children badly housed and fed while the director scooped out as much profit as he could and then split for Chicago. I saw a flow chart of the organization once, in the shape of a pyramid, with the director at the top and the students squeezed in at the bottom, falling off the page. George did not think it a good place for children, and so as often as he could he brought the teenage boys he worked with home. Weekends our house was filled with thieves and muggers, I suppose; one boy, I recall, had put his stepmother through a plate-glass window. He was large for his age. In our house the boys were good-humored, often deferential, and very hungry.

George and I suffer from an adoption complex. Usually we have been able to assuage our urge to shelter homeless creatures by a visit to the local Humane Society, whence we have rescued such members of our household as Freya and Gwydion and Vanessa Bell and Lionel Tigress and Clifford-the-Small-Black-Dog. But occasionally we have found ourselves taking in people for weeks, even months. To a German student who wanted to improve her English we gave room and board in exchange for some help with Anne and Matthew when they were small. One summer a Brown student lived with us while he worked for a political candidate we supported. For a year or so we rented a room to a poor and rather helpless young woman recovering from Hodgkin's disease.

These were all, in a sense, transients, however: people with lives of their own, welcome as sojourners to whatever encouragement and companionship we had to offer until they chose to move elsewhere. At Chazen, we found people without the power—legal, moral, emotional—to make any such choice. They might leave, if anyone were willing to take them (many were wards of the state, which meant that their families, if they had any, were either unwilling or unable to take them), but they'd likely be back, to this place or one like it, until they were old enough to be sent to prison. In light of these realities, we were probably destined, from the moment George started teaching there, to try to rescue at least one of the dozens of children he watched come and go and come.

That one was Ron, but how he came to be Ron and not some other I don't remember. He spent one weekend with us, then another, and another, and gradually a ritual evolved wherein George, who was by now teaching at another school, would drive every Friday afternoon out to Chazen to get him. (The school was located in an area, remote at that time, of the Tucson Mountain foothills, and thus needed no barbed wire. Runaways simply had their shoes taken away. But even faced with acres of rocky ground, cholla and saguaro and prickly pear, rattlesnakes, scorpions, a good many of them went "over the hill.") Friday night, Saturday, Saturday night, Sunday, Ron would spend stretched out in front of the television; often he slept right where he lay, though we had a bed for him in the study. Each Sunday night George would drive him back.

At Christmas that year, 1973 it must have been, he told us he was going home for good. His father hadn't actually said so, but he had sent him a plane ticket, and Ron was sure that once he was home, his father would want him to stay. We had him to our house for an early Christmas before taking him to the airport. I don't recall now just what we gave him—clothes, I think, because he was bursting out of the few articles he owned—but I do remember that after opening his gifts, he disappeared. I found him in the back yard, in the dark, crying softly. "You shouldn't have given me anything," he blurted as I put my arms around him. "I don't have anything for you." "Oh, Ron," I told him, "we don't care. You don't have to give us anything for us to love you." He quieted, but I think now that he didn't believe me. Even after he'd lived with us for a couple of years, he didn't understand why we'd taken him in. "Why do you want me?" he shouted through his tears during one of our rare but agonizing fights. "We love you" was never answer enough. In a life in which survival is based on barter, love can be a pitifully small coin.

Shortly after New Year's, the telephone rang. "I'm at the airport," Ron told George. "Can you come get me?" Despite our hopes, George and I were not surprised, although we didn't tell Ron so. What we did tell him was that when he felt ready to leave the Chazen Institute, he was welcome to live with us. We had to tell him that. Clearly his father wasn't about to take him. And the longer he stayed at Chazen, the more dangerous the lessons he learned. He'd been sent there in the first place for truancy, and already while there he'd been busted for shoplifting a carton of cigarettes. Too, because the system of behavior modification used by the school was teaching him that the only real power he had was the power of manipulating the wielders of the system, he spent increasing amounts of his energy gauging what he could or couldn't get away with. He was a shy sad abandoned child, grieving for his dead mother, tossed out by his father and his new stepmother, growing steadily more sullen and grim and unattractive. We had no idea whether he could survive with us, but plainly he wasn't likely to survive without us.

He took a long time to say yes. I don't mean moments or days. I mean months. During that time he continued to live with us on weekends. In the summer we took him East with us for several weeks as we visited friends and relations. People were polite, but they obviously considered us more than a little gaga: First we'd moved so far west we'd practically dropped off the edge of the earth, and now we reappeared towing this grubby, gawky figure, with neither impeccable genes nor impeccable jeans, his straight black hair to his shoulders and a gold hoop in one ear, who almost never spoke and never, never smiled. Ron, in turn, was faced with a complicated itinerary among clusters of a large and somewhat bumptious family none of whom he could see clearly, his glasses having broken just before the trip. Had we been testing his mettle by this ordeal, he'd have passed with colors soaring.

At the end of the summer he came to stay.

And it was awful. Let there be no doubt about that. Lest anyone be tempted to sentimentalize the situation (and many have), to exclaim about our generosity in taking him in or his good fortune in being taken in, I must make clear that much of what followed was painful and maddening and exhausting for all of us. George and I were faced with sole and full responsibility for a troubled fifteen-year-old in whose upbringing we had had no hand, whose values and attitudes were alien to us, whom, all in all, we could love all right but didn't much like. Anne and Matthew, then nine and five, were faced with a jealous big brother who tormented them in ways limited only by his imagination, which luckily wasn't very resourceful. And Ron was faced with an established family, whose rituals and demands were often beyond him, and whose motives for incorporating him remained obscure and baffling.

The first demand that we made of him was that he stop watching television, and it was very nearly a killer. I find the noise of a television unbearably irritating—after a while it drives me to clenched teeth and tears—and I might have been able to survive his weekends silently weeping and gnashing, but I was never going to make it seven days a week. Anyway, like many parents, George and I worry about the effects of television, and so Anne and Matthew had grown up with restrictions on weekday viewing: PBS from four to six o'clock, special shows by petition. Cooperatively, our elderly black-and-white set blew a tube the day Ron moved in, and George was leisurely in replacing it. He took about a month, if I remember correctly. During that time Ron spent most of his hours out of school lying on his back on his bed, staring at the blank ceiling as though to will on it images of Gomer Pyle. The rest of us read books and magazines. Before that month was out, Ron had started to pick up books and magazines too, and although he returned to the television every permissible hour once it was mended, logging hours of *Sesame*

Street and *The Electric Company*, which may have given him some much-needed skills, as well as the grisly collection of Saturday-morning cartoons, he usually spent some part of each day reading as well.

His lack of basic skills worried us a good deal. One day as we were driving along Speedway Boulevard, surely one of the most hideously commercial main thoroughfares in the country, we realized that he could not read most of the signs we were passing but was identifying the stores and restaurants by appearance and logos. Neither George nor I had ever known anyone except tiny children who couldn't read, and we were dismayed. A psychologist at Chazen had told us that although Ron's tests revealed average intelligence, his emotional problems would probably keep him from realizing his full abilities. But at least, we thought, he had got to be able to read. Functional literacy took on lively meaning for us. We began to set him tasks we thought would give him survival skills in a literate society. When we traveled, he read the maps and gave directions, and we never got hopelessly lost. We encouraged him to use the bus system, figuring out times and connections. We ate everything he cooked for us except the batch of brownies for which he misread one-half teaspoon as one-half cup of baking soda; those heaved and crawled up the sides of the pan and all over the oven and were thereby lost to us.

His schooling helped some, of course. We sent him to the Catholic high school of not quite a thousand students where George and I were teaching, in the hope that the atmosphere there would be less daunting than that at the public high school, about three times Salpointe's size, to which he would have been assigned. He had, after all, been incarcerated for truancy, and school obviously held for him terrors that we didn't know but certainly believed. In his two years at Salpointe, he missed two half-days, both with my permission. And although his ability to read and write and figure was still marginal when he graduated, it was at least sufficient to satisfy the Navy.

In many ways, his lack of social skills was more troubling than his lack of academic skills. He had no idea how to form and sustain relationships either within the family or without. Over time, as we began to piece together from various sources the details of his history, we began to understand why he was able neither to give nor to receive the ordinary gestures of human warmth and attachment. What we learned took us well beyond our experiential and conceptual boundaries.

According to a letter from a woman, located by our lawyer as she tried to trace Ron's origins to satisfy guardianship requirements, little "Roddy" was born on 1 October 1958 in Fort Yukon, Alaska, the illegitimate child of an American soldier and an Athabaskan woman. The Athabaskan woman, married with several children already, took him home, but after about a year the tribe told her that she could no longer keep him because he was too white. She took him, hungry and covered with sores, to the woman, who agreed to keep him; but when he was about four, she and her husband divorced. She then gave him to friends who had no children of their own. How accurate this information is we don't know, since we have copies of both a baptismal certificate from St. Stephen's Episcopal Church in Fort Yukon for Elwood Roderick Gabriel, dated 23 November 1958, and a certificate of live birth, dated 3 October 1958, of Elwood Roderick Rose.

At any rate, the couple took him in and renamed him Ronald William DuGay, according to a copy of a baptismal certificate dated 3 July 1962. They raised him, and eventually the man legally adopted him, though not until 8 November 1973. Some time before, his wife had died of some neurological disease. Within six months, he had remarried, a woman with a teenaged son of her own, who wanted nothing to do with Ron; and so Ron was made a ward of the state of Colorado and sent to Chazen (whose stiff fees were paid for by the federal government since the man was an Army veteran) for refusing to go to school. While Ron was there, we discovered in the elaborate course of obtaining guardianship, which required the man's permission, he moved from Colorado to California without leaving a forwarding address. The sum of these events was a sharp message: Don't settle in too deep, don't put out tendrils of affection: The tendrils will be hacked away: Whoever you love will leave you. I have said that Ron had some learning difficulties, but he was not stupid. He learned this lesson by heart.

Our relationship with Ron's father, whom we never met, was complicated and bitter. I had forgotten, in fact, just how painful it was until I dug out Ron's file and old furies flew out of the folder and gripped me in talons amazingly sharp for all their age. Once we had tracked him down, the man was glad enough to sign the guardianship papers, a legal necessity in case Ron ever needed emergency medical care. Indeed, clearly he wanted to be quit of Ron altogether. He refused to support Ron, or even to send him the few possessions—a bicycle, a Boy Scout backpack and mess kit, an old pony bridle—that Ron had laid up. To get these I used, in one of the ugliest machinations of my life, the only leverage I knew I had: "Unless Ron's things are in his possession by Thanksgiving," I wrote him, "we will return Ron to you. . . . If you will not *share* the responsibility for your son with us, then you must assume *full* responsibility for him." They arrived by Greyhound within a week.

The issue of support was not so readily resolved. Both teachers, George and I made too little money to enable us to take on another mouth to feed, another frame to clothe, especially one that ate and grew prodigiously. But because the man was not an Arizona resident, we could not be paid foster parents under the Arizona Department of Economic Security. The authorities in California rejected a reciprocal agreement, though they would have supported Ron in a foster home in their own state. Our point was not just to get Ron foster care, however; it was to care for him in our own family. At one point the man agreed to send us twenty-two dollars a month, but after two months the checks stopped. Finally, the Veterans Administration arranged garnishment of twenty-five dollars a month from his retirement check, and we had to make do with that. Ron always had enough to eat, I think, but he had few clothes, and with five dollars a week for allowance he could afford few indulgences.

Ron's father may not have been very much to blame in his negligence. He was, according to one of his daughters by his first marriage, a "weak" man who had to have a woman to lean on, and so she was not surprised that he remarried precipitously without caring whether his new wife and Ron could get along. Anyway, I think Ron had been pretty much his mother's child, and she was dead. The man's intelligence and education seemed limited, and he certainly knew nothing of child psychology: It seems never to have occurred to him that Ron's behavior was connected to what was going on in his life. Too, he was aging, with a heart condition; all he wanted was peace and ease. And Ron, smoldering with grief, resentment, rage, was a difficult and threatening presence. I know. I lived with him.

The people who suffered most immediately from that presence were Anne and Matthew. He resented them, of course: They were the "real" children, whose places in the family could never be doubted, whereas he was among us by sufferance, in a position more tenuous in his perception than in actuality. We did not want to get rid of him, but nothing in his experience had taught him that human ties could be so tenacious. I think he always lived on the edge of expulsion. Nothing had taught him gentleness either. The only words he knew to reach the children were threat—"I'm gonna break your arm"—and the only touch a swat, a pinch, the quick wrench of a limb, the yank at a lock of hair. One night he so menaced Matthew that Matthew, in flight, smashed one arm through a glass door, severing the ulnar artery and two tendons.

We were asking a lot of two quite young children. Today I wonder whether we asked too much. The scar on Matthew's wrist is, after seven years, a thin silvery thread. But are there other scars, I wonder, elsewhere than in the flesh, puckers in mind, in emotions, from those years of living with an almost aimless meanness? When I ask the children their feelings about the time Ron lived with us, Matthew's memories are fond, Anne's bitter. Matthew is glad Ron was there, he says—Ron was "fun." Anne makes the kind of face I have learned to associate with her refusal to express strong anger openly. "Do you wish he hadn't come to live with us?" I ask. "I was so young," Matthew explains, "that it never occurred to me that Ron wasn't just part of the family." "And I," says Anne, "was used to beating up on Matthew but not to getting beaten up on myself." We laugh at this discovery of different perceptions according to place in the family. Matthew, at the bottom of the pecking order anyway, seems to have figured that Ron's bullying was just part of family life; for Anne he shifted the entire familial structure. She punished him cruelly for his intrusion, though she looks surprised now when I tell her so. Far brighter and more self-assured than he, she outwitted him at turn after turn, jeered at his mistakes in reading, pronunciation, and simple math, lashed him verbally. Many of his pinches and slaps may have been retaliatory, as a bear swats at the bees that sting his ears and nose when he raids their honey. Matthew, with the lovely warmth he has had since he was a toddler, overwhelmed him in quite another way: He forgave Ron every blow, every trick, and loved him relentlessly, mean spirit and all.

From Ron's point of view, life in our family must have been a sore trial. We were told by his counselor at Chazen that he needed a firmly structured environment, but even without such a caution, the need would have been clear. He was the most passive child I have ever known—emotionally, intellectually, even physically inert. When he stood and walked, his small bony frame seemed to be melting; whenever he could, he lay limply on his bed or in a chair. He could not think of things to do, even to amuse himself; he lay still for hours, as though waiting for something to happen to him. He rarely laughed, and then—a quick bark—only if someone were hurt or humiliated in some way. Nor did he cry as a rule, or complain, or rebel. He was the only student George had known at Chazen who never once tried to run away. He was unnervingly tractable. He would do whatever one demanded. Of course he would do it as quickly and badly as he could get away with, but so will most children; his carelessness was, in an odd way, a healthy sign. His pliancy was scary. The firm structure we were advised to give him seemed necessary literally to give him a form, keep him intact, so that he wouldn't dissolve and ooze away.

And so we were strict in our requirements and regulations. Ron had to attend school every day and a counseling session once a week. He had to do enough work in his classes to enable him to pass. His fixed household chores were to wash the dishes and to keep his room decent, though not necessarily spotless; in addition, we expected him to pitch in for routine cleaning, shopping, and yard work. If he went out, as he too seldom did, he had to tell us where he was going and when he'd be back. Phone calls were limited to fifteen minutes, though often, after he'd begun to make friends, he trotted to the nearest pay phone and chatted to his adolescent heart's content. He was not to drink alcohol, smoke dope, or take anything that didn't belong to him; on these points we were adamant, knowing that, with his record, he could be whisked at the slightest infraction into the juvenile-detention system and we would be helpless to keep him. Anne and Matthew must meet a nearly identical set of demands now that they are teenagers—we didn't create them especially for Ron—but Anne and Matthew have grown up with our expectations, under our discipline. For Ron, adapting to them, suddenly and wholesale, must have been a harsh and often bewildering task.

Living closely with him, we could not always tell whether he was making progress. But gradually he was. His first quarter at Salpointe he was enrolled in the physical education course required for graduation. He had, it turned out, some sort of hang-up about PE, the nature of which we never discovered, though we gathered that it was partly responsible for his earlier truancy. At mid-quarter we received notice that Ron was failing PE because he had never attended. Confronted with the failure warning, he acknowledged that he had just gone off and sat under a tree every day during first period.

"What did you think would happen when we found out?" we asked him.

"I thought I'd get to the mail first," he said.

"But we'd still have found out at the end of the quarter."

He seemed nonplussed. He probably hadn't thought that far ahead. He was even more nonplussed when we told him he'd simply have to take PE another time. Evidently he believed that by his failure he'd cleared himself of the obligation somehow. Quarter after quarter he put it off, waiting, I suppose, for some sign of our relenting. In the last quarter of his senior year, dressing out with a flock of freshmen and sophomores, he took PE, and passed it. He passed all his other courses as well, though perhaps he shouldn't have. We refused to teach him ourselves, but his teachers were our friends in this small, intimate faculty, and they may have been more kind than honest. He made a few friends, and began to wander off campus at lunch to sneak cigarettes and "fool around." He even got hauled into the dean's office one day for getting into a fight. Our bony lump, who had never dared take on anything bigger than a ten-year-old girl, lashed out at another boy just before religion class. We could not condone the act, but we rejoiced in the energy behind it.

As Ron's senior year waned, we grew increasingly worried about his future. Clearly he was going to graduate, with only marginal skills and even poorer initiative. He didn't seem capable of college-level work, even at our local community college. And although one of our demands when he came to live with us had been that he get a part-time job, he had never done so; he claimed to have tried, but we doubted that he had ever screwed his courage so far as to request and fill out an application. He seemed an unlikely candidate for success in the tightening job market. But we would not keep him, we were sure. We were still financially distressed; Anne was old enough to need a room of her own instead of sharing one with Matthew; most of all, we were exhausted. At least by the time he was eighteen, Ron would have to go off on his own.

We were rescued in the most ironic way possible. Ron was incapable of independent action, but he would do as he was told. He needed, then, a situation in which every aspect of his life and work would be regulated. Holy orders offered one alternative, but on the basis of his overweening interest in girls, he did not seem in the least cut out to be a priest. The second most paternalistic organization we could think of after the Catholic church was the military. Two pacifists, radicalized by the grinding ugliness of Vietnam, George and I found ourselves recruiting our foster son for Uncle Sam. His father had been in the Army, of course, and Ron would not, even fleetingly, consider enlistment in the same branch of the service; by this time his fury at his betrayal by his father was flinty. But George had been a naval officer for three years in the early sixties, and George was apparently—though Ron could probably not have said so—okay. Ron took himself to the Naval Recruitment Office, passed the tests, signed the papers. We were all free.

Or almost. We had tried to teach Ron to be scrupulous. Soon after he came to live with us, while we were waiting in line one day at McDonald's, Ron showed me a pair of sunglasses he had lifted from a nearby Circle K. Why is it that children choose to administer these tests in the agora, while you are trying to order three Big Macs and two Quarter-Pounders, two Cokes, a Dr. Pepper, a root beer, and a Sprite, and no thank you, you wouldn't like some hot apple turnovers for dessert, with walls of polyestered shoulders on every side and your five-year-old unloading an entire napkin-holder just beyond your clutching fingers? I told Ron quietly but, I hoped, emphatically that he was not to take things that didn't belong to him, because shoplifting was against the law and we would lose him if he were caught, and that he was to return the sunglasses to the Circle K. I don't know whether he did, but I never saw them again. Nor did I see evidence of other booty, though he was painfully poor compared to most of his classmates and may have succumbed to temptation, especially with regard to a turquoise ring I had given to George which disappeared without a trace. We were equally strict about truthfulness, and I remember him blazing with anger once when I lied to the telephone company, telling them I didn't have an illicit extension phone, to save myself some embarrassment. He accused me of being no better than he had been when he tried to cover up his failure in PE; and he was right. How often our children keep us honest. So it was not surprising that, when the Navy recruiter asked him whether he had ever smoked marijuana, he said that he had. There was a six-month waiting period after the last incident, he was told, and so he could not go into the Navy in August as planned but would have to wait till October.

   I nearly wept when I heard of the delay. I was tired—I had just finished a difficult school year, I had not been rehired, the summer heat that aggravates multiple sclerosis symptoms was in full force—and one of the things I was tired of was Ron's presence, especially his ceaseless bickering with the children. And now I was faced with two extra months of it. But as I look back, I'm glad he had the extra time. He still claimed that he couldn't find a job, but once he had graduated I was no longer willing to let the matter slide. He was now, I told him, an adult, and adults had to assume responsibility in society; if he couldn't find a paid job, he'd have to do volunteer work. So he spent several months at the Red Cross, lugging bags of blood about twenty hours each week, and the people there seemed to think well of him. He needed that success. Also, Anne had been promised her own room for her eleventh birthday in September; rather than renege, we simply moved Ron in with Matthew, freeing his room to be redecorated for Anne. Ron was rather nice about his own space and possessions, and I think he began to be eager to escape Matthew's miasma. By the end of the summer, too, his friends had drifted away, into college or jobs. Without the familiar structure of high school, without his own room, without old friends or any way to make new ones, he could look forward to the Navy with some enthusiasm.

Shortly after his eighteenth birthday, we put him on a Greyhound for basic training in San Diego, a skinny, slouching, silent young man with shaggy dark hair and dark-framed glasses, wearing jeans and an open-necked shirt, though as I recall the earring was gone. I don't know whether he was terrified, but I know that I was. He was, after all, my eldest child, the first one to go off, and he seemed more fragile and vulnerable than either of the others. George and I had tried to make the world solid for him and to give him some of the skills we thought he'd need to survive, but we'd had so little time, and we'd made so many mistakes: Most parents get eighteen years; we'd had, all told, not much more than three. I watched the bus pull out of the station and down the narrow street, and when I couldn't see it any more, I watched the point at which it had disappeared, as though I could fix myself to it somehow and travel with Ron across the desert, over the rubbly mountains, down to the blue sweep of San Diego Harbor where once, on a vacation, we had all gone onto the base and stood under the looming gray ships.

The first separation was short, for he was allowed to come home at Christmas. At the airport we couldn't find him; he had to find us. Who was this man in the shirt and tie, the dark uniform and white cap, black stubble covering his round pink head, almost smiling as we reached out to pull him close, almost hugging us back? He was our Ron, and he wasn't. Already he was different. Quiet, not sullen, but quiet, at ease. He teased the children, not as one child taunting others but as a big brother show-ing off a bit. He brought us fine presents — I still keep my jewelry in the handsome white case with the red satin lining. He talked to us. And then suddenly he was gone again.

We saw him only once more, the following fall, when he had finished radio school and was on his way to a ship in Norfolk. In May 1978 he called to tell us he'd just gotten married to a girl called Angel. In June 1979 his first son was born: Alexander William Randall DuGay. In August 1980, about to be transferred to Keflavik, Iceland, the three got as far as Waco, Texas, to visit Angel's mother, but they couldn't afford the trip to Tucson and we couldn't afford the trip to Waco. In Keflavik, in October 1980, Christopher Jason Allen DuGay was born. Now George and I had a daughter-in-law and two grandbabies we'd never seen. And then at last this summer, between Keflavik and their new duty station in Key West, they came to us.

How strange to see Ron with his wife and children. In five years he has changed some — filled out, grown self-assured — though not so drastically as he did during that first brief separa-tion. Angel I have come to know and like through her good let-ters. She is the kind of person I enjoy: alert, thoughtful, an enthusiastic tourist, who loves to read and keeps a journal. I worry about her a good deal because, like me, she is easily depressed, and I think that her life, with two such small children, is difficult just now; but so far her courage hasn't failed. At least while he's on leave, Ron takes turns with her watching the boys, who need surprisingly little watching; I've tried to childproof the house, putting our few fragile treasures out of reach, and the only thing that seems in any danger is Lionel Tigress, the new kitten, whom they plaster with pats and sticky kisses. Ron's involvement seems natural, genuine. Almost immediately the night they arrived, Alex threw up all over the dining room, and while Angel raced him to the bathroom, Ron grabbed a roll of paper towels and started mopping. I know a good many men who'd have sat frozen waiting for some woman — and although Angel was other-wise occupied, Anne and I were both available for duty — to cope with the mess. I liked him a lot then. I liked his calm, his compe-tence.

They act like a family. They are a family. Ron has for the first
time in his conscious life his own kin, people whose relationship
is clear and unequivocal, who belong to him, to whom he
belongs, not by sufferance but by right. And he has brought them
home to us—home, here, where we are—because we are part of
the family, eight of us under one roof. I sense that he has owned
us—really owned us, with that matter-of-fact boldness with
which children recognize their parents and their siblings—at
last. Us: Grandma, Grandpa, Aunt Anne, Uncle Matthew, to
whom Alex and Chris, through their father, now have every
claim.

People have asked me often whether I regret taking Ron in,
whether I'd do so again if I had it to do over. Hard questions to
face, the answers risky to the ways I like to think of myself.
Because I did regret taking him in, many times. I lack the largeness of spirit that enables someone like George to transcend daily
inconveniences, lapses in behavior, even alien values, and to
cherish a person without condition. I often judged Ron harshly,
by standards inappropriate to his peculiar situation; I was often
grudging of approval and affection; I made him work too hard
for the privilege of being my son. He suffered, I'm afraid, for my
regrets. And no, I think, I wouldn't do it again, knowing what I
now know. But then, I wouldn't have Anne and Matthew again
either. Might not even marry George again. Such ventures seem
now, in the wisdom of hindsight, to demand a woman of more
than my mettle. That's how we get wise, by taking on in ignorance the tasks we would never later dare to do.

No. Yes.

RICHARD RODRIGUEZ

GOING HOME AGAIN

At each step, with every graduation from one level of education to the next, the refrain from bystanders was strangely the same: "Your parents must be so proud of you." I suppose that my parents were proud, although I suspect, too, that they felt more than pride alone as they watched me advance through my education. They seemed to know that my education was separating us from one another, making it difficult to resume familiar intimacies. Mixed with the instincts of parental pride, a certain hurt also communicated itself—too private ever to be adequately expressed in words, but real nonetheless.

The autobiographical facts pertinent to this essay are simply stated in two sentences, though they exist in somewhat awkward juxtaposition to each other. I am the son of Mexican-American parents, who speak a blend of Spanish and English, but who read neither language easily. I am about to receive a Ph.D. in English Renaissance literature. What sort of life—what tensions, feelings, conflicts—connects these two sentences? I look back and remember my life from the time I was seven or eight years old as one of constant movement away from a Spanish-speaking folk culture toward the world of the English-language classroom. As the years passed, I felt myself becoming less like my parents and less comfortable with the assumption of visiting relatives that I was still the Spanish-speaking child they remembered. By the time I began college, visits home became suffused with silent embarrassment: there seemed so little to share, however strong the ties of our affection. My parents would tell me what happened in their lives or in the lives of relatives; I would respond with news of my own. Polite questions would follow. Our conversations came to seem more like interviews.

A few months ago, my dissertation nearly complete, I came upon my father looking through my bookcase. He quietly fingered the volumes of Milton's tracts and Augustine's theology with that combination of reverence and distrust those who are not literate sometimes show for the written word. Silently, I watched him from the door of the room. However much he would have insisted that he was "proud" of his son for being able to master the texts, I knew, if pressed further, he would have admitted to complicated feelings about my success. When he looked across the room and suddenly saw me, his body tightened slightly with surprise, then we both smiled.

For many years I kept my uneasiness about becoming a success in education to myself. I did so in part because I wanted to avoid vague feelings that, if considered carefully, I would have no way of dealing with; and in part because I felt that no one else shared my reaction to the opportunity provided by education. When I began to rehearse my story of cultural dislocation publicly, however, I found many listeners willing to admit to similar feelings from their own pasts. Equally impressive was the fact that many among those I spoke with were *not* from nonwhite racial groups, which made me realize that one can grow up to enter the culture of the academy and find it a "foreign" culture for a variety of reasons, ranging from economic status to religious heritage. But why, I next wondered, was it that, though there were so many of us who came from childhood cultures alien to the academy's, we voiced our uneasiness to one another and to ourselves so infrequently? Why did it take *me* so long to acknowledge publicly the cultural costs I had paid to earn a Ph.D. in Renaissance English literature? Why, more precisely, am I writing these words only now when my connection to my past barely survives except as nostalgic memory?

Looking back, a person risks losing hold of the present while being confounded by the past. For the child who moves to an academic culture from a culture that dramatically lacks academic traditions, looking back can jeopardize the certainty he has about the desirability of this new academic culture. Richard Hoggart's description, in *The Uses of Literacy*, of the cultural pressures on such a student, whom Hoggart calls the "scholarship boy," helps make the point. The scholarship boy must give nearly unquestioning allegiance to academic culture, Hoggart argues, if he is to succeed at all, so different is the milieu of the classroom from the culture he leaves behind. For a time, the scholarship boy may try to balance his loyalty between his concretely experienced family life and the more abstract mental life of the classroom. In the end, though, he must choose between the two worlds: if he intends to succeed as a student, he must, literally and figuratively, separate himself from his family, with its gregarious life, and find a quiet place to be alone with his thoughts.

After a while, the kind of allegiance the young student might once have given his parents is transferred to the teacher, the new parent. Now without the support of the old ties and certainties of the family, he almost mechanically acquires the assumptions, practices, and style of the classroom milieu. For the loss he might otherwise feel, the scholarship boy substitutes an enormous enthusiasm for nearly everything having to do with school.

How readily I read my own past into the portrait of Hoggart's scholarship boy. Coming from a home in which mostly Spanish was spoken, for example, I had to decide to forget Spanish when I began my education. To succeed in the classroom, I needed psychologically to sever my ties with Spanish. Spanish represented an alternate culture as well as another language — and the basis of my deepest sense of relationship to my family. Although I recently taught myself to read Spanish, the language that I see on the printed page is not quite the language I heard in my youth. That other Spanish, the spoken Spanish of my family, I remember with nostalgia and guilt: guilt because I cannot explain to aunts and uncles why I do not answer their questions any longer in their own idiomatic language. Nor was I able to explain to teachers in graduate school, who regularly expected me to read and speak Spanish with ease, why my very ability to reach graduate school as a student of English literature in the first place required me to loosen my attachments to a language I spoke years earlier. Yet, having lost the ability to speak Spanish, I never forgot it so totally that I could not understand it. Hearing Spanish spoken on the street reminded me of the community I once felt a part of, and still cared deeply about. I never forgot Spanish so thoroughly, in other words, as to move outside the range of its nostalgic pull.

Such moments of guilt and nostalgia were, however, just that—momentary. They punctuated the history of my otherwise successful progress from *barrio* to classroom. Perhaps they even encouraged it. Whenever I felt my determination to succeed wavering, I tightened my hold on the conventions of academic life.

Spanish was one aspect of the problem, my parents another. They could raise deeper, more persistent doubts. They offered encouragement to my brothers and me in our work, but they also spoke, only half jokingly, about the way education was putting "big ideas" into our heads. When we would come home, for example, and challenge assumptions we earlier believed, they would be forced to defend their beliefs (which, given our new verbal skills, they did increasingly less well) or, more frequently, to submit to our logic with the disclaimer, "It's what we were taught in our time to believe. . . ." More important, after we began to leave home for college, they voiced regret about how "changed" we had become, how much further away from one another we had grown. They partly yearned for a return to the time before education assumed their children's primary loyalty. This yearning was renewed each time they saw their nieces and nephews (none of whom continued their education beyond high school, all of whom continued to speak fluent Spanish) living according to the conventions and assumptions of their parents' culture. If I was already troubled by the time I graduated from high school by that refrain of congratulations ("Your parents must be so proud. . . ."), I realize now how much more difficult and complicated was my progress into academic life for my parents, as they saw the cultural foundation of their family erode, than it was for me.

Yet my parents were willing to pay the price of alienation and continued to encourage me to become a scholarship boy because they perceived, as others of the lower classes had before them, the relation between education and social mobility. Lacking the former themselves made them acutely aware of its necessity as prerequisite for the latter. They sent their children off to school in the hopes of their acquiring something "better" beyond education. Notice the assumption here that education is something of a tool or license—a means to an end, which has been the traditional way the lower or working classes have viewed the value of education in the past. That education might alter children in more basic ways than providing them with skills, certificates of proficiency, and even upward mobility, may come as a surprise for some, but the financial cost is usually tolerated.

Complicating my own status as a scholarship boy in the last ten years was the rise, in the mid-1960s, of what was then called "the Third World Student Movement." Racial minority groups, led chiefly by black intellectuals, began to press for greater access to higher education. The assumption behind their criticism, like the assumption of white working-class families, was that educational opportunity was useful for economic and social advancement. The racial minority leaders went one step further, however, and it was this step that was probably most revolutionary. Minority students came to the campus feeling that they were representative of larger groups of people—that, indeed, they were advancing the condition of entire societies by their matriculation. Actually, this assumption was not altogether new to me. Years before, educational success was something my parents urged me to strive for precisely because it would reflect favorably on *all* Mexican-Americans—specifically, my intellectual achievement would help deflate the stereotype of the "dumb Pancho." This early goal was only given greater currency by the rhetoric of the Third World spokesmen. But it was the fact that I felt myself suddenly much more a "public" Mexican-American, a representative of sorts, that was to prove so crucial for me during these years.

One college admissions officer assured me one day that he recognized my importance to his school precisely as deriving from the fact that, after graduation, I would surely be "going back to [my] community." More recently, teachers have urged me not to trouble over the fact that I am not "representative" of my culture, assuring me that I can serve as a "model" for those still in the *barrio* working toward academic careers. This is the line that I hear, too, when being interviewed for a faculty position. The interviewer almost invariably assumes that, because I am racially a Mexican-American, I can serve as a special counselor to minority students. The expectation is that I still retain the capacity for intimacy with "my people."

This new way of thinking about the possible uses of education is what has made the entrance of minority students into higher education so dramatic. When the minority group student was accepted into the academy, he came—in everyone's mind—as part of a "group." When I began college, I barely attracted attention except perhaps as a slightly exotic ("Are you from India?") brown-skinned student; by the time I graduated, my presence was annually noted by, among others, the college public relations office as "one of the fifty-two students with Spanish surnames enrolled this year." By having his presence announced to the campus in this way, the minority group student was unlike any other scholarship boy the campus had seen before. The minority group student now dramatized more publicly, if also in new ways, the issues of cultural dislocation that education forces, issues that are not solely racial in origin. When Richard Rodrigeuz *became* a Chicano, the dilemmas he earlier had as a scholarship boy were complicated but not decisively altered by the fact that he had assumed a group identity.

The assurance I heard that, somehow, I was being useful to my community by being a student was gratefully believed, because it gave me a way of dealing with the guilt and cynicism that each year came my way along with the scholarships, grants, and, lately, job offers from schools which a few years earlier would have refused me admission as a student. Each year, in fact, it became harder to believe that my success had anything to do with my intellectual performance, and harder to resist the conclusion that it was due to my minority group status. When I drove to the airport, on my way to London as a Fulbright Fellow last year, leaving behind cousins of my age who were already hopelessly burdened by financial insecurity and dead-end jobs, momentary guilt could be relieved by the thought that somehow my trip was beneficial to persons other than myself. But, of course, if the thought was a way of dealing with the guilt, it was also the reason for the guilt. Sitting in a university library, I would notice a janitor of my own race and grow uneasy; I was, I knew, in a rough way a beneficiary of his condition. Guilt was accompanied by cynicism. The most dazzlingly talented minority students I know today refuse to believe that their success is wholly based on their own talent, or even that when they speak in a classroom anyone hears them as anything but *the* voice of their minority group. It is scarcely surprising, then, though initially it probably seemed puzzling, that so many of the angriest voices on the campus against the injustices of racism came from those not visibly its primary victims.

It became necessary to believe the rhetoric about the value of one's presence on campus simply as a way of living with one's "success." Among ourselves, however, minority group students often admitted to a shattering sense of loss—the feeling that, somehow, something was happening to us. Especially from students who had not yet become accustomed, as by that time I had, to the campus, I remember hearing confessions of extreme discomfort and isolation. Our close associations, the separate dining-room tables, and the special dormitories helped to relieve some of the pain, but only some of it.

Significant here was the development of the ethnic studies concept—black studies, Chicano studies, et cetera—and the related assumption held by minority group students in a number of departments that they could keep in touch with their old cultures by making these cultures the subject of their study. Here again one notices how different the minority student was from other comparable students: other scholarship boys—poor Jews and the sons of various immigrant cultures—came to the academy singly, much more inclined to accept the courses and material they found. The ethnic studies concept was an indication that, for a multitude of reasons, the new racial minority group students were not willing to give up so easily their ties with their old cultures.

The importance of these new ethnic studies was that they introduced the academy to subject matter that generally deserved to be studied, and at the same time offered a staggering critique of the academy's tendency toward parochialism. Most minority group intellectuals never noted this tendency toward academic parochialism. They more often saw the reason for, say, the absence of a course on black literature in an English department as a case of simple racism. That it might instead be an instance of the fact that academic culture can lose track of human societies and whole areas of human experience was rarely raised. Never asking such a question, the minority group students never seemed to wonder either if as teachers their own courses might suffer the same cultural limitations other seminars and classes suffered. Consequently, in a peculiar way the new minority group critics of higher education came to justify the academy's assumptions. The possibility that academic culture could encourage one to grow out of touch with cultures beyond its conceptual horizon was never seriously considered.

Too often in the last ten years one heard minority group students repeat the joke, never very funny in the first place, about the racial minority academic who ended up sounding more "white" than white academics. Behind the scorn for such a figure was the belief that the new generation of minority group students would be able to avoid having to make similar kinds of cultural concessions. The pressures that might have led to such conformity went unexamined.

For the last few years my annoyance at hearing such jokes was doubtless related to the fact that I was increasingly beginning to sense that I was the "bleached" academic the minority group students found so laughable. I suppose I had always sensed that my cultural allegiance was undergoing subtle alterations as I was being educated. Only when I finished my course work in graduate school and went off to England for my dissertation year did I grasp how far I had traveled from my cultural origins. My year in England was actually my first opportunity to write and reflect upon the kind of material that I would spend my life producing. It was my first chance, too, to be free simultaneously of the distractions of course work and of the insecurities of trying to find my niche in academic life. Sitting in the reading room of the British Museum, I no longer doubted that I had joined academic society. Ironically, this feeling of having finally arrived allowed me to look back to the community whence I came. That I was geographically farther away from my home than I had ever been lent a metaphorical resonance to the cultural distance I suddenly felt.

But the feeling was not pleasing. The reward of feeling a part of the world of the British Museum was an odd one. Each morning I would arrive at the reading room and grow increasingly depressed by the silence and what the silence implied—that my life as a scholar would require self-absorption. Who, I wondered, would find my work helpful enough to want to read it? Was not my dissertation—whose title alone would puzzle my relatives— only my grandest exercise thus far in self-enclosure? The sight of the heads around me bent over their texts and papers, many so thoroughly engrossed that they wouldn't look up at the silent clock overhead for hours at a stretch, made me recall the remarkable noises of life in my family home. The tedious prose I was writing, a prose constantly qualified by footnotes, reminded me of the capacity for passionate statement those of the culture I was born into commanded—and which, could it be, I had now lost.

As I remembered it during those gray English afternoons, the past rushed forward to define more precisely my present condition. Remembering my youth, a time when I was not restricted to a chair but ran barefoot under a summer sun that tightened my skin with its white heat, made the fact that it was only my mind that "moved" each hour in the library painfully obvious.

I did need to figure out where I had lost touch with my past. I started to become alien to my family culture the day I became a scholarship boy. In the British Museum the realization seemed obvious. But later, returning to America, I returned to minority group students who were still speaking of their cultural ties to their past. How was I to tell them what I had learned about myself in England?

A short while ago, a group of enthusiastic Chicano undergraduates came to my office to ask me to teach a course to high school students in the *barrio* on the Chicano novel. This new

literature, they assured me, has an important role to play in helping to shape the consciousness of a people currently without ade-
quate representation in literature. Listening to them I was struck
immediately with the cultural problems raised by their assumption. I told them that the novel is not capable of dealing with
Chicano experience adequately, simply because most Chicanos
are not literate, or are at least not yet comfortably so. This is not
something Chicanos need to apologize for (though, I suppose,
remembering my own childhood ambition to combat stereotypes
of the Chicano as mental menial, it is not something easily
admitted). Rather the genius and value of those Chicanos who
do not read seem to me to be largely that their reliance on voice,
the spoken word, has given them the capacity for intimate conversation that I, as someone who now relies heavily on the written word, can only envy. The second problem, I went on, is more
in the nature of a technical one: the novel, in my opinion, is not
a form capable of being true to the basic sense of communal life
that typifies Chicano culture. What the novel as a literary form
is best capable of representing is solitary existence set against a
large social background. Chicano novelists, not coincidentally,
nearly always fail to capture the breathtakingly rich family life of
most Chicanos, and instead often describe only the individual
Chicano in transit between Mexican and American cultures.

I said all of this to the Chicano students in my office, and
could see that little of it made an impression. They seemed only
frustrated by what they probably took to be a slick, academic
justification for evading social responsibility. After a time, they
left me, sitting alone. . . .

There is a danger of being misunderstood here. I am not suggesting that an academic cannot reestablish ties of any kind with
his old culture. Indeed, he can have an impact on the culture of
his childhood. But as an academic, one exists by definition in a
culture separate from one's nonacademic roots and, therefore,
any future ties one has with those who remain "behind" are complicated by one's new cultural perspective.

Paradoxically, the distance separating the academic from his
nonacademic past can make his past seem, if not closer, then

clearer. It is possible for the academic to understand the culture from which he came "better" than those who still live within it. In my own experience, it has only been as I have come to appraise my past through categories and notions derived from the social sciences that I have been able to think of Chicano life in cultural terms at all. Characteristics I took for granted or noticed only in passing—the spontaneity, the passionate speech, the trust in concrete experience, the willingness to think communally rather than individually—these are all significant phenomena to me now as aspects of a total culture. (My parents have neither the time nor the inclination to think about their culture as a culture.) Able to conceptualize a sense of Chicano culture, I am now also more attracted to that culture than I was before. The temptation now is to try to preserve those traits of my old culture that have not yet, in effect, atrophied.

The racial self-consciousness of minority group students during the last few years, evident in the ethnic costumes, the stylized gestures, and the idiomatic though often evasive devices for insisting on one's continuing membership in the community of the past, is also an indication that the minority group student has gained a new appreciation of the culture of his origin precisely because of his earlier alienation from it. As a result, Chicano students sometimes become more Chicano than most Chicanos. I remember, for example, my father's surprise when, walking across my college campus one afternoon, we came upon two Chicano academics wearing serapes. He and my mother were also surprised—indeed offended—when they earlier heard student activists use the word "Chicano." For them the term was a private one, primarily descriptive of persons they knew. It suggested intimacy. Hearing the word shouted into a microphone by a stranger left them bewildered. What they could not understand was that the student activist finds it easier than they to use "Chicano" in a more public way, for his distance from their culture and his membership in academic culture permits a wider and more abstract view.

The Mexican-Americans who begin to call themselves Chicanos in this new way are actually forming a new version of what it means to be a Chicano. The culture that didn't see itself as a culture is suddenly prized and identified for being one. The price one pays for this new self-consciousness is the knowledge of just that—it is *new*—and this knowledge is not available to those who remain at home. So it is knowledge that separates as well as unites people. Wanting more desperately than ever to assert his ties with the newly visible culture, the minority group student is tempted to exploit those characteristics of that culture that might yet survive in him. But the self-consciousness never allows one to feel completely at ease with the old culture. Worse, the knowledge of the culture of the past often leaves one feeling strangely solitary. At home, I hear relatives speak and find myself analyzing too much of what they say. It is embarrassing being a cultural anthropologist in one's own family's kitchen. I keep feeling myself little more than a cultural voyeur. I often come away from family gatherings suspecting, in fact, that what conceptions of my culture I carry with me are no more than illusions. Because they were never there before, because no one back home shares them, I grow less and less to trust their reliability: too often they seem no more than mental bubbles floating before an academic's eye.

Many who have taught minority group students in the last decade testify to sensing characteristics of a childhood culture still very much alive in these students. Should the teacher make these students aware of these characteristics? Initially, most of us would probably answer negatively. Better to trust the unconscious survival of the past than the always problematical, sometimes even clownish, re-creations of it. But the cultural past cannot be assured of survival; perhaps many of its characteristics are lost simply because the student is never encouraged to look for them. Even those that do survive do so tenuously. As a teacher, one can only hope that the best qualities in his minority group students' cultural legacy aren't altogether snuffed out by academic education.

More easy to live with and distinguishable from self-conscious awareness of the past are the ways the past unconsciously survives—perhaps even yet survives in me. As it turns out, the issue becomes less acute with time. With each year, the chance that the student is unaware of his cultural legacy is diminished as the habit of academic reflectiveness grows stronger. Although the culture of the academy makes innocence about one's cultural past less likely, this same culture, and the conceptual tools it provides, increases the desire to want to write and speak about the past. The paradox persists.

Awaiting the scholarship boy who finally acknowledges the fact that his perceptions of reality have changed is the dilemma of action. The sentimental reaction to this knowledge entails merely a refusal to renew contact with one's nonacademic culture lest one contaminate it. The problem, however, with this sentimental solution is that it overlooks the way academic culture renders one capable of dealing with the transactions of mass society. Academic culture, with its habits of conceptualization and abstraction, allows those of us from other cultures to deal with each other in a mass society. In this sense academic culture does have a profound political impact. Although people intent upon social mobility think of education as a means to an end, education does become an end: its culture allows one to exist more easily in a society increasingly anonymous and impersonal. The truth is, the academic's distance from his own experience brings the capacity for communicating with bureaucracies and understanding one's position in society—a prerequisite for political action.

If the sentimental reaction to nonacademic culture is to fear changing it, the political response, typical especially of working-class and lately minority group leaders, is to see higher education solely in terms of its political and social possibilities. Its cultural consequences, in this view, are disregarded. At this time when we are so keenly aware of social and economic inequality, it might seem beside the point to warn those who are working to bring about equality that education alters culture as well as economic status. And yet, if there is one main criticism that I, as a minority group student, must make of minority group leaders in their past attacks on the "racism" of the academy, it is that they never distinguished between my right to higher education and the desirability of my actually entering the academy—which is another way of saying again that they never recognized that there were things I could lose by becoming a scholarship boy.

Certainly, the academy changes those from alien cultures more than it is changed by them. While minority groups had an impact on higher education, largely because of their advantage in coming as a group, within the last few years students such as myself, who finally ended up certified as academics, also ended up sounding very much like the academics we found when we came to the campus. I do not enjoy making such admissions. But perhaps now the time has come when questions about the cultural costs of education ought to be delayed no longer. Those of us who have been scholarship boys know in our bones that our education has exacted a large price in exchange for the large benefits it has conferred upon us. And what is sadder to consider, after we have paid that price, we go home and casually change the cultures that nurtured us. My parents today understand how they are "Chicanos" in a large and impersonal sense. The gains from such knowledge are clear. But so, too, are the reasons for regret.

ANNIE DILLARD

LIVING LIKE WEASELS

A weasel is wild. Who knows what he thinks? He sleeps in his underground den, his tail draped over his nose. Sometimes he lives in his den for two days without leaving. Outside, he stalks rabbits, mice, muskrats, and birds, killing more bodies than he can eat warm, and often dragging the carcasses home. Obedient to instinct, he bites his prey at the neck, either splitting the jugular vein at the throat or crunching the brain at the base of the skull, and he does not let go. One naturalist refused to kill a weasel who was socketed into his hand deeply as a rattlesnake. The man could in no way pry the tiny weasel off, and he had to walk half a mile to water, the weasel dangling from his palm, and soak him off like a stubborn label.

And once, says Ernest Thompson Seton—once, a man shot an eagle out of the sky. He examined the eagle and found the dry skull of a weasel fixed by the jaws to his throat. The supposition is that the eagle had pounced on the weasel and the weasel swiveled and bit as instinct taught him, tooth to neck, and nearly won. I would like to have seen that eagle from the air a few weeks or months before he was shot: was the whole weasel still attached to his feathered throat, a fur pendant? Or did the eagle eat what he could reach, gutting the living weasel with his talons before his breast, bending his beak, cleaning the beautiful airborne bones?

I have been reading about weasels because I saw one last week. I startled a weasel who startled me, and we exchanged a long glance.

Twenty minutes from my house, through the woods by the quarry and across the highway, is Hollins Pond, a remarkable piece of shallowness, where I like to go at sunset and sit on a tree trunk. Hollins Pond is also called Murray's Pond; it covers two acres of bottomland near Tinker Creek with six inches of water and six thousand lily pads. In winter, brown-and-white steers stand in the middle of it, merely dampening their hooves; from the distant shore they look like miracle itself, complete with miracle's nonchalance. Now, in summer, the steers are gone. The water lilies have blossomed and spread to a green horizontal plane that is terra firma to plodding blackbirds, and tremulous ceiling to black leeches, crayfish, and carp.

This is, mind you, suburbia. It is a five-minute walk in three directions to rows of houses, though none is visible here. There's a 55-mph highway at one end of the pond, and a nesting pair of wood ducks at the other. Under every bush is a muskrat hole or a beer can. The far end is an alternating series of fields and woods, fields and woods, threaded everywhere with motorcycle tracks—in whose bare clay wild turtles lay eggs.

So, I had crossed the highway, stepped over two low barbed-wire fences, and traced the motorcycle path in all gratitude through the wild rose and poison ivy of the pond's shoreline up into high grassy fields. Then I cut down through the woods to the mossy fallen tree where I sit. This tree is excellent. It makes a dry, upholstered bench at the upper, marshy end of the pond, a plush jetty raised from the thorny shore between a shallow blue body of water and a deep blue body of sky.

The sun had just set. I was relaxed on the tree trunk, ensconced in the lap of lichen, watching the lily pads at my feet tremble and part dreamily over the thrusting path of a carp. A yellow bird appeared to my right and flew behind me. It caught my eye; I swiveled around—and the next instant, inexplicably, I was looking down at a weasel, who was looking up at me.

Weasel! I'd never seen one wild before. He was ten inches long, thin as a curve, a muscled ribbon, brown as fruitwood, soft-furred, alert. His face was fierce, small and pointed as a lizard's; he would have made a good arrowhead. There was just a dot of chin, maybe two brown hairs' worth, and then the pure white fur began that spread down his underside. He had two black eyes I didn't see, any more than you see a window.

The weasel was stunned into stillness as he was emerging from beneath an enormous shaggy wild rose bush four feet away. I was stunned into stillness twisted backward on the tree trunk. Our eyes locked, and someone threw away the key.

Our look was as if two lovers, or deadly enemies, met unexpectedly on an overgrown path when each had been thinking of something else: a clearing blow to the gut. It was also a bright blow to the brain, or a sudden beating of brains, with all the charge and intimate grate of rubbed balloons. It emptied our lungs. It felled the forest, moved the fields, and drained the pond; the world dismantled and tumbled into that black hole of eyes. If you and I looked at each other that way, our skulls would split and drop to our shoulders. But we don't. We keep our skulls. So.

He disappeared. This was only last week, and already I don't remember what shattered the enchantment. I think I blinked, I think I retrieved my brain from the weasel's brain, and tried to memorize what I was seeing, and the weasel felt the yank of separation, the careening splash-down into real life and the urgent current of instinct. He vanished under the wild rose. I waited motionless, my mind suddenly full of data and my spirit with pleadings, but he didn't return.

Please do not tell me about "approach-avoidance conflicts." I tell you I've been in that weasel's brain for sixty seconds, and he was in mine. Brains are private places, muttering through unique and secret tapes—but the weasel and I both plugged into another tape simultaneously, for a sweet and shocking time. Can I help it if it was a blank?

What goes on in his brain the rest of the time? What does a weasel think about? He won't say. His journal is tracks in clay, a spray of feathers, mouse blood and bone: uncollected, unconnected, loose-leaf, and blown.

I would like to learn, or remember, how to live. I come to Hollins Pond not so much to learn how to live as, frankly, to forget about it. That is, I don't think I can learn from a wild animal how to live in particular—shall I suck warm blood, hold my tail high,

walk with my footprints precisely over the prints of my hands?—
but I might learn something of mindlessness, something of the
purity of living in the physical sense and the dignity of living
without bias or motive. The weasel lives in necessity and we live
in choice, hating necessity and dying at the last ignobly in its
talons. I would like to live as I should, as the weasel lives as he
should. And I suspect that for me the way is like the weasel's:
open to time and death painlessly, noticing everything, remembering nothing, choosing the given with a fierce and pointed
will.

I missed my chance. I should have gone for the throat. I should
have lunged for that streak of white under the weasel's chin and
held on, held on through mud and into the wild rose, held on
for a dearer life. We could live under the wild rose wild as weasels, mute and uncomprehending. I could very calmly go wild. I
could live two days in the den, curled, leaning on mouse fur,
sniffing bird bones, blinking, licking, breathing musk, my hair
tangled in the roots of grasses. Down is a good place to go, where
the mind is single. Down is out, out of your ever-loving mind
and back to your careless senses. I remember muteness as a prolonged and giddy fast, where every moment is a feast of utterance
received. Time and events are merely poured, unremarked, and
ingested directly, like blood pulsed into my gut through a jugular
vein. Could two live that way? Could two live under the wild
rose, and explore by the pond, so that the smooth mind of each
is as everywhere present to the other, and as received and as
unchallenged, as falling snow?

We could, you know. We can live any way we want. People
take vows of poverty, chastity, and obedience—even of silence—
by choice. The thing is to stalk your calling in a certain skilled
and supple way, to locate the most tender and live spot and plug
into that pulse. This is yielding, not fighting. A weasel doesn't
"attack" anything; a weasel lives as he's meant to, yielding at
every moment to the perfect freedom of single necessity.

I think it would be well, and proper, and obedient, and pure,
to grasp your one necessity and not let it go, to dangle from it
limp wherever it takes you. Then even death, where you're going

no matter how you live, cannot you part. Seize it and let it seize you up aloft even, till your eyes burn out and drop; let your musky flesh fall off in shreds, and let your very bones unhinge and scatter, loosened over fields, over fields and woods, lightly, thoughtless, from any height at all, from as high as eagles.

SCOTT RUSSELL SANDERS

The Inheritance of Tools

At just about the hour when my father died, soon after dawn one February morning when ice coated the windows like cataracts, I banged my thumb with a hammer. Naturally I swore at the hammer, the reckless thing, and in the moment of swearing I thought of what my father would say: "If you'd try hitting the nail it would go in a whole lot faster. Don't you know your thumb's not as hard as that hammer?" We both were doing carpentry that day, but far apart. He was building cupboards at my brother's place in Oklahoma; I was at home in Indiana putting up a wall in the basement to make a bedroom for my daughter. By the time my mother called with news of his death—the long distance wires whittling her voice until it seemed too thin to bear the weight of what she had to say—my thumb was swollen. A week or so later a white scar in the shape of a crescent moon began to show above the cuticle, and month by month it rose across the pink sky of my thumbnail. It took the better part of a year for the scar to disappear, and every time I noticed it I thought of my father.

The hammer had belonged to him, and to his father before him. The three of us have used it to build houses and barns and chicken coops, to upholster chairs and crack walnuts, to make doll furniture and bookshelves and jewelry boxes. The head is scratched and pockmarked, like an old plowshare that has been working rocky fields, and it gives off the sort of dull sheen you see on fast creek water in the shade. It is a finishing hammer, about the weight of a bread loaf, too light really for framing walls, too heavy for cabinetwork, with a curved claw for pulling nails, a rounded head for pounding, a fluted neck for looks, and a hickory handle for strength.

The present handle is my third one, bought from a lumber-yard in Tennessee down the road from where my brother and I were helping my father build his retirement house. I broke the previous one by trying to pull sixteen-penny nails out of floor joists—a foolish thing to do with a finishing hammer, as my father pointed out. "You ever hear of a crowbar?" he said. No telling how many handles he and my grandfather had gone through before me. My grandfather used to cut down hickory trees on his farm, saw them into slabs, cure the planks in his hayloft, and carve handles with a drawknife. The grain in hickory is crooked and knotty, and therefore tough, hard to split, like the grain in the two men who owned this hammer before me.

After proposing marriage to a neighbor girl, my grandfather used this hammer to build a house for his bride on a stretch of river bottom in northern Mississippi. The lumber for the place, like the hickory for the handle, was cut on his own land. By the day of the wedding he had not quite finished the house, and so right after the ceremony he took his wife home and put her to work. My grandmother had worn her Sunday dress for the wed-ding, with a fringe of lace tacked on around the hem in honor of the occasion. She removed this lace and folded it away before going out to help my grandfather nail siding on the house. "There she was in her good dress," he told me some fifty-odd years after that wedding day, "holding up them long pieces of clapboard while I hammered, and together we got the place cov-ered up before dark." As the family grew to four, six, eight, and eventually thirteen, my grandfather used this hammer to enlarge his house room by room, like a chambered nautilus expanding his shell.

By and by the hammer was passed along to my father. One day he was up on the roof of our pony barn nailing shingles with it, when I stepped out the kitchen door to call him for supper. Before I could yell, something about the sight of him straddling the spine of that roof and swinging the hammer caught my eye and made me hold my tongue. I was five or six years old, and the world's commonplaces were still news to me. He would pull a nail from the pouch at his waist, bring the hammer down, and a moment later the *thunk* of the blow would reach my ears. And that is what had stopped me in my tracks and stilled my tongue, that momentary gap between seeing and hearing the blow. Instead of yelling from the kitchen door, I ran to the barn and climbed two rungs up the ladder—as far as I was allowed to go—and spoke quietly to my father. On our walk to the house he explained that sound takes time to make its way through air. Suddenly the world seemed larger, the air more dense, if sound could be held back like any ordinary traveler.

By the time I started using this hammer, at about the age when I discovered the speed of sound, it already contained houses and mysteries for me. The smooth handle was one my grandfather had made. In those days I needed both hands to swing it. My father would start a nail in a scrap of wood, and I would pound away until I bent it over.

"Looks like you got ahold of some of those rubber nails," he would tell me. "Here, let me see if I can find you some stiff ones." And he would rummage in a drawer until he came up with a fistful of more cooperative nails. "Look at the head," he would tell me. "Don't look at your hands, don't look at the hammer. Just look at the head of that nail and pretty soon you'll learn to hit it square."

Pretty soon I did learn. While he worked in the garage cutting dovetail joints for a drawer or skinning a deer or tuning an engine, I would hammer nails. I made innocent blocks of wood look like porcupines. He did not talk much in the midst of his tools, but he kept up a nearly ceaseless humming, slipping in and out of a dozen tunes in an afternoon, often running back over the same stretch of melody again and again, as if searching for a way out. When the humming did cease, I knew he was faced with a task requiring great delicacy or concentration, and I took care not to distract him.

He kept scraps of wood in a cardboard box—the ends of two-by-fours, slabs of shelving and plywood, odd pieces of molding—and everything in it was fair game. I nailed scraps together to fashion what I called boats or houses, but the results usually bore only faint resemblance to the visions I carried in my head. I would hold up these constructions to show my father, and he would turn them over in his hands admiringly, speculating about what they might be. My cobbled-together guitars might have been alien spaceships, my barns might have been models of Aztec temples, each wooden contraption might have been anything but what I had set out to make.

Now and again I would feel the need to have a chunk of wood shaped or shortened before I riddled it with nails, and I would clamp it in a vise and scrape at it with a handsaw. My father would let me lacerate the board until my arm gave out, and then he would wrap his hand around mine and help me finish the cut, showing me how to use my thumb to guide the blade, how to pull back on the saw to keep it from binding, how to let my shoulder do the work.

"Don't force it," he would say, "just drag it easy and give the teeth a chance to bite."

As the saw teeth bit down the wood released its smell, each kind with its own fragrance, oak or walnut or cherry or pine — usually pine, because it was the softest and the easiest for a child to work. No matter how weathered and gray the board, no matter how warped and cracked, inside there was this smell waiting, as of something freshly baked. I gathered every smidgen of sawdust and stored it away in coffee cans, which I kept in a drawer of the workbench. When I did not feel like hammering nails I would dump my sawdust on the concrete floor of the garage and landscape it into highways and farms and towns, running miniature cars and trucks along miniature roads. Looming as huge as a colossus, my father worked over and around me, now and again bending down to inspect my work, careful not to trample my creations. It was a landscape that smelled dizzyingly of wood. Even after a bath my skin would carry the smell, and so would my father's hair, when he lifted me for a bedtime hug.

I tell these things not only from memory but also from recent observation, because my own son now turns blocks of wood into nailed porcupines, dumps cans full of sawdust at my feet and sculpts highways on the floor. He learns how to swing a hammer from the elbow instead of the wrist, how to lay his thumb beside the blade to guide a saw, how to tap a chisel with a wooden mallet, how to mark a hole with an awl before starting a drill bit. My daughter did the same before him, and even now, on the brink of teenage aloofness, she will occasionally drag out my box of wood scraps and carpenter something. So I have seen my apprenticeship to wood and tools reenacted in each of my children, as my father saw his own apprenticeship renewed in me.

The saw I use belonged to him, as did my level and both of my squares, and all four tools had belonged to his father. The blade of the saw is the bluish color of gun barrels, and the maple handle, dark from the sweat of hands, is inscribed with curving leaf designs. The level is a shaft of walnut two feet long, edged with brass and pierced by three round windows in which air bubbles float in oil-filled tubes of glass. The middle window serves for testing whether a surface is horizontal, the others for testing whether it is plumb or vertical. My grandfather used to carry this level on the gun rack behind the seat in his pickup, and when I rode with him I would turn around to watch the bubbles dance. The larger of the two squares is called a framing square, a flat steel elbow so beat up and tarnished you can barely make out the rows of numbers that show how to figure the cuts on rafters. The smaller one is called a try square, for marking right angles, with a blued steel blade for the shank and a brass-faced block of cherry for the head.

I was taught early on that a saw is not to be used apart from a square: "If you're going to cut a piece of wood," my father insisted, "you owe it to the tree to cut it straight."

Long before studying geometry, I learned there is a mystical virtue in right angles. There is an unspoken morality in seeking the level and the plumb. A house will stand, a table will bear weight, the sides of a box will hold together only if the joints are square and the members upright. When the bubble is lined up between two marks etched in the glass tube of a level, you have aligned yourself with the forces that hold the universe together. When you miter the corners of a picture frame, each angle must be exactly forty-five degrees, as they are in the perfect triangles of Pythagoras, not a degree more or less. Otherwise the frame will hang crookedly, as if ashamed of itself and of its maker. No matter if the joints you are cutting do not show. Even if you are butting two pieces of wood together inside a cabinet, where no one except a wrecking crew will ever see them, you must take pains to insure that the ends are square and the studs are plumb.

I took pains over the wall I was building on the day my father died. Not long after that wall was finished—paneled with tongue-and-groove boards of yellow pine, the nail holes filled with putty and the wood all stained and sealed—I came close to wrecking it one afternoon when my daughter ran howling up the stairs to announce that her gerbils had escaped from their cage and were hiding in my brand-new wall. She could hear them scratching and squeaking behind her bed. Impossible! I said. How on earth could they get inside my drum-tight wall? Through the heating vent, she answered. I went downstairs, pressed my ear to the honey-colored wood, and heard the scritch scritch of tiny feet.

"What can we do?" my daughter wailed. "They'll starve to death, they'll die of thirst, they'll suffocate."

"Hold on," I soothed. "I'll think of something."

While I thought and she fretted, the radio on her bedside table delivered us the headlines. Several thousand people had died in a city in India from a poisonous cloud that had leaked overnight from a chemical plant. A nuclear-powered submarine had been launched. Rioting continued in South Africa. An airplane had been hijacked in the Mediterranean. Authorities calculated that several thousand homeless people slept on the streets within sight of the Washington Monument. I felt my usual helplessness in face of all these calamities. But here was my daughter weeping because her gerbils were holed up in a wall. This calamity I could handle.

"Don't worry," I told her. "We'll set food and water by the heating vent and lure them out. And if that doesn't do the trick, I'll tear the wall apart until we find them."

She stopped crying and gazed at me. "You'd really tear it apart? Just for my gerbils? The *wall*?" Astonishment slowed her down only for a second, however, before she ran to the workbench and began tugging at drawers, saying, "Let's see, what'll we need? Crowbar. Hammer. Chisels. I hope we don't have to use them—but just in case."

We didn't need the wrecking tools. I never had to assault my handsome wall, because the gerbils eventually came out to nibble at a dish of popcorn. But for several hours I studied the tongue-and-groove skin I had nailed up on the day of my father's death, considering where to begin prying. There were no gaps in that wall, no crooked joints.

I had botched a great many pieces of wood before I mastered the right angle with a saw, botched even more before I learned to miter a joint. The knowledge of these things resides in my hands and eyes and the webwork of muscles, not in the tools. There are machines for sale—powered miter boxes and radial arm saws, for instance—that will enable any casual soul to cut proper angles in boards. The skill is invested in the gadget instead of the person who uses it, and this is what distinguishes a machine from a tool. If I had to earn my keep by making furniture or building houses, I suppose I would buy powered saws and pneumatic nailers; the need for speed would drive me to it. But since I carpenter only for my own pleasure or to help neighbors or to remake the house around the ears of my family, I stick with hand tools. Most of the ones I own were given to me by my father, who also taught me how to wield them. The tools in my workbench are a double inheritance, for each hammer and level and saw is wrapped in a cloud of knowing.

All of these tools are a pleasure to look at and to hold. Merchants would never paste NEW NEW NEW! signs on them in stores. Their designs are old because they work, because they serve their purpose well. Like folksongs and aphorisms and the grainy bits of language, these tools have been pared down to essentials. I look at my claw hammer, the distillation of a hundred generations of carpenters, and consider that it holds up well beside those other classics—Greek vases, Gregorian chants, *Don Quixote*, barbed fishhooks, candles, spoons. Knowledge of hammering stretches back to the earliest humans who squatted beside fires chipping flints. Anthropologists have a lovely name for those unworked rocks that served as the earliest hammers. "Dawn stones" they are called. Their only qualification for the work, aside from hardness, is that they fit the hand. Our ancestors used them for grinding corn, tapping awls, smashing bones. From dawn stones to this claw hammer is a great leap in time, but no great distance in design or imagination.

On that iced-over February morning when I smashed my

thumb with the hammer, I was down in the basement framing the wall that my daughter's gerbils would later hide in. I was thinking of my father, as I always did whenever I built anything, thinking how he would have gone about the work, hearing in memory what he would have said about the wisdom of hitting the nail instead of my thumb. I had the studs and plates nailed together all square and trim, and was lifting the wall into place when the phone rang upstairs. My wife answered, and in a moment she came to the basement door and called down softly to me. The stillness in her voice made me drop the framed wall and hurry upstairs. She told me my father was dead. Then I heard the details over the phone from my mother. Building a set of cupboards for my brother in Oklahoma, he had knocked off work early the previous afternoon because of cramps in his stomach. Early this morning, on his way into the kitchen of my brother's trailer, maybe going for a glass of water, so early that no one else was awake, he slumped down on the linoleum and his heart quit.

For several hours I paced around inside my house, upstairs and down, in and out of every room, looking for the right door to open and knowing there was no such door. My wife and children followed me and wrapped me in arms and backed away again, circling and staring as if I were on fire. Where was the door, the door, the door? I kept wondering. My smashed thumb turned purple and throbbed, making me furious. I wanted to cut it off and rush outside and scrape away the snow and hack a hole in the frozen earth and bury the shameful thing.

I went down into the basement, opened a drawer in my workbench, and stared at the ranks of chisels and knives. Oiled and sharp, as my father would have kept them, they gleamed at me like teeth. I took up a clasp knife, pried out the longest blade, and tested the edge on the hair of my forearm. A tuft came away cleanly, and I saw my father testing the sharpness of tools on his own skin, the blades of axes and knives and gouges and hoes, saw the red hair shaved off in patches from his arms and the backs of his hands. "That will cut bear," he would say. He never cut a bear with his blades, now my blades, but he cut he cut deer, dirt, wood. I closed the knife and put it away. Then I took up the hammer and went back to work on my daughter's wall, snugging the bottom plate against a chalkline on the floor, shimming the top plate against the joists overhead, plumbing the studs with my level, making sure before I drove the first nail that every line was square and true.

BARRY LOPEZ

Grown Men

I returned from a week of camping in the high desert of eastern Oregon, a respite from the twilight and winter rains on the west side of the Cascade Mountains where I live, to find a letter with a straightforward message, that Odey Cassell was dead.

It had been a year for deaths. My mother had died of cancer in Lenox Hill Hospital in New York. An uncle I was close to died of a heart attack among strangers in the Atlanta airport. I had lost with their fading a sense of family, as though the piers had suddenly gone out from under the veranda of an ancestral southern home and revealed it abandoned. I was brooding over that sense of emptiness when the letter about Odey came, written in Nettie's fine, neat hand.

He had gone unremarkably one morning, wrote his wife, in his own bed in a house he had lived in since he was born in its living room in 1885. I was weary of deaths, but this passing stunned me. I spent the evening trying to answer Nettie's letter, trying half the night to say how grateful I was to have known him.

I first met Odey in the spring of 1964. A friend, Peter, and I drove down from Notre Dame, where I was in school, to spend a week with the Cassells. Their farm lay northeast of Cass, West Virginia, beneath Back Allegheny Mountain on the Greenbrier River. Its cleared fields were cut out square against the hills, in a dense second growth of oak, maple and white pine. Peter had first met them in 1961, when he saw a card on a bulletin board in Cass—"Home cooked meals and overnight, $1 per meal, $1 for bed"—and found his way out to them, to a two-story clapboard house, white paint faded to light gray, a large unpainted barn, a woodshed, split-rail and wire fences, Nettie's garden, and, overhead, a 125-kV power line that passed through their lives, over chickens, a few cows, twenty-five or thirty sheep, some pigs and their border collie, Topsy.

What Nettie put on her table for a single meal was more than most people saw in three. Farm meals, plain food meant for working people. Tomatoes and green beans, yellow squash, potatoes, carrots and sweet corn. Mutton and ham. Fresh milk, churned butter and honey, fresh bread and biscuits. All of it, save the grains, from the farm.

The guest beds upstairs were hard to match in our minds for comfort: feather mattresses on box springs with layers of quilts and sun-stiffened sheets. Their home was wood-heated; the water system gravity-fed from a stream on a hill behind the house. Hot water ran out of a circulating pipe in a wood stove in the kitchen. A loaded .30 / 30 leaned against the pale yellow wall by the front door, for bears and feral dogs, for the sake of the sheep.

We went to Odey's farm because it was so different from what we knew, because we were eighteen and sensed adventure in it.

In the evenings Odey would tell stories, dozens of them, on visit after visit, never the same one twice unless he was asked. He drew us in, sitting wide-eyed and silent in his living room. We never heard enough; later we barely understood how to retell them.

Whenever we came we brought him two cans of Prince Albert pipe tobacco and a little Jack Daniel's. Nettie didn't approve of the whiskey. Odey's eyes would sparkle behind his wire-frame glasses, a look of boyish surprise would come over him and he'd affect astonishment and delight at her disapproval. And he'd say, "Well, boys, I declare. . . ." He studied the gifts, turning them slowly in his hands as though they were as exotic for him as ostrich eggs. "Thank you," he would say. He was the first man I knew who was not accustomed to receiving inexpensive gifts.

Odey was slow to begin a session of stories, as the art required, but once under way the range of his historical experience, the touch for revealing detail, his timing and rhythmic pace took you and lulled you. Almost every incident of which he spoke—the time a wounded owl punctured his hand, the way they cut ice on the river with horse-drawn saws—had occurred within twenty miles of the house we sat in. He'd cleared the land around it with his father and a team of oxen before the turn of the century. He'd seen commercial logging for white pine and spruce come and go, and with it the railroad and the town. Cass now supported only a clothes-pin factory, and in summer rides to a nearby hilltop behind an antique Shay logging engine. In spring the half-dozen wheelless cars in vacant lots sat strangling in vines. His children had gone on to become a university professor, a state trooper. Another son, the youngest, had stayed on to help his parents, working part-time in the Green Bank Observatory, nine miles east by foot or thirty by West Virginia mountain road.

At seventy-eight, six-feet-four-inches tall, with hands so large he had to take a doorknob in his fingertips, with physical strokes perfectly measured to whatever work had to be done—splitting wood or winding the stem of his pocket watch—he strode down the road with us on an evening walk at a pace we couldn't catch. And he knew it.

Odey was outsize for us, in part because he hardly made himself the subject of conversation, and we felt this a quality to admire. In the years we visited we heard stories of his prodigious physical strength and his generosity only from friends, neighbors with names like Walter Beverage and Charles Seabolt. It pleased us to think that they thought of him as we did, though to them he was only what they were to him, all of value in that country, neighbors, ones who went way back.

At the time, the largest unexplored cave in West Virginia lay under Odey's land. With the aid of some crude maps made by a U.S. Geological Survey crew, Peter and I went down into its tunnels and caverns, an adventure of self-induced terror and, to be sure, of awesome sights. When we unraveled our stories that evening Odey listened as keenly as we had to him, strengthening the flow of our narrative with a gentle question or two, helping us shape it, though we could not understand this at the time.

We stumbled into rattlesnakes in the nearby hills (he told us once their dens smelled like cucumbers, and he was right); and we watched, stunned, one night from a second-story window as a black bear tore up his sheep pens and most of his cash income for the year. The next morning he fired up the stove, milked the cow and went to work on the sheep.

I don't ever remember getting up earlier than he did.

I learned more than I comprehended at Odey's, about hardware disease in cows and how to shoot crows; about a farmer's life eighty years long, set dead against half as many bitter winters, violent economic loss, forest fires, friends chewed up in farm machinery, and stillborn children; about backwoods skills thought unremarkable, and a capacity for improvisation—quick and sharp in men with little income who work alone. He was, of course, like a grandfather to me, in part because I had never known grandfathers. He was orthodox in that he never spoke in our presence of religion or politics. In general, he moved us by his own example toward a respect for people for whatever they might do well, and to recall that different people lived in different ways. I never saw bitterness or resentment in him. Or meanness.

In later years, when I read about Appalachia in books like Harry Caudill's *Night Comes to the Cumberlands* or heard a man like Doc Watson sing of hard lives in the hills, I would think of the thing Odey had given us: we had lived that time like willow shoots with a man rooted in the earth like a tan oak. We had repaired his fences and milked his cows and run his sheep and brought him whiskey; and he had told us well-fetched stories of young ladies met at county fairs, or bear-hunting for meat, and of practical jokes to break the back of a terrible winter, about what he thought were the courtesies and obligations in life, in short to be self-reliant and neighborly, and grateful for what there was. And then he sent us on our way.

Some things Odey said about integrity didn't bloom in me for years. For the most part they came in time.

There was another man. During the summers after my sophomore and junior years at Notre Dame, I moved West to work in Wyoming, some of that time with a man in his sixties named Bill Daniels. We cleared forest trails together and I wrangled horses on a few trips on which he was employed as a cook. He took a liking to me. On our days off he took me into places in the Teton Wilderness Area he felt not many men had seen.

At the request of the Museum of Natural History in New York, Bill Daniels had prepared an exhibit on Sheepeater Indians, people banished to the Rocky Mountain ranges by their respective tribes for heinous crimes, people who lived on bighorn sheep the way Plains Indians lived on buffalo. As far as I know, he was the only man around at the time who knew the location of several of their caves and could easily find evidence of their vanished culture. My time with him was less keen and shorter than that with Odey but he introduced me to a perception of America's indigenous people more complex than anything I was later to read about them, and he formed in me a sympathy for mountain men.

I realized later that he saw, without motive or design, to a part of my education that required his attention.

There was a third man who affected me as much as these two, though years later, a kind of frontier roustabout named Dave Wallace. As a young man he had hunted wolves and coyotes for bounty in North and South Dakota. He later moved to eastern Montana where he worked on cattle ranches and drilled for oil before going north to crew on a commercial fishing boat in the Gulf of Alaska. I met him, crippled by accidents sustained in those and other jobs, living in the southeastern Oregon desert where he was making a living mining and trapping coyotes.

I spent several days with Dave in the winter of 1976. He lived in a shack and adjacent trailer without electricity or running water, in a sheltered spot beneath cottonwoods on a stream called Pike Creek. From his door you looked across sixty or seventy square miles of bleached playa desert south into the Trout Creek Mountains. It was dry country, with an annual temperature range of from one hundred degrees above to thirty-five degrees below zero. Dave subsisted mostly on canned foods, was kind toward his infrequent visitors, congenial, and he shared whatever he had without making a fool of himself.

I've met several men like Wallace in the West, but few of such varied background who were as clearheaded and energetic. When I asked him he agreed to a series of long interviews.

What Dave Wallace, Bill Daniels and Odey Cassell represented I thought was vanishing. Before it was gone I wanted to speak with them, formally, as a writer; to make extensive notes; to try to elicit those things in them that were so attractive and give them names. For men who had had difficult times, without money and companionship, they were uncommonly free of bitterness. There was a desire in them to act to help when something went wrong rather than to assign blame, even when the trouble was over. When something went very wrong they reached down into a reservoir of implacable conviction, as a man puts his hands into a cold, clear basin of water. And they wrenched humor—impish in Odey, raw in Bill, laconic in Dave—out of the bleakest of these things.

I wanted to speak with them. Because there are lives, near and distant, wearing out too quickly, without plan or laughter.

I received word through a mutual friend the week I was making ready for the trip that Dave had died. He had apparently had a heart attack while driving down the dirt road past his place and had slumped across the steering wheel. The pickup had slowed, drifted off the road and come to rest against a thick tuft of rabbit brush. The engine must have run until it emptied the gas tank.

I made the three-hundred-mile drive a week later. His cabin had already been vandalized, by the same sort of people he had made welcome and fed from his meager garden.

A month later I learned of Bill Daniels's death in Dubois, Wyoming, at his brother's ranch. He had taken with him his extensive knowledge of the Sheepeaters. He had told me once that after seeing what had been done to other Indian sites he would die without telling the rest of what he knew.

When I read, a few weeks after this, Nettie's letter—". . . he hadn't been able to be out on the place for a long time, which he wanted to do so much . . ."—I felt the loss of what Odey had been, and that his life, like Daniels's and Wallace's, was now irretrievable. The heart of my pain, and anger, I think, was that, unproclaimed, these men would have seemed to so many like failures.

I was, of course, very fond of them, as young men are fond of their grandfathers by blood or not; I realized just before they died that there was something of transcendent value in them, fragile and as difficult to extract as the color of a peach. I wanted to be able to have it and pass it on, and so their deaths left me burdened and confused, as though something had been stolen that I owned. The silence and obscurity that were so essential to their lives escaped me entirely. I could not leave them alone in their deaths.

In the days following, no longer charged with a responsibility to describe them, I began to drift back to older, more personal feelings. One evening when I was out walking along the edge of a river that runs near my home I stopped and became absorbed in the swirling current of jade-colored water. Close by in the Douglas fir and cedar trees was a roaring, a white-water creek sheathed in mist where it hit the river in an explosion, and was absorbed in that massive, opaque flow. I took Nettie's letter out of my pocket, gently unfolded it and let it go.

The river flows I do not know how many miles, Odey, to another, which flows farther on to the Columbia, and on to the Pacific. There are whales there—they lead obscure and exemplary lives. They are as long as your barn, and speak with voices like the sound of the wind in the cave beneath your pasture. They are for the most part undisturbed. They seem to me to be at home.

VICKI HEARNE

Oyez à Beaumont

A student of mine called two days ago and asked, "What do the experts do when their dogs die?"

He developed a calcium deposit on his upper spine, did my good Airedale Gunner, and it would hurt him to track, so Gunner and I stopped tracking, stopped retrieving and jumping, not because he wouldn't have gone on if it were up to him, and awhile after that he was very ill with cancer, and after a time of that, too much of that, I had him killed. Gallant Gunner, brave Gunner, gay Gunner. Once, late one evening on a beach in Malibu, he took down a man who was attacking me with a knife. The vet had to patch Gunner up some, but he didn't turn tail the way my assailant did. Brave Gunner. Harken to Gunner. Twenty-four hours later, bandaged, he clowned and told jokes for the kids at Juvenile Hall, performing for the annual Orange Empire Dog Club Christmas party. Oh, rare and dauntless Gunner. Even his hip, broken when a prostate tumor grew right through the bone, did not stop the courage of his gaiety, but I did. My friend Dick Koehler said, "He is lucky to have a good friend like you," to encourage me, you see, to get on with it, kill him, and Dick was right, of course, right, because when there is nothing much left of a dog but his wounds you should bury those decently.

Until he died, he was immortal, and the death of an immortal is an event that changes the world. That is all for now about Gunner, because what it does to you when such a dog dies is not fit to print. "Der Tod ist groß," writes Rilke. "Death is huge." But

443

various psychologists deny that it is as huge as all that when it is an animal that is mourned. I have read statistically studded reassurances that mourning for a cat lasts at most one month, for a dog three. I have read that when an animal dies there are no regrets, no rehearsal of the wail, "If only I had," and also that the splendid thing about animals, what is said to make them so convenient to our hearts, like antidepressants, is that when we mourn them, we are only mourning a personal loss and not "the loss of life and potential," according to Professors Beck and Katcher, authorities on all of this at the University of Pennsylvania.

That is the way psychological authorities talk—"Eventually an animal *can* be replaced," they write in their books, but this is not how the experts talk. (I realize that psychologists and such like are generally understood to be experts, but I have met none who were experts in the various ways my good Gunner's work with scent developed, especially when he started scenting out the human heart.) But I am just a dog trainer. My thinking, such as it is, I learned from the animals, for whom happiness is usually a matter of getting the job done. Clear that fence, fetch in those sheep, move those calves, win that race, find that guy, retrieve that bird. The happiness of animals is also ideologically unsound, as often as not, or at least it is frequently wanting in propriety, as when your dog rolls in something awful on his afternoon walk, or your cat turns off your answering machine.

In over a quarter of a century of training I have never met an animal who turned out to be replaceable, and Dick says, "Hell, even trees are irreplaceable, but we don't know that, and *that* is our loss." The loss the dog trainer has in mind is the loss of eternity, for, as Wittgenstein put it: "Denn lebt er ewig, der in der gegenwart lebt." "So he lives forever, who lives in the present," wrote the philosopher, and this is how the animals live, in the present, which is why the expert's difficult and apparently harsh advice, advice they occasionally take themselves, is: "Another dog. Same breed, as soon as possible." Not because another dog of the same breed will be the same, but because that way you can pick up somewhere near where you left off, say that you have it in you.

In a children's book called *Algonquin: The Story of a Great
Dog*, there is a quarrel between two brothers, old men they were,
grandfather and great-uncle to the boy who tells the story. Grandsir is angry because Uncle Ovid is going to take on the training
of the grand young Pointer named Algonquin; he is angry
because he wants no more of the "grief and the rage and the
ashes." He shouts at his brother, "Do you know what it does to
you? Do you know what it does every time one of them dies?"
but Uncle Ovid just says, "Don't tell me. I am an old man and
it would not be good for me to know," and he trains that Pointer
who turns out to be something else again at the field trials. Mr.
Washington says, "I think sometimes that he would pity his
bracemates, were he not enough of a gentleman to know that
they would rather die than be pitied," and Algonquin wins and
wins and wins and then Algonquin starts to get a lung disease
and can't work well, is distressed therefore, because he is losing
his work, his happiness, and Uncle Ovid sends him out on his
last run and shoots him while he is on point, while there is still
something more to him than his wounds.

At the end of that story, when Grandsir suggests that it is time
for the boy who has been witness to all of this to get another dog,
he says to his grandfather, "Irish Setters don't win field trials, do
they? I mean, you are not in much danger of getting a great
dog?" Grandsir purses his lips and agrees, "Not much." The boy
says, "Then an Irish Setter would be nice."

There exist mighty dogs, the dangerous kind who take hold of
your heart and do not let go. But avoiding the great ones does
not get you out of it. If, like the boy in *Algonquin*, you already
know what a great dog is, then the knowledge marks you. If you
do not know, then you are still in danger, for if you give her a
civilized upbringing, every collie is Lassie *in propria persona*,
killing that snake in your heart, driving off the cougar that lurks
there, sending for help. This is not because all dogs are great
dogs but rather because all dogs are both irreplaceable and
immortal and as Rilke says, "Der Tod ist groß."

One day I talked about death with my friend—my teacher
and friend, for these are synonyms in the trainer's world—Dick
Koehler. I had told him about the results obtained at the Univer-

sity of Pennsylvania. "Dick! The news is out! There are no regrets when a dog dies," and Dick said, "Oh, then my several thousand students who say to me, 'If only I had done what you said, Mr. Koehler,' or 'If only I had worked with her more'—they're all hallucinating, right?"

"Must be," I reply, "for it says here that dogs are replaceable, and grief for them lasts no more than three months," and right before my eyes Dick Koehler starts looking a little funny; he startles me. He is thinking of Duke, dead several decades now. Hallucinating that Duke had been irreplaceable. Duke was a Great Dane, one of your great dogs, too. Duke was a movie dog; some of you may remember him from *The Swiss Family Robinson*.

"What was so irreplaceable about Duke?" I asked.

"Well, it's not every day you find a Great Dane who thinks a 255-pound tiger is a kitty cat. Not every day you find a Great Dane who will hit a sleeve and go through a second-story window, not just once, not just twice, but seven times and it was as good the last time as the first time."

Soon after Duke died, there was Topper, of *The Ugly Dachshund*, various TV series. "Topper paid the rent for about three years there," said Dick. "I mean, he did all the work on that series." Topper died like this: the great dog and his son were playing, horsing around after a day's work, and his son slammed into him and ruptured his spleen and Dick realized it too late for the vet to fix things up, and so had him put down. That was over two decades ago, Dick's most recent Great Dane.

Dick talks about Duke and Topper and the thing starts to happen to me again, the merging of all of the elegies, all of the great dogs. "There is nothing left but his name . . . but there never was a dog like Algonquin," or, "It's all regrets," or, "After he got in his car and drove away I dug a grave and lined it with the bright fallen leaves and there I buried all that could die of my good Fox," or "He was allus kind to the younguns and he kilt a rattlesnake onct," or one of my favorites, the passage in T. H. White's *The Sword in the Stone*. The great hound named Beaumont is on the ground, his back broken by the boar, and the expert, the Master of Hounds, William Twyti, has been hurt also. Twyti limps over to Beaumont and utters the eternal litany, "Hark to Beaumont. Softly, Beaumont, mon amy. Oyez à Beaumont the valiant. Swef, le douce Beaumont, swef, swef." Then he nods to Robin Wood, and holds the hound's eyes with his own, saying "Good dog, Beaumont the valiant, sleep now, old friend Beaumont, good old dog," while the huntsman kills the dog for him: "Then Robin's falchion let Beaumont out of this world, to run free with Orion and to roll among the stars."

What next, though? The narrator of *Algonquin* decides to go for an Irish Setter. But that is not what the experts say to do. They say, "Another dog, same breed, right away." It takes courage, courage that Master Twyti seems to have had, for he rose from beside Beaumont's wounds and "whipped the hounds off the corpse of the boar as he was accustomed to do. He put his horn to his lips and blew the four long notes of the Mort without a quaver." He called the other hounds to him.

Another dog, same breed, right away. Or a pack of them, and not because there were any replacements for Beaumont in that pack. The other hounds were all right, but there were no Beaumonts among them, and there is no point in saying otherwise. I don't mean by that that there are not plenty of great dogs around. "There are a lot of them," says Dick. Yeah. They're a dime a dozen. So are great human hearts; that's not the point. We are by way of being connoisseurs of dogs, some of us, but one falls into that, and a dog is not a collector's item, not for Dick Koehler, anyhow, whom I have seen risk himself in more ways than one, over and over, day in and day out, ever since I met him when I was nineteen and he straightened out Stevie, a German Shepherd cross I had then, who was charging children but was a nice dog after we took care of that, who lived for twelve years after Dick showed me how to train him, who shook the ground just as hard as Beaumont did when he died. My teacher and friend Dick Koehler is a maniac for training dogs instead of killing them. Deaf dogs, three-legged dogs, dogs with chartreuse spots on their heads. He hasn't gotten around to getting another Dane, though there have been other dogs, of course. Of *course*.

But "Master William Twyti startled The Wart, for he seemed to be crying," and this book, *The Sword in the Stone*, is about the education of great hounds and of a great king, King Arthur in fact. Immortal Beaumont, douce, swef, swef. And immortal Arthur—douce, douce, harken to Arthur, they would say in time about: *Regis quondam regisque futuri*. The once and future king. Which is to say, this is all of it about the education of any hound and any boy.

"But won't it hurt?" my student asked me recently when I gave that advice: *another dog, same breed, as soon as possible.* "Won't it hurt my daughter again?" Oh, it hurts, especially when, as is so often the case, you have a part in the dog's death. Perhaps because you were careless and he got run over, or because, like Master Twyti, you gave the nod to the vet or to the huntsman with his falchion.

There is the falchion, and then sometimes you must speak abruptly into the face of grief, for grief gives bad advice. Grief will tell you to throw your heart into the grave with the dog's corpse, and this is ecologically unsound. The ants will take care of the corpse in a few weeks, but a discarded heart stinks for quite some time. Two days ago that student of mine called, a woman in her late thirties. She had gotten a new pup for her eight-year-old daughter, and at a few months of age the pup had died because she had been left in her crate with her collar on, and the collar got caught on the handle of the crate. "My daughter is so upset, my husband says it would be too bad to get another dog and have something else happen. What do the experts do?"

I said in tones of vibrant command, "Another dog, same breed, right away." Nothing else, for wordiness is not in order when you are discussing, as we so often are, the education of a queen.

A decade went by between the death of Gunner and the purchase of the new Airedale pup. That was as soon as I could get to it, what with one thing and another.

ON BEING BLACK AND MIDDLE CLASS

Not long ago a friend of mine, black like myself, said to me that the term "black middle class" was actually a contradiction in terms. Race, he insisted, blurred class distinctions among blacks. If you were black, you were just black and that was that. When I argued, he let his eyes roll at my naiveté. Then he went on. For us, as black professionals, it was an exercise in self-flattery, a pathetic pretension, to give meaning to such a distinction. Worse, the very idea of class threatened the unity that was vital to the black community as a whole. After all, since when had white America taken note of anything but color when it came to blacks? He then reminded me of an old Malcolm X line that had been popular in the sixties. Question: What is a black man with a Ph.D.? Answer: A nigger.

For many years I had been on my friend's side of this argument. Much of my conscious thinking on the old conundrum of race and class was shaped during my high school and college years in the race-charged sixties, when the fact of my race took on an almost religious significance. Progressively, from the mid-sixties on, more and more aspects of my life found their explanation, their justification, and their motivation in race. My youthful concerns about career, romance, money, values, and even styles of dress became a subject to consultation with various oracular sources of racial wisdom. And these ranged from a figure as ennobling as Martin Luther King, Jr., to the underworld elegance of dress I found in jazz clubs on the South Side of Chicago. Everywhere there were signals, and in those days I considered myself

so blessed with clarity and direction that I pitied my white classmates who found more embarrassment than guidance in the fact
of *their* race. In 1968, inflated by my new power, I took a mischievous delight in calling them culturally disadvantaged.

But now, hearing my friend's comment was like hearing a
priest from a church I'd grown disenchanted with. I understood
him, but my faith was weak. What had sustained me in the sixties
sounded monotonous and off the mark in the eighties. For me,
race had lost much of its juju, its singular capacity to conjure
meaning. And today, when I honestly look at my life and the
lives of many other middle-class blacks I know, I can see that
race never fully explained our situation in American society.
Black though I may be, it is impossible for me to sit in my single-
family house with two cars in the driveway and a swing set in the
back yard and *not* see the role class has played in my life. And
how can my friend, similarly raised and similarly situated, not
see it?

Yet despite my certainty I felt a sharp tug of guilt as I tried to
explain myself over my friend's skepticism. He is a man of many
comedic facial expressions and, as I spoke, his brow lifted in
extreme moral alarm as if I were uttering the unspeakable. His
clear implication was that I was being elitist and possibly (dare
he suggest?) anti-black—crimes for which there might well be
no redemption. He pretended to fear for me. I chuckled along
with him, but inwardly I did wonder at myself. Though I never
doubted the validity of what I was saying, I felt guilty saying it.
Why?

After he left (to retrieve his daughter from a dance lesson) I
realized that the trap I felt myself in had a tiresome familiarity
and, in a sort of slow-motion epiphany, I began to see its outline.
It was like the suddenly sharp vision one has at the end of a
burdensome marriage when all the long-repressed incompatibili-
ties come undeniably to light.

What became clear to me is that people like myself, my friend,
and middle-class blacks generally are caught in a very specific
double bind that keeps two equally powerful elements of our
identity at odds with each other. The middle-class values by
which we were raised—the work ethic, the importance of educa-

tion, the value of property ownership, of respectability, of "getting ahead," of stable family life, of initiative, of self-reliance, etc.—are, in themselves, raceless and even assimilationist. They urge us toward participation in the American mainstream, toward integration, toward a strong identification with the society—and toward the entire constellation of qualities that are implied in the word "individualism." These values are almost rules for how to prosper in a democratic, free-enterprise society that admires and rewards individual effort. They tell us to work hard for ourselves and our families and to seek our opportunities whenever they appear, inside or outside the confines of whatever ethnic group we may belong to.

But the particular pattern of racial identification that emerged in the sixties and that still prevails today urges middle-class blacks (and all blacks) in the opposite direction. This pattern asks us to see ourselves as an embattled minority, and it urges an adversarial stance toward the mainstream, an emphasis on ethnic consciousness over individualism. It is organized around an implied separatism.

The opposing thrust of these two parts of our identity results in the double bind of middle-class blacks. There is no forward movement on either plane that does not constitute backward movement on the other. This was the familiar trap I felt myself in while talking with my friend. As I spoke about class, his eyes reminded me that I was betraying race. Clearly, the two indispensable parts of my identity were a threat to each other.

Of course when you think about it, class and race are both similar in some ways and also naturally opposed. They are two forms of collective identity with boundaries that intersect. But whether they clash or peacefully coexist has much to do with how they are defined. Being both black and middle class becomes a double bind when class and race are defined in sharply antagonistic terms, so that one must be repressed to appease the other.

But what is the "substance" of these two identities, and how does each establish itself in an individual's overall identity? It seems to me that when we identify with any collective we are basically identifying with images that tell us what it means to be a member of that collective. Identity is not the same thing as the fact of membership in a collective; it is, rather, a form of self-definition, facilitated by images of what we wish our membership in the collective to mean. In this sense, the images we identify with may reflect the aspirations of the collective more than they reflect reality, and their content can vary with shifts in those aspirations.

But the process of identification is usually dialectical. It is just as necessary to say what we are *not* as it is to say what we are — so that finally identification comes about by embracing a polarity of positive and negative images. To identify as middle class, for example, I must have both positive and negative images of what being middle class entails; then I will know what I should and should not be doing in order to be middle class. The same goes for racial identity.

In the racially turbulent sixties the polarity of images that came to define racial identification was very antagonistic to the polarity that defined middle-class identification. One might say that the positive images of one lined up with the negative images of the other, so that to identify with both required either a contortionist's flexibility or a dangerous splitting of the self. The double bind of the black middle class was in place.

The black middle class has always defined its class identity by means of positive images gleaned from middle- and upper-class white society, and by means of negative images of lower-class blacks. This habit goes back to the institution of slavery itself, when "house" slaves both mimicked the whites they served and held themselves above the "field" slaves. But in the sixties the old bourgeois impulse to dissociate from the lower classes (the "we-they" distinction) backfired when racial identity suddenly called for the celebration of this same black lower class. One of the qualities of a double bind is that one feels it more than sees it, and I distinctly remember the tension and strange sense of dishonesty I felt in those days as I moved back and forth like a bigamist between the demands of class and race.

Though my father was born poor, he achieved middle-class standing through much hard work and sacrifice (one of his favorite words) and by identifying fully with solid middle-class values—mainly hard work, family life, property ownership, and education for his children (all four of whom have advanced degrees). In his mind these were not so much values as laws of nature. People who embodied them made up the positive images in his class polarity. The negative images came largely from the blacks he had left behind because they were "going nowhere."

No one in my family remembers how it happened, but as time went on, the negative images congealed into an imaginary character named Sam, who, from the extensive service we put him to, quickly grew to mythic proportions. In our family lore he was sometimes a trickster, sometimes a boob, but always possessed of a catalogue of sly faults that gave up graphic images of everything we should not be. On sacrifice: "Sam never thinks about tomorrow. He wants it now or he doesn't care about it." On work: "Sam doesn't favor it too much." On children: "Sam likes to have them but not to raise them." On money: "Sam drinks it up and pisses it out." On fidelity: "Sam has to have two or three women." On clothes: "Sam features loud clothes. He likes to see and be seen." And so on. Sam's persona amounted to a negative instruction manual in class identity.

I don't think that any of us believed Sam's faults were accurate representations of lower-class black life. He was an instrument of self-definition, not of sociological accuracy. It never occurred to us that he looked very much like the white racist stereotype of blacks, or that he might have been a manifestation of our own racial self-hatred. He simply gave us a counterpoint against which to express our aspirations. If self-hatred was a factor, it was not, for us, a matter of hating lower-class blacks but of hating what we did not want to be.

Still, hate or love aside, it is fundamentally true that my middle-class identity involved a dissociation from images of lower-class black life and a corresponding identification with values and patterns of responsibility that are common to the middle class everywhere. These values sent me a clear message: be both an individual and a responsible citizen; understand that the quality of your life will approximately reflect the quality of effort you put into it; know that individual responsibility is the basis of freedom and that the limitations imposed by fate (whether fair or unfair) are no excuse for passivity.

Whether I live up to these values or not, I know that my acceptance of them is the result of lifelong conditioning. I know also that I share this conditioning with middle-class people of all races and that I can no more easily be free of it than I can be free of my race. Whether all this got started because the black middle class modeled itself on the white middle class is no longer relevant. For the middle-class black, conditioned by these values from birth, the sense of meaning they provide is as immutable as the color of his skin.

I started the sixties in high school feeling that my class-conditioning was the surest way to overcome racial barriers. My racial identity was pretty much taken for granted. After all, it was obvious to the world that I was black. Yet I ended the sixties in graduate school a little embarrassed by my class background and with an almost desperate need to be "black." The tables had turned. I knew very clearly (though I struggled to repress it) that my aspirations and my sense of how to operate in the world came from my class background, yet "being black" required certain attitudes and stances that made me feel secretly a little duplicitous. The inner compatibility of class and race I had known in 1960 was gone.

For blacks, the decade between 1960 and 1969 saw racial identification undergo the same sort of transformation that national identity undergoes in times of war. It became more self-conscious, more narrowly focused, more prescribed, less tolerant of opposition. It spawned an implicit party line, which tended to disallow competing forms of identity. Race-as-identity was lifted from the relative slumber it knew in the fifties and pressed into service in a social and political war against oppression. It was redefined along sharp adversarial lines and directed toward the goal of mobilizing the great mass of black Americans in this warlike effort. It was imbued with a strong moral authority, useful for denouncing those who opposed it and for celebrating those who honored it as a positive achievement rather than as a mere birthright.

The form of racial identification that quickly evolved to meet this challenge presented blacks as a racial monolith, a singular people with a common experience of oppression. Differences within the race, no matter how ineradicable, had to be minimized. Class distinctions were one of the first such differences to be sacrificed, since they not only threatened racial unity but also seemed to stand in contradiction to the principle of equality which was the announced goal of the movement for racial progress. The discomfort I felt in 1969, the vague but relentless sense of duplicity, was the result of a historical necessity that put my race and class at odds, that was asking me to cast aside the distinction of my class and identify with a monolithic view of my race.

If the form of this racial identity was the monolith, its substance was victimization. The civil rights movement and the more radical splinter groups of the late sixties were all dedicated to ending racial victimization, and the form of black identity that emerged to facilitate this goal made blackness and victimization virtually synonymous. Since it was our victimization more than any other variable that identified and unified us, moreover, it followed logically that the purest black was the poor black. It was images of him that clustered around the positive pole of the race polarity; all other blacks were, in effect, required to identify with him in order to confirm their own blackness.

Certainly there were more dimensions to the black experience than victimization, but no other had the same capacity to fire the indignation needed for war. So, again out of historical necessity, victimization became the overriding focus of racial identity. But this only deepened the double bind for middle-class blacks like me. When it came to class we were accustomed to defining ourselves against lower-class blacks and identifying with at least the values of middle-class whites; when it came to race we were now being asked to identify with images of lower-class blacks and to see whites, middle class or otherwise, as victimizers. Negative lining up with positive, we were called upon to reject what we had previously embraced and to embrace what we had previously rejected. To put it still more personally, the Sam figure I had been raised to define myself against had now become the "real" black I was expected to identify with.

The fact that the poor black's new status was only passively earned by the condition of his victimization, not by assertive, positive action, made little difference. Status was status apart from the means by which it was achieved, and along with it came a certain power—the power to define the terms of access to that status, to say who was black and who was not. If a lower-class black said you were not really "black"—a sellout, an Uncle Tom—the judgment was all the more devastating because it carried the authority of his status. And this judgment soon enough came to be accepted by many whites as well.

In graduate school I was once told by a white professor, "Well, but . . . you're not really black. I mean, you're not disadvantaged." In his mind my lack of victim status disqualified me from the race itself. More recently I was complimented by a black student for speaking reasonably correct English, "proper" English as he put it. "But I don't know if I really want to talk like that," he went on. "Why not?" I asked. "Because then I wouldn't be black no more," he replied without a pause.

To overcome his marginal status, the middle-class black had to identify with a degree of victimization that was beyond his actual experience. In college (and well beyond) we used to play a game called "nap matching." It was a game of one-upmanship, in which we sat around outdoing each other with stories of racial victimization, symbolically measured by the naps of our hair. Most of us were middle class and so had few personal stories to relate, but if we could not match naps with our own biographies, we would move on to those legendary tales of victimization that came to us from the public domain.

The single story that sat atop the pinnacle of racial victimization for us was that of Emmett Till, the Northern black teenager who, on a visit to the South in 1955, was killed and grotesquely mutilated for supposedly looking at or whistling at (we were never sure which, though we argued the point endlessly) a white woman. Oh, how we probed his story, finding in his youth and Northern upbringing the quintessential embodiment of black innocence, brought down by a white evil so portentous and apocalyptic, so gnarled and hideous, that it left us with a feeling not far from awe. By telling his story and others like it, we came to *feel* the immutability of our victimization, its utter indigenousness, as a thing on this earth like dirt or sand or water.

Of course, these sessions were a ritual of group identification, a means by which we, as middle-class blacks, could be at one with our race. But why were we, who had only a moderate experience of victimization (and that offset by opportunities our parents never had), so intent on assimilating or appropriating an identity that in so many ways contradicted our own? Because, I think, the sense of innocence that is always entailed in feeling victimized filled us with a corresponding feeling of entitlement, or even license, that helped us endure our vulnerability on a largely white college campus.

In my junior year in college I rode to a debate tournament with three white students and our faculty coach, an elderly English professor. The experience of being the lone black in a group of whites was so familiar to me that I thought nothing of it as our trip began. But then halfway through the trip the professor casually turned to me and, in an isn't-the-world-funny sort of tone, said that he had just refused to rent an apartment in a house he owned to a "very nice" black couple because their color would "offend" the white couple who lived downstairs. His eyebrows lifted helplessly over his hawkish nose, suggesting that he too, like me, was a victim of America's racial farce. His look assumed a kind of comradeship: he and I were above this grimy business of race, though for expediency we had occasionally to concede the world its madness.

My vulnerability in this situation came not so much from the professor's blindness to his own racism as from his assumption that I would participate in it, that I would conspire with him against my own race so that he might remain comfortably blind. Why did he think I would be amenable to this? I can only guess that he assumed my middle-class identity was so complete and all-encompassing that I would see his action as nothing more than a trifling concession to the folkways of our land, that I would in fact applaud his decision not to disturb propriety. Blind to both his own racism and to me—one blindness serving the other—he could not recognize that he was asking me to betray my race in the name of my class.

His blindness made me feel vulnerable because it threatened to expose my own repressed ambivalence. His comment pressured me to choose between my class identification, which had contributed to my being a college student and a member of the debating team, and my desperate desire to be "black." I could have one but not both; I was double-bound.

Because double binds are repressed there is always an element of terror in them: the terror of bringing to the conscious mind the buried duplicity, self-deception, and pretense involved in serving two masters. This terror is the stuff of vulnerability, and since vulnerability is one of the least tolerable of all human feelings, we usually transform it into an emotion that seems to restore the control of which it has robbed us; most often, that emotion is anger. And so, before the professor had even finished his little story, I had become a furnace of rage. The year was 1967, and I had been primed by endless hours of nap-matching to feel, at least consciously, completely at one with the victim-focused black identity. This identity gave me the license, and the impunity, to unleash upon this professor one of those volcanic eruptions of racial indignation familiar to us from the novels of Richard Wright. Like Cross Damon in *Outsider*, who kills in perfectly righteous anger, I tried to annihilate the man. I punished him not according to the measure of his crime but according to the measure of my vulnerability, a measure set by the cumulative tension of years of repressed terror. Soon I saw that terror in *his* face, as he stared hollow-eyed at the road ahead. My white friends in the back seat, knowing no conflict between their own class and race, were astonished that someone they had taken to be so much like themselves could harbor a rage that for all the world looked murderous.

Though my rage was triggered by the professor's comment, it was deepened and sustained by a complex of need, conflict, and repression in myself of which I had been wholly unaware. Out of my racial vulnerability I had developed the strong need of an identity with which to defend myself. The only such identity available was that of me as victim, him as victimizer. Once in the grip of this paradigm, I began to do far more damage to myself than he had done.

Seeing myself as a victim meant that I clung all the harder to my racial identity, which, in turn, meant that I suppressed my class identity. This cut me off from all the resources my class values might have offered me. In those values, for instance, I might have found the means to a more dispassionate response, the response less of a victim attacked by a victimizer than of an individual offended by a foolish old man. As an individual I might have reported this professor to the college dean. Or I might have calmly tried to reveal his blindness to him, and possibly won a convert. (The flagrancy of his remark suggested a hidden guilt and even self-recognition on which I might have capitalized. Doesn't confession usually signal a willingness to face oneself?) Or I might have simply chuckled and then let my silence serve as an answer to his provocation. Would not my composure, in any form it might take, deflect into his own heart the arrow he'd shot at me?

Instead, my anger, itself the hair-trigger expression of a long-repressed double bind, not only cut me off from the best of my own resources, it also distorted the nature of my true racial problem. The righteousness of this anger and the easy catharsis it brought buoyed the delusion of my victimization and left me as blind as the professor himself.

As a middle-class black I have often felt myself *contriving* to be "black." And I have noticed this same contrivance in others—a certain stretching away from the natural flow of one's life to align oneself with a victim-focused black identity. Our particular needs are out of sync with the form of identity available to meet those needs. Middle-class blacks need to identify racially; it is better to think of ourselves as black and victimized than not black at all; so we contrive (more unconsciously than consciously) to fit ourselves into an identity that denies our class and fails to address the true source of our vulnerability.

For me this once meant spending inordinate amounts of time at black faculty meetings, though these meetings had little to do with my real racial anxieties or my professional life. I was new to the university, one of two blacks in an English department of over seventy, and I felt a little isolated and vulnerable, though I did not admit it to myself. But at these meetings we discussed the problems of black faculty and students within a framework of victimization. The real vulnerability we felt was covered over by all the adversarial drama the victim/victimized polarity inspired, and hence went unseen and unassuaged. And this, I think, explains our rather chronic ineffectiveness as a group. Since victimization was not our primary problem—the university had long ago opened its doors to us—we had to contrive to make it so, and there is not much energy in contrivance. What I got at these meetings was ultimately an object lesson in how fruitless struggle can be when it is not grounded in actual need.

At our black faculty meetings, the old equation of blackness with victimization was ever present—to be black was to be a victim; therefore, not to be a victim was not to be black. As we contrived to meet the terms of this formula there was an inevitable distortion of both ourselves and the larger university. Through the prism of victimization the university seemed more impenetrable than it actually was, and we more limited in our powers. We fell prey to the victim's myopia, making the university an institution from which we could seek redress but which we could never fully join. And this mind-set often led us to look more for compensations for our supposed victimization than for opportunities we could pursue as individuals.

The discomfort and vulnerability felt by middle-class blacks in the sixties, it could be argued, was a worthwhile price to pay considering the progress achieved during that time of racial confrontation. But what may have been tolerable then is intolerable now. Though changes in American society have made it an anachronism, the monolithic form of racial identification that came out of the sixties is still very much with us. It may be more loosely held, and its power to punish heretics has probably diminished, but it continues to catch middle-class blacks in a double bind, thus impeding not only their own advancement but even, I would contend, that of blacks as a group.

The victim-focused black identity encourages the individual to feel that his advancement depends almost entirely on that of the group. Thus he loses sight not only of his own possibilities but of the inextricable connection between individual effort and individual advancement. This is a profound encumbrance today, when there is more opportunity for blacks than ever before, for it reimposes limitations that can have the same oppressive effect as those the society has only recently begun to remove.

It was the emphasis on mass action in the sixties that made the victim-focused black identity a necessity. But in the eighties and beyond, when racial advancement will come only through a multitude of individual advancements, this form of identity inadvertently adds itself to the forces that hold us back. Hard work, education, individual initiative, stable family life, property ownership—these have always been the means by which ethnic groups have moved ahead in America. Regardless of past or present victimization, these "laws" of advancement apply absolutely to black Americans also. There is no getting around this. What we need is a form of racial identity that energizes the individual by putting him in touch with both his possibilities and his responsibilities.

It has always annoyed me to hear from the mouths of certain arbiters of blackness that middle-class blacks should "reach back" and pull up those blacks less fortunate than they—as though middle-class status were an unearned and essentially passive condition in which one needed a large measure of noblesse oblige to occupy one's time. My own image is of reaching back from a moving train to lift on board those who have no tickets. A noble enough sentiment—but might it not be wiser to show them the entire structure of principles, effort, and sacrifice that puts one in a position to buy a ticket any time one likes? This, I think, is something members of the black middle class can realistically offer to other blacks. Their example is not only a testament to possibility but also a lesson in method. But they cannot lead by example until they are released from a black identity that regards that example as suspect, that sees them as "marginally" black, indeed that holds *them* back by catching them in a double bind.

To move beyond the victim-focused black identity we must learn to make a difficult but crucial distinction: between actual victimization, which we must resist with every resource, and identification with the victim's status. Until we do this we will continue to wrestle more with ourselves than with the new opportunities which so many paid so dearly to win.

AMY TAN

MOTHER TONGUE

I am not a scholar of English or literature. I cannot give you much more than personal opinions on the English language and its variations in this country or others,

I am a writer. And by that definition, I am someone who has always loved language. I am fascinated by language in daily life. I spend a great deal of my time thinking about the power of language—the way it can evoke an emotion, a visual image, a complex idea, or a simple truth. Language is the tool of my trade. And I use them all—all the Englishes I grew up with.

Recently, I was made keenly aware of the different Englishes I do use. I was giving a talk to a large group of people, the same talk I had already given to half a dozen other groups. The nature of the talk was about my writing, my life, and my book, *The Joy Luck Club*. The talk was going along well enough, until I remembered one major difference that made the whole talk sound wrong. My mother was in the room. And it was perhaps the first time she had heard me give a lengthy speech, using the kind of English I have never used with her. I was saying things like, "The intersection of memory upon imagination" and "There is an aspect of my fiction that relates to thus-and-thus"—a speech filled with carefully wrought grammatical phrases, burdened, it suddenly seemed to me, with nominalized forms, past perfect tenses, conditional phrases, all the forms of standard English that I had learned in school and through books, the forms of English I did not use at home with my mother.

Just last week, I was walking down the street with my mother, and I again found myself conscious of the English I was using, the English I do use with her. We were talking about the price of new and used furniture and I heard myself saying this: "Not waste money that way." My husband was with us as well, and he didn't notice any switch in my English. And then I realized why. It's because over the twenty years we've been together I've often used the same kind of English with him, and sometimes he even uses it with me. It has become our language of intimacy, a different sort of English that relates to family talk, the language I grew up with.

So you'll have some idea of what this family talk I heard sounds like, I'll quote what my mother said during a recent conversation which I videotaped and then transcribed. During this conversation, my mother was talking about a political gangster in Shanghai who had the same last name as her family's, Du, and how the gangster in his early years wanted to be adopted by her family, which was rich by comparison. Later, the gangster became more powerful, far richer than my mother's family, and one day showed up at my mother's wedding to pay his respects. Here's what she said in part:

"Du Yusong having business like fruit stand. Like off the street kind. He is Du like Du Zong—but not Tsung-ming Island people. The local people call putong, the river east side, he belong to that side local people. That man want to ask Du Zong father take him in like become own family. Du Zong father wasn't look down on him, but didn't take seriously, until that man big like become a mafia. Now important person, very hard to inviting him. Chinese way, came only to show respect, don't stay for dinner. Respect for making big celebration, he shows up. Mean gives lots of respect. Chinese custom. Chinese social life that way. If too important won't have to stay too long. He come to my wedding. I didn't see, I heard it. I gone to boy's side, they have YMCA dinner. Chinese age I was nineteen."

You should know that my mother's expressive command of English belies how much she actually understands. She reads the *Forbes* report, listens to *Wall Street Week*, converses daily with her stockbroker, reads all of Shirley MacLaine's books with ease—all kinds of things I can't begin to understand. Yet some of my friends tell me they understand 50 percent of what my mother says. Some say they understand 80 to 90 percent. Some say they understand none of it, as if she were speaking pure Chinese. But to me, my mother's English is perfectly clear, perfectly natural. It's my mother tongue. Her language, as I hear it, is vivid, direct, full of observation and imagery. That was the language that helped shape the way I saw things, expressed things, made sense of the world.

Lately, I've been giving more thought to the kind of English my mother speaks. Like others, I have described it to people as "broken" or "fractured" English. But I wince when I say that. It has always bothered me that I can think of no way to describe it other than "broken," as if it were damaged and needed to be fixed, as if it lacked a certain wholeness and soundness. I've heard other terms used, "limited English," for example. But they seem just as bad, as if everything is limited, including people's perceptions of the limited English speaker.

I know this for a fact, because when I was growing up, my mother's "limited" English limited *my* perception of her. I was ashamed of her English. I believed that her English reflected the quality of what she had to say. That is, because she expressed them imperfectly her thoughts were imperfect. And I had plenty of empirical evidence to support me: the fact that people in department stores, at banks, and at restaurants did not take her seriously, did not give her good service, pretended not to understand her, or even acted as if they did not hear her.

My mother has long realized the limitations of her English as well. When I was fifteen, she used to have me call people on the phone to pretend I was she. In this guise, I was forced to ask for information or even to complain and yell at people who had been rude to her. One time it was a call to her stockbroker in New York. She had cashed out her small portfolio and it just so happened we were going to go to New York the next week, our very first trip outside California. I had to get on the phone and say in an adolescent voice that was not very convincing, "This is Mrs. Tan."

And my mother was standing in the back whispering loudly,

"Why he don't send me check, already two weeks late. So mad he lie to me, losing me money."

And then I said in perfect English, "Yes, I'm getting rather concerned. You had agreed to send the check two weeks ago, but it hasn't arrived."

Then she began to talk more loudly. "What he want, I come to New York tell him front of his boss, you cheating me?" And I was trying to calm her down, make her be quiet, while telling the stockbroker, "I can't tolerate any more excuses. If I don't receive the check immediately, I am going to have to speak to your manager when I'm in New York next week." And sure enough, the following week there we were in front of this astonished stockbroker, and I was sitting there red-faced and quiet, and my mother, the real Mrs. Tan, was shouting at his boss in her impeccable broken English.

We used a similar routine just five days ago, for a situation that was far less humorous. My mother had gone to the hospital for an appointment, to find out about a benign brain tumor a CAT scan had revealed a month ago. She said she had spoken very good English, her best English, no mistakes. Still, she said, the hospital did not apologize when they said they had lost the CAT scan and she had come for nothing. She said they did not seem to have any sympathy when she told them she was anxious to know the exact diagnosis, since her husband and son had both died of brain tumors. She said they would not give her any more information until the next time and she would have to make another appointment for that. So she said she would not leave until the doctor called her daughter. She wouldn't budge. And when the doctor finally called her daughter, me, who spoke in perfect English—lo and behold—we had assurances the CAT scan would be found, promises that a conference call on Monday would be held, and apologies for any suffering my mother had gone through for a most regrettable mistake.

I think my mother's English almost had an effect on limiting my possibilities in life as well. Sociologists and linguists probably will tell you that a person's developing language skills are more influenced by peers. But I do think that the language spoken in the family, especially in immigrant families which are more insular, plays a large role in shaping the language of the child. And I believe that it affected my results on achievement tests, IQ tests, and the SAT. While my English skills were never judged as poor, compared to math, English could not be considered my strong suit. In grade school I did moderately well, getting perhaps B's, sometimes B-pluses, in English and scoring perhaps in the sixtieth or seventieth percentile on achievement tests. But those scores were not good enough to override the opinion that my true abilities lay in math and science, because in those areas I achieved A's and scored in the ninetieth percentile or higher.

This was understandable. Math is precise; there is only one correct answer. Whereas, for me at least, the answers on English tests were always a judgment call, a matter of opinion and personal experience. Those tests were constructed around items like fill-in-the-blank sentence completion, such as, "Even though Tom was _____, Mary thought he was _____." And the correct answer always seemed to be the most bland combinations of thoughts, for example, "Even though Tom was shy, Mary thought he was charming," with the grammatical structure "even though" limiting the correct answer to some sort of semantic opposites, so you wouldn't get answers like, "Even though Tom was foolish, Mary thought he was ridiculous." Well, according to my mother, there were very few limitations as to what Tom could have been and what Mary might have thought of him. So I never did well on tests like that.

The same was true with word analogies, pairs of words in which you were supposed to find some sort of logical, semantic relationship—for example, "*Sunset* is to *nightfall* as _____ is to _____." And here you would be presented with a list of four possible pairs, one of which showed the same kind of relationship: *red* is to *stoplight*, *bus* is to *arrival*, *chills* is to *fever*, *yawn* is to *boring*. Well, I could never think that way. I knew what the tests were asking, but I could not block out of my mind the images already created by the first pair, "*sunset* is to *nightfall*"— and I would see a burst of colors against a darkening sky, the moon rising, the lowering of a curtain of stars. And all the other pairs of words—red, bus, stoplight, boring—just threw up a mass of confusing images, making it impossible for me to sort out something as logical as saying: "A sunset precedes nightfall" is the same as "a chill precedes a fever." The only way I would have gotten that answer right would have been to imagine an associative situation, for example, my being disobedient and staying out past sunset, catching a chill at night, which turns into feverish pneumonia as punishment, which indeed did happen to me.

I have been thinking about all this lately, about my mother's English, about achievement tests. Because lately I've been asked, as a writer, why there are not more Asian Americans represented in American literature. Why are there few Asian Americans enrolled in creative writing programs? Why do so many Chinese students go into engineering? Well, these are broad sociological questions I can't begin to answer. But I have noticed in surveys — in fact, just last week — that Asian students, as a whole, always do significantly better on math achievement tests than in English. And this makes me think that there are other Asian-American students whose English spoken in the home might also be described as "broken" or "limited." And perhaps they also have teachers who are steering them away from writing and into math and science, which is what happened to me.

Fortunately, I happen to be rebellious in nature and enjoy the challenge of disproving assumptions made about me. I became an English major my first year in college, after being enrolled as pre-med. I started writing nonfiction as a freelancer the week after I was told by my former boss that writing was my worst skill and I should hone my talents toward account management.

But it wasn't until 1985 that I finally began to write fiction. And at first I wrote using what I thought to be wittily crafted sentences, sentences that would finally prove I had mastery over the English language. Here's an example from the first draft of a story that later made its way into *The Joy Luck Club*, but without this line: "That was my mental quandary in its nascent state." A terrible line, which I can barely pronounce.

Fortunately, for reasons I won't get into today, I later decided I should envision a reader for the stories I would write. And the reader I decided upon was my mother, because these were stories about mothers. So with this reader in mind—and in fact she did read my early drafts—I began to write stories using all the Englishes I grew up with: the English I spoke to my mother, which for lack of a better term might be described as "simple"; the English she used with me, which for lack of a better term might be described as "broken"; my translation of her Chinese, which could certainly be described as "watered down"; and what I imagined to be her translation of her Chinese if she could speak in perfect English, her internal language, and for that I sought to preserve the essence, but neither an English nor a Chinese structure. I wanted to capture what language ability tests can never reveal: her intent, her passion, her imagery, the rhythms of her speech and the nature of her thoughts.

Apart from what any critic had to say about my writing, I knew I had succeeded where it counted when my mother finished reading my book and gave me her verdict: "So easy to read."

BIOGRAPHICAL NOTES

JAMES BALDWIN, novelist and playwright, is most highly regarded for his essays, which have been collected in *Notes of a Native Son, The Fire Next Time*, and other books. An important figure during the civil rights movement of the 1960s and early 1970s, he was, at his best, a distinctive and powerful prose stylist.

MAX BEERBOHM, the author of *Zuleika Dobson, A Christmas Garland*, and *Around Theatres*, is the greatest English essayist of the twentieth century, a brilliant draftsman, and the master parodist in all of English literature.

JEREMY BERNSTEIN, a theoretical physicist, was for many years a staff writer at *The New Yorker* and a columnist for *The American Scholar*. He is the author of *The Tenth Dimension, Quantum Profiles*, and *Cranks, Quarks, and the Cosmos*, among other books.

TRUMAN CAPOTE, novelist and short-story writer, is the author of *Breakfast at Tiffany's* and *In Cold Blood*, the latter a work he described as a "nonfiction novel." He published his first novel, *Other Voices, Other Rooms*, in his early twenties, wrote much journalism, and had a lifelong genius for attracting attention to himself and to his work.

WILLA CATHER, the great American novelist, is the author of *My Antonia, A Lost Lady, The Professor's House, Death Comes for the Archbishop*, and other novels.

BRUCE CHATWIN, who worked at Sotheby's and for the London *Sunday Times*, wrote the novels *Songlines, On the Black Hill*, and *Utz* as well as *In Patagonia*, a work of nonfiction. A brilliant young writer, his talent was eclipsed by an early death.

WINSTON CHURCHILL, author of *History of the English-Speaking People* and *The Second World War*, is rightly accredited, when he was prime minister of England, with saving the Western world from fascism.

CYRIL CONNOLLY, the English literary critic who made a great success over his self-declared failure to write a masterpiece, is the author of the novel *Rock Pool* and of *The Unquiet Grave*, and of several collections of literary criticism.

JOAN DIDION is the author of the novels *Play It as It Lays, Run River, Democracy*, and *The Book of Common Prayer* as well as of the essay collections *Slouching towards Bethlehem, The White Album*, and *After Henry*. Along with her husband, John Gregory Dunne, she has written several screenplays.

ANNIE DILLARD, novelist and essayist, is the author of *Pilgrim at Tinker Creek, Mornings Like This,* and *The Writing Life.* She won the Pulitzer Prize in 1975 for *Pilgrim at Tinker Creek.*

JOHN GREGORY DUNNE is the author of the novels *True Confession* and *The Red, White, and Blue* and the nonfictional *Vegas* and *Quintana and Friends.* With Joan Didion, he writes screenplays, and has, in his essays of recent years, functioned as a historian of behind-the-scenes life in Hollywood.

LOREN EISELEY, who for many years was chairman of the Department of Anthropology at the University of Pennsylvania, wrote *The Immense Journey, The Invisible Pyramid, The Night Country,* and other works of philosophical physical-anthropology that have gained the status of literature. He has often been described, not inaccurately, as a scientist with the soul of a poet.

RALPH ELLISON, whose novel *Invisible Man* is often thought the best American novel of the past half century, is also the author of two collections of essays, *Shadow and Act* and *Going to the Territory.*

JOSEPH EPSTEIN is the author of five collections of familiar essays, among them *Once More Around the Block, A Line Out for a Walk,* and *With My Trousers Rolled,* and a book of short stories titled *The Goldin Boys.*

M. F. K. FISHER, best known as the author of *How to Cook a Wolf, Consider the Oyster,* and other books on cookery, also wrote novels and memoir. She translated Brillat-Savarin's *The Physiology of Taste* and, in her own writing about food, elegantly amalgamated the best of Old and New World culture.

F. SCOTT FITZGERALD, one of the central figures in the cultural and social history of the 1920s, is the author of *This Side of Paradise, Tender Is the Night, The Last Tycoon,* and, above all, *The Great Gatsby,* his classic American novel.

GRAHAM GREENE, the distinguished English novelist, is the author of more than twenty books, among them books of poems, short stories, travel, essays, and movie criticism. He wrote the screenplay for *The Third Man.*

EMILY HAHN has written the novels *Beginner's Luck* and *Affair* and the nonfiction works *Animal Gardens* and *China Only Yesterday.* For many years her reports from China and from zoos around the world appeared in *The New Yorker.*

VICKI HEARNE, who has written extensively about the training of animals, is the author of *Adam's Task, Bandit,* and *Parts of Light.* Her work has appeared in *Harper's, Raritan,* and other magazines.

L. RUST HILLS, editor of the anthologies *How We Live* and *New York, New York,* has for many years been an editor at *Esquire.*

JEAN HOLLANDER, poet and translator, is the director of the annual writers' conference at Trenton State College in New Jersey. Her writing has appeared in *Sewanee Review, The American Scholar,* and *Literary Review.*

ZORA NEALE HURSTON, folklorist and storyteller, is the author of, among other works, *Dust Tracks on a Road, Mules and Men, The Gilded Six-Bits,* and *Folklore, Memoirs, and Other Writings.* Her work is now more widely read than at any period during her lifetime.

DAN JACOBSON, who was born in South Africa but has lived for many decades in England, is a novelist, short-story writer, essayist, and literary critic. Among his books are *The Zulu and the Zeide, The Confessions of Josef Baisz, The God-Fearer,* and *Time and Time Again.*

DORIS LESSING, born in Rhodesia, is the author of *The Golden Notebook, African Stories, Summer before Dark,* and *London Observed.* She has written science fiction, autobiography, and political essays.

A. J. LIEBLING, for most of his career a leading figure at *The New Yorker,* where he wrote on boxing, food, and literature, is the author of two posthumous collections, *Liebling Abroad* and *Liebling at Home.*

BARRY LOPEZ is the author of *Of Wolves and Men, Arctic Dreams, Crossing Open Ground,* and *Field Notes.* He is a contributing editor of *Harper's,* and has also written a number of novels.

NANCY MAIRS, who lives in Arizona, has written *Ordinary Time, Plaintext,* and *Remembering the Bone House.*

H. L. MENCKEN, America's most famous journalist, is the author of the series of essays known under the collective title of *Prejudices,* of three classic autobiographical volumes *(Happy Days, Heathen Days,* and *Newspaper Days),* and of *The American Language.*

NANCY MITFORD is the author of *Love in a Cold Climate* and *Noblesse Oblige, Voltaire in Love,* and of biographies of Madame de Pompadour and Frederick the Great. Her letters to and from Evelyn Waugh show her to have been a woman of wit and divine patience.

V. S. NAIPAUL, born in Trinidad though long resident in London, is the author of the novels *A House for Mr. Biswas, A Bend in the River,* and *The Enigma of Arrival* as well as such works of nonfiction as *The Loss of El Dorado, An Area of Darkness,* and *Among the Believers.*

FLANNERY O'CONNOR, who died of lupus at the age of thirty-nine, is the author of *A Good Man Is Hard to Find, The Violent Bear It Away,* and *Mystery and Manners.* Her work, including her splendid correspondence, has been published in the Library of America.

FRANK O'CONNOR, chiefly known for his short stories, is the author of *A Set of Variations, A Short History of Irish Literature,* and *My Father's Son.* His correspondence with William Maxwell, *The Happiness of Getting It Down Right,* has recently been published.

GEORGE ORWELL, most famous for his two political novels, *Animal Farm* and *1984,* is generally thought to be at his best in his essays, personal and political. He was of the generation of European literary intellectuals that included Arthur Koestler, André Malraux, and Ignazio Silone.

CYNTHIA OZICK has written *The Messiah of Stockholm* and *The Cannibal Galaxy,* novels, and *Art and Ardor, Memory and Metaphor,* and *Fame and Folly,* collections of essays. She has also written *The Shawl,* a play.

DOROTHY PARKER, a member of the Algonquin Round Table, wrote short stories, light verse, and screenplays, but she is undoubtedly most famous for the various and devastating witty remarks attributed (and sometimes mis-attributed) to her.

KATHERINE ANNE PORTER, who was born in Indian Creek, Texas, is the author of, among other books, *Pale Horse, Pale Rider,* a collection of stories; *Ship of Fools,* a novel; and *The Days Before*, a collection of essays. She was elected a member of the National Institute of Arts and Letters in 1943, and won both the Pulitzer Prize and the National Book Award for her work.

DAWN POWELL, the author of fifteen novels, numerous short stories, and half a dozen plays, has enjoyed a revival in reputation with the republication in the 1990s of several of her novels and *The Diaries of Dawn Powell, 1931–1965*.

RICHARD RODRIGUEZ, author of *Hunger of Memory*, writes for *Harper's*, *The American Scholar*, and other magazines. He lives in San Francisco and regularly writes about life in that city.

PHYLLIS ROSE has written *Parallel Lives*, *Woman of Letters*, and *Jazz Cleopatra*, a biography of Josephine Baker. She is professor of English at Wesleyan University in Middletown, Connecticut.

BERTRAND RUSSELL, the famous English philosopher, is the author of *Principia Mathematica*, *Mysticism and Logic*, and *Why I Am Not a Christian*, among a vast number of other books.

OLIVER SACKS, a neurologist by training, is the author of *Anthropologist on Mars*, *Seeing Voices*, and *The Man Who Mistook His Wife for a Hat and Other Writings*. His writing is in the tradition of physicians of literary sensibility who bring a human touch to scientific subjects.

SCOTT RUSSELL SANDERS, who teaches at Indiana University, has written *The Paradise of Bombs*, *Stone Country*, *Secrets of the Universe*, and *Bad Man Ballad*, a novel.

SHELBY STEELE, author of *Content of Our Character*, has written for *Harper's*, *Commentary*, and *The American Scholar* on the subject of race in American life.

AMY TAN, the youngest contributor to this book, is the author of the novels *The Joy Luck Club*, *The Kitchen God's Wife*, and *The Moon Lady*.

LEWIS THOMAS, for many years president of the Sloan-Kettering Cancer Center in New York City, is the author of several essay collections, among them *The Lives of the Cell* and *The Medusa and the Snail*.

BARBARA TUCHMAN, the American historian whose works enjoyed an immense commercial as well as critical success, is the author of *Guns of August*, *The Proud Tower*, and *The Distant Mirror*.

MARK TWAIN is perhaps too famous to require a biographical note. Nevertheless, he is the author of various books, preeminent among them *The Adventures of Huckleberry Finn*, much occasional comedy, and seven full columns of memorable remarks in the most recent edition of *Bartlett's Familiar Quotations*.

EUDORA WELTY, best known for her many collections of short stories, most of them set in her native Mississippi, also wrote the novels *Delta Wedding*, *The Ponder Heart*, and *Clock Hands*. She has won the Pulitzer Prize and just about every other literary award her nation has to confer.

REBECCA WEST, the English novelist, is well known also for her extraordinary works of nonfiction, among them *The Meaning of Treason*, *St. Augustine*, and *Black Lamb and Grey Falcon*, her study of Yugoslavia. The theme of betrayal pervades her writing, and her love affair with the novelist H. G. Wells seems to have added to her interest in the subject.

E. B. WHITE, a founding figure at *The New Yorker*, has long been regarded as one of America's foremost essayists. He is also the author of two enduring books for children, *Stuart Little* and *Charlotte's Web*.

EDMUND WILSON, the doyen of literary criticism in twentieth-century America, also wrote poetry, fiction, history, autobiography, and extensive journals that run from the twenties through the sixties. He is the author of, among more than thirty books, *Memoirs of Hectate County*, *To the Finland Station*, and *Shores of Light*.

VIRGINIA WOOLF, the renowned English essayist and a central figure in the English intellectual and artistic coterie known as Bloomsbury, is also the author of the novels *To the Lighthouse*, *The Waves*, and *Mrs. Dalloway*.

WILLIAM ZINSSER, author of *Writing Well* and other books, has written for *The Atlantic*, *The New Yorker*, and *The American Scholar*. He taught for many years at Yale and is currently at work on a new book recounting his lifelong devotion to travel.

CREDITS

James Baldwin, "Stranger in the Village" from *Notes of a Native Son*. Copyright © 1955 and renewed 1983 by James Baldwin. Reprinted with the permission of Beacon Press.

Max Beerbohm, "Something Indefeasible" from *And Even Now* (London: Wm. Heinemann, 1921). Reprinted with the permission of Sir Rupert Hart-Davis on behalf of Mrs. Eva Reichmann and The Estate of Max Beerbohm.

Jeremy Bernstein, "Take the 'A' Train" from *The American Scholar*. Reprinted with the permission of the author.

Truman Capote, "Tangier" from *Local Color*. Copyright 1950 by Truman Capote. Reprinted with the permission of Random House, Inc.

Willa Cather, "A Chance Meeting" from *Not Under Forty*. Copyright 1936 by Willa Cather, renewed © 1964 by Edith Lewis and the City Bank Farmers Trust Company. Reprinted with the permission of Alfred A. Knopf, Inc.

Bruce Chatwin, "The Bey" from *What Am I Doing Here*. Copyright © 1989 by The Estate of Bruce Chatwin. Reprinted with the permission of Viking Penguin, a division of Penguin Books USA Inc. and Aitken, Stone & Wylie, Limited.

Winston Churchill, "The Dream" from *Winston Spencer Churchill*, Volume VIII (London: Wm. Heinemann, 1987). Reprinted with the permission of Curtis Brown, Ltd. on behalf of The Estate of Sir Winston Churchill.

Cyril Connolly, "Revisiting Greece" from *Previous Convictions* (New York: Harper & Row, 1963). Reprinted with the permission of The Estate of Cyril Connolly, c/o Rogers, Coleridge & White, Ltd., 20 Powis Mews, London W11 1JN, UK.

Joan Didion, "On Keeping a Notebook" from *Slouching towards Bethlehem*. Copyright © 1966, 1968 by Joan Didion. Reprinted with the permission of Farrar, Straus & Giroux, Inc.

Annie Dillard, "Living Like Weasels" from *Teaching a Stone to Talk: Expeditions and Encounters*. Copyright © 1982 by Annie Dillard. Reprinted with the permission of HarperCollins Publishers, Inc.

John Gregory Dunne, "Quintana" from *Quintana & Friends*. Copyright © 1977 by John Gregory Dunne. Reprinted with the permission of Dutton Signet, a division of Penguin Books USA Inc.

B 5/15/97